Public Grievances and the Lokpal

(2nd Revised Edition)

Dr. R.K. Dhawan

Synergy Books India
(A Unit of M/s Bookwell Publication)
New Delhi

First Published 1981
Second Revised Edition 2012

ISBN: 978-93-82059-07-3

Published by:
Synergy Books India
(A Unit of M/s Bookwell Publications)
24/4800 Ansari Road, Darya Ganj
New Delhi-110002
Phone: 011-23268786, 23257264
Fax: 011-23281315
E-Mail: synergybooksindia@gmail.com
bookwell@vsnl.net

Printed and bound in India by :
D.K. Fine Art Press (P) Ltd

Contents

Preface

The conflict between the liberty of man and the authority of organized society has characterized human civilization in all ages. This conflict has been aggravated in recent times with the assumption of progressively larger responsibility by the state for beneficent purposes. The modern welfare state, which aims at not only "hindering the hindrances" in the path of good citizenship, but also creating positive conditions for its growth, has also failed to reconcile this rather perennial conflict. In the welfare state, which aims to contribute to the all-round enrichment of the human personality, the interventions of the Central and local authorities in the lives and affairs of ordinary citizens inevitably multiply. The acceptance of planned economy and socialism has further extended the area of state action in a vast field demanding the existence of a huge, sprawling bureaucracy. This touches the personal and occupational life of the citizens, both individually and collectively, in a manner and on a scale unprecedented in human history The state action, and consequently the power of the state officials, has come to cover the whole vista of citizens' life from cradle to grave. It is an era where no aspect of citizens' life from cradle to grave. It is an era where no aspect of citizens' life remains untouched and unaffected by the state. "In many fields such as hospital services and the operation of public utilities, governmental supervision or control was by no means a novelty", as the Whyatt Committee has pointed out, "but the important new feature which emerged with the establishment of comprehensive state services was the almost complete disappearance of alternatives." This makes citizens totally dependent upon the state services, and consequently upon the government officials.

Representative democracy inevitably creates a class of intermediaries between the state and the citizens. This is a class of salaried officials. The state depends upon this vast corps of officials for the execution of its policies. The social and welfare legislations augment their powers to such an extent that the layman is simply overawed by hem. The officials are vested with considerable discretionary powers. The statutes which establish these comprehensive social services often enable the officials to decide any question of appeal which may be laid against their execution. For this, reliance is put upon the administrative tribunals or ministerial decisions. It has been alleged that officials develop a strong solidarity and help each other in case of trouble. Ministers also act upon the advice of the officials who feed the former with facts and figures in such a way that the former often find no alternative but to approve of latter's actions. This shows the power of the officials, which assumes a formidable proportion in a welfare state.

Moreover, the development of a social service state has also necessitated delegated legislation. Legislature has neither the time nor the requisite competence for providing technical details relating to the laws of a modern state. It cannot foresee every event. Therefore, it has become a general practice of the legislature to indicate the broad principles and pass laws in skeleton form, leaving rule-making power to the officials to fill up the details. The officials in a modern state, thus, combine in themselves not only executive power but also judicial and legislativc powers to some extent. Specially during the period of war and national emergencies, the powers of the "ruling servants" expand tremendously. The relationship between the administrator and the citizen has proved particularly intriguing and crucial to many theorists.

The dawn of Independence in 1947 and the introduction of the Constitution in 1950 set in motion a long process of efforts to change he former "law and order state" into a "welfare state". This goal was sought to be achieved through democratic planning. Many schemes, big and small, were initiated in various fields such a agriculture, community development, irrigation, industry, mining, social services, which increased the burden on the administration. The phenomenal increase in the points of contact between the officials and the public necessitated a change in the administrators' attitude towards the public. They were no longer he "rulers" and the public no longer the "ruled". The administration has not only to work for the people, but with the people.

The present study is an attempt to look at the problems objectively. The author had to carry out intensive field studies in order to prove his occlusions. Among other things, the present study aims at identification of the major causes for public grievances and an objective appraisal of the administrative machinery for their prompt and effective redressal at the Central, State and District levels. The increasing complexity of administrative processes and inadequacy of management personnel to cope with the ever-growing developmental activities of the government are the primary reasons for generating public complaints. A need for an independent machinery for redress of public grievances like Ombudsman-type of institutions such as Lokpal and Lokayuktas in generally felt.

The credit for steering this work to a successful conclusion mainly goes to my esteemed friend late Professor B.S. Narula, for his valuable contribution in this endeavour.

I am deeply indebted to Dr. J.N. Khosla, former Director of the Indian Institute of Public Administration for his constant inspiration and guidance to me throughout, and to the Indian Council of Social Science Research for their financial support for this publication.

R.K. DHAWAN

Foreword

Latest Trends- 2010-11 was a bad patch for the Government as corruption was rampant in almost all the departments of Government of India and state Governments. The rich and middle class did not mind paying extra money for getting their needs and aspirations attended to expeditiously, but it really hurt the poor and downtrodden, who raised hue and cry. They were forced to pay illegal gratification for getting licenses, permits, ration cards, or any other small things attended to on their behalf. However people were so frustrated with corruption particularly after recent episodes like 2 G scam, Common- wealth games, Adarsh cooperative society, Mumbai and many other incidents of corruptions that once a call was given by a Gandhian, lakhs of people followed him all over the country

Seeing such a huge crowd of followers both young and old the Government invited Anna Hazare and his team of civil movement to join them in drafting the Lokpal Bill. There were five persons from the Government and five from civil society. Copy of Government Notification is at Annexure I. Without taking into account the recommendations of the civil society members, Government came out with its own recommendations and drafted its own Bill. Civil Society was not happy with this action of the Government. The Government however went ahead with their draft and placed before the Parliament the Lokpal Bill 2011. Independently, Civil Society also sent a separate draft called Jan Lokpal Bill. The Government was not willing to send Jan Lokpal to the Parliament and agitation started, once again.

Anna Hazare was arrested and a public uproar started. The Government had to yield, because of agitation all over the country and released him from Tihar jail. They also agreed to send Jan Lokpal bill to Parliament.

The demand of civil society was that; a) Prime Minister should be covered under the Lokpal Bill, b). Judiciary should also be similarly covered; c) People's grievances should be part of Lokpal.

The Society demanded that Lokpal should give protection to whistle blowers. Lokpal should not only investigate a few high profile cases of

Anna Hazare came down on his demands and raised only three issues before both Houses of Parliament. These issues are:-

1. Inclusion of lower Bureaucracy in Lokpal's ambit,
2. To appoint Lokayuktas in states,
3. Citizens Charter

With these three demands and keeping in view similar agitation and fast by Baba Ramdev in June 2011 against corruption, which was broken up in the midnight scoop, by the police, the Government had to yield. In a response both the Houses of Parliament agreed on a 'Sense' of the respective Houses accepting in principle the three demands mentioned above. It was resolved by both the Houses to send these three issues of Anna Hazare to Standing Committee of Parliament, with all the papers, including the debates of the respective Houses.

The author is of the view that Lokpal alone will not be able to eradicate corruption and there is a strong need to bring about changes in the system of governance.Lokpal is likely to be flooded with complaints and grievances, there is a need to have a number of lokayuktas (Deputy Lokpal) to assist the lokpal.

There should be a Lokpal of the stature of Chief Justice of India, both in terms of power, status and emoluments. There should be a number of Lokayukttas at the Centre, depending upon the work load. Lokayukttas should be equal in rank to the Chief Justice of a High Court.

The work load needs to be divided in terms of Lokayukta (investigations) and Lokayukta (grievances). The Central Bureau of Investigation and Central Vigilance Commission should be part of the Lokayukta investigations. Similar set up of Lokayukta should be at the state level. It is felt that Chief Minister of the State should be covered under the Lokayukta ambit. As regards, the Prime Minister, being the top most functionary of the Government of India, could be outside the Jurisdiction of Lokpal as, he is answerable to Parliament and his functioning depends on his majority in the Parliament. He is also dealing with sensitive issues of the Government of India and some confidentiality needs to be maintained.

Citizens Charter- Under the Right of Citizens to Time Bound Delivery of Services Act 2011, 28 services rendered by 32 Departments and Agencies of Delhi Administration, including MCD, NDMC, Power Discoms and Police have decided to provide time bound delivery of services. Incase, of default in time bound services, officials concerned will have to pay a penalty of Rs. 10 per day upto Rs. 200 per application, which will be deducted from their salary and paid to the applicant.

Delhi Administration is the first Government to start this service under the new act. It may further add some more departments under the time bound delivery of services. Applicants can now monitor their applications on internet, for which they will be provided an ID number.

Government of India has decided to set up 71 fast track Special CBI courts. A Committee will be set up to look into CBI cases of corruption that have been pending for more than 10 years. Guilty officials can lose upto 20 percent of their pension. Even private sector companies have started roping in retired high court judges to be appointed as independent ombudsmen in different regions to resolve cases filed against the company by its suppliers, distributors, stockist and retailers. This is a new trend, which will resolve public complaints outside the courts. The Government has also decided to set up Grievance Commissioners at district level to resolve pending issues. The Government needs a strong and effective institutional infrastructure to deal with corruption and grievances, but it has to be seen that such an institution does not override the Constitution of India and ensures independent judiciary for, which Judicial Accountability Commission is the answer. The Government started another important scheme under the Right to Information Act. Any information not covered, under restrictions contained in Section 8 and 9 of Act can be obtained under the Right to Information Act 2005. There is also a Provision of Appeal under the section 19 (1) of the Right to Information Act 2005, One Officer is designated as Central Public Information officer in each Ministry or Department for this purpose. Incase, the Departmental Officer doesnot provide information under the RTI act, case can be filed before Information Commissioner. An appeal against the Commissioner lies with the Chief Information Commissioner.

The bill since has been passed by Lok Sabha and is pending in Rajya Sabha for its approval

RK Dhawan,
MA, Ph.D

CHAPTER I

Introduction

With the phenomenal growth during the past few decades of the developmental and nation-building activities of the Central and the State governments in India, proliferation of the machinery of the government and increase in the complexities of the administrative process, the citizens' dissatisfaction with administration has mounted up significantly. The increase in public grievances is partly the result of the rising expectations, which have followed in the wake of the spread of general education and political awakening after the attainment of Independence. While efficiency and discipline among the public employees have gone down the activities of the government, particularly the developmental tasks, have expanded in scope and scale and there has been no commensurate strengthening of the administrative machinery.

The vast responsibilities that the government has assumed in the field of development and welfare have led to the multiplication of the administrative agencies and vesting in them wide discretionary powers. There is a wide field of administrative action in which administrative authority may act outside the strict scope of law and propriety without the injured citizens being in a position to obtain effective redress. Where there is a power and discretion there is always a possibility of its abuse; more so when the power and discretion have to be exercised in the context of economic controls and scarcity of goods and raw materials. "The progressive regulation of a citizen's life through the acts and policies of Government and through institutions set up to implement them, has made very substantial encroachment into the spheres of individual liberty and consequently the citizen is much more affected now, than in the past, by the activities of the administration today. He is exposed at numerous points to the impact of the multifarious activities of the administration ranging over a vast field, e.g., the operation of controls relating to the various commodities which he needs, the provision of many services intended for general benefit and welfare, the operation of the contractual relations between himself and the Government in various spheres, and the regulation of property rights and of the various social services, such as, labour, banking, insurance and provident funds."[1]

Since the early sixties, the need for developing an adequate machinery for the redress of public grievances has attracted increased attention in the media among the public, in the Parliament and State legislatures, and in the reports of the various administrative reorganization enquiry committees and commissions. Even though the problem of redress of citizens' grievances has been under the public gaze in recent years, it has hardly received any detailed and comprehensive treatment either at the hands of the political leaders and administrative reformers or from scholars and professional associations.

Adequate machinery for the redress of citizens' grievances is essential for several reasons. In the first place, administration exists not for itself but for the citizens. "... Administration like most things is, in the final analysis, a human problem-- to deal with human beings, not with some statistical data... there is the danger that pure administrators at the top—not so much at the bottom—because they came into contact with human beings—may come to regard human beings as mere abstractions. The administrator may think in abstract of the people he deals with, come to conclusions which are justifiable apparently, but which miss the human element. After all whatever department of Government you deal with, it is ultimately a problem of human beings, and the moment we forget them, we are driven away from reality".[2] Again, "If, in the prosperity of the people lies the strength of a Government,

[1] Government of India, Administrative Reforms Commission, *Interim Report on Problems of Redress of Citizens' Grievances,* 1966, pp. 4 and 6.

[2] Jawaharlal Nehru, "Administration—A Human Problem" address delivered at the inaugural meeting of the Indian Institute of Public Administration, New Delhi, 29 March 1954, *The Indian Journal of Public Administration, January-March, 1955, p.2.*

it is in their contentment that lie the security and stability of democracy."[3]

Secondly, if the citizens' grievances are allowed to mount up, their dissatisfaction with the administration is likely to add to the existing social unrest and tensions. The phenomenon of growing social discontent which erupts into sporadic acts of violence, gheraos, and work-stoppages, finds sustenance in the citizens' frustration with the administration. It is necessary that the citizens' faith in the government, of which administration is the chief executive agency, should not be allowed to deteriorate but should be reinforced adequately. This is important for both political stability and preservation of the social fabric.

Thirdly, the large-scale programme of development which the government has taken upon itself requires people's cooperation and even collaboration in many fields of governmental activity. If citizens' grievances continue to rise at the present rate, their cooperation in the developmental effort may be seriously affected. Such cooperation is indispensable for further expansion of the developmental programmes which are inevitable for accelerating the pace of economic development and raising the living standards. For example, the lack of cooperation from the people in the family planning programme of the government was not only a complete failure but also threw the government out which started its implementation.

Fourthly, it is by now well established that as the bureaucratic organization grows in scale and its activities sprawl out, it is likely to ride rough-shod over the citizens' rights. Even a welfare state is a leviathan and its activities criss-cross the citizens' daily life at innumerable points. The citizens, more so in a developing country and particularly those who belong to the poor or backward sections, cannot protect themselves against the inroads of the almighty state. Even in the U.K. this aspect of the problem has attracted special attention in cases such as the Crichel Down, Sachsen-hausen etc. In India, for example, the Citizens of Democracy, a non-official organization had appointed a Civil Rights Committee under the

[3]Government of India, Administrative Reforms Commission, *Interim Report on Problems of Redress of Citizens' Grievances*, op. cit., p. 7.

chairmanship of Justice V.M. Tarkunde to go into the alleged encounters between the police and the Naxalites in Andhra Pradesh. The Committee has submitted two reports to the government in which a prima facie case of cold-blooded murder of some Naxalites by the police has been made out.

BACKGROUND OF THE PROBLEM

In considering the problem of the citizens' grievances in India, certain special features of the economic, social, and political conditions of the country will need to be borne in mind. These briefly are as follows:

1. The general standard of living of the people is low; the country is over populated and there is considerable unemployment and underemployment. India is the seventh largest and the second most populous country in the world. It has a population of 1,210,193,422 (2011 census), and over 82.3 per cent people in villages. The national per capita income is very low. About 9.6 million persons are unemployed[4] and underemployed. The proportion of the unemployed and the underemployed in the rural areas is sizeable and the per capita income of the rural people is much lower. The facilities and amenities provided in the urban areas greatly fall short of the needs, and the problems of industrial congestion, shortage of housing, growth of slums and insanitary conditions have intensified. The rural side, despite some significant progress made in recent years, still suffers from lack of roads, means of communication, transport, educational facilities and the like.

2 Despite efforts made by the government during the past sixty five years, the proportion of illiteracy is quite high. The Indian society is passing through a transitional phase from a traditional and rural society to an industrial and

[4] Relate to persons mostly from urban areas, registered with the Employment Exchanges in 1966. These do not fully reflect the number of the unemployed in the country, as they include some employed people seeking better jobs. Many of the unemployed do not come forward to register themselves. *Reserve Bank of India Bulletin,* December 1969, p. 13.

modern polity. The tradition of looking up to the government for help in every walk of life where the citizen runs into a difficulty still continues to hold strong. The expectations of the people from the government have risen substantially in recent years in the wake of political and social awakening. These expectations are not only for the satisfaction of genuine needs of the people, but also for concessions and favours. The latter aspect of the problem is an inheritance from the British rule and the earlier feudalistic regimes.

3. In the circumstances, the demands made by the citizens on the administration are too enormous compared to the capacity of the administration. The stupendous responsibilities in the field of development and welfare taken upon itself by the government have to an extent helped in raising the living standards of the people and placing at their disposal more amenities and facilities. However, notwithstanding the several measures taken by the government to strengthen the administrative machinery, the general level of efficiency has gone down. But the people's aspirations and expectations from the government continue to rise, and the gap between the delivery capacity of the administration and the people's demand is likely to increase during the next 15 years.

4. As already noted, the government's intervention in the daily life of the citizens has increased substantially as a result of a vast network of regulatory controls found necessary for giving effect to the five year plans of development. The discretionary powers enjoyed by the administrative agencies have increased substantially, thereby widening the scope for encroachment upon the citizens' rights.

5. Even though India has been able to maintain and strengthen a parliamentary form of democratic government, intervention by elected public officials in the day-to-day administration has been on the increase. And this development has tended to demoralize the civil service. While some of such interventions emanate from the desire to give relief to the aggrieved citizens or community groups, for the most part these are prompted by considerations of helping friends and supporters, accommodating sectional interests and building political strength.

6. The general attitude of the civil service, as inherited from

the past, has been authoritative and paternalistic, and shows a singular lack of belief in the dignity of the individual and want of regard for his felt-needs and difficulties. Indian administration continues to be characterized by the imperialist tradition of master-servant relationship. The facade of relationship between the citizen and the administration has outwardly changed, but not in spirit. The citizen today feels greatly frustrated due to the inconvenience caused to him as a result of tortuous administrative procedures. True, a difference in the attitude of the civil servants is perceptible. But there is little concern for the discomfort and harassment caused to the citizens by methods and procedures which were evolved during the British days and are repeated mostly for the convenience of the bureaucracy and a handful of political leaders. Service is rendered to the citizens as a "favour" and not as a "duty". In some ways, the paternalistic attitudes of the Indian bureaucracy has its roots in the authoritarian social norms and the low value attached to the dignity of the illiterate and the poor individuals.

EXISTING LITERATURE ON THE SUBJECT

Though the problem of citizens' grievances has been exercising the minds of people and the government for the past several years, the existing research studies on the subject are only a few. Though several government reports have dealt with the problem since Independence, from the historical perspective the impetus to initiation of measures for the redress of citizens' grievances has come from the three main sources as follows:

1. The need for the adaptation of the administrative system to the requirements of plans of economic and social development.
2. The fight against corruption that followed the growing public criticism of lowering of standards of integrity in high places and "delicate" areas of administration.
3. The spiralling public dissatisfaction with the administration.

Government reports

Several of the reports on administrative reforms made by individual experts and administrative enquiry committees appointed by the government, touch upon the problem of citizens' grievances mostly from the point of view of improvement of procedures and systems, prevention of delay, and better public relations.

The five year plan documents have not dealt with the problem of citizens' grievances directly, but as one of the ingredients in the policy of evoking public cooperation and involvement in the developmental effort. The question of setting up a suitable redress machinery or streamlining of the machinery which already exists has received attention only in a few of these reports.

A.D. Gorwala, who was asked in 1952 by the Planning Commission to make a report on the health of the public administration system of the country, observed that the principal cause of lack of confidence in the government and administrative machinery was the many tales of improper behaviour of those in power. The psychological atmosphere produced by such persistent and unfavourable comment was leading to further moral deterioration, for the people would try to adapt their methods, even for securing a legitimate right, to what they believed to be the tendency of men in power and office. He added that it was not surprising that when grave allegations by responsible parties were made against people holding positions of high authority and they continued to remain in power without being cleared of the accusations, the public generally felt that anybody really influential could get away with anything. In 1953, Paul H. Appleby, who was specially invited by the government to survey the Indian adminisirative system, remarked that "an administrative method that permits letters from citizens to go unanswered, poorly answered, or long delayed is not properly considerate or responsive . . . a method that underestimates the value of citizens' criticisms merely because the citizen knows only what displeases him and not the difficulties in the way of pleasing him, is not sufficiently responsive."[5]

After the advent of planning, there were set up a plethora

[5]Government of India, Cabinet Secretariat, *Report of Survey on Public Administration in India*, Paul H. Appleby 1953, pp. 63-4.

of working groups on the functional aspect of administration and administrative enquiry committees in several States such as Maharashtra, Rajasthan, Orissa, Kerala, Karnataka and Andhra Pradesh. But citizens' grievances hardly received any worthwhile attention in these efforts at administrative reforms prior to 1962.

A committee was appointed by the government in 1962 (known as Santhanam Committee) to look into the problem of corruption.

This committee also took note of the increasing dissatisfaction of the citizens with administration and recommended the setting up, at the Centre, of a Directorate General of Complaints and Redress. The committee added, "the problem of maintaining integrity in administration cannot be viewed in isolation from the general administrative processes. In order to deal effectively with the problem, it is necessary to take into account the root cause of which the most important is the wide discretionary power which has to be exercised by the executive in carrying on the complicated work of modern Administration."[6]

The Santhanam Committee report aroused a good deal of interest in the press, the Parliament and State legislatures. Following the report, a network of vigilance commissions came up at the Centre and in the States, but the proposal of the Santhanam Committee for a Central Directorate of General Complaints and Redress was postponed on the ground that the problem of public complaints was a big one and would require a separate agency or machinery. It would be too much to burden the vigilance machinery with public complaints of all kinds.

At the State level, for the first time, a detailed examination of the problem of public complaints was made by the Rajasthan Administrative Reforms Committee (1963), under the chairmanship of H.C. Mathur. The Committee recommended the establishment of an independent high-powered body on the lines of the institution of the Ombudsman obtaining in the

[6] D.O. No.1/4/63CPC dated 22 February 1963 from K. Santhanam, Chairman, Committee on Prevention of Corruption, to Lal Bahadur Shastri, Home Minister, Government of India.

Scandinavian countries. It emphasized that such a body would also help give adequate protection to those who were unnecessarily maligned. It would also provide the legislature with adequate means for effectively discharging their functions as guardians of the people's rights and privileges. The Punjab Administrative Reforms Committee (1964-66) under the chairmanship of K. Hanumanthaiya, however, recommended a system of grievances' tribunals and also suggested greater delegation of authority, reduction in number of stages of decision-making, and accessibility of officers to the people. The Andhra Pradesh Administrative Reforms Committee (1964) under the chairmanship of K.M. Unninathan, and the Kerala Administrative Reorganization and Economy Committee (1965-67) under the chairmanship of M.K. Vellodi made some general recommendations having a bearing on the problem of citizens' grievances, e.g. acknowledgement of all applications, appointment of receptionists, improvement in the speed of disposal, etc.

The public debate that had been set in motion by the report of the Santhanam Committee and the heightened interest of the Members of Parliament in administrative reforms following the administrative failures in the implementation of the Third Five Year Plan highlighted by its mid-term appraisal, led to the constitution in early 1965 of a Special Consultative Group of Members of Parliament on administrative reforms. This group appointed three sub-committees, namely sub-committee on controls, sub-committee on administrative tribunals and machinery for the redress of grievances at the Centre, and a sub-committee on district administration and removal of citizens' grievances. The group, however, could not conclude its work on the matter of citizens' grievances. There was a growing demand in Parliament and in the press for the appointment of an all-India Administrative Reforms Commission (A.R.C.). The Commission was appointed on 6 January 1966 under the chairmanship of Morarji Desai and on the suggestion of the Special Consultative Group of Members of Parliament on administrative reforms, the government included among the terms of reference of the A.R.C. two important aspects of public grievances: (i) the adequacy of the existing arrangements for the redress of grievances; and (ii) the need for introduction of any new machinery or special institution for redress of grievances.

The A.R.C. gave the highest priority to the question of citizens' grievances and submitted a special report to the government in October 1966. The Commission's main finding was that the district channels of redress were too much loaded against ordinary citizens in securing prompt and fair redress of their grievances. The Commission was of the view that the creation of the Ombudsman-type of institutions of Lokpal and Lokayukta was a "must" for developing the people's confidence and faith in the capability of the administration to deliver the goods. Though the Commission's proposals for the Indian Ombudsman included both the Centre and the States, several of the State Governments did not want to be covered by the proposal, legislation for which was brought forward by the Government of India in 1969. Accordingly, the Lokpal and Lokayuktas Bill 1969 provided for the creation of an Ombudsman-type of institution at the Centre only. This Bill, however, lapsed on the dissolution of the Lok Sabha which preceded the mid-term general election of March 1971. The Bill was reintroduced but the Congress Government gave it very low priority with the result that it was never put through. The Janata Government reintroduced this Bill on 28 July 1977 but with limited functions.

However, in more recent times, the advantages likely to accrue from the creation of an Ombudsman-type of institutions are catching up the attention of the State governments. The Maharaṣhtra Administrative Reforms Enquiry Committee recommended in 1968 the appointment of the States Ombudsman with two tiers called Lokayukta and Uplokayukta. The Committee was of the view that it was important to take immediate cognizance of the problem of public grievances and provide machinery for relief to the citizens against improper exercise of discretionary powers. The Governments of Maharashtra, U.P., and Orissa have enacted legislation for the appointment of Lokayuktas.

The problem of prevention of citizens' grievances has also received attention as a part of some of the studies of the district administration sponsored by the Planning Commission. A study of Sabarkantha district, made in 1962-64 by G.D. Patel, examined the existing administrative procedures of different departments at the district level and suggested measures for removing the prevailing procedural difficulties, malpractices, and delays. Another important study worth mentioning is the Administrative Survey of the Surat district by N.B. Desai. This study mostly deals with the existing machinery at different levels in Surat district from the point of view of improvement of procedures and practices. The study revealed that the delays in the disposal of the citizens' applications were largely due to the reference to subordinate offices for their furnishing the information without specifically indicating the points on which information was required. The studies of Sabarkantha and Surat districts are largely concerned with the delay in the disposal of cases at different levels.

Academic studies

Exclusive studies of the problem of citizens' grievances are only a few and these have been conducted mostly by the Indian Institute of Public Administration. The main studies are:

1. "Citizens' Grievances in Development Administration" by A.P. Barnabas.
2. "The Experience of Citizens in getting Water Connections" by A.P. Barnabas.
3. "Machinery and Procedures for Redress of Citizens' Grievances" by V. Jagannadham and H.R. Makhija.
4. "Citizen and the Municipal Bureaucracy—A Survey of the Building Department of the Delhi Municipal Corporation" by V. Jagannadham and N.S. Bakshi.
5. "Citizen and the Municipal Bureaucracy—A Study of the Assessment and Collection Department of the Delhi Municipal Corporation" by V. Jagannadham and N.S. Bakshi.
6. "The Citizens and Administration in a Developing Democracy—An Empirical Study in Delhi State" by S.J. Eldersveld, V. Jagannadham and A.P. Barnabas.
7. "Lokpal Ombudsman in India" by M.P. Jain.

The first study by A.P. Barnabas is concerned mostly with

the perceptions and attitudes of the officials and villagers towards each other felt by the citizens in their dealings with officials. The study emphasizes that the public support or alienation depends on the way the rules are applied. The study suggests the appointment of a Commissioner for Grievances at the Centre to help restore the confidence of the people in administration. The second study by Barnabas reveals that the majority of the respondents were unaware of the procedures and the conditions governing the provision of the water connections, and there was a general feeling that unless "speed" money was paid the files would not move. The study concludes that "one of the most important things that needs to be done is to develop greater communication between the administration and the public with regard to administrative procedures.

The study by Jagannadham and Makhija is at present the only piece of research which deals with the machinery for the redress of citizens' grievances. This study was conducted in 1966-67 in a block each in four States, namely, Andhra Pradesh, Maharashtra, Orissa, and Rajasthan. The object of the study was to identify the existing weaknesses in the machinery and procedures for the redress of citizens' complaints and to suggest appropriate remedial measures. The study was confined to five departments, viz. revenue, irrigation, industries, cooperation, and health. A sample of applications of the citizens (covering requests, complaints, representations, petitions, etc.) were selected from each department/office for the purpose of examination. The study covers the nature of the citizens' requests and complaints, the processing of the applications in the government offices, the time taken in disposal, and the reasons for delay. The study makes a number of suggestions for procedural improvements for taking prompt action on citizens' applications. A special feature of the study is the presentation of 13 short case studies of processing of applications.

The Jagannadham and Makhija study does not favour the creation of a separate State Directorate of Public Grievances and would like that the responsibility in this regard should rest with the departmental head who may, if necessary, be provided with full-time or part-time grievances officer to assist him. The study examines the relationship between the proposed institution of Lokpal and Lokayukta (the Indian Ombudsman) and the departmental redress machinery and suggests a detailed procedure for the functioning of the offices of Lokpal and Lokayukta.

The two studies conducted by V. Jagannadham and N.S. Bakshi (nos. 4 and 5 above) mostly deal with administrative improvements in certain specific segments of municipal administration and, in this connection, touch upon the nature of citizens' grievances and the possible measures for their redress. The study on building department of the Delhi Municipal Corporation examines in detail the hardships which the citizens have to put up with in securing the approval of the building plans, the delays in the processing of the citizens' applications, and the prevalence of corrupt practices. It highlights the inadequacies of the communication from the government to the citizens which open up opportunities for the unscrupulous civil servants to harass the citizens. The study recommends the creation of Citizens' Advice and Service Bureau to protect the common man from exploitation by the routine-ridden and secrecy-worshipping administration. The second study examines the difficulties experienced by the citizens in regard to over-assessment of their property, delays in the disposal of their representations, and the inconvenience caused in getting rebates for the additional facilities provided by them. The study emphasizes the importance of training in public relations and of regular inspections.

The study on "The Citizen and the Administrator in a Developing Democracy" by Samuel J. Eldersveld, V. Jagannadham, and A.P. Barnabas deserves a special mention. It contains a survey of the mental attitudes of 700 citizens and 220 administrators selected from five government departments, namely, health, police, posts and telegraphs, community development, and the Delhi Transport Undertaking. The study is mainly focussed on congruence in perspectives of the citizens and the administrators which is very necessary to mobilize the people's support in developmental and other nation-building activities. This study goes deep into job perspectives of the officials and their authoritarian or democratic predispositions. The study reveals that there exists a big gap between the administrators and the public in their perceptions and in their evaluation of the administrative system. Indices have been constructed to assess the administrative contacts of the citizens, contacts with political leaders, general communication exposure, and authoritarian and democratic orientations in personal predispositions. An interesting finding of the study is that administrators who are latently authoritarian can take on general democratic orientations concerning their jobs and the latter can predominate when reinforced by organizational expectations and performance demands. The study thus provides an analytical and conceptual framework of the interaction between the citizens and the administrators, as the backdrop for public grievances.

In recent years, there has also appeared some literature bearing on the suitability of the Ombudsman institution in India. In addition, there exists a considerable number of news items and special features in daily papers and articles in periodicals which deal with the problem of citizens' grievances. A study on "Lokpal Ombudsman in India" by M.P. Jain presents a critical analysis of the main features of the institution of the Ombudsman in the Scandinavian and some other countries vis-a-vis the proposals for the appointment of Lokpal and Lokayuktas in India. The study examines in detail the recommendations of the Administrative Reforms Commission on the subject, the provisions of the lapsed Bill on Lokpal and Lokayukta, and the proposals of the Joint Select Committee. For the effective functioning of the proposed institution of Lokpal and Lokayukta the study recommends the constitution of a watchdog committee of Lok Sabha members on the lines of the Select Committee appointed by the House of Commons in the U.K. to look into the reports of the Parliamentary Commissioner. There are also some other studies and write-ups on the suitability of the Ombudsman institution in India. Worth mentioning here is the study on "Corruption: Control of Maladministration" by John B. Monteiro. It probes into the nature and causes of corruption in the government, examines the working of the vigilance machinery, and also examines the validity of the Ombudsman-type of institutions in Indian conditions.

The above brief analysis of the existing academic studies shows that there is hardly any study which deals with the machinery for the redress of grievances at the district, State, and

Central levels in a comprehensive manner and from an integrated perspective. Taken together, the existing studies give an idea about the nature of grievances and the type of the redress machinery available; but they largely present a fragmented and blurred picture with several hazy patches and underexposed spots. The government reports and documents hardly give in detail the character and dimension of the citizens' grievances. The statistics they contain do not throw any light on these aspects of the problem. Such an approach on the part of the government departments or administrative reforms committees and commissions is understandable if we take note of the fact that policy-making in the government lacks, for the large part, a comprehensive empirical base.

BASIC ISSUES

In embarking upon the present study, the author kept in view the following basic issues:

1. What is the nature of citizens' grievances and what are their underlying causes?
2. How adequate is the existing administrative machinery for the redress of citizens' complaints and how effective is it in providing relief and inspiring the confidence of the people in its functioning?
3. Is there any integrated policy in the government's efforts at redress of citizens' complaints at the district, State, and Central levels? To what extent has there been a unified and systematic approach on the part of the government to the problem of redress of citizens' grievances?
4. To what extent is there a need for an independent machinery for the redress of public complaints? How far will the Ombudsman-type of institutions of Lokpal and Lokayukta proposed to be set up, be useful and workable in Indian conditions?

The present study differs from the previous studies in as much as its scope is much large and its approach quite comprehensive. In the first place, it tries to examine the nature of citizens' grievances and the factors and forces that give rise to them. It then attempts a critical appraisal of the machinery set up by the government for the redress of grievances from an integrated perspective, covering the entire gamut of administration—the District level, the State level, and the Central level. The study also deals in detail with the proposal for the Indian Ombudsman, the inadequacies of the provisions of the Bills on the subject introduced in the Lok Sabha in 1971 and 1977 and the improvements that are needed for making the new institutions of Lokpal and Lokayukta a success.

The study is largely based on the following:

1. Study of the existing published government reports and documentation including debates and discussions in the Parliament.
2. Study of selected official records covering the functioning of the existing machinery for the redress of complaints.
3. Study of existing non-official published literature, including research studies, articles in periodicals, and news reports.
4. Two special field studies carried out by the author—one of the citizens' grievances in eight villages in the Barabanki district of the State of Uttar Pradesh and the other of six treasuries in four States. The first field study was conducted through an open-ended questionnaire and covered 425 respondents, 320 citizens and 105 officials.
5. Interviews with select groups of officials and citizen leaders.

Thus, the present study is largely based on documented material. Quite a bit of the material has been collected from government records, which are not available to the public. The two field studies have helped in enriching the findings of the study.

The main theme of the study is the administrative machinery for the redress of public grievances. Administrative machinery, for purposes of this study, may be defined as institutional arrangements and procedures set up in the executive branch of the government for looking into the citizens' complaints. The various agencies and channels for the redress of citizens' grievances can be classified as follows:

1. Normal departmental channels of redress
2. Special departmental redress machinery
3. Supra-departmental redress machinery

The above-mentioned channels exist at the following levels:
—under the Union government
—under the State government
—at the district level
—under municipal administration
—in public sector undertakings

4. Judicial and semi-judicial channels:
—the courts
—administrative tribunals
5. Legislative and other channels:
—legislative channels
—citizens' associations and voluntary organizations
6. Special independent machinery

The main focus of the study is on the administrative redress machinery, i.e. items 1 to 3 and 6 above. The role of courts, administrative tribunals, the legislature, and citizens' associations (items 4 and 5) has also been covered but in a broad manner, as these do not strictly fall within the definition of administrative machinery. In the context of the recent debate about the usefulness of special independent machinery, such as the Ombudsman, three chapters have been devoted to it. The study, however, does not cover the problem of citizens' grievances in municipal administration and in public sector undertakings, which mostly operate on their own.

MACHINERY OF THE GOVERNMENT

For a fuller understanding of the problem of citizens' dissatisfaction with administration and the nature of their grievances, it seems necessary to outline very briefly the overall structure of the machinery of the government and to highlight the critical administrative inadequacies that give rise to citizens' grievances. Both these points are treated here to provide the setting for the discussion that follows in the following chapters.

Central administrative machinery

India is a Union of States. The Indian Constitution is neither purely unitary nor purely federal. The Seventh Schedule to the Constitution enumerates matters in respect of which the Union and the States respectively have exclusive powers to make laws. It also sets out in the Concurrent List certain other matters in respect of which legislation can be enacted by the Centre as well as by the States. The residuary legislative powers rest with the Union. This distribution of legislative powers also forms the basis for the distribution of the executive functions between the Centre and the States. It is heavily weighed in favour of the Union. The jurisdiction of the Union government under the Seventh Schedule covers matters such as defence, foreign affairs, railways, posts and telegraphs, airways, currency and banking, income-tax, central excise and customs, international trade and commerce, national highways, inter-State waterways, ports and the like. With the undertaking of economic and social planning a subject included in the Concurrent List the Union government has taken an active role in the formulation and the overseeing of the execution of Plan programmes in fields which fall in the Concurrent and the State Lists.

The executive machinery of the government at the Union level is headed by the President and under the Constitution all the executive powers vest in him. These powers are exercised by the President on the advice of the Council of Ministers through civil servants. The Union Cabinet has supreme control and directing powers over the civil servants. A similar position obtains in Sates which are headed by a Governor appointed by the President.

The machinery of the executive branch of the Union government consists of a secretariat and a number of field agencies. Where the Union government operates in its original jurisdiction, most of the work involved is in the nature of direct administration, although there are instances of the Union List work being handled through the States on agency arrangements. The role of the Central administration in matters falling in the State List is mainly that of coordinator, that of pioneer guide, disseminator of information, overall planner, and evaluator.

The secretariat comprises ministries and departments. Some of these ministries and departments have no field agencies.

A ministry or a department is headed by a secretary to the government. It is divided into a number of wings, each under a joint secretary. A wing has normally three divisions, each in a deputy secretary's charge. A division consists of about two under secretaries, each having two or three branches under him. A branch has a section officer or superintendent and about five dealing hands, four assistants and one upper division clerk. Each section constitutes an office. An important feature of Indian administration is the differentiation between the officer and the office. The Indian administrative system has thus sharp hierarchical structures and there are generally as many as five or six levels of processing and consideration before a decision is arrived at. This makes for delay. The number of offices functioning under the secretariat runs into thousands. There are about 570 non-secretariat offices having the attributes of the headquarters units. The field agencies are of two types: attached offices and subordinate offices. In the Indian scheme of administration, the field agencies are generally headed as a separate entity from the secretariat with the object of keeping the policy formulation function separate from the executive work. The secretariat personnel, being near the seat of political power, have come to enjoy higher informal status The secretariat is mostly staffed by generalists and this has in some way affected the quality of policy-making. The scales of pay and benefits of the personnel working in the field agencies are generally lower than those of the secretariat staff. Financial and administrative powers enjoyed by the heads of the field agencies are normally inadequate for the discharge of their duties; though lately there has been a trend towards their enhancement. The distinction between the secretariat and the field agencies acts as a great drag on the feedback from the field, and as a result the secretariat is hardly well posted with the difficulties of the citizens and the progress in the implementation of programmes and policies.

Administrative set-up in the States

There are in India, as of today, 28 States and 7 Union Territories. The latter are administered by the Union Government, though some of them have representative assemblies of advisory character. The individual citizen comes in much more contact with the administrative machinery of the State than of the Centre. Under the present division of executive powers between the Union and the States, subjects such as law and order, prisons, local governments, public health, excise, agriculture, etc., fall within the purview of the legislative and executive branches of the State governments.

In the States, the basic unit of administration is the district. There are in India, 6934 towns and 640867 villages in 640 districts. The district-level general administration comprises the district collector-cum-magistrate and his office known as the collectorate, district offices of different executive authorities, such as the police, public works, irrigation, cooperatives, agriculture, industry, health, etc. Each district is divided into sub-districts or sub-divisions, tehsils or talukas. The district collector-cum-magistrate and the sub-divisional officer and the talukdar/tehsildar are primarily concerned with such matters as maintenance of law and order, assessment and collection of land revenue, land tenure, etc. In some States the sub-divisional officer also looks after the development work. Apart from the traditional district machinery, district administration today covers a vast range of officials and functionaries dealing with developmental functions in areas such as public works, health, industry, agriculture, etc. The district collector is also responsible for coordination of all developmental activity of the government in the district except in the States of Maharashtra and Gujarat. He is assisted in this task by a district development officer.

In many States, districts are organized into divisions which are regional units of administration. Each division is headed by a divisional commissioner. At the State headquarters is located the State secretariat, consisting of several administrative departments. The internal set-up of an administrative department is largely similar to a secretariat department at the Centre except that it is much smaller in size. Under each administrative department, there are executive agencies known as executive departments. The field offices of these executive agencies run through the entire State territory. All of them invariably have district offices and many of them also have regional offices. The jurisdiction of the regional offices of the executive agencies, however, does not always coincide with that of the divisions.

Most of the towns have municipal committees— the larger

ones have municipal councils and the large cities have municipal corporations. The municipal government is autonomous within a certain statutory framework. However, certain powers of control are vested in the local government directorate/department of the State government. Some limited supervisory powers are also vested in the district collector. It needs to be specifically mentioned that the grievances of citizens in the matter of facilities and amenities provided by the municipal administration and machinery for their redress are not specifically covered by the present study. In each district, and even at the regional level, there also exist field agencies of certain executive departments of the union government such as income-tax, Central excise, food department, Central labour inspectorate, Central public works department, etc. These offices, though located in the States, are vested with the responsibility of carrying out certain functions of the Central administration.

Popular bodies known as panchayati raj (people's) institutions have come up at the village, block/taluk, and district levels. Village panchayats (village councils), panchayat samitis (at the block or tehsil level), and zila parishads (at the district level) exist in most of the States. The pattern of panchayati raj administration is slightly different in the States of Maharashtra and Gujarat. While in many other States the zila parishad has only a coordinating or supervisory role, in Gujarat and Maharashtra the administration of the development programme has been handed over entirely to the district-level popular body. In these two States, the district heads of all development departments have been placed under the zila parishad's chief executive officer who is responsible for coordinating and supervising all the development programmes those funded by the government as well as those which are financed from the funds raised by the popular bodies.

The panchayat samiti constitutes the intermediate level of panchayati raj bodies. This body is at the block level in all States except in Gujarat, Maharashtra, and Karnataka. In these States, the samitis have been constituted at the taluk level. The nomenclature of the samiti varies. The panchayat samiti at the block level is the focal point of the people's institutions. It looks after (i) civic amenities, (ii) social welfare activities, and (iii) development work. There is attached to each panchayat samiti a block development officer who is assisted by a team of six or seven extension workers in the field of agriculture, social education, industry, cooperatives, etc.

At the village level, there is the gram panchayat (village council) which is responsible for civic amenities and implementation of the village welfare and development programmes. The main officials at the grass-roots level for group of villages are the patwari (revenue clerk), the village panchayat secretary, and the gram sevak (village-level worker). There is a police station at each tehsil and there are police chowkies for a group of villages, manned by policemen and junior police officials.

Public sector undertakings

Since the advent of economic planning in the early fifties, there has been a phenomenal expansion of the public sector. It today covers more than 277 operating units spread over the length and breadth of the country. These undertakings enjoy autonomy within the broad policy framework set by the government, though intervention by the ministers or administrative departments is said to be on the increase. The public sector undertakings are mostly engaged in manufacturing and providing services, though some are also engaged in external trade and promotional activities. Some notable lacunae in the management of public sector undertakings are unbusiness-like methods of work, manning of a large proportion of senior positions by civil servants on loan, and lack of adequate managerial capability. So far as the citizens are concerned, the main problem is that the monopolistic public enterprises can show profits in spite of inefficient operations at the expense, so to say, of the consumers. However, the present study does not go into the problem of citizens' grievances relating to public sector undertakings set up as corporations or companies. But it covers posts and telegraphs and railways, which are departmentally managed. In any case after economic liberalisation in 90s. some of the public sector units have been privatised.

By and large, the machinery of the government moves at a snail's pace. The secretariat at the Centre and in the States have taken up various unimportant tasks and even executive functions. The secretariat is, for a large part, an unwieldy and over-staffed organization. There is blurring of responsibilities and choking of administrative machinery, leading to dilatoriness. The number of agencies has proliferated and there is considerable overlapping and fragmentation of functions. The methods of work are mostly outmoded. For instance, in the villages, patwari still works by antiquated methods and nobody has ever thought of providing him with a typewriter. The district collectorate presents an unhappy picture of heaps of arrears, protracted delays, and over-congestion. The secretariat offices exhibit a woeful lack of sense of urgency. The pattern of staffing lacks in quality and competence. The main burden of work in the secretariat continues to be borne by the "dealing assistants" who comprise the office, and the officer level does not appear to make much contribution. In one of the research studies conducted for the Punjab Administrative Reforms Commission it was found that the original contribution from secretaries to the government was about five to six per cent.

The non-secretariat organizations which are the field-arm of the administration find the secretariat control frustrating and meaningless. "To them, the secretariat largely acts as a drag on the execution of schemes and programmes by delaying sanctions and insisting on meticulous observance of rules and procedures. Unfamiliarity with the field conditions, particularly among the assistants concerned with the initial scrutiny of and noting on their proposals adds to discontent."[7] The personnel in the field are handicapped in several respects, particularly in the matter of adequate facilities and good service conditions. It is the junior personnel in the field who are mostly unsympathetic to the citizens' needs and difficulties and in many cases have fallen a prey to corrupt practices. The working of the field agencies is marked by slackness, inefficiency, and indifference.

It will not be an exaggeration to state that the Indian bureaucracy works largely for the influential and the powerful, and for itself. In due course it does meet some of the demands of

[7]Government of India, *Report of the Administrative Reforms Commission on the Machinery of the Government of India and Its Procedures of Work*, 1968, p. 31.

the citizens and a measure of complaints are also redressed. But the delay which takes place in the process, the harassment which is caused to the citizen, and the evils which surround the bureaucratic working appear to overshadow whatever good work the Indian administration does. The benefits which the citizen gets are large by way of doles, something which he receives as a matter of mercy from officials, after a great deal of persistence and suffering great hardships.

One of the most difficult principles for the average civil servant to appreciate and to honour is his complete dependence on the will of the people. Having achieved his post, he is quite understandably inclined to resent any intrusions upon his time and his authority that appear to sway him from pursuing his mission as he understands it. He has trouble in seeing how any legislator or any citizen could possibly have an interest in what he does. He forgets that in exercising those discretions that are left to him he is obliged in his deliberations to listen to, to consider carefully, and to weigh the viewpoints of others as to the meaning, intent, and spirit of the law he administers.[8]

SOCIO-POLITICAL CONTEXT

The social and political setting of the administration is hardly conducive to the efficient functioning of the Indian bureaucracy. The working of parliamentary system established after Independence has created new stresses and strains. Political development in India has not proceeded on healthy lines in as-much as the political parties have come to depend a good deal on power patronage for winning the elections and continuing in office. Party cohesion is maintained by being skilful in providing rewards to diverse factions and communities. The emergence of the unstable coalition governments in several States with different party ideologies has in some ways adversely affected the making of speedy decisions on policy matters and the quality of coordination in programme planning and implementation. The disintegrating forces of regionalism and linguism tend to disrupt social stability and if today the grow-

[8]O. Glenn Stahl, *Public Personnel Administration*, New York, Harper & Row, 1971, pp. 248-9.

ing discontent in the political, social, and economic fields has found expressions in riots, strikes, pressure tactics, and damage to life and property, the attention of the government is being increasingly devoted to the more critical political and social problems leaving little time for attending to mundane matters such as administrative reforms. And the problem of citizens' grievances is only one of the many items in the field of administrative improvement and reorganization. But this does not explain adequately the ambivalent approach of the government to the citizens' problems and difficulties. It is a part of the wider problem of the gap between the promise and the performance which is pronounced in the matter of implementation of the five year plans and the schemes. In all traditional societies there is decidedly a considerable gap between intentions and actions. "There is reluctance to face up to the realities of power to use it to achieve certain social ends. This attitude is based on the belief that use of power is not consistent with belief in man's goodness and reasonableness, or with the democratic rights and harmonious relations deemed to have been characteristic of traditional India and to be essential to a socialistic society."[9]

Viewing the problem of public grievances from the political perspective, we find that though sovereignty rests with the people, administration is not directly responsible to the people but to the elected representatives who enjoy the majority in the legislature. It is the bounden duty of the administration to carry out the policies and programmes as proposed by the political executive and framed or approved by the legislature. Administration is supposed to function in public interest, but its responsibility to the people's needs is only indirect. When we speak of the responsiveness of administration to the people's needs and demands, we have also to keep in view that intervening between the people and the administration are the government and the legislature.

A bureaucratic organization operates mostly by a set of

[9]Joseph P. Spangler, "Allocation and Development, Economic and Political", in *Political and Administrative Development*, Duke University Press, 1969, pp. 602-3.

objective and impersonal rules and this characteristic tends to make it "faceless" and "lifeless" in its dealings with its people. Bureaucracy also tends to develop, in the process of its working, some dysfunctional and unintended consequences or displacement of its goals and the means tend to become ends in themselves. In a developing country this problem is even more acute, as the social and political controls over the administration are not strong enough to make it fully responsive to the citizens' needs and difficulties. From the point of view of ecology and administration, the system in India can be said to be more or less on the lines of Prismatic model formulated by Fred W. Riggs. The differentiation of functions in the society under this model is incomplete and its chief characteristics are uneven distribution of services, institutionalized corrupt practices, inefficiency in rule application, bureaucratic clusters dominated by motives of self-protection and a high degree of formalism, i.e., a pronounced gap between formal expectations and actual behaviour.[10]

"Only by building effective instrumentalities for imposing real control over the State bureaucracy can the sanctions needed to insure administrative efficiency be brought into being. But, effective political institutions are a more delicate and fragile growth than bureaucratic agencies. The path of least resistance for transitional elites bent on rapid modernization is the expansion of bureaucracy and the mere imposition, by fiat, of a facade of official 'parties', rubber-stamp legislatures, pliable courts, and administered interest groups. Thus what appears to be the quickest way to create political and administrative institutions results, in practice, in the fateful appearance of negative politco-administrative processes."[11]

The problem of the effective functioning of the machinery for the redress of citizens' grievances is, thus, a part of the wider end more complex problem of taming the bureaucratic machine. Unless the latter is properly tackled, the creation of a new grievance redress agency or strengthening of the existing

[10]Fred W. Riggs, *Administration in Developing Countries: The Theory of Prismatic Society*, Boston, Houghton Mifflin Company, 1964, pp. 260-85.

[11]*Ibid.*, pp. 423-4.

agency is not going to make any meaningful difference, provided, of course, such machinery serves as a control mechanism.

One fruitful approach to reinforcing the social infrastructure will be the creation of a network of voluntary organizations, citizens' associations, consumers' councils, and the like. Since the advent of economic planning, voluntary organizations have proliferated, but their functioning is, by and large, hardly up to the mark, and they do not wield much influence over the government in the matter of redress of public complaints.

Some other types of socio-political controls over the bureaucracy can also be thought of. In the U.S.A., most of the top positions in the government are held by political appointees. In Germany, the appointments to the first two administrative levels at the top go by political considerations. Whatever may be the demerits of such arrangements, they do help in building into the administrative resilience and adaptability to meet the environmental challenges. The Indian bureaucracy is largely a closed system,[12] and parliamentary control over administration is hardly adequate to make it development-minded and responsive to the citizens' needs. As pointed out by an eminent scholar, "The essence of administration in developing countries is smooth and creative management of rapid social and political change. This requires among other things a major innovational role on the part of the higher civil service which is crucial link between the political elites and the rank-and-file bureaucrats. To secure such a contribution from the higher civil service, however, takes more than the mere presence of some innovational elements within it. It requires a parallel presence of enlightened political leadership with an adequate measure of 'Developmentalist' orientation."[13] It is important that one of the two political elite groups, either the power elite which control or the task political elite which are in charge of action programmes, must be "developmentalists", preferably

[12]An interesting discussion of closed, mixed, and open bureaucracy will be found in "Bureaucratic Models and Administrative Reform" by Hahn-Been Lee, *Development and Change*. The Hague, Institute of Social Studies, Volume II, 1970-71, No. 2, pp. 56-9.

[13]Hehn-Been Lee, "The Role of the High Civil Service under Rapid Social and Political Change" in Edward W. Weidner (ed.), *Development Administration in Asia*. Durhan, Duke University Press, 1970, p. 131.

the latter because the higher bureaucracy is more influenced by it than by the power elite.

From the wider perspective, the problem of citizens' grievances is intimately connected with that of closely inter-relating together the efforts at social, economic, political, and administrative change or development. Development is a process of upward multi-dimensional change and amalgam of modernity, nation-building, and socio-economic progress. India has embarked upon "planned directional growth with system change". But "such planned change requires prior basic alteration in the political and administrative systems. On occasions major changes may be embraced temporarily by politicians or the bureaucracy, for forgetting the past and looking to the future are popular things to support. When faced with the details of executing such changes they find the difficulties great. Without the alterations, the administrative system and the political support base are likely to be inadequate to the task of carrying through major system change and growth."[14] Any proposal for the reform of the existing machinery for the redress of grievances or the creation of a new, independent redress agency, therefore, needs to be scrutinized adequately in terms of the role of such an agency in the context of the overall process of development.

We must, accordingly, try to look at the administration as a total system and try to delineate the role of the machinery for the redress of citizens' grievances in the administration as a whole. In the effort at administrative reforms in India, the general approach has been to treat the administration as a closed system. The wider perspective of administration as a social sub-system, interacting on the environment, has mostly evaded the administrative reformers. The problem of citizens' grievances has thus received only peripheral attention, even though the citizens' satisfaction constitutes a major goal of administration. However, if we follow the systems approach[15] to administration we can conceive of the citizens'

[14]Edward W. Weidner, "The Elements of Development Administration", in Edward W. Weidner (ed.), *Development Administration in Asia*, op. cit., p. 12.

[15]Systems approach presents a useful framework for the examination of a recurrent pattern of interaction which is interdependent or comple-

grievances as a part of the feedback on the effectiveness of the system in goal achievement, i.e. citizens' satisfaction and welfare. The conceptualization of administrative reforms in terms of systems approach will also have a far-reaching impact on the entire pattern of planned administrative change. It would imply that the administrative system must be able to meet the environmental demands effectively and its different components would have a justification only in so far as they contribute to this objective. The main emphasis in such a perspective will be on correcting the functioning of the system. Machinery for the redress of grievances will be treated as a special mechanism designed to take care of the inadequacy of the system in adapting itself or meeting the environmental demands completely. Such a role of the redress machinery as a feedback device and as a compensating mechanism will be more realistic and useful. The redress machinery will be considered as an integral part of the administrative system, and not as an adjunct which is the general treatment accorded to it in India today.

mentary with respect to some common purpose or function and which is thus separated from the rest of the environment. The interrelated activities of the system are directed to achieving some desired behaviour. Beginning with the goals, the systems approach is directed to processing of the inputs into outputs through a set of interrelated decisions. In the systems approach, the feedback occupies a key place in as much as it reveals errors in estimates, unexpected events, and new possibilities, leading to the reformulation of the earlier policies or decisions. Saul M. Katz "A Systems Approach to Development Administration". Special Series No. 6 (Washington, D.C.), American Society for Public Administration, *Papers in Comparative Public Administration*, 1965, pp. 4-10. "The Systems approach stresses the way in which the action of the parts is structured by the system's need for stability and goal-consensus, and emphasizes the processes of integration and adaptation." David Silverman, *The Theory of Organizations*, London, Heinemann, 1970, p. 39. The four main elements in the systems approach are system, environment, feedback, and response. David Beston, *A Framework for Political Analysis*. Engle-wood Cliffs, N.J., Prentice-Hall, 1965, pp.24 -5.

CHAPTER II

Nature of Grievances

The dissatisfaction of the citizens with the district level machinery has grown in recent years due to its proliferation, the growth in the expectations and demands of the people, and the lowering of standards of efficiency and discipline in the administration. There is a "complex and paradoxical mosaic of support and hostility of consensus and critique" in the attitude of citizens towards the government. There is a general agreement that district administration has been unable to render efficient and timely service. The rural people, being illiterate and poor, do not have the capacity to secure satisfaction of their genuine needs and demands from administration. The rural population constitutes at present 92 per cent of the total population of the country.

The main areas of citizens' contact with administration in the district relate to the supply of services in developmental fields such as agriculture (supply of agricultural inputs such as fertilizers, pesticides, seeds, etc.), animal husbandry, land conservation and development, consolidation of land holdings, supply of water and power, provision of credit for purposes of agriculture; handicrafts and small-scale industry, provision of essential commodities the supply of which has been controlled by the government, facilities for education and medical care, development of roads, post and telegraph facilities and transport services such as railways, and measures of sanitation and preventive health. In addition, the district administration also renders traditional services, e.g., protection against damage to individual life and property (provided by the police), maintenance of land records and land tenure system, etc.

SAMPLE SURVEY OF GRIEVANCES OF VILLAGERS AND ATTITUDE OF OFFICIALS

Rural development has an important place in the national plans of economic and social development. The problem of citizens' grievances in rural areas is not just of making the administration streamlined and efficient and providing for their effective redress, it is equally a problem of adaptation and extension of administrative machinery to the new task of rural development and to the rising expectations of the people. The distribution of the gains of development during the past twenty-five years has been uneven and the benefits of the green revolution which has appeared on the scene about a decade ago have also not been spread widely to benefit all sections of the rural society.

In view of the political awakening and increasing expectations of the rural people, any attempt at administrative reorganization and improvement must take into account the nature and magnitude of their grievances. Empirical studies of this problem have so far been too few. The author was, therefore, very keen to gain some first-hand knowledge about the character and the quantum of the grievances of the villages, and a special study was undertaken for the purpose. Care was taken to select a district that was "backward" in terms of socio-economic development. A backward district was selected purposively as it was felt that the emerging problem of the citizens' relations with the administration could be better appreciated by a study of a unit of district administration where the impact of development programmes has been impeded by several factors including the inadequacies of the administration.

The sample

The district chosen was Barabanki in the State of Uttar Pradesh. The district has about 1,414,500 population. It has an area of 4,440 sq. km. Its economy is predominantly agricultural. Two villages were selected at random from each of the four tehsils. The population of each village ranged between 3,000 and 7,000. For each village, a sample of 1 per cent population was selected, with a minimum of 40 villagers, giving a total sample of 350. However, of these only 320 could be interviewed.

As regards the officials, they were selected on the basis of stratified sampling from among those working at the tehsil and block offices and as well as those stationed at the district headquarters and dealing with rural areas. From a total of 516 of such officials,129 (25 per cent) were selected, but only 105 of them could be interviewed, 50 at the district headquarters and 55 in the field. The study was conducted through an open-ended questionnaire, with some questions prepared separately for the villagers and for the officials (see Appendix I). The questionnaire was administered personally and this opportunity was also availed of to find out the general views of the villagers and officials. Some of the respondents in both the groups showed hesitation in expressing their opinions freely and frankly. This hesitation was but natural. The villagers were afraid that a frank expression of their grievances might annoy the government functionaries concerned and there might be victimization in the future. The officials had the feeling that their acceptance of the shortcomings of administration could amount to admission of their own inefficiency. However, by explaining the purpose of the enquiry and by giving the respondents the assurance that their views would be kept strictly confidential and their identity would not be disclosed, it was found possible to establish rapport, and when once they were able to overcome their initial hesitation, it was not difficult to get their frank and honest views.

Characteristics of the respondents

A brief description of the main characteristics of the villager-respondents is as follows:

Age: Thirty per cent of the respondents were above the age of 50 years, 35 per cent between the ages of 40 and 49 years, 20 per cent in the age-group of 30-39 and 15 per cent were below the age of 30 years.

Profession: About 80 per cent of the respondents were engaged in agriculture (35 per cent owned agricultural lands and 65 per cent were landless labours); 20 per cent were artisans, traders, government servants, etc.

Land-holding: About 68 per cent respondents owned either less than 5 acres of land or no land; 6.4 per cent possessed land between 10 and 20 acres; and 5.6 per cent owned land above 20 acres.

Education: Seventy per cent respondents were illiterate; 15 per cent had studied up to primary level. The remaining had studied up to middle. There were no respondents living in the village who possessed high school education.

Panchayat membership: Seventy-eight per cent of the respondents were members of panchayats and cooperative societies.

Caste: Sixty-seven per cent of the respondents belonged to farming castes; 8 per cent were Brahmins; 13 per cent were Harijans; and 10 per cent were Muslims.

Among the officials interviewed, 55 per cent had been in service for more than ten years, 25 per cent had joined government service some 7 to 9 years back, 13 per cent had service experience of 4 to 6 years and 7 per cent were in the service group of 1 to 3 years.

About 60 per cent of the officials were holding the position they occupied for less than 3 years, 25 per cent for 4 to 7 years, and the remaining 15 per cent had been there for more than 7 years.

Officials interviewed were collector, deputy collectors, superintendent of police, deputy superintendents of police, inspectors of police, head constables, constables, panchayat officers, electoral officers, block development officers, gram sewaks, executive engineers, magistrates, vigilance officers, superintendent, assistants, clerks, peons, etc.

Sixty-nine per cent of the officials had their education up to the high school or less, 12 per cent possessed college education, 13 per cent technical qualifications and 6 per cent post-graduates.

Fifty-five per cent of the officials were in the age-group of 24 to 35 years, 25 per cent in the age-group of 36 to 55 years, 3 per cent were above 55 years, and the remaining were below 24 years of age.

Nature of grievances

The villagers were asked a set of questions about the nature and type of their grievances against the administration. Of the 320 respondents, only 97 per cent replied to these questions. Their reactions regarding the intensity of their complaints were as follows:

Serious complaints	52 per cent
Complaints of moderate intensity	31 per cent
Minor complaints	8 per cent
No complaints	6 per cent

The study has revealed that the citizens' complaints are largely of the following type:

Non-availability or inadequacy of supplies: The most pronounced complaints relate to non-availability or inadequacy of supplies such as kerosene oil, cement, tyres and tubes, medicines (in hospitals), fertilizers, seeds, pesticides, power for working tubewells, credit for agricultural purposes and for starting and extending arts and crafts and small industries, and inadequate facilities for education and vocational training. It was a common experience that either the supplies were not available or if they were available some of these either found their way into the black market or were given only on the payment of some illegal gratification. For instance, the villagers of Danyalpur complained that they had to regularly pay extra money to the irrigation staff, and whosoever paid the maximum would get preference in the allotment of water from the canal. Twenty-four per cent of the respondents complained of short or late supply of fertilizers and one-third of them attributed this to the unsatisfactory distribution and callousness of officials. Another one-third were of the view that the shortage in fertilizers were due to the misuse of supplies, i.e. giving more supplies to friends and influential farmers, selling them in black market, etc. The villagers had to obtain permits from the district supply office to get fertilizers and the distribution of these permits was made on several considerations including the influence of political power, money, status, etc.

Delays in provision of supplies and services: The study showed that delays in the provision of supplies and services were quite marked and the problem was much intense in the case of supply of fertilizers, seeds, agricultural credit, pesticides, and power for tubewells. The weaker and illiterate villagers were thus forced to purchase sugar, maida, kerosene oil, cement, cycle tyres and tubes, etc. in black market. In the case of fertilizers delays were also due to late arrival of stocks from the factories. The main fault was that the available stocks were not equitably distributed and this was particularly emphasized by the respondents. Many of them felt disgusted when they were openly discriminated against in a free and democratic country. It is common knowledge that how much in short supply a commodity may be, the influential people secure permits to get it at the controlled prices while the less fortunate are left with the option of buying it in the black market or going without it. It is this type of discrimination which leads to heart burning among the people, and there is certainly the need for looking into the working of the civil supplies department and to recognize the system of distribution of essential commodities on a more equitable basis in rural areas. The villagers of Barabanki district were greatly frustrated over these delays.

Inconvenience and harassment: It is not only that the supplies of essential commodities, services, and facilities are inadequate and are often delayed, the villagers are put to great inconvenience, hardship, and even harassment in trying to secure the fulfilment of their legitimate demands on the administration. They have to pay frequent visits to the block and tehsil offices and to the district-level officials, and wait long hours outside their doors. Visits to dispensaries and hospitals involve waiting for hours only to discover many a time at the end of a long wait that the medicines needed are not available. The illiterate villagers are harassed by the petty officials and it is not uncommon to demand small sums of graft money. They even fall a prey to professional touts and have to shell out a portion of their hard-earned savings. What is worse is that the villagers are generally treated with great rudeness and callousness by the officials. The relations between the rural people and the administration are, by and large, characterized by an utter lack of regard for the dignity of the poor and the backward sections of the rural society.

Issue of quotas and permits: With the advent of development plans a number of regulatory controls have been imposed on economic activity. In the system of economic controls, the ordinary citizens, the farmers, the artisans and the craftsmen, and the self-employed find it difficult to secure permits and quotas. The securing of these permits is an uphill task and all sorts of influence have to be mobilized for the purpose. The expansion of the system of quotas and permits has given rise to corrupt practices of several kinds. A considerable proportion of the citizens' grievances can be traced to this system.

Lack of fair play under political and parochial influence: The vast majority of the villager-respondents felt that the decisions of the administration on citizens' requests for services and facilities were mostly based on political and parochial considerations. Lack of impartiality and fair play in decisions had vitiated the citizens' faith in the ability of the administration to deliver the goods, and further tended to increase their sense of dissatisfaction with the administration even where minor complaints or requests had been turned down on legitimate grounds. Smooth and healthy citizen-administration relations are at present greatly marred by the growing favouritism and patronage which is being shown by both the civil servants and the elected representatives.

The vast majority of the villagers interviewed (71 per cent) expressed dissatisfaction with the working of the community development programmes. Two-thirds of the officers interviewed, on the other hand, felt that the inadequate progress of the community development programmes was due to the apathetic attitude of the people and lack of proper facilities for the functionaries of the community development department in rural areas. However, one-fifth of them conceded that the officials had failed to arouse popular enthusiasm and to establish rapport with the villagers.

The emergence of panchayati raj institutions, with control over a major segment of developmental activity in the rural areas, has let loose new evils such as injudicious distribution of the common village land among the supporters of the ruling clique, growth of factions and strife in the panchayati raj leadership, and even increase in litigation and minor crime.

The psychological aspect of the citizens' grievances is as important as other aspects and the remedy perhaps lies in the creation of an independent agency to look into citizens' complaints.

Major findings of the study

The villager-respondents were asked to state their degree of satisfaction with the general working of the rural administrative machinery. Only 14 per cent of them said that they were "satisfied", about 38 per cent were "dissatisfied", and 48 per cent were "highly dissatisfied".

Attitude of officials: The villagers as well as officials were asked a set of questions concerning the attitude of officials towards rural people. As would be evident from Table 1, about one-fourth of the officials agreed that the officials' attitudes were marked by haughtiness and lack of concern for the people's welfare, and about one-third of them admitted that the officials were generally callous and unsympathetic. A good

TABLE 1

Perception of villagers (N-320) and officials (N--105) regarding attitudes of officials

1. General behaviour towards citizens

	Courteous		*Formal*		*Haughty*	
	N	%	*N*	%	*N*	%
Villagers	43	13	277	87	270	85
Officials	87	82	18	17	20	20

2. Attitude towards citizens' needs and difficulties

	Sympathetic		*Indifferent*		*Unsympathetic*		*Obstructive*	
	N	%	*N*	%	*N*	%	*N*	%
Villagers	43	13	255	82	260	81	264	82
Officials	75	71	38	37	37	36	34	33

3. Concern for people's welfare

	Little		*Moderate*		*High*	
	N	%	*N*	%	*N*	%
Villagers	269	84	11	4	32	10
Officials	13	12	19	18	74	71

many grievances of the citizens spring from the incorrect relationship of the administrative personnel with the citizens. In a democratic set-up like India's, the citizens, in theory, are the masters and the government officials are their servants, but in actual practice the concept often appears to operate in the reverse direction.

Delay: Delays are the common bane of Indian administration. In the case of villagers, delays in decisions on their applications are all the more significant in view of the absence, for the most part, of organized interest groups to articulate their demands and the widespread illiteracy among the rural people. In the present study, 75 per cent of the villager-respondents stated that they could seldom get their work done within a reasonable time. About 58 per cent of the officials agreed that timely services were not being provided to the people.

Lengthy and involved procedures are responsible for delays in the opinion of three-fifths of the villagers and four-fifths of the officials. In regard to inefficiency and overwork as causes of delay, the perceptions of the two groups differed significantly: 45 per cent of the villagers attributed delay to inefficiency against 27 per cent of officials; 94 per cent of the officials considered that excessive load of work was responsible for delays but only 23 per cent of the villagers agreed with this proposition (see Table 2).

There is also difference of opinion in regard to the contribution made to delays by lack of knowledge of procedure on the part of applicants. Only 38 per cent of the villagers against 62 per cent officials agreed that this was a delaying factor. It may be mentioned here that one of the studies of the Indian Institute of Public Administration shows that the knowledge among the rural people of the procedures to be followed for obtaining facilities such a taccavi loans, maternity and child welfare and family planning services, etc., is very poor. Villagers are even paying for the cost of medicines at the government dispensaries even though these services are to be provided free of charge.

A study of the causes of delay carried out by the Department of Removal of Public Grievances in Rajasthan State indicated that some important causes of delay were lack of adequate or

TABLE 2

Perception of villagers (N--320) and officials (N--105) regarding the causes of delay in rendering timely services

Cause	*Perception of* *Officials*		*Villagers*	
	N	%	*N*	%
1. Inefficiency	28	27	144	45
2. Lengthy and involved procedures	83	80	192	60
3. Inadequate delegation of power	88	91	288	90
4. Overworked staff	97	94	76	23
5. Corrupt practices	42	40	166	52
6. Lack of knowledge of procedures by applicants	64	62	121	38

efficient staff, posts lying vacant for long periods, frequent transfers of officials, inadequate knowledge of rules and regulations, and want of proper attention by the supervisory officials to the notings on the files and neglect of reminders. The study shows that the delay is perceived as more due to laxity of administration and supervision, lack of interest and sensitiveness to public interest than due to the complexity of rules and procedures.

Inefficiency: In view of the considerable importance attached by both the categories of respondents to inefficiency as a cause of delay, the respondents were probed further about the causes of inefficiency. The overall picture that emerged was that inefficiency was due to several factors. Here again, the differences between the viewpoints of the officials, the villagers were quite pronounced, and even within the officials, the district-level civil service attributed inefficiency more to such factors as political intervention, faulty methods of recruitment, and lack of provision to reward efficient workers (see Table 3).

A significant proportion of district-level officials appear to attribute faulty methods of recruitment, inadequate education, and intervention by elected representatives to the causes of

TABLE 3

Perception of villagers and officials on causes of inefficiency

Causes of inefficiency	*Villagers* N=14	*Officials* District level N=50	Village/block level N=55	*Total*
1. Faulty methods of recruitment	119 (82.64)	21 (42.00)	9 (16.36)	149
2. Inadequate education	105 (72.92)	19 (38.00)	10 (18.18)	134
3. Lack of adequate training	124 (86.11)	9 (18.00)	25 (45 45)	158
4. Lack of supervision and guidance	132 (91.76)	4 (8.00)	26 (47.27)	162
5. Faulty methods of promotion	95 (65.97)	14 (28.00)	30 (54.50)	139
6. Frequent transfers	109 (75.69)	20 (40.00)	23 (41.02)	152
7 Intervention by elected representatives and political leaders	86 (59.72)	29 (56.00)	16 (29.09)	131
8. Intervention by senior civil servants	43 (29.86)	4 (8.00)	21 (38.18)	68
9. Lack of incentive for good work	49 (34.00)	11 (22.00)	22 (40.00)	82
10. Lack of delegation of power for decision-making	76 (52.78)	8 (16.00)	32 (56.18)	116
11. Inadequacy of office equipment and facilities	108 (75.00)	5 (10 00)	24 (43.64)	137

inefficiency. On the other hand, a large number of village and block-level officials perceive that the main reasons for inefficiency are faulty methods of promotions, lack of power, inadequate training, lack of supervision and guidance, want of adequate equipment, lack of incentives, and intervention by senior civil servants. Two-fifths of both the groups agree that frequent transfers are having a damaging effect on efficiency.

Use of influence: About 85 per cent of the villager-respondents felt that it was difficult to have a fair decision from the government machinery without the use of some sort of influence.

One-tenth of them, however, thought that things had improved significantly in recent years and in the majority of the cases fair decisions could be expected and were also given, though there were invariably long delays and influence was necessary to get things done quickly.

As regards the type of influence which was effective to produce results, two-fifths of the villagers thought that political contacts were most rewarding. One-third of the villagers attached importance to the acquaintance with the officials, and the major device favoured for winning support of the officials was an appeal to the official's feeling of authority and paternalism. About 32 per cent were of the view that it was impossible to secure their acceptance of legitimate claims without offering some gratification to the officials. About 7 per cent of the villager-respondents added that parochial considerations such as caste, creed, etc., weighed considerably with the officials in granting citizens' requests.

Intervention by elected representatives: Out of 45 per cent villager-respondents whose applications did not receive prompt action (144 persons of the total number of villagers interviewed) said that they had contacted the elected representatives to speed up action. The intervention of the members of panchayats/panchayat samitis/zila parishads/legislatures was useful to the extent shown in Table 4.

TABLE 4

Villagers' (N=144) perception of helpfulness of elected representatives

Intervention by elected representatives	*Proportion of villagers*	
	N	%
Very much helpful	26	18
Moderately helpful	54	38
Not at all helpful	64	44

About one-third of the 144 villagers who had contacted the elected representatives said that they offered gifts and presents such as wine, wheat, rice, vegetables, etc., to the elected representatives. A very limited proportion of them also paid cash, apparently to meet the costs of journey and other incidental expenses of the elected representatives at the district and state headquarters. In 15 cases the respondents complained that the elected representatives virtually took no action on their requests.

It will be seen that an overwhelming majority of villagers as well as officials thought political intervention by elected representatives and other political leaders as a real growing menace. Many of the villagers interviewed conceded that they had no choice for the most part except to approach the elected representatives. But they did not look favourably upon the increasing political intervention, even though in their personal cases it had brought them some benefits. As regards the officials, the large majority of them were emphatic that political intervention was a major cause of lowering of morale and efficiency in the rural administration. This intervention had increased in the wake of the growth of panchayati raj institutions.

An overwhelming majority (80 per cent) of the officials complained that they were often approached by the politicians to go out of their way to help their relatives, friends, and supporters and that if some official did not oblige them, they used their influence with the ministers to get them transferred. Various other instances of interference by the politicians in the day-to-day administration were also cited by some respondents. Such interference ranged from getting permits and quotas to admission in hospitals and schools for their relatives, friends and supporters. An overwhelming majority of the officials stated that this type of interference tended to undermine integrity and to develop a pathetical attitude among the officials who were beginning to feel that even their honest administrative decisions would be reversed.

Corruption: An important finding of the study is that the problem of corruption in the rural administration has assumed a significant dimension. The vast majority (84 per cent) of the villagers felt that there was substantial corruption (i.e., 51 per cent or more) among the officials and it was not easy to get the work done without greasing the palm of the officials. On the other hand, only 28 per cent of the officials interviewed agr ed with such a view of the dimensions of corrupt practices. Only 21 per cent of the officials and 11 per cent of the villagers interviewed felt that the corrupt officials were 5 per cent or less.

The detailed responses of the officials and the villagers on this issue are shown in Table 5.

TABLE 5

Villagers' (N=176) and officials' (N=80) estimate about the percentage of corrupt officials

Percentage of corrupt officials	*Villagers holding the view*		*Officials holding the view*	
	N	%	*N*	%
Up to 5	27	11	23	29
Up to 25	4	2	30	38
26 to 50	7	3	20	25
51 to 75	52	30	18	23
76 and above	113	64	12	15

If corruption was treated to be the most important problem in rural administration, the researcher was naturally interested in finding out its underlying causes, and asked the respondents as to what they thought about its underlying causes. The answers of the respondents were quite revealing as shown in Table 6.

TABLE 6

Villagers' (N=320) and officials' (N=105) views regarding the reasons for the prevalence of corruption

Factors responsible for corruption	*Perception of respondents*			
	Villagers		*Officials*	
	N	%	*N*	%
1. Low emoluments	261	81	94	91
2. Low professional standards	256	79	23	22
3. Lack of strict enforcement of rules	265	83	61	58
4. Quota/permit system	279	87	84	83
5. Social and political pressures	54	17	49	48
6. Declined to answer	39	13	9	8

It will be seen from Table 6 that there is a general agreement that low emoluments and quota/permit system constitute two important causes of corruption. About four-fifths of the villagers attached importance to the lack of strict enforcement of rules and low professional standards as factors contributing to corruption. About half of the officials thought social and political pressures to be an important cause of corrupt practices. One plea put forward by the officials was that they had to spend a large amount on the entertainment of the senior officials and ministers that came on tour.

During the interviews many of the villager-respondents pointed out that the growing malaise of corruption was due to long delays in the grant of citizens' requests. The ordinary citizen often approaches the juniormost officials and it is at this level that the corruption is more rampant. Many of the rural people, being illiterate, have often to employ contact men and pay them a significant amount of money. Corrupt practices constitute a vicious circle and it is difficult to say who is the real culprit—the officials or the citizens. These findings are supported by some other studies also. There prevails among the public a considerable degree of feeling that there is deliberate delay, harassment, and discourtesy in many departments of the local bodies. On the contrary, the officials feel that the public want to get things done expeditiously or out of turn and even without completing all the formalities. To a significant extent, corruption is becoming a matter of habit, a way of life. The president of a panchayat samiti applied over a year ago for getting electric connection for his tubewell, but he could not get it. When he approached an M.L.A., the latter gave him to understand that he himself had to pay Rs.100 through his clerk to the official for getting the connection and he advised the president of the panchayat samiti to do likewise.

The Barabanki study of the citizens' grievances has highlighted the importance of a fundamental reorientation of the attitudes of the officials towards the felt-needs and difficulties of the citizens. It has pinpointed that the existing organization and staffing patterns are singularly inadequate to meet the citizens' legitimate demands. Improvements in both these directions are going to be a continuing challenge to the government.

TREASURIES AND CITIZENS' GRIEVANCES

An important area of the citizens' grievances relates to the deposit of money in the treasury for payments due to the government from the citizens, and securing refunds of money due from the government by the citizens. The existing procedure of receiving payments from and depositing money in the treasury is extremely tortuous and dilatory and helps generate considerable corruption at lower levels. The citizen passes through the following channels for receiving payment from the government or for making payment to the government exchequer.

For receiving payment from the government

Citizen
|
Department (or treasury for the collection of form)
|
Treasury (when he is issued a token and asked to come after about a week)
|
Bank (for receiving cash, if all goes well at the treasury. Otherwise goes back to the department for correction and stands in the queue again at the treasury and waits for a week before going to the bank)

For making payment to the government

Citizen
|
Department (or treasury for the collection of form)
|
Treasury (for counter-signature)
|
Bank (for deposit, receipt of which is issued after a day or so)

The treasuries are under the charge of the district collector. With the extension of the branches of the State Bank of India, many of the treasuries have become non-banking treasuries. The citizens have, by and large, also to visit the bank and this adds to their inconvenience significantly. The Administrative Reforms Commission has observed:

The satisfaction which an administration may bring to a citizen is not so immediate by what is proposed or done at the higher levels as by the action and behaviour of the officials at lower levels with whom the citizen directly comes into contact. The Treasuries which are the pivot of our financial system affect almost every citizen of the country. The present systems and procedures of the Treasuries, in matters of payments and receipts, are irksome and dilatory and they cause considerable inconvenience, even harassment.[1]

In view of the magnitude of the citizens' difficulties in this area, the author carried out a study of six treasuries, one each in the district of Rohtak (Haryana State), Ahmedabad (Gujarat State), Hazur Treasury (Bangalore), and Ramanagaram district treasury (Karnataka State) and the treasuries of Delhi and New Delhi (a Union Territory). The study confirmed that the present procedures for depositing money into and securing refunds from the treasuries were causing great harassment to the citizens. Take, for instance, the collection of refund of money due from a government department. On presentation of the refund voucher to the treasury, the party is asked to come after about eight days. If by then the intimation from the department concerned is not directly received by the treasury, the party is asked to visit a second time. Many a time it is found that the head of account in the refund voucher has not been properly filled in by the department. The party has to go back to the concerned department for necessary correction. For the mistakes of the department, the party is made to suffer.

It will be of interest to mention here one of the several case studies collected by the author. When the author visited Rohtak treasury, a person Mr. X told him, that he had built his house in Sonepat, which was requisitioned by the supply department. After three months of labour he got the rent fixed. Then, finally he went to the supply department, Rohtak, to get a cheque for Rs.126 as rent for three months. He got the cheque from the department after producing an identification by paying some money to the advocate. This cheque was to be endorsed by the treasury after its issue by the department. When he approached the clerk at the treasury counter, he was

[1]Government of India, Administrative Reforms Commission, (*Report Treasuries*, 1970, p. 3.

ill-treated. He was made to sit for a few hours only to be told that the treasury closes at 2 p.m. When he came the next day, the clerk demanded money for endorsing the cheque. He had to "satisfy" the clerk. When he went to the State Bank, he was asked to bring an identification. He was an illiterate person. He had no account in the bank. He went back to Sonepat and endorsed the cheque to a third party who had an account in the Bank. Transfer of treasury cheques to third parties is not allowed. The cheque came back. He again had to go to Rohtak. This time he got an identification of an advocate after paying him the fee, but in the bank he was told that there were too many endorsements on the cheque which should be countersigned by the treasury officer. He again approached the clerk in the morning at 10 a.m. The author met Mr. X at the counter at 12.30 p.m. that day and at 2 p.m., on the pleading of his case by the author, the cheque of Mr. X was countersigned. He was required to visit Rohtak once again as the bank was closed at 2 p.m. For Rs.126, the poor man had to come to Rohtak 4 to 5 times from Sonepat which was about 40 miles. Difficulties of this type can be met by suitable changes in the system and procedure, e.g., payment of refunds directly by the department concerned or through the money orders.

Where the major function of receipt and disbursement has been taken over by the banks, the public is put to great inconvenience by having to visit the treasury as well as the bank. The distance between the treasury and the State Bank in some cases is more than three miles. Illiterate people are harassed by the bank/treasury employees in order to extract money from them. Identification of the man is required at three places—the first time when he gets the refund voucher from the department, the second time when he presents the voucher at the treasury, and the third time when he goes to the bank to cash the cheque. It is very difficult for an illiterate person who comes to the treasury, which is situated in some cases about 40 miles away from his village, to find somebody known to the treasury, department, or bank to identify him.

Similar hardship is experienced by the pensioners. Though there is an option that pension can be obtained through postal money order from the treasury, most of the pensioners prefer to collect personally. Payments by postal money order take

5 to 6 days in some cases to reach a village, whereas the pensioner would like to take his pension immediately when it is due. In the study of the Rohtak district treasury, it was found that 2,000 pensioners come to the treasury every month to draw their pensions. Sometimes it takes the whole day to get the amount as there is only one guard file maintained by the treasury. This file contains the necessary details of the pensioners. Pensions can be paid only after the scrutiny of the guard file. Extra employees cannot be deputed to cope with the rush as there is only one guard file. This difficulty can be overcome by maintaining a card index or one card for each pensioner.

The study of the six treasuries carried out by the author has underlined the importance of streamlining of procedures not only from the point of view of cutting delays but also for removing the general inconvenience caused to the citizens. The transactions between the citizens and the treasuries are generally of a routine character. Their number is so enormous that any machinery for redress of complaints is not likely to be very effective. The solution obviously lies in making innovations in the existing system and procedures. A wider study of the treasuries by the Indian Institute of Public Administration has come to the conclusion that "if a citizen is to be relieved of his botheration and inconvenience in the matter of receiving money from the government or depositing money in government account, it is necessary that one organization alone is made entirely responsible for making payment to or receiving payments from him." The study has suggested ways and means for ensuring speedy and accurate transmission of accounting information to appropriate levels of financial and programme management in order to promote efficiency at the minimum cost and to alleviate the enormous difficulties and inconveniences experienced by the public under the existing arrangements.

The need for a new approach to the problem of citizens' difficulties and for finding solution without any inhibitions was emphasized by the Chairman of the Administrative Reforms Commission in the following words:

If we realise that the citizen is the master and all of us are his servants, you will see how perverse these procedures are: the master is made to petition, wait, beg and if need be, bribe the servant. All payments, never mind what department it is, the citizen must receive at his door.

This is not such a revolutionary idea. Even today, all revenue collections are made at doors of peasants. But the payment authority or refund-voucher is handed over to the citizens mostly at the desk of the officer concerned. In many cases, a payment order to be obtained from the Treasury and where there is a Banking Treasury, the citizen has also to go to the Bank to receive the cash payment. The Post Office makes payment by money orders at the door of the citizens. If we were to make payments directly in a similar manner, the citizen would be saved from going through a veritable maze of procedures and all the harassment he is now put to. If land and some other tax collections are made by the concerned officers without any commission being charged, why, I ask in the name of fair-play, should any money be charged or deducted when payments are made by Government.[2]

Citizens' relations with the treasuries represent only one of the areas where the bureaucratic procedures are oriented towards the comforts of the officials at the cost of the citizens' convenience and interest. Some basic changes were made by the government in the treasury procedures in order to minimize the inconvenience to the citizens. Changes of a basic character in the procedures may be of some help. Departmental machinery for the redress of complaints may be useful in a limited way. However, the basic malady of the Indian bureaucracy a socio-psychological gap in the values and outlook of the people and the officials is not likely to be cured by these adaptations and improvements. Training in human relations may be of some help. If the values and attitudes of the officials have to be reoriented actively towards serving the citizens, it may be necessary to create some independent machinery to look into the causes of maladministration and trampling over the citizens' legitimate claims and demands. The harassment to which the citizen continues to be put in his relations with the treasuries, despite all the recent talk of administrative reforms, bears out that a socio-psychological change in the tone of administration cannot take place without providing for an independent agency which can take the administration to task for its failures in rendering prompt and effective service to the citizens.

[2]Inau ural address by Shri K. Hanumanthaiya, Chairman, Administrative Reforms Commission, at the Joint Seminar of the Regional Branches of the Indian Institute of Public Administration, Hyderabad, 20-21 November 1971, pp. 4-5.

LARGER CONTEXT

The problem of citizens' grievances is not confined to the rural area only. The grievances in urban areas can be classified, for purposes of analysis, into two categories. In the first place, there are grievances relating to the inadequacy or inferior quality of the various services provided by the municipal bodies in matters such as sanitation, water supply, electricity, street lighting, roads, etc. Again, grievances also arise in regard to different taxes and controls imposed by the municipal administration such as assessment of property tax, approval of building plans, regulation of land use, control on street hawkers, etc.

The second type of grievances in urban areas mostly concern persons of middle and higher income groups who have to deal with the executive departments of the State government, the office of the district collector or agencies of the Central government in pursuit of their vocations or for payment of taxes of various kinds. This category of grievances will include matters such as erroneous assessment of tax dues, grant of permits and quotas for scarce raw materials, purchase of government land for starting an industry or a trade, permits for running bus transport on specific routes, permits for construction of cinema houses, and the like.

The nature of citizens' grievances in the urban areas is not different from that of the rural side. Most of the grievances are about delays, inadequacy or poor quality of facilities and services, inconvenience and harassment, lack of impartiality in administrative decisions, etc. The weaknesses in administration which give rise to complaints in urban areas are for the most part similar to those in the rural administration. However, certain administrative ailments appear to flourish more in the urban climate. These include excessive workload (leading to long delays, more tossing of papers upward and across different administrative agencies, more articulate political pressures, and greater capacity and willingness of the interest groups to get things done through speed money. The citizen clientele in the urban areas are also better educated and informed and more articulate. Broadly speaking, the administrative matters do tend to move faster than in the rural areas. But the overwhelming burden of work acts as a big constraint. On the whole, the citizens' grievances in the rural and the urban areas differ in their intensity and not in their character.

For a proper understanding of the nature of citizens' grievances it is necessary to view the problem in the larger context of the value system of the citizens and the administrators. "There appears to be a complex attitudinal and perceptual set of expectations about the citizens' relationship with administrators. The components of this syndrome are: lack of self-confidence on the part of the ordinary citizens in dealing directly with officials; a feeling that the best way to deal with administrators is by enlisting the support of others, particularly individuals with the right contacts and 'political pull' that administrators do not and will not treat all people equally and that these administrative actions are final, complaints availing very little or being difficult to process."[3] There is also another allied dimension of the citizens' attitudes. The traditions left behind by two hundred years of the British rule and the earlier feudalistic society of looking up to the government machinery for favours and concessions still persist. A sizeable proportion of citizens' grievances, therefore, relate to the turning down of their requests for favours and concessions. It needs, however, to be borne in mind that the need for favours and concessions to a large part arises from the rigidity of administrative procedures.

The administrator's value system, on the other hand, is, as mentioned earlier, predominantly authoritarian and power-oriented. Some change in attitudes is perceptible. The facade of public relations is changing but not the spirit. Services are rendered to the citizens "as a favour" and not "as a duty". There is little real concern for the discomfort and harassment caused to the citizens by methods and procedures which were evolved during the British days mostly for the convenience of the Indian bureaucracy. Administration lacks significantly in motivation to render service to the people on its own. The callousness and disregard of the citizens' needs which characterize the lower rungs of the administration is supplemented

[3]S.J. Eldersveld, *et al.*, *The Citizen and the Administrator in a Developing Democracy*, Delhi, IIPA, 1968, p. 29.

at the higher levels by a superiority complex, high-brow attitude and a kind of elite casteism in dealings with the citizens and even with the junior officials. The value system of the Indian bureaucracy needs to be fully borne in mind in examining the problem of machinery for the redress of citizens' grievances, to which we turn in the subsequent chapters.

CHAPTER III

Redress Machinery at the District and State Levels

The callousness, indifference, and delay that characterize the State administrations in dealing with citizens' applications and requests for services and facilities are equally marked in the processing of their complaints. The traditional remedy of the redress consists of departmental channels, i.e. filing of complaints with the higher departmental authorities. A complaint may relate to delay in the grant of an application or of request already made or to reconsideration of an application or a request which has been rejected. In regard to the latter, the citizens can even file an appeal with the higher authorities.

During the past decade, a number of measures have been taken by the State governments to improve the machinery for prompt and speedy disposal of citizens' requests and claims as well as for the redress of their grievances. It is proposed to discuss in this chapter the role and working of the existing redress machinery in the States. (The functions and effectiveness of redress machinery under the Union government are examined in the next chapter.) The discussion of the redress machinery in the States may, for the purposes of analysis, be divided into the following three main parts:

1. Departmental channels of redress
2. Special public complaints machinery at the district level
3. Redress machinery at the State headquarters.

CURRENT INADEQUACIES

The overwhelming majority of the citizens are very much dissatisfied with the working of the departmental machinery for redress of their complaints. The nature of the complaints has already been examined in detail in the preceding chapter.

The study of citizens' grievances of eight villages of Barabanki district has thrown up interesting data about the hesitation on the part of the citizens in rural areas to lodge complaints and the fate which the complaints meet when lodged.

Only about 40.6 per cent (130) of the villager-respondents said that they had lodged complaints even though 272 out of 320 (85 per cent) interviewed had some or the other specific grievance. Of the respondents 44.4 per cent (142) agreed that they had a complaint to lodge, but they did not file because of certain considerations. The remaining 15 per cent (48) said that they had no occasion to complain. Of those who complained, 63 per cent (82/130) filed a complaint on grounds of delay, 32 per cent (42/130) for reasons of rejection of their requests, and about 5 per cent for miscellaneous reasons. About two-fifths (33/82) of those who had complained of delays also mentioned in their appeals that the officials who were sitting over their applications had either demanded or were accepting illegal gratification.

As regards the disposal of complaints, the respondents were highly dissatisfied. Only 23 per cent (30/130) of the complainants said that their complaints had been acknowledged; and the proportion of complainants who received an intimation of the decision on their complaints was 55 per cent (72/130), the decision being favourable only in one-fourth (18/72) of the cases of intimation (i.e. 14 per cent of the total complaints lodged).

It would have been noted that 44.4 per cent (142/320) of the citizen-respondents did not lodge a complaint even though they had reasons to do so. When asked about the factors which prevented them from lodging a complaint, about two-fifths of them felt that no useful purpose would have been served by lodging a complaint and they would have only wasted their time, energy and money. About one-fourth of them could not lodge a complaint due to lack of knowledge about the appropriate authority to be approached; and one-fifth of the respondents had hesitated to lodge a complaint for fear of various kinds such as harassment, victimization by the officials, etc. Three-twentieths could not give any definite reason for their failure to file a complaint.

The above findings of the Barabanki study, even though they relate to citizens' complaints in the rural areas, are, more or less, equally valid in the matter of complaints of the citizens residing in the urban areas. It is no doubt true that the urban citizens are more articulate in ventilating their grievances and can muster greater influence to bear upon their redress. This, however, does not make any significant difference in the matter of innate deficiencies in the redress machinery.

The study, by and large, reveals that there is at present a high level of dissatisfaction with the administration, and that the existing machinery for the redress of citizens' complaints is inadequate in several respects, ineffective for the most part and hardly inspires confidence.

At the Conference of the Chief Secretaries of various States held in June 1976, it was decided that States should take concrete steps including simplification of procedures and direct involvement of officers and ministers to ensure quick redress of citizens' grievances. Among the suggestions made was periodic visits by ministers/senior officers to the field offices/courts to ensure that citizens were not unduly harassed. Other suggestions envisaged appointment of a Director of Citizens' Grievances at headquarters, allotment of individual districts to individual ministers to ensure adequate arrangements for the redress of public grievances at the district, block and village level, imparting of proper training to officials coming in contact with the public, giving appropriate publicity to the rules and procedures with a view to assisting the public. But unfortunately these decisions remained only on paper and the States got busy with the general elections and change of governments in most of the States.

DEPARTMENTAL CHANNELS OF REDRESS

The normal channel of redress for a citizen's grievance is filing of a complaint to the next higher level. The citizen can go up to the successive higher levels and even submit a petition to the concerned minister. For the most part, the citizen does not believe that a complaint to the level immedi-

HIERARCHICAL CHANNELS OF REDRESS

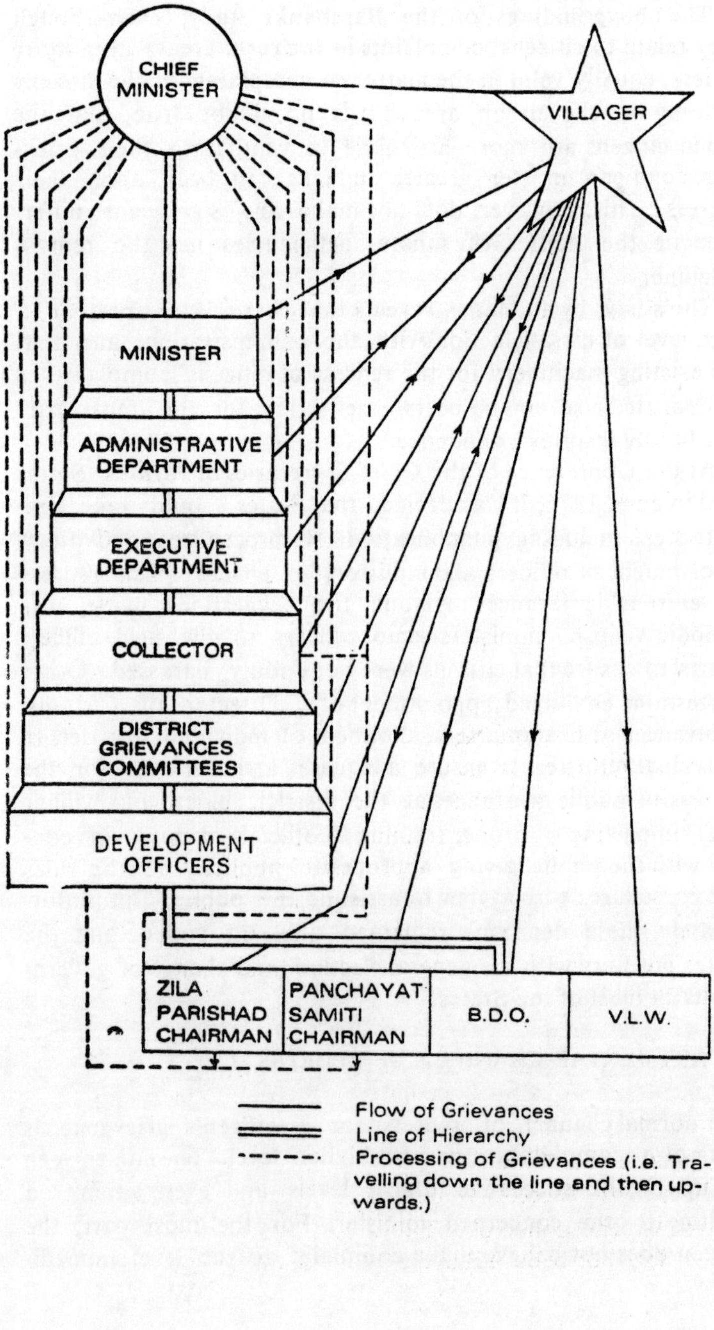

ately above the officer against whom the complaint is made can be of any material help in redressing his grievance. There is, therefore, a growing tendency on the part of citizens to take their complaints to the headquarters of the executive departments and even to the secretariat departments and the minister in charge. A recent study of the problem of citizens' grievances has revealed that over 25 per cent of the citizens prefer to take their complaints directly to the ministers and members of the State legislatures. Notwithstanding this trend the departmental remedy still remains the most common channel of redress for the ordinary citizen. The tragedy is that the departmental channels do not provide any effective means for the consideration of the citizens' complaints on an objective and impartial basis. This is because the officer complained against is, for the large part, directly involved in considering the complaint of the citizens.

If a complaint is received in the secretariat department directly, it is mostly referred down to the executive department concerned and the latter transmits it, by and large, to its district office for the supply of information or for appropriate remedial action. The higher the level at which the complaint is initially received, the more the chances that it may receive better attention. The senior officers do at times take some interest and this results in suitable redress. However, for the most part, the approach of the officials is to take a defensive view of the action or decision already made and treat the complaints of delays in a routine and perfunctory manner.

Increasing efforts have been directed in recent years, to improve the departmental channel of redress. The main directions of improvement have been as follows:

1. establishment of complaint cells and designating each head of the office as the complaints officer in respect of that office;
2. streamlining of procedures for receipt, processing, and disposal of complaints (including fixation of time limits for completion of action on applications and complaints);
3. setting aside specified hours for receiving, listening to the citizens' complaints;
4. setting up of reception-cum-enquiry counters for helping the

citizen with the information which he needs in filing an application or complaint as well as for receiving applications and complaints;

5. installation of complaint boxes at the reception counters or outside the executive or administrative offices; and
6. strengthening of the public relations units or cells and their increasing involvement in receiving complaints from the citizens and in promoting their redress.

Complaint cells and complaint officers

An important new dimension of the strengthening of the departmental channels of redress concerns the establishment of special complaint cells in major executive and secretariat departments in several States and the appointment of departmental public grievance officers. This development is more marked at the headquarters level than in the field.

Several States have also set up complaint cells at the district level, headed by the collector. Generally, at the divisional commissioner's office, one of the gazetted officers is put in charge of the cell for assisting the public. In Punjab and Haryana, a senior magistrate at the district level has been designated as the public grievances officer. He is assisted by two assistants. In Tamil Nadu, there is in each district an officer who is responsible for receiving complaints and processing action on them till a final decision is reached. In Karnataka, an officer of the status of tehsildar, working as general assistant or revenue assistant to the deputy commissioner, looks after the public grievances cell. He receives the petitions and representations and arranges to hear the petitioners and sees that suitable and prompt replies are given to the petitioners. This officer also refers to superior officers any particular problem which does not admit of an easy solution. The deputy commissioners and assistant commissioners have been requested to inspect periodically these cells and to review the work done by them. Similar arrangements have also been made in the State of Jammu and Kashmir in the district collectorates and district offices. An officer immediately below the head of office is designated as the complaints cell officer. In the offices of the district collectors, the personal assistant to the collector (administration) functions as the complaints cell officer.

The Study Team of the Administrative Reforms Commission on State Administration has emphasized that the district collector should be designated as district grievances officer with jurisdiction extending over every department of the district. It has urged that the district collector should be invested with special powers to inquire into complaints against any government agency at the district level. Incidentally the Administrative Reforms Commission has not agreed with this proposal, as in its view the problem of citizens' grievances at the district level is much more complex and elaborate. The solution suggested by the Administrative Reforms Commission is the appointment of a Lokayukta the Indian Ombudsman at the State level.

The movement for the creation of special departmental complaint cells in the States has received impetus and encouragement from the Union government. In 1964, the Union Ministry of Home Affairs issued guidelines to the Central Ministries and departments for reviewing the existing arrangement for handling complaints and outlining how the complaint cells should work in collaboration with the enquiry-cum-reception counters. Copies of these guidelines were also sent to the States. The guidelines emphasize that the system of handling complaints and grievances in the existing hierarchy of offices should be tightened up to ensure that every complaint received quick and sympathetic attention. It was also urged that in each big organization having substantial contacts with the public, there should be a district cell under a specially designated senior officer, which would function as a sort of "outside complaints agency" within the organization and thus act as a second check on the adequacy of disposal of complaints. The guidelines issued by the Ministry of Home Affairs also give a list of check points for reviewing the existing arrangements for handling complaints.

In practice, however, the several advantages claimed for the complaint cells have not much been realized. Due to inadequacy of staff, the complaint cells have not been able to do justice to the enormous number of complaints received by them. The guidelines prepared by the Union Ministry of Home Affairs stress that the cell should investigate only selected cases in which the normal hierarchical channels have failed to give satisfaction or cases of patently hard kind. The guidelines also emphasize that each cell should be headed by a senior officer. It has been very difficult to observe both of these instructions. The complaint cells have tended to deteriorate into more or less an agency for receiving the complaints at a central point and distributing them to the departments concerned. Again, it has not been found possible to spare the competent officials to man the complaint cells. For the most part an officer who is not wanted elsewhere is sent to the complaint cell and it is obviously too much to expect of him to have a detailed knowledge of government procedures, a freshness of outlook, and an earnestness to provide redress—qualities that are essential for the effective working of the complaint cells. Furthermore, in many cases the officers designated to head the complaint cells have additional administrative or executive responsibilities. This factor, by itself, is sufficient to render them ineffective in their role as public complaints or grievance officers.

Streamlining of procedures

The effort of streamlining of procedures has as its objectives the elimination of delay in the processing of the applications as well as complaints and giving satisfaction to the citizens. For instance, the State Government of Karnataka has issued detailed instructions that all petitions received from the public should normally be acknowledged within 24 hours and action should be initiated by the competent authority at its own level without waiting for report from the lower level. Most of the States have constituted a system of registers for keeping track of processing of citizens' complaints. An application or complaint received is first diarized or entered in the register and it is acknowledged on a prescribed printed or roneoed acknowledgement form. The petition is then passed on to the concerned officer for examination. If it is addressed to the secretary by designation it will be sent by the central registry to the concerned section where it will be processed and then put up to a level depending upon the importance of the contents of the petition. A reply is to be sent to the petitioner at the time of the final disposal.

Many of the States have prescribed time limits for the

disposal of complaints. For instance, in Punjab when a complaint is received through a minister, a report is required to reach him within 21 days if it pertains to his own department and within 30 days (through the minister concerned) if it pertains to another department. Each complaint is normally required to be disposed of speedily and in any case within a period of one month to three months, depending upon the nature of its contents. In some States, a system of monthly meetings of the departmental officers has also been evolved to discuss the pending complaints. This system is working advantageously at the level of the district collector.

Specified hours to meet the public

Most of the States have issued orders that every day during office hours, head of offices should set apart some specified time to hear representations from the public. The district collector sets apart normally one hour daily to grant interview to the members of public who wish to see him with some complaint or other official work. For instance, in U.P. the district magistrate is required to specify a magistrate to receive on working days, at fixed hours, complaints against all classes of officials posted in the district. In Tamil Nadu, instructions have been issued to collectors and revenue divisional officers to allocate one day in a week to listen to complaints and representations of the public. The collectors have also been instructed to receive complaints or representations from the public on any other day also, either at the district headquarters or at the divisional headquarters. Other district officers such as the director of agriculture, district industries officer, civil supplies officer, etc., are required to set aside some specified hours each day for receiving the citizens and hearing their complaints.

A register showing details of the interviews, such as the name and address of the person granted interview, particulars of grievance, action taken, etc., is supposed to be maintained by all officers who have substantial dealings with the public. This register is subjected to surprise inspection by superior officers.

The device of granting interviews to the public during specified hours has generally proved to be quite useful for redress of grievances of a routine character and for giving the citizens a feeling of accessibility to the administration. But for complex cases and in the matter of the citizens' convenience the arrangements are very much unsatisfactory. The citizen has to wait quite for some time in getting an interview. But for a lone bench lying in the corridor in some cases, there is hardly any convenient waiting place. And when he gets an interview, for the most part the previous papers having a bearing on his complaint are not traceable or the assistant/clerk concerned is not on his seat. The timings for public interviews have been fixed more for the convenience of the bureaucrats than of the citizens.

Reception-cum-enquiry offices and complaint boxes

Many of the executive and secretariat departments which have large dealings with the public have set up reception-cum-enquiry offices. These offices give information to the citizens about the appropriate authorities to be contacted for filing complaints. They also help the citizens in making their applications for particular facilities by providing them the needed information, application form, etc.

Complaint boxes have been installed by many departments at the district collectors' offices to receive complaints from the public. Some of the Raj Bhavans (State Governors' offices) too have set up complaint boxes. The complaint box is generally kept at the main entrance to the office. Complaints collected are removed periodically from the boxes and attended to by the senior officers of the department concerned.

However, not much use is being made by the people of this device of lodging complaints; the reason being the lack of confidence. Filing a complaint in the box does not get the citizen a receipt and he is not sure whether the complaint so lodged will be considered by the departmental machinery.

Role of public relations units

In some States, the public relations units of the executive or the secretariat departments also assist in a general way in the redress of the citizens' grievances. This role is mostly limited to receiving complaints, and articulating of and placing the citizens' point of view before the government department concerned.

In some States the role of public relations unit is much wider. A public relations unit has been set up by the Government of Gujarat in the general administration department under the minister for public relations for the expeditious disposal of complaints and grievances of the public. The unit deals with complaints received by it as well as with the grievances pending with various departments in the secretariat for long periods. It also attends to the applications of government servants regarding pay bills, allowances, pay fixation, pension and gratuity when there has been unusual delay in their disposal.

The public relations unit of the general administration department in Gujarat is mainly concerned with the early finalization of cases of grievance which are reported to it as unduly delayed. It obtains a report on the reasons for delay and arranges for its expeditious disposal by the concerned department by bringing it to the notice of higher authority, if necessary. The unit does not deal with cases of corruption, cases covered by statutory provisions or disciplinary rules, and cases referred to the government for the first time.

Official tours and redress on the spot

During the British regime, collectors used to go on horse back to inspect the villages and to camp there for a few days. One of the important functions of the collector during such camps was to hear and remove public difficulties, complaints and grievances on the spot. Many of the States have found it useful to strengthen this system. Other district officers such as the director of agriculture, district education officer, district industries officer, etc. also tour the district and hear public complaints. The commissioner of the division and regional/circle officers of various executive departments visit the district headquarters but their role in redress of citizens' complaints is less marked. The official tours of the deputy commissioner or the district collector are equally meant for inspection. The tours by the collectors and other officials are useful but this channel is not adequate enough to cope with the growing number of complaints and can be effective mostly in cases of severe hardship or gross injustice caused to the citizens.

Ministers in States also tour the districts. In some of the States such as Punjab, Haryana, and Maharashtra each minister has been allotted some districts for the purposes of overseeing the working of its administration. During their tours to the districts allotted to them, the collector of the district has to accompany the minister. The applications, petitions, etc., received by the ministers during their tours are handed over to the district officers for disposal. When the district officers find that the matter is not within their competence, the case is referred by them to their immediate superior officer who sends it to the concerned secretariat department, if necessary.

During their district tours, the ministers also try to dispose of as many public complaints as possible on the spot. The practice of on-the-spot disposal has been very much systematized in Gujarat though it obtains in some other States also. Every minister and deputy minister in Gujarat pays a visit to each district at suitable intervals for the purpose of disposing of on-the-spot applications of members of the public concerning the subjects which come within the perview of his ministry. The chief minister is free to look into complaints concerning any department. Intimation to the public is given by the collector sufficiently in advance through the local press and circulars about the date of the visit of ministers and deputy ministers. Along with such intimation the local people are informed that they may send their applications in advance regarding matters which they wish to bring before the minister/deputy minister. However, not all types of applications can be entertained for such disposal. The following matters cannot be considered and decided on the spot: (a) complaints on matters pending before any court, tribunal, or other similar authority or regarding which proceedings can be taken in such courts, tribunals, or authority, (b) complaints in which any criminal offence is disclosed, (c) complaints where the applicant has omitted to approach the competent head of department for redress (except where there are reasonable grounds for such omission), (d) matters which have been considered and decided by the Government in the past and no new facts have been brought to light.

The scheme of on-the-spot disposal of the people's grievance in Gujarat is said to have been quite a success. About 60 to 80 per cent of the citizens' applications are generally disposed of by the ministers during their tours. The people line up in dozens to get their difficulties resolved by ministers and deputy ministers. This method is proving usefu for the large number of routine type of applications; the complex and complicated cases left over are referred to the regular departmental channels.

The main advantages of on-the-spot disposal scheme are as follows:

1. The minister remains in direct contact with the people who submit their grievances to him personally.
2. The minister can understand the difficulties of the people and try to solve them.
3. The officers tend to become more vigilant and thereby unnecessary delay is avoided.
4. The people gain confidence in the administration.

Among the several advantages of the system, the most important one perhaps is that ministers are in a position to explain the correct position to the citizens as their applications and complaints have been scrutinized in detail in advance. Whether or not the final decision is in favour of the applicant, he at least has the satisfaction of having been heard at the highest level in the government. The ministers also get a chance to identify the weak spots in the administrative machinery and initiate action for improvement.

In Gujarat, a minister during his tour can look into grievances relating to the deparments under his charge only. But under the scheme of allocation of a district to each minister for overseeing its administration, a minister in States such as Haryana, Maharashtra and Punjab, can hear grievances relating to any department of the government. This creates difficulties of inter-departmental jurisdiction. Even though difficult and complex cases are not decided on-the-spot but are referred to the minister in charge of the subject concerned, the justification for a single minister overseeing the entire administration of a district lies in the doctrine of collective ministerial responsibility.

Another difficulty which has come up is that many ministers are inclined to pass oral orders on the spot and such a manner of disposal does not admit of all relevant administrative rules and regulations to be taken into account. At times, the oral orders passed may not be fully "regular", i.e. within the bounds of the rules and regulations. The scheme of disposal of grievances on the spot by ministers has not found favour with some of the administrative reforms committees and commissions. For instance, the Punjab Administrative Reforms Commission (1964-65) felt that oral orders by the ministers, on-the-spot, for the redress of grievances were likely to create complexities and difficulties. It recommended that any such oral orders must be reduced to writing. The Central Administrative Reforms Commission had taken a similar view. The Punjab Administrative Reforms Commission was also of the view that a minister, while on tour, would indeed be making a very useful contribution if, instead of listening to unrepresentative, stray, and doubtful people about the truth or otherwise of a complaint or about the functioning of the administration in the field, he consulted the local elected representatives.

District grievances committees

The trend towards democratic decentralization during the past 25 years has led to the setting up of district level committees of officials and non-officials. Some of these committees are exclusively concerned with the public complaints. Others have a wider function of associating the representatives of the public in district administration, particularly with the developmental activities.

District-level committees which look into the citizens' grievances are generally of three types. Firstly, in some of the States such as Punjab, Haryana, Madhya Pradesh, etc. there have been constituted district grievances committees consisting of both officials and non-officials. The non-official members include all M.L.A.s and M.P.s representing the district and a few citizen-leaders, nominated by the government. The total strength of these committees generally does not exceed 25. The district collector functions as the convener of the district grievances committee, which meets once a month.

The main function of a district grievances committee is to scrutinize all the petitions and complaints received by it. It tries to ensure that all grievances are properly looked into. Periodic reports of the action taken are placed before the committee. Where some members of the committee are not satisfied with the result of an enquiry, the collector will entrust the matter to the public grievances officer of the district and get it reinvestigated in consultation with the member complaining.

In Madhya Pradesh, there are two complaints committees, one of the officials, and the other of non-officials. The committee of non-officials consists of all members of Parliament and the Legislative Assembly from the district and a few nominated non-officials, with the collector as the convener. The role of this committee is to screen the complaints received from the citizens and interest groups. The committee of officials consists of all the district officers of the various departments except the district and sessions judge. The collector acts as the chairman of the committee. The committee takes expeditious action on all complaints and petitions received from the committee of non-officials.

The second type of district level committees concerned with the citizens' grievances are coordination committees. They inquire into citizens' grievances so far as they relate to inter-departmental coordination committee at the district level. A district coordination committee consists normally of both officials and non-officials. The non-officials include president and secretary of the district congress committee, members of Parliament, members of Legislative Assembly representing the district, representatives of farmers and traders, president of the zila parishad, etc. The committees of this category are found in the States of Assam, Madhya Pradesh and Punjab. In Punjab and Assam there are also sub-divisional grievances committees. A sub-divisional grievances committee comprises the sub-divisional officer, deputy superintendent of police and other supervisory police officers. The non-official members are the chairmen of all panchayat samitis and urban local bodies.

The third category of the district level committees comprise public relations committees or public relations and grievances committees. These committees treat the citizens' grievances as a special aspect of public relations. They focus the attention of the district administration on the general difficulties experienced by the citizens in their contacts with the administrative machinery and make suggestions for its improvement. They also receive complaints from the citizens and send them to the officers concerned. Important cases of general interest are, however, taken up for discussion in the meeting.

Anti-corruption committees consisting of officials and non-officials have also come up in several States. But these committees perform only a limited role in the matter of citizens' complaints—they concern themselves with only allegations of corruption.

The study team of the Administative Reforms Commission on district administration has pointed out that the main usefulness of the district level grievances committees lies in associating enough non-officials with the steps being taken by the administration for the redress of grievances. It points out, "On the one hand, non-official members can bring to the notice of the collector and other officials, grievances and complaints of a general nature and seek redress; on the other, the officials can place before such influential non-officials as M.P.s, M.L.A.s etc. important policies of government and seek their cooperation in implementation." The study team has noted that the experiment with district-level committees in the merged State areas of Orissa did not succeed due to their unwieldy size. The study team has, however, favoured a broad-based district-level grievances committee and suggested a model composition. In its view, the district-level committee should consist of members of Parliament, members of Legislative Assembly and members of Legislative Council of the district; president of the zila parishad; two presidents/mayors of municipal committees or corporations to be nominated by the State Government; representatives of the Bar Association, traders, transport, labour, industry and such others as the State Government may consider appropriate; chief executive officer of the zila parishad; all district heads of departments and collector as chairman.

The district-level committees are supposed to provide a channel for the articulation of the grievances, to focus the attention of the district administration on the more important grievances, to serve as an instrument of review of action taken and to act as a catalyst to speed up action. They have been effective in removing the bottlenecks in inter-departmental coordination at the district level and in the redress of individuals' grievances which find the special support of the non-official element.

The approach of the non-officials represented on the committees is generally narrow and parochial. They show concern mostly for those individual or community grievances the redress of which is likely to advance their personal interest and the interests of their friends and supporters, and they are not very appreciative of the difficulties of the administrative agencies. Their interest, again, is of an ephemeral character. The non-official members have not shown the spirit of team work, and have even formed factions.

The presence in the district-level committees in some States of the office-bearers of the district unit of the ruling party (and not of other political parties) tends to make the district complaints committees an adjunct of the government machinery and the party in power. The officials generally treat the committees as a cog of the government machine and do not take them seriously. All this has limited greatly the usefulness of the district-level complaint committees and rendered them mostly ineffective so far as the grievances of the ordinary citizens go. The district-level complaints committees seem to have outlived their purpose and are tending to become a superfluous limb of the district administration.

However, the Administrative Reforms Commission has not favoured the idea that a grievances committee should deal with complaints in the district. It feels that the entrusting of the redress of grievances to a committee, instead of a single person, is likely to make for confusion and delay, if, as is bound to be, there is a difference of opinion among the members of the committee.

REDRESS MACHINERY AT STATE HEADQUARTERS

Role of ministers

The State Chief Minister and ministers, as the elected representatives of the people holding ministerial positions, are the highest forum available to the citizens for redress of their complaints. In the Cabinet form of parliamentary government, ministers are supposed to deal mostly with policy and leave its actual implementation to the administrative and executive agencies. But they have also the duty to ensure that the execution of policies serves the objective in view and brings satisfaction to the citizens. Ministers have to be, and are, accessible to the general public, as they depend, both individually and as a group, for their continuation in office on the support of the people.

Every minister has specified hours for granting interviews to the members of the public; and interviews are frequently given even outside these hours to the influential citizens or the elected representatives of the people who may have a grievance of the citizens to ventilate. Some ministers even hold "darbars" or open courts in the evening to listen to the citizens.

In a democratic set-up, even the ordinary citizen feels that he has a right to see the minister who comes from his area or is in charge of the department to which his complaint relates. This approach has led to an endless stream of citizens flocking to the State capital to meet the chief minister, other ministers and secretariat officials.

To cope with this growing problem, some new arrangements have come up in recent years. In the first place, the minister's personal staff has been expanded and a special number of it earmarked for purposes of arranging interviews of the people with ministers. The minister's personal office receives a large number of complaints, and these are sent down the administrative hierarchy to be enquired into. Once a while, particularly where the minister is interested for one reason or another, he records a couple of words or lines on the complaint, asking that the case be fully investigated and reported back to him or that he would like to see the previous papers. But, for the large part, the complaints, received in the minister's office are just distributed to the appropriate administrative agency, and there is no follow-up by the minister's office on the action taken on them in due course unless the personal staff of the minister has an interest in a particular complaint.

Another important device the use of which has increased

substantially in recent years is the tours of the district and sub-districts by the ministers and the chief minister. These tours are used for both political purposes and meeting the citizens and listening to their complaints. The merits and demerits of redress of grievances on the spot by minister during their tours have already been discussed in a preceding section.

SPECIAL COMPLAINTS UNITS AT SUPRA-DEPARTMENTAL LEVEL

In view of the growing volume of public complaints and increasing dissatisfaction of the citizens with administration, it has been found necessary to set up special units or cells in the chief minister's office or in the organisation of the chief secretary who is the top-most civil service adviser to the chief minister. In several of the States such as Punjab, Haryana and Rajasthan there is a special complaints unit or section attached to the office of the chief minister. This unit is generally under the charge of an officer of the level of under secretary or assistant secretary. Complaints received are sent to the concerned quarters for necessary action, enquiry, disposal or report. At times, the officer in charge also decides the level at which a complaint should be looked into. He may himself conduct an enquiry and send the report of that enquiry to the secretary of the department concerned.

In Rajasthan, a petition officer is attached to the chief minister who processes the complaints and refers them to the various heads of departments concerned with the complaints. After scrutiny of a case, if it is felt that justice has been denied, reports are called for in the matter. On an average 44,000 petitions are received every year out of which about 50 per cent can be considered as complaints. The chief minister has set apart every morning an hour or so for hearing public grievances.

Some States have also experimented with the device of a full-fledged supra-departmental agency to look into the citizens' complaints. A director of public grievances was appointed in Punjab in June 1965. This directorate was assigned the following functions:

1. to receive complaints directly from public (including retired government servants) or through ministers or secretaries to government and to conduct enquires directly or through the department;
2. to advise the heads of departments and deputy commissioners in setting up arrangements for quick disposal of public grievances;
3. to ensure that government instructions for proper redress of public grievances are carried out in all departments and districts;
4. to undertake enquiries in cases of undue delay and of urgent nature;
5. to study causes of major grievances and to propose remedies and to recommend changes in law, rules, etc., where necessary;
6. to suggest ways and means to improve the machinery for removal of public grievances;
7. to recommend to the concerned departments action against defaulting officials and if these recommendations are not complied with or agreed to, to bring the fact to the notice of the chief secretary or the chief minister;
8. to ask the concerned departments to send reports to the police or the vigilance department if a criminal case is made out; and
9. to ensure effective supervision and submit annual review on the receipt and disposal of complaints.

The Punjab Government has since abolished the directorate for reasons of financial stringency and political considerations. Its functions are now looked after by the director of public relations who has also been designated as the director of public grievances.

A similar experiment was carried out in Rajasthan during the years 1964-66. A department for removal of public grievances was set up in April 1964 on the recommendations of the State Administrative Reforms Committee (Chairman, the late H.C. Mathur). The main functions of this Department were:

1. to enquire into the causes of delay in disposal and inattention to public grievances by various departments of the State Government;

2. to oversee the implementation of the orders of the government and particularly the Cabinet and bring out instances of gross delay in this respect; and
3. to look into such cases, as especially remitted to it by the government, involving corruption and malpractices or cases of alleged impropriety in the decisions made by the various departments.

The department was also authorized to entertain enquiries into the following four categories of complaints by government servants: (1) cases of non payment of salaries, travelling allowance, and daily allowance; (2) cases of fixation of pay; (3) cases in which pensions had been continuing temporarily for long periods; and (4) cases of delay in payment of pension and gratuity. Corruption cases and complaints about judicial delays were normally outside the purview of the public grievances department.

The Rajasthan experiment with a central complaints organization did not succeed for several reasons. There was criticism in the State legislature that the expenditure on the organization was not commensurate with the results achieved and financial stringency with which the State was faced did not allow its continuation. Again, as the complaints organization operated at the supra-departmental level, it made inroads into the role of the individual ministers as well as members of the State legislature in the matter of the redress of citizens' complaints and tended to reduce their importance in this regard. The administrative departments also did not take a favourable attitude and did not like an outside agency (even though it was a limb of the government machinery) to probe into their internal affairs. The Rajasthan department for removal of public grievances was abolished in 1966.

The failure of the Punjab and Rajasthan experiments with a separate supra-department grievances redress machinery is a pointer to the need for the creation of an independent organization outside the government machinery for the purpose. A study conducted by the Indian Institute of Public Administration has come to the conclusion that a separate State directorate of public grievances is not needed for the simple reason that such a directorate is neither able to function on behalf of the citizens nor is it in a position to bring to bear an objective mind on the subject of complaints. A separate department for public grievances, being a part of the governmental machinery, cannot pull on with the departments in which the grievances originate. The study recommends that the secretary to government in each secretariat department and the heads of departments in the attached and subordinate offices should be designated as the ex-officio grievance officer for that particular department or agency.

HONORARY ENQUIRY OFFICERS

The Government of Gujarat has tried an interesting experiment with the system of appointing honorary officers for looking into public grievances. A start was made in this direction in 1964 by appointing seven honorary officers each of whom is attached to a minister. The appointments are made by the chief minister in consultation with the concerned ministers from amongst retired government servants of good reputation and with wide administrative experience or suitable social workers. The posts carry a fixed honorarium up to Rs.500 per month plus travelling and daily allowances. The honorary enquiry officers investigate complaints and grievances remitted to/remittable to them by the chief minister or the minister concerned and have access to all departmental officials and local offices for securing the needed information. Certain types of complaints such as, matters pending before any court or tribunal or similar other authority, or cases in which the applicant has failed to approach the competent authority for redress are, however, excluded from their purview. The report of the investigations conducted by the honorary officers is considered by the appropriate administrative department and placed before the chief minister or the minister concerned. The institution of the honorary officers has hardly been a success. The honorary officers are exposed to all kinds of pressures and they look up to the senior civil servants and the ministers for continuation of their tenure. The selection of the honorary officers has also not been made entirely on merit. The scheme has a resemblance of the institution of honorary magistrates which was inherited from the British days and all the weaknesses of the latter are equally valid in the present case.

VIGILANCE AND ANTI-CORRUPTION MACHINERY

Following the lead given by the Government of India, almost all states have set up, a special machinery for enquiring into charges of corruption made by government departments themselves, or the citizens or their elected representatives. Several of the State governments set up vigilance commissions modelled on the pattern of the Central Vigilance Commission. Some States have anti-corruption boards or units. The institution of vigilance commission has come up in pursuance of the implementation of the recommendations of the Santhanam Committee on Prevention of Corruption (1963). The creation of a central agency, independent of government is to deal comprehensively with two of the major problems of administration, namely, prevention of corruption and maintenance of integrity and ensuring just and fair exercise of administrative powers vested in various authorities by statutory rules or by non-statutory executive orders. The government memorandum on the setting up of the Central Vigilance Commission fully recognized the importance and urgency of providing a machinery for looking into tne grievances of citizens against the administration and for ensuring just and fair exercise of administrative power. The government, however, decided that to begin with attention should be concentrated on the prevention of corruption and maintenance of integrity in the public services. The Central Vigilance Commission was set up in 1964 and this development was soon followed by constitution of vigilance commissions at the State level.

The State vigilance commission consists of a vigilance commissioner, a chief executive officer, a police officer of the rank of deputy inspector general of police, and a commissioner for departmental enquiries. The commission can look into any transaction in which a public servant is suspected or alleged to have acted for any improper purpose or in a corrupt manner. It also causes an enquiry for investigation to be made into (a) any complaint that a public servant has exercised or abstained from exercising his powers for improper or corrupt purposes; and (b) any complaint of corruption, misconduct, lack of integrity or other kinds of malpractices or misdemeanour on the part of a public servant including members of the all India services, who are serving in connection with the affairs of the State government.

Furthermore, in every department of the secretariat and in all major offices of the heads of department, there are vigilance officers, mostly part-time, who are charged with the following duties:

1. to examine the existing organization and procedures so as to eliminate or minimize factors leading to corruption or malpractices;
2. to organize regular inspections and surprise visits for detecting causes of corruption or malpractices;
3. to take prompt action in cases where reasonable ground for suspicion of corruption or malpractices exists against any official;
4. to scrutinize monthly statements of disposal of cases with a view to locating chronic delays and suggesting remedial measures;
5. to receive and register complaints of delays, discrimination, etc.;
6. to take expeditious action for the grievance or the complaint, under the orders of the head of the department or on his own within the powers delegated to him by the head of the department; and
7. to investigate the cause of grievance and take remedial action in consultation with the head of the department.

In Jammu and Kashmir State, the anti-corruption organization is headed by a deputy inspector-general of police with powers of inspector-general. In addition there are two anti-corruption commissioners (one for the gazetted and the other for the non-gazetted government servants) who deal with prima facie cases established against the government servants under the Jammu and Kashmir Government Servants' Prevention of Corruption (Commission) Act, 1962.

As public grievances are mostly due to the prevalence of corruption, Maharashtra has combined the functions of looking into the corruption charges and the redress of public grievances into a single departmental agency. It has combined vigilance and public relations offices in each part of the secretariat and major executive agencies. In recent years, in quite a few States charges of corruption against ministers have been enquired into by one-man commissions of inquiry under the Commissions of Inquiry Act, 1952. The vigilance machinery is accountable to the home department of the State government. The vigilance machinery has no jurisdiction to inquire into allegations of corruption against political executives. By and large, the anti-corruption machinery has been quite useful in checking corrupt practices in the lower levels but its efficacy in regard to corruption obtaining in the higher echelons has been limited. The anti-corruption machinery does help in bringing to book the corrupt civil servants against whom the citizens may have levelled allegations but anti-corruption machinery does not bring any direct benefit to the citizens in the matter of the redress of their complaints.

Under the scheme for setting up Ombudsman-type of machinery at the State level, namely, the institution of Lokayukta (which is discussed in Chapter VIII of the present study), as recommended by all-India Administrative Reforms Commission, it is proposed to abolish the State vigilance commissions and entrust their anti-corruption responsibilities to the Lokayuktas. Following this recommendation the vigilance commissions in most of the states have become defunct. In three States Punjab, Bihar, and Uttar Pradesh the vigilance commissions have been abolished. In Maharashtra the commission ceased to function since the death of the last vigilance commissioner. In Kerala, the coalition Government abolished the organization on coming in power. In States like Madhya Pradesh, Rajasthan, Assam, and Tamil Nadu the vigilance commissions are functioning with limited jurisdiction, e.g. in Tamil Nadu an inquiry by the vigilance commission into the charges against a secretary or a minister must be cleared by the Government first. West Bengal and Karnataka are the only States where vigilance commissions are functioning on the model of the Central Vigilance Commission. In the light of the wide dimensions of the problem of corruption at the State level, it is doubtful whether the abolition of state vigilance commissions will be a useful proposition. What is needed is to bring the vigilance commissions into the fold of the Ombudsman machinery. This aspect of the problem is discussed in detail later.

EXTRA-BUREAUCRATIC CHANNELS

The elected representatives, viz., members of the State legislatures and of Parliament and members and heads of panchayati raj institutions of a particular district, also act as an important channel for the purpose of redress of grievances. Members and heads of the panchayati raj institutions have been taking more active interest in recent years in ventilating citizens' grievances and securing their redress. Intervention by the elected representatives to secure redress of public complaints has been on the increase lately. There is a general feeling that such intervention is promoted mostly by consideration of obliging particular citizens, castes, groups, political factions or other parochial interests.

As already stated earlier, in Barabanki District an overwhelming majority of the officials complained that they were often approached by the politicians to go out of their way to help latter's relatives, friends, or supporters, and if some officials did not oblige them they would use their influence with the ministers to get them transferred. An interesting case cited was of a senior officer who in his 27 years of service has served in 23 districts of the State. In another case, head of a department had transferred a very junior member of the staff because of some administrative considerations. The junior staff member had some connections with an influential political leader, who put pressure on the senior officer concerned to cancel the transfer order. When the senior officer did not yield to such pressure, he was transferred and his successor cancelled the transfer orders of the junior member of the staff.

Broadly speaking, the political channels can serve as a very useful instrument for the redress of public complaints and in the process lead to political cohesion and maturity. However, in the context of patronage politics as developing in India, their usefulness as a mechanism of redress of citizens complaint gets vitiated. Political intervention by the elected representatives does not discriminate between the genuine and the unreasonable requests and complaints against the civil servants. In a way, it obstructs the in-building of the right relationship between the administration and the citizen.

THE PROBLEM OF EFFECTIVENESS

By and large, the existing redress machinery at the State level has been unable to deliver the goods. It has already been noted that the experiments with the creation of special directorates of public grievances did not succeed. The other innovating devices, i.e. the special complaints cells, public relations units, etc., play only a limited role and are inadequate to cope with the wide dimensions of the problem of citizens' grievances. The departmental channals have built in bias and constraints against an effective redress of public complaints. The district level committees are useful only for community grievances and that too when their non-official members are articulate and dynamic enough to press the case. Redress on the spot during the tours of officials and ministers and the "darbars" or public audience held by ministers are somewhat effective but their scope is narrow. This, however, does not mean that all these channels have no use whatsoever. They have their own utility but their effectiveness is considerably constrained by several limiting factors.

There are several directions for affecting substantial improvements in the existing redress machinery.[1] In the first place, the various ad hoc innovations which have come up in recent years in the departmental channels of redress need to be consolidated and integrated. The special complaint cells should

[1]A study conducted by the Indian Institute of Public Administration has suggested, inter alia, that (a) each State government should have a central grievance officer common to all departments as well as a grievance officer in each government department; (b) the number of dealing levels should be reduced: (c) more information and education should be provided both to the public and to the officials about the services provided by government and the procedures to be followed by the citizens for availing of them; (d) training programmes of officials at all levels should be reviewed; and (e) there should not be too much probe or interference by ministers in the power or discretion of officers. A.P. Barnabas, *Citizens' Grievances in Development Administration*, New Delhi, IIPA, 1966, p. 149.

be manned by a full-time senior official. This departmental grievance officer should be provided with the assistance of a deputy grievance officer to enable him to discharge his duties effectively. He should be able to win the respect of his colleagues in the department and should be sufficiently reputed for his integrity so that he may also win the confidence and respect of the public. He should be of amiable disposition and of helpful attitude towards the public. The decisions on all major complaints should be taken by a departmental grievance officer, and not by an officer, even though a senior one, of the branch or segment of the department to which the grievance relates.

The existing arrangement for acknowledging complaints and for their timely disposal within specified time limits needs to be reinforced adequately. It is not enough to have departmental redress machinery. The public must have confidence and faith in the impartiality and effectiveness of such machinery. The system of departmental grievance officer will have an edge over a scheme of a central directorate of public grievances, such as those tried in Rajasthan and Punjab without much success. The new departmental system, in which the decisions on grievances are taken by an officer other than the set of officers involved in administrative activity of which a complaint relates is likely to arouse a lot of bureaucratic resistance but it will help ensure a degree of independence in adjudging the complaints.

The system of district-level grievances committees has by now lost all its shine and glory with which it started. Its basic philosophy, however, is sound and the system needs to be renovated. The nomination of the non-officials on the district public grievances committees needs to be made on a more selective but wider basis so as to involve all sections of the community. The discussions in these committees should be steered to more purposeful conclusions. Their effectiveness would perhaps be enhanced if the secrecy which surrounds the discussions is removed.

As regards the redress of grievances on the spot, there is already appearing on the scene a reaction against the misuse of this mechanism for furthering of their political ends by the ministers. This channel of redress is important enough in the case of far-flung rural areas where it is difficult for the citizens to approach the officials. It has great potentiality in dealing with emergencies such as flood, famines, outbreak of epidemics resettlement of refugees, etc. However, in more mundane matters, involving the rights of other citizens to the use of public funds or property, this device has obvious serious limitations.

At present, little advantage is taken of the experience with the processing of the public complaints through departmental channels to improve the tone of administration, particularly, administrative systems and methods having a bearing on rendering of service of different kinds to the citizens. An important function of the grievances machinery should be to analyse the possible causes which underlie the citizens' complaints. The results of these findings should be fed back to the departments concerned. Such an analysis will also help to diagnose the deficiencies and foibles in the attitudes of the public towards the administration. Again, in fixing the time-limits for the disposal of complaints, it will be foolhardy not to take into account the differences in nature and complexity of complaints. Accordingly, varying time limits need to be prescribed for different kinds of complaints.

The effectiveness of the departmental redress machinery is obviously circumscribed by the general quality of administration. Such machinery cannot succeed beyond a certain point unless the administration is capable of meeting the citizens' claims in prompt, fair and judicious manner and rendering effective services. The wider question of modernization of the administrative system and procedures is, for the most part, outside the scope of the present study, though some suggestions in this regard are made in a subsequent section.

The suggestions made earlier for improving the effectiveness of the existing redress machinery will not, however, help in resolving a fundamental deficiency which characterizes the present mechanism for the removal of the public grievances. The Indian bureaucracy is more or less a closed system. The values, attitudes and the outlook of civil servants continue to be authoritarian with little regard for the felt-needs and difficulties of the unorganized body of citizens. Any administrative machinery for redress of grievances which is a part of the bureaucratic system is not likely to be really effective. It is natural for the bureaucracy to defend itself and fight for the preservance of the status and dignity of the officials. There has been a growing realization in recent years that the real solution to the problem of citizens' grievances lies in the creation of an agency outside the normal governmental machinery, e.g., an Ombudsman-type of institution.

CHAPTER IV

Cenrtal Adminitsration and the Citizen

Under the constitutional scheme of division of powers between the Centre and the States, the Union Government has the legislative as well as the executive authority in matters specified in List I of the Schedule VII to the Constitution. With the acceptance of planning as the chief instrument of economic and social development during the past three decades, the Centre's involvement in a number of subjects falling within the purview of States under the Concurrent List has increased considerably. The Centre now administers a number of controls such as regulation of imports and exports, industrial licensing, control of prices of essential commodities, drugs control, preventive detention of persons who are a risk to the security of the state, and the like. As a result, the contact points between the citizen and the Central administration have multiplied.

The citizens' principal contacts with the Central administration fall under four broad categories as follows:

1. Provision of services or goods by a multitude of semi-independent State enterprises operating within the framework of the Central Government and other undertakings managed departmentally.
2. Provision of special services and facilities, in matters like higher technical education, specialized health services, supply of information, technical guidance and scarce raw materials, provisions of subsidies and loans, housing sites, etc.
3. Grant of Government's clearances, quotas or permits under the various types of economic controls (such as industrial licensing, import and export trade control, price controls, etc.)
4. Collection of various taxes levied by the Central Government

COMPOSITION OF THE DEPARTMENTS OF GOVERNMENT OF INDIA

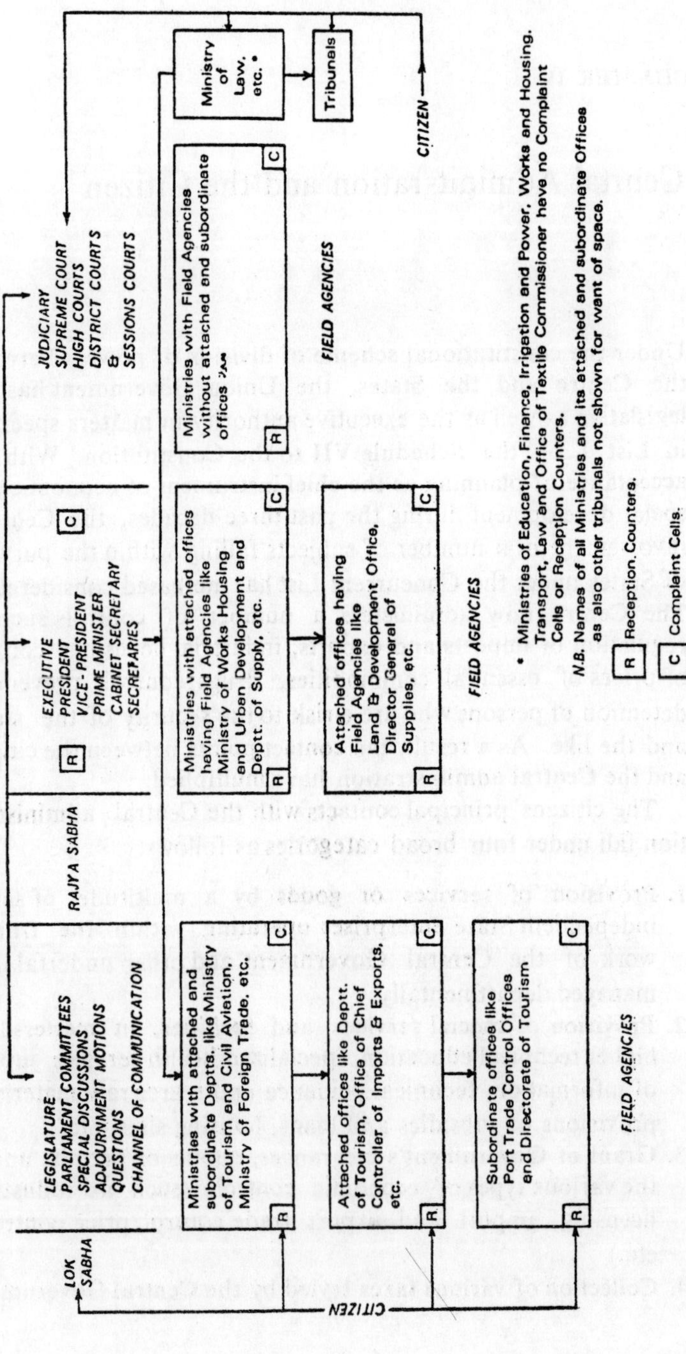

such as income-tax, corporation tax, customs and excise.

The relationship between the citizen and the Central administration is, by and large, characterized by inadequacy or lack of facilities and services, protracted delays, citizens' harassment, and a lack of impartiality in decision-making. The story of hardships to which the citizen is put in his relations with the Central Government is not different from what happens at the State and district level. The procedure regarding the working of various controls is cumbersome and dilatory and the anxiety on the part of the citizens to get things done quickly has led to the growth of corrupt practices, like speed money, political interference, etc. Apart from the inconvenience caused to the citizen by the tortuous and elaborate procedure, the attitude of the officers of the Central Government is unsympathetic and overbearing. For the most part, there is an utter indifference towards the citizens' convenience and difficulties. The problem of civil servants' callousness towards the citizens' felt-needs and convenience has already been noted in the earlier chapter dealing with the "Nature of Grievances". As regards fairplay and impartiality in decisions affecting the citizen, the position on the whole is better than what obtains in the States. However, the citizen, for the most part, does not have confidence in the objectivity and impartiality of decision-making in Central government.

TRADITIONAL REMEDIES

The hierarchical remedy available to the citizen aggrieved by a particular decision is to approach the higher authority to the one against whose action he is aggrieved. This departmental channel of redress is generally not much effective. In the first place, formal procedures do not generally exist for the purpose of approaching a higher official to review a decision taken at the lower level, and in most of the cases the matter is left to the departmental practice. It is only in exceptional cases that the statute, or the rules made thereunder, lay down intra-departmental review procedures. Secondly, very often, the complaint against a particular officer is processed by the same officer. The senior officer in looking through the complaint normally consults him to find out the reasons which prompted him to take a particular decision. The office, in putting up the previous papers, mostly re-states the old position. Thirdly, experience shows that the higher official is too busy to apply his own mind to the matter. Instead of bringing to bear a fresh approach on the issue in dispute, he generally prefers to go by the decision already taken unless he finds that the exercise of discretion has been mala fide or there is some serious omission in applying the rules. This analysis of the existing position is also confirmed by the report of the Commissioner of Public Grievances to the Ministry of Home Affairs made in 1966. According to this report "Government replies to the public follow a 'laconic' and 'brusque' pattern. The replies normally are on these lines: 'The matter is receiving attention' or 'is being looked into' or 'is under consideration' or 'we have nothing to add to what has already been stated in our last letter' or 'as already stated, nothing can be done for you and you are advised to desist from writing again."

The change in the environmental context, the establishment of a parliamentary form of government based on adult franchise, spread of education, social and political awakening and the increased demands on the Government for raising living standards—has provided a broad framework for focussing of increasing attention on satisfaction of citizens' legitimate demands and redress of their grievances. The taking up by the Government of increasing responsibilities for development and welfare brought in its wake the problem cf adaptation of the traditional administrative system to the new demands and challenges. However, notwithstanding a series of ad hoc enquiries and improvements in Government procedures, the real efforts at administrative reforms in India started in 1963. The mid-term appraisal of the Third Five Year Plan indicated some serious shortfalls in implementation of plan schemes and programmes and pin-pointed some significant administrative weaknesses. A full-fledged department of administrative reforms was set up by the Government of India early in 1964 which drew up a comprehensive plan of studies and review.

A stimulus to streamlining of procedures and machinery for redress of citizens' grievances was provided by the report of the Santhanam Committee on Prevention of Corruption (1963).

This Committee recommended the creation of a Central directorate general of complaints and redress as a part of the organization of the Central Vigilance Commission.

While initiating action on the recommedation of the Santhanam Committee regarding the machinery to be set up to look into the complaints of corruption, the Government of India felt that the broader issue of citizens' grievances will be required to be considered separately. The Santhanam Committee Report stimulated some constructive thinking in the Government circles and in the Parliament on the problem of citizens' grievances.

In June, 1964, detailed instructions were issued to the Central Ministries and Departments for initiating a review of the existing system of handling complaints and grievances. These instructions emphasized the need for streamlining the procedures and machinery for redress of citizens' grievances as follows:

> It is a basic proposition that the prime responsibility of dealing with a complaint from the public lies with the Government organisation whose activity, or lack of activity, gives rise to the complaint. Thus, the higher levels of the hierarchical structure of an organisation are expected to look into complaints against the lower levels. If the internal arrangements within each organisation are effective enough, there should be no need for a special 'outside' machinery to deal with complaints. The fact that there has been a growing demand for a special machinery indicates that the present arrangements within departments are not good enough from the point of view of giving satisfaction to the public. It is, therefore, necessary to devise measures that will give substantial satisfaction to the public in the matter of grievances against the administration.[1]

The Government instructions of 1964 were directed at not only streamlining the procedures for handling of complaints, but also creation of such internal machinery as would make possible the consideration of complaints by officers other than those who are involved in the original decision against which the complaint had arisen. The main purposes of the new policy as set out in the Government instructions, were as follows:

[1]Government of India, Ministry of Home Affairs (Department of Administrative Reforms) Office Memorandum No. 30/1/64-AR dated 29 June 1964.

(i) to tighten-up the existing system of handling complaints and grievances so as to ensure that every complaint receives quick and sympathetic attention, and (ii) to set up, in every big organization, having substantial contacts with the public, a distinct "cell" under specially designated officers to function as a sort of "outside" complaints agency within the organization and thus to act as a second check on the adequacy of disposal of complaints.

Complaint cells

The instructions of June 1964 stipulated that the complaint cells would be placed under the charge of a senior officer, generally the Joint Secretary dealing with administration in the ministry, and the officer next in line after the head in the case of attached offices. It was also visualized that only selected cases would be taken up for investigation by the cells themselves and, that the rest would be dealt with by normal hierarchical channels.

Following the government's instructions, complaint cells were set up in several Central ministries, departments and attached organizations, generally under the part-time charge of a dupty secretary. As the ministries and departments differed in their functions and organization, the structure of the complaint cells vary. The overall pattern which emerged by the end of 1968 was as follows:

1. Central Administrative Agency with separate complaint cells:

(a) Central Ministries and departments:

—Ministry of Commerce, Civil Supplies & Cooperation
—Posts and Telegraphs Board
—Department of Company Affairs
—Ministry of Agriculture and Irrigation
—Ministry of Industry
—Department of Supply
—Ministry of Labour and Employment
—Directorate General of Technical Development
—Ministry of Petroleum and Chemicals
—Ministry of Railways

— Department of Rehabilitation
— Department of Social Welfare
— Department of Iron and Steel
—Department of Mines

(b) Attached administrative organizations or field agencies:

— Chief Controller of Imports and Exports (Now Directorate General of Foreign Trade)
— Directorate General of Supplies and Disposals and Pay and Accounts Office
— Central Public Works Department

2. Central administrative agencies having combined complaint and vigilance cells:
— Ministry of Tourism and Civil Aviation
— Office of the Textile Commissioner
— Ministry of Education and Social Welfare
— Ministry of Finance (Department of Economic Affairs)
— Rehabilitation Finance Administration and the National Savings Organization closely follow the procedure as that of the main departments
— Ministry of Finance (Department of Expenditure)
— Ministry of Energy
— Ministry of Works, Housing and Urban Development
— Ministry of Shipping and Transport

3. Centeral Ministries and departments without complaint cells but having a complaint officer:
— Department of Rural Development
— Department of Co-operation
— Ministry of Defence
— Union Public Service Commission

The combination of the vigilance and the complaint cells in the Central administrative agencies listed under (2) above was felt necessary for reasons of economy and small magnitude of citizens' grievances arising in these agencies. Fifteen ministries and departments did not set up any complaint cells though they have complaint officers of appropriate status.[2]

[2] These Ministries/Departmetns are—Department of Atomic Energy, Cabinet Secretariat (Departments of cabinet Affairs and Statistics), Department of Communications including Overseas Comunications Service, Ministry of External Affairs, Ministry of Finance (Department

These ministries and departments normally do not have much direct dealings with public.

The constitution of the complaint cells in various ministries and departments was supplemented by creation of enquiry-cum-reception offices. These offices were meant to serve as focal points for contact with the public—feeding the public information as well as for receiving complaints. Enquiry-cum-Reception offices were set up in all important ministries and departments having substantial dealings with public, i.e. Import and Export Control Organization, Customs and Central Excise Department, Income-tax Department, etc.

A review of the working of the new arrangements for the redress of citizens' complaints, namely, the complaint cells and Enquiry-cum-Reception offices was made in 1966 by the Central Commissioner for Public Grievances. He found that the existing government machinery was not adequate to deal with complaints from the public. He was further of the view that the Cabinet's expectation that in each ministry an independent person not connected with the original government decision which gave rise to the complaint would bring to bear upon the grievances a corrective had not been fulfilled in as much as a complaint was being generally examined by the same person against whose decision, or the decision in which he had a hand, the complaint had been made. The Commissioner was also not satisfied with the working of the complaint cells. He felt that if officers of the level of Joint Secretaries could not be spared for looking into the complaints, the new institution of complaint officer should be scrapped. He further recommended that the complaints officer or public relations officer should bring out handy literature on policies

---

of Expenditure), Ministry of Finance (Revenue) (complaints in respect of Income-tax, Customs and Central Excise Departments are passed on to the Director of Inspections concerned for necessary action), Ministry of Finance (Defence), Ministry of Health including Directorate General of Health Services, Ministry of Home Affairs, Ministry of Information and Broadcasting (complaint cells, however, exist in Directorate of Advertising and Visual Publicity and Directorate General of All India Radio), Ministry of Law (Legal Affairs and Legislative), President's Secretariat, Prime Minister's Secretariat, Department of Parliamentary Affairs and Planning Commission.

and procedures of their ministeries so that the public knows how and whom to approach regarding a particular grievance.

Following the report of the Commissioner of Public Grievances, the Government asked in 1968 all the ministries and departments to make inspection of the complaint cells. It was urged that the complaint cells should be set up where they did not already exist. Ministries and departments were further advised that wide publicity be given to the arrangements made for dealing with public grievances, indicating the names of the complaint officers. It was also emphasized that a separate register should be maintained to watch the quick disposal of the public complaints which were received. The scope of the new instructions was widened to include public undertakings. A new feature of these instructions was that each ministry was asked to identify the kinds of grievances in relation to the business allocated to it, which were likely to come under the "grievances" jurisdiction of the proposed institutions of Lokpal/Lokayukta. It was emphasized that every effort should be made to initiate measures so as to prevent grievances from arising, as far as possible, and to provide quick and effective redress for such grievances as would still arise. It was pointed out that efficient arrangements would not only fulfil the underlying purpose of the proposed legislation on the Lokpal and Lokayuktas, but would also help to ensure that the ministry's actions would not come under criticism from the new institution of Lokpal and Lokayukta.

The government's instructions of July 1968 in particular emphasized following points:

1. It should be ensured that every communication from 'citizen' is replied to, on the substance of the communication, as quickly as possible. The citizens should be informed of the outcome within a month of filing the representation.

2. As far as possible, every representation from a citizen against a previous decision affecting him should be processed in accordance with broad principles of natural justice. The final order on his representation should be a "speaking" order, i.e. it should give reasons for the decision, and this hould be communicated to him.

3. The representation should be considered by an authority

higher than the one which took the original decision unless it has been specifically addressed to the lower authority. If the nature of the case so warrants, he should be given an opportunity to explain his point of view personally. If there are papers which are essential for him to see and there is no over-riding objection, he should be allowed to see them.

4. The complaints officer appointed in each ministry should inspect periodically the complaint cell set up in the ministry and its attached and subordinate offices and bring about such improvements in their working as may be necessary.

The complaints cells should also investigate/examine a certain percentage of public complaints directly, particularly where normal hierachical channels have failed to give satisfaction, or cases of a patently hard kind.

Till to date no review has been made of the action taken by the various departments on the instructions of July, 1968. By and large, the position regarding the functioning cf the complaint cells and the reception-cum-enquiry offices remained unchanged. It was felt that these checks have, however, never proved completely adequate for ensuring administrative consistency or citizens' satisfaction with the administration. A need has always been felt, and efforts have continuously been made for evolving agencies which are external to the administrative organization; and yet, which have the right to voice the citizens' grievances to ask questions, to examine official records and, if necessary, to criticise administration for the way it acted or failed to act.

Systems of appeals

In some of the departments, a set procedure has been laid down to provide a channel for appeal by the citizens against the decisions taken by the administration. For instance, in the Department of Customs and Excise, an aggrieved citizen can go in appeal to the collector against the decision of Assistant Collector. Similarly, in Income Tax Department, an aggrieved citizen can go to Appellate Assistant Commissioner against the decision of Income Tax Officer. He can also go to the Income Tax Commissioner in appeal if he is not satisfied with the decision of Appellate Assistant Commissioner. In certain cases appeal is made to the Board of Direct Taxes in the Ministry of Finance. The matter can also be taken to the Income tax. Appellate Tribunal. The procedure of appeals and review in the departments is statutorily laid down by the Sea and Customs Act and Indian Income Tax Act 43 of 1961.

Important and Export Trade Control Organization: A similar appeal procedure has also been provided for in the case of Import and Export Trade Control Organization. This procedure is explained at some length below to illustrate the system of appeal obtaining at the Centre.

The citizens come in contact with this organization for obtaining licences for import of raw material, capital equipment and other goods. The Import and Export Control Organization is also approached by the exporters claiming incentive in the shape of import licences for raw material required for manufacture of export products.

If a person is not satisfied with the decision of a licensing authority, he may make an appeal on a prescribed form against the decision in respect of an application of import licence. An appeal, in the first instance, will lie with the head of the office in which the application was initially dealt with. This is known as "first appeal". Normally, the authority to whom the first appeal is made is the Joint Director General of Foreign Trade at the regional offices located at various cities in India. The first appeal has to be made within 45 days of the date of order appealed against. It is to be accompanied by a copy of the decision against which the appeal is made and the necessary relevant information. No fee is charged for the first appeal. The appeals are dealt with not in the normal licensing sections, but by an appropriate branch of a separate appeal division. Personal hearing to the parties is also granted on request.

It has been a common experience that in first appeal the Joint Director General can provide redress if the application has been rejected on procedural grounds or if its handling has been defective. He has no discretionary powers and in 90 per cent of the cases first appeals are turned down.

A "second appeal" lies with the Director General of

Foreign Trade, New Delhi (Appeal Wing), if the applicant is not satisfied with the decision of the first appellate authority. The second appeal must be made within 45 days of the rejection of the first appeal. The second appeal is heard by an officer of the status of Joint Director General at the headquarters in New Delhi. There is a third and final departmental channel of removal of grievances also. An application for review of the decision taken on second appeal can be made to the Director General of Foreign Trade, New Delhi, within 45 days.

The system of appeals at successive levels provides for quick and methodical handling of grievances of citizens who are not satisfied with the initial decisions of the Import and Export Trade Control Organization. It is in second appeal and review that most of the cases are decided. In such cases the officers of the Directorate General of Foreign Trade have discretionary powers and they can waive the normal rules in exceptional cases. Broadly speaking, the first appeal succeeds in about 10 per cent cases; the second appeal succeeds in about 55 per cent cases and only about 5 per cent of the reviews are made in favour of the citizens.

Apart from the procedure of appeal, there is a public relations officer of the rank of Joint Director General of Foreign Trade in the Port Offices. A public relations committee was constituted by the Imports Trade Control Organization in 1967 with the object of suggesting measures for improvement of public relations. The organization has also a system of granting interviews to the citizens to provide them with answers on the spot to their queries and to listen to their pleas for quick disposal of their applications. The number of interviews normally ranges between 1.2 and 1.5 million during a year. In addition there is a standing grievance committee which takes care of grievance redressal mechanism.

Notwithstanding the prescribed procedures, the appeal systems have several loopholes. The opportunities given to the citizens for their successive appeals increase the work of the organization considerably. Appeal of each of the three categories takes about 3 to 4 months. There is thus virtually no finality of the administrative decision for a long period. Secondly, the officers continue to enjoy wide discretionary powers, which provide scope for arbitrary decisions and corrupt practices. Thirdly, the officers who deal with appeals or review are generally disinclined to sit in judgment over their colleagues and are influenced significantly by administrative convenience. According to the report of the Study Team on Economic Administration (ARC), "There is a feeling, never explicitly mentioned but frequently implied, that officers at high levels have a tendency to support the actions of their subordinates. Above all, it is a matter of clientele satisfaction and creating public confidence. We would, therefore recommend, that a Board of Referees should be constituted to hear appeals on orders issued under Import Trade Control.

These deficiencies of the present system of appeals have attracted special notice of the Administrative Reforms Commission. It has taken the view that consideration of the appeals exclusively by a set of departmental officers has inherent limitations of its own. The Commission has recommended that "provision should be made for filing review applications to Government against second appellate orders relating to permits and licences, including punitive orders and a Board of Referees should be set up for advising Government before the applications for review are disposed of. Where the decision on a review application is not in favour of the applicant the reasons underlying the decision should clearly be brought out and that the review applications should be disposed of within a period of three months."

It has been urged that the composition of the Board should be such as to inspire public confidence. Besides very senior officers, the members should include some representatives of recognized bodies in the field of industry and commerce like the Federation of Indian Chambers of Commerce and Industry and Associated Chambers of Commerce.

Industrial licensing organization

Another important area which touches upon the middle and higher income groups of industry and business relates to grant of industrial licences for the purposes of starting new factories or expansion of old ones. Citizens' grievances in this area generally relate to protracted delays in the grant of licences, demand for speed money, etc. In recent years, the government has initiated several steps to remove the grievances of the industrialists.

Case studies carried out by a Study Team (chairman late H.C. Mathur) set up in 1966 by the then Union Ministry of Supply, Technical Development and Material Planning in collaboration with the Union Department of Administrative Reforms, show that the average time of disposal of applications for industrial licences is 180 days as against 90 days prescribed in the appropriate rules. Earlier, the Industries Development Procedure Committee (Chairman; T. Swaminathan) had found in 1964 that the majority of applications for industrial licences took more than five to six months. The Study Team recommended a number of measures for streamlining the procedures and eliminating unnecessary stages of consideration or consultation and fixation of time limits for acknowledgments of applications as well as for their disposal.

COMPLAINTS ORGANIZATIONS IN RAILWAYS AND POSTS AND TELEGRAPHS DEPARTMENT— TWO CASE STUDIES

Complaints organization in Indian Railways

Two important and big services which are managed departmentally by the Government of India, are Railways and Posts and Telegraphs. It will, therefore, be of interest to examine the arrangements which exist in these organizations for the redress of citizens' complaints. In some respects, these arrangements are typical of other major agencies of the Centre.

Indian Railways are the biggest public undertaking in India with a route kilometrage of 114500. The Railways, divided into 17 zones employ about 1.36 million persons. Each zonal railway administration has a Complaints organization which generally works under a Senior Deputy General Manager. He is aided by one Assistant Secretary (Public Complaints). In each Division, the responsibility for looking after complaints is of the Divisional Commercial Superintendent. He is assisted by a Public Complaints Inspector and a complement of clerical staff.

Complaints are recorded by the public in the complaints

books provided at the Railway stations and with the Guards of the trains. Facilities have also been provided to the public to drop their complaints in the "Complaint and Suggestion Boxes" located at all important stations and at Divisional and Headquarters offices. Extracts of such complaints are sent within 48 hours to the Divisional Commercial Superintendent for enquiry and for sending a reply to the complainant. Each complaint has to be acknowledged within three days of its receipt either in the Divisional or in the Headquarters office.

The complaints received by the Railway Board[3] through Members of Parliament and from the people directly are transmitted to the Divisional Commercial Superintendents concerned. The complaints unit in the Board, however, keeps a watch over the progress of their disposal. Complaints received through the Railway Board and from VIPs[4] are directly enquired into by the zonal complaint cell through demi-official correspondence with the Divisional Officers concerned or through the two Inspectors attached to the Complaint Cell of the zonal office. Replies to the Members of Parliament are sent under the signature of Divisional Superintendent if they are addressed to the Divisions, and under the signature of an officer not below the rank of the Junior Administrative Officer if received by the headquarters offices. The General Manager himself replies to those complaints from Members of Parliament which are addressed to him by name. The average time fixed by the Railway Board for enquiries in public complaint cases is 15 days except when a confronted enquiry is conducted in which case the time limit is 45 days.

[3]In 1905, Railway Board was set up with railway experts as its members. In 1908 it was converted into an autonomous department. Railways are divided into nine zones. Railway Board which functions as Secretariat of the Government in the Ministry of Railways is a central controlling authority coordinating the functions of the zonal railways and ensures planned development of the railway system in India. The Railway Board consists of a Chairman who is ex-officio Principal Secretary to the Government of India. It has four other Members; Member-Finance (also known as Financial Commissioner), Member-Transportation, Member-Mechanical and Member-Staff.

[4]Ministers of the Government of India and State Governments, Members of Parliament etc. come under the category of Very Important Persons.

The citizens' complaints against the Railway administration are generally of the following types: (a) complaints of misbehaviour and discourtesy; (b) complaints concerning catering, reservations, late opening of booking offices and irregularities thereof, irregularities in goods offices, lack of amenities at stations and demands for additional facilities, late placement of carriages on platforms, etc. (c) complaints regarding late running of trains, pilferage of consignments, and bad maintenance of coaches.

In dealing with complaints, efforts are also made by the Railway administration to plug the loopholes that give rise to them, e.g. action against the delinquent staff, provision of additional amenities where justified, etc. In addition, the following measures have been adopted in recent years to reduce complaints and give greater satisfaction to the users:

1. Surprise checks are made by the divisional officers and inspectorate staff to ensure timely opening of booking windows and other offices.
2. Public complaints inspectors have been instructed to inspect the reservation offices and reservation charts to ensure that reservations are made on first come first served basis and that no irregularities are committed in providing reservations in the trains by the reservation staff and the conductors.
3. During the inspection of the divisional Offices, the Senior Deputy General Managers and Assistant Secretary (Public Complaints) examine complaint books to ensure that prompt replies to the complainants have been sent.
4. Severe punishments are imposed on the staff in proved cases of misbehaviour.
5. "No Complaint Weeks" are organized at the various important stations every six months.

The problem of the redress of citizens' complaints against Railway administration is quite stupendous. The Railways carry on an average 30 million passengers and 2.8 million tonnes of goods every day. Some of the complaints are due to inefficiency and irregularities but in more recent years outburst of labour tensions, pilferage of copper wire and other small but essential items of railway equipment, etc., have been on the increase, giving rise inevitably to public complaints. The existing redress machinery in the railways is predominantly of departmental character. However, railway users' Committees have been set up at national, zonal and divisional levels and these perform useful functions in articulating the public complaints and focussing attention of the railway administration on their early redress.

The Railway Users' Committee at the national level is presided over by the Railway Minister, and includes representatives of all the user ministries of the Government of India, businessmen and 30 Members of Parliament, 18 from the Lok Sabha and 12 from the Rajya Sabha.

The zonal Railway Users' Consultative Committees consist of Members of Parliament, representatives of coal, iron and steel, mineral ores, jute, cotton, sugar, cement, and salt industries, one member each from the federated chambers of commerce, the Associated Chambers of Commerce and the All India Manufacturers' Organization, one representative of agricultural interest. The zonal users' consultative committee looks into the following kinds of problems:

1. Matters relating to services and facilities provided by the railways to the general public;
2. matters relating to the services and facilities on railways which the individual members may like to take up;
3. any other subject of general public interest or public convenience or state matters affecting the services and facilities which have been the subject of representation by the users.

Each zonal railway has also a railway users' amenities committee, a time-table committee, catering supervisory committee, and a book stall committee. At the station level there are 323 consultative committees. In addition, there are 57 local catering advisory committees. At the divisional level there are 50 railway users' consultative committees.

The detailed composition of the Railway Users' Consultative Committees at the three levels—national, zonal and divisional —is shown in Table 1.

TABLE 1

Table showing the members representing principal interests among railway users of the area on the Railway Users Consultative Committees

Type of representation	*Divisional level*	*Zonal level*	*National level*
1. Name of appointing authority	G.M. of respective zone	Minister of Railways	Minister of Railways
2. Chambers of commerce, trade associations, industries and agriculture associations	6	7	12
3. Passengers' associations	2	2	Any number
4. Representatives from legislature/ Parliament	3	5	18
5. Special interests	2	3	Any number
6. Government representatives	1	3	12
7. Representatives of divisional/zonal committees	—	1	1

The past experience with the working of the railway users' committees has not been much encouraging. They are mostly interested in taking up those complaints which are either backed by some sort of influence or which will serve to give publicity to the members. For the large part, a continuing and persistent interest in improving the railway administration and providing greater satisfaction to the citizens is lacking.

At present there is no special complaints organization in the Railway Board as compared to a well-knit organization set up by the Posts and Telegraphs Department. The official opinion in the Railway Board is not in favour of the establishment of a full-fledged separate organization for complaints. It is felt that such an agency will become another routine type of machinery. Nor will it be possible for it to look into the large volume of public grievances which arise in the Railways. The officials of the Railway Board, however, agree that a small complaints unit in the office of the Board will be useful. This unit could look into, say 10 per cent or so, of the complaints picked up at random. The sample complaints picked up at random should be examined in detail from all angles, e.g., (i) whether the case has been processed within the rules framed by the government, (ii) whether the citizen has a case against the Railway administration, (iii) whether the government official has used his discretion judiciously, and (iv) whether there is any mala-fide intention which can be proved after investigating such a case. The results of the analysis of 10 per cent of cases should be a guideline for the Railways as a whole.

A peculiar feature of the Railway administration is a sizeable amount of intervention by the Members of Parliament and State Legislatures in ventilating the citizens' grievances. On an average, the Union Railway Minister receives about 350 to 400 letters per month from members of Parliament and other elected representatives of the people. Table 2 shows a monthly profile of the types of grievances in the communications to the Railway Minister by elected representatives.

The receipt of such a large number of public complaints every month from Members of Parliament and State Legislatures poses quite a problem for the Railway administrations. Obviously, it is not feasible to look into each complaint within a short period of time. Again many of the grievances forwarded by the elected representatives are of favours and concessions sought for certain groups, individuals or railway employees.

Posts and Telegraphs

The Posts and Telegraphs department is a huge organization having 155333 post offices, and 520191 employees. In addition to the work relating to wireless licences the P & T department discharges certain agency functions with respect to the government saving bank, national savings certificates, postal life insurance and collection of duties on postal articles on behalf of other departments of the Government of India.

In India, the Posts and Telegraphs services are managed by a Posts and Telegraphs Board under the administrative control of the Department of Communications of the Government of India. The Secretary of the Department is an ex-officio Director-General, Posts and Telegraphs, and is also the Chairman of the Posts and Telegraphs Board. This Board exercises

TABLE 2

Monthly profile of complaints by Members of Parliament and other elected representatives against Railway administration

Nature of complaints	*Number*
Complaints about corruption and mal-practices by Railway staff	62
Requests for transfers and postings of Railway staff	48
Requests for Railway travel concessions, complimentary passes, etc.	68
Complaints against late running of trains, lack of proper attention to lights and fans in the compartments etc.	18
Scarcity of drinking water, lack of catering arrangement, insufficient accommodation in the dining car, non-compliance of orders regarding service of food, tea etc.	17
Shortage of reserved accommodation non-display of reservation charts etc.	29
Supply of dirty bedding, dirty conditions in retiring rooms etc.	11
Discourteous behaviour of Railway staff	31
Non-availability of porters at stations	7
Defects in Railway coaches, trains and engines running without lighting	19
Non-availability of the complaint books with the conductor guards and at the Railway Stations etc.	9
Requests for halting facilities at certain stations	12
Miscellaneous	28
	359

These statistics relate to one of the months of 1971.

all the powers of the Government of India in administrative matters and is responsible for the development, maintenance and extension of postal, telegraph, telephone and wireless communications throughout the country.

The Posts and Telegraphs department is the only Central Government agency which has set up a special Directorate of Public Complaints, headed by the Deputy Director-General, Vigilance. The Posts and Telegraphs complaints organization initially came up after World War II. Its main role is to investigate complaints of all kinds against the postal, telegraph and telephone services. At the end of each quarter, a detailed analytical study is made into the causes of the complaints with a view to evolving effective measures to keep the incidence of complaints to the minimum. The post of Director (complaints) has since been revived under whom three Assistant Directors-General work, one of them looks into personal complaints, the other is in charge of investigations and the third is in charge of telephones and telegraph complaints. There are also circle complaint officers attached to each Circle. Complaints are again divided into three sections, dealing with postal complaints, investigation and telephone and telegraph complaints. In addition, there is, at each of the 303 postal divisions, a sub-inspector who looks after public complaints. In the telegraph engineering divisions, a similar arrangement has been made by making one of the engineering supervisors at the headquarters responsible for complaint work. At circle headquarters, two officers, one technical and other non-technical, have been provided exclusively for looking into complaints.

A connected major recommendation of the Administrative Reforms Commission is that "the existing orders and instructions on the subject of public complaints should be reviewed by the P & T Board and reduced to a compendious form and incorporated in the manuals." At present, instructions on the manner in which different kinds of public complaints are to be handled, are scattered in innumberable orders memoranda, instructions, circulars etc., accumulated over last three decades. This creates quite a considerable difficulty in view of the fact that the clerical and supervisory staff in the divisional offices who ultimately have to deal with the complaints are rotated after three or four years. The Administrative Reforms Commission have also found that not much use is made of all the complaint books which are maintained in the post offices. It has proposed that the availability of complaint books should be published through suitable notices, posters, etc. These books should be scrutinized regularly by all inspecting officers.

Another channel for redress of the citizens' grievances against the P & T department is the institution of advisory bodies set up by the department. At present there is a National P & T Advisory Council and there are regional P & T Advisory Committees at the circle levels. There are 68 Telephone Advisory Committees functioning all over the country. The role played by the advisory bodies has so far been rather limited. These Committees need to be revitalized. It is also necessary to revive Divisonal Advisory Committees (which are abolished in 1956). The members of the Advisory Bodies should be authorised to examine the complaint books maintained in the offices and take up with the authorities the cases which they consider to be deserving.

Two important areas of public complaints against the P & T department are delay in getting through trunk calls and delay in securing new telephone connections.

It would be of interest to mention that the official figures furnished by the department show that while the rate of disposal has remained more or less the same, the size of complaints received has shown a tendency to go down, in recent years. The Working Group on Posts and Telegraphs of the Administrative Reforms Commission have reported that the percentage of complaints to the total traffic of all kinds thus works out to only 0.01 per cent. It adds that "our enquiries from the public reveal that the image of the P & T Department is not as good as it ought to be. There are complaints of delays in delivery of letters and telegrams, pilferage of registered packets and parcels, wrong delivery of articles, mis-direction of money orders, wrong billing of telephone charges, rude behaviour across the counter or at the other end of the telephone line or link, etc." Commenting on the report of the Working Group, the Administrative Reforms Commission observed that "in absolute numbers the figures of complaints are quite high. Moreover, they represent grievances of only those who have taken the trouble of putting down their complaints in writing.

There may be many more who refrain from doing so on account of innate inertia or cynical lack of faith in securing prompt redress."

SUPRA-DEPARTMENTAL MACHINERY

Even though the departmental channels of redress are open to the average citizen, he is apt to nurse a feeling of not having received an impartial treatment when the superior authority confirms the decision of the lower authority, thereby turning down the complaint. It is important that such a feeling of having been denied justice should not be allowed to grow. The special Complaints Cells in the Central ministries and departments, though, in some ways, a check-post, are still a part of the inter-departmental machinery. There is, thus, need for a supra-departmental agency to oversee the working of the inter-departmental machinery and to ensure that the complaints receive an impartial and objective treatment.

The Committee on Prevention of Corruption, 1963, (Santhanam Committee) recommended, *inter alia,* the setting up of a Central Directorate General of Complaints and Redress.[5] This Directorate of General Complaints and Redress was to be a part of the Central Vigilance Commission. It was to be vested with the duty of inquiring into, investigating or causing an inquiry or investigation to be made into: (a) all complaints forwarded by the Committee on Petitions of the Lok Sabha and the Rajya Sabha; (b) all complaints remitted by the public vigilance committees; (c) all complaints forwarded by Members

[5]Under the Santhanam Committee scheme, there were to be three directorates as follows and they were to be a part of the Central Vigilance Commission: (i) Directorate of General Complaints and Redress, (ii) Directorate of Vigilance, and (iii) Central Police Organization which would exercise the powers then exercised by the Delhi Special Police Establishment, till such time as the Central Bureau of Investigation was set up. The Central Bureau of Investigation was created on 1 April 1963 and in December of that year the Central Vigilance Commission was constituted, but without a Directorate of General Complaints and Redress. The reason for not including such a Directorate in the organization of the Central Vigilance Commission was that the proposed functions of such a Directorate were such as would justify the establishment of a separate agency for undertaking them.

of Parliament; (d) other complaints in respect of matters falling within the purview of the vigilance committees and deserving to be investigated or inquired into.

When the Report of the Santhanam Committee was considered by the government, as noted earlier, it took the view that the question of evolving a suitable machinery for redress of the citizens' grievances needed to be dealt with in detail separately and that it would not be appropriate to burden the Central Vigilance Commission with grievances other than those relating to corruption.

As a follow-up on the general measures initiated by the government to strengthen and streamline the departmental complaints machinery, the Government of India appointed in February, 1966, a Commissioner of Public Grievances with the status of Additional Secretary in the Ministry of Home Affairs. His main functions are to coordinate and keep under review the working of the Complaint Cells and of the complaints officers under the various ministries and departments. He also oversees the arrangements made in each department for receiving and dealing with citizens' grievances and sees to their efficient working. He is generally concerned with the policy matters arising in any ministry in the matter of the citizen's grievances. He can look into such individual complaints also as come to his notice or are remitted to him by the ministries and departments. When a rule, regulation, practice or procedure is found to work harshly in individual cases, the Commissioner is free to place the matter before the ministry/minister for reconsideration of rule etc., and to see that the grievance has been dealt with properly, i.e., whether the officer concerned applied his mind to it and dealt with the points involved and whether the case was at all stages handled with reasonable expedition.

The first Commissioner for Public Grievances submitted a report to Government in July, 1967. This report was in the form of a review note and has been treated as 'confidential' by the Government of India. As noted earlier, the Commissioner for Public Grievances found that the machinery for redress of the citizens' grievances was not upto the mark and the complaints continued to be examined by the person complained against notwithstanding the Cabinet directive against such an arrangement. The Commissioner was emphatic that senior officers should be spared for looking into public complaints. He also suggested that suitable literature on policies and procedures should be brought out by each ministry "so that the public knows how and whom to approach regarding a particular grievance."

In July 1967, Government of India abolished the separate post of Commissioner for Public Grievances and assigned its responsibilities to Secretary (Personnel) in the Ministry of Home Affairs. In this work, he was assisted by an Under Secretary and a full section, called Public Grievances Section. With the transfer of Services Wing to the new Department of Personnel, the work of the former Commissioner of Public Grievances is now handled by the Secretary in the Department of Personnel. The reasons for the abolition of the post of the Commissioner of Public Grievances are not known. According to certain sources, the post was abolished in view of the unsavoury observations made by the former Commissioner on the processing of complaints by the Central ministries and departments. However, another view is that the post was abolished as there was really not enough work to be handled by a full-time Commissioner.

In recent years, the public complaints received by the Central ministries and departments have been mounting up. The total number of complaints, as reported by the various ministries/departments and offices during the years 1968 and 1969 ending 30 June 1969 was 4,40,035. About 53 per cent of these complaints related to delays. The number of complaints received during the year 1975-76 was 12,27,691 out of which 10,07,724 were disposed of in that year.

The institution of the Commissioner of Public Grievances, even though it functions as supra-departmental level, has certain built-in constraints. One of the objectives of the creation of complaint cells was that there should be in each ministry an independent person, unconnected with the original decision who could "bring to bear upon a grievance on objective mind and thus provide a corrective to the limitations from which hierarchical remedies suffer." However, complaints still find their way mostly to the same persons against whose decision the complaint is being made, with the result that the required objectivity in examining a case is not forthcoming. The existence of the Commissioner of Public Grievances does not help much to improve matters in this regard as he is an officer of the government and cannot pull much weight; the public does not get a feeling that their grievances have been impartially examined as would be the case if their complaints were looked into by an organization independent of the government.

Further, if the Commissioner of Public Grievances is unable to get his recommendation in favour of the complainant accepted by the department concerned, it is embarrassing for him to inform the complainant that in spite of his best efforts he has not succeeded in securing redress. The position would be different if he could report the results of the action taken by him to Parliament. His responsibility for bringing into the open the facts of the case as reviewed by him would have been then discharged. Any genuine difference of opinion between him and the department would not be a cause for embarrassment, because the department could, if called upon to do so, openly defend its position through the minister before Parliament. The complainant will also have the satisfaction that his grievance had been gone into at a very high level by an independent functionary.

Redress of complaints of corruption

An important recent development in the field of administration which touches vitally upon the life of the citizen is the increase in corrupt practices. Corruption, conceived broadly, implies not only the acceptance of money and gift but also taking some administrative decision or action or withholding it for some personal gain. It is commonly accepted that the extent of corruption in administration in India has gone up during the last twenty-five years. Economic controls of different kinds, which have come in the wake of five year plans of economic and social development, have widened the opportunities for corrupt practices. Corruption is said to prevail in the civil services as well as among the ministers and other elected representatives. In his speech before the AICC on 5 May 1977, Shri T.A. Pai, former Industry Minister has rightly described this as: "Our system of working itself creates considerable black money, encouraged smuggling and corruption became rampant. By denying the existence of corruption, people who have been victim of these practices cannot be deprived of their right to say so. In fact, it became a joke that if a peon accepted money it was called "bakshish", if a clerk accepted money, it was called "mamool", if an officer accepted, it was called "bribe" and if a minister accepted, it became "party fund". Corruption not merely means injustice for the large body of the citizens; it demoralizes both the administration and the people. In India, the movement for improving the machinery for the redress of the citizens' grievances has emerged from the larger demand for fighting the evils of corruption in administration. It will therefore, be pertinent to trace very briefly the developments relating to the growth of anti-corruption and vigilance machinery as well as the machinery for looking into complaints against ministers.

There has come up in recent years a net work of anti-corruption and vigilance agencies at the Centre charged with the responsibility of looking into complaints of corruption against public officials. The main government agencies working in this field are:

(a) Special Police Establishment,
(b) Central Bureau of Investigation, and
(c) Central Vigilance Commission.

The Special Police Establishment was created by the Government of India in 1941 to investigate cases of bribery and corruption. In 1953, an Enforcement Wing was added to the Special Police Establishment to deal with offences relating to breach of import and export regulations. The Central Bureau of Investigation was established in April 1963, and Special Police Establishment became one of its Divisions. The Bureau investigates complaints of corruption received from the public. On an average, the Central Bureau of Investigation investigates about 1,200 cases every year, of a very serious nature, out of which about 18 per cent cases relate to bribery, corruption, misappropriation, cheating, etc., involving public servants. Till now 2200 cases are pending trial for 10 years 71 special CBI courts are being set up.

The Central Vigilance commission was set up in 1964, following the recommendations of the Santhanam Committee.

The Central Vigilance Commissioner is appointed by the President by a warrant under his hand and seal, is removable in the same manner as the Chairman or Member of the Union Public Service Commission. He holds office for a term of six years, but is ineligible for any further employment under the Union or State Governments.

The Vigilance Commission's role is confined to undertaking inquiries on receiving a reference from the concerned Government department, about lack of integrity or a malpractice on the part of a public servant. It can enquire into any transaction in which a public servant is suspected or alleged to have acted for an improper purpose or in a corrupt manner. Where it appears, after a preliminary inquiry, that a public servant had acted or refrained from acting for an improper or corrupt purpose, the Commission advises the appropriate disciplinary authority regarding suitable action to be taken against the public servant concerned. The Commission has also given the responsibility of excercising a general check and supervision over vigilance and anti-corruption work in the ministries/departments and public sector undertakings, etc. The Commission can call from administrative authorities such reports and returns as it may consider necessary.

The staff of the Vigilance Commission includes eight Commissioners for Departmental Enquiries. These Commissioners hold oral enquiries in vigilance cases against (i) gazetted officers and (ii) officers of public undertakings, etc. drawing a salary of Rs.1,000 or above.

The Central Vigilance Commission's functions are advisory and it enjoys the same measure of independence and autonomy as the Union Public Service Commission. The Commission submits an annual report to the Union Ministry of Home Affairs about its activities drawing particular attention to any recommendation made by it which have not been accepted or acted upon by government. A copy of the annual report is required to be laid by the Ministry of Home Affairs before the two Houses of Parliament, together with a memorandum explaining the reasons for non-acceptance of the recommendations of the Commission, if any.

An additional dimension of the anti-corruption machinery is the establishment of a vigilance organization comprising vigi-

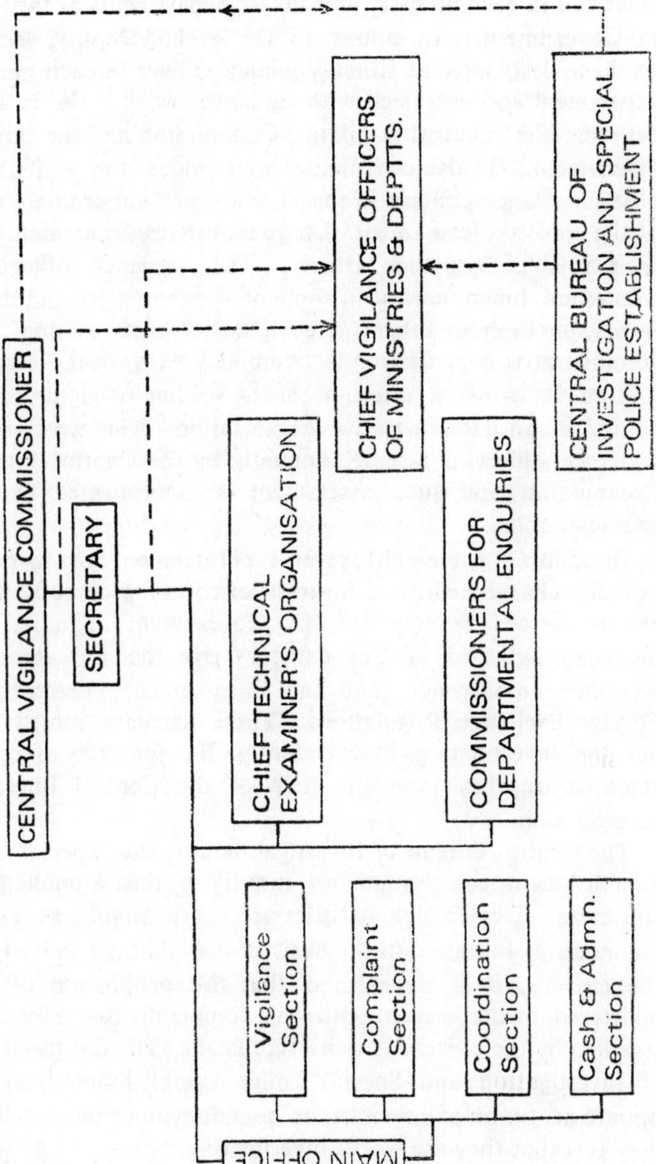

ORGANISATIONAL SET UP OF THE CENTRAL VIGILANCE COMMISSION

lance cell in each ministry and major departments of the Central Government. An officer of the level of Deputy Secretary has been designated as Chief Vigilance Officer in each ministry/department and entrusted with vigilance work. He is a link between the Central Vigilance Commission and the ministry/department. He also coordinates and guides the activities of other Vigilance Officers in the attached and subordinate offices of the ministry/department. Large ministries/departments even have a Chief Vigilance Officer. The vigilance officers are wholetime functionaries in some of the ministries and departments, but in many others, the vigilance work arising in an administrative organization is combined with other responsibilities. It is all a question of the volume of vigilance work arising in an administrative organization. The work of the vigilance officers is assessed annually by the Central Vigilance Commission and such assessment is incorporated in their character rolls.

In addition, there exist several enforcement or inspection agencies charged with the function of checking corrupt practices in various branches of the Government of India. Some important agencies of this category are the Directorate of Revenue Intelligence and the Enforcement Directorate of Foreign Exchange Regulations. These agencies mostly carry out the investigations independently. But for cases of complicated nature, they take the help of the Central Bureau of Investigation.

The Central Bureau of Investigation and the Special Police Establishment can initiate an inquiry against a public officer suo motu. Even though statistics are not available as regards the inquiries initiated on the basis of complaints received from the citizens, it is understood that the proportion of cases registered on the basis of citizens' complaints or information supplied by the citizens is quite significant. The Central Bureau of Investigation and Special Police Establishment can even initiate action on anonymous or pseudonymous complaints if they feel that they are worth investigating.

Cases of corruption are on the increase if one goes by the number of complaints made to the Central Vigilance Commission. From 426 cases in which advise of the Commission was sought by the Central Government in 1964-65—the first year of the Commission's existence— the number rose to 713 in 1975-76. Corruption in government departments has apparently increased over the last decade for several reasons which need not be gone into here. The Postal department, for instance, which was comparatively free of corruption, has become a victim of corrupt practices. The Central Bureau of Investigation received the highest number of complaints against the postal officials and employees. Other government agencies covered by the Bureau were the office of the Director General of Foreign Trade, the Central Public Works Department and the Directorate General of Supplies and Disposal.

As regards the redress of the citizens' complaints in the matter of corrupt practices, the anti-corruption machinery, the vigilance organization and the enforcement agencies play a limited and indirect role. The anti-corruption machinery and the enforcement agencies initiate action on receiving a complaint from the citizen and conduct investigations which may result in bringing the offenders to book. This may not bring any direct benefit to the complainant in most of the cases, but it does help to curb the corrupt practices and thereby make the administration clean.

COMPLAINTS AGAINST MINISTERS

The adoption of the Cabinet system of parliamentary government has brought in its wake the problem of lack of integrity among the holders of the elected public offices.

The Santhanam Committee (1963) which went into the problem of corruption was very much exercised over the deterioration of standards of integrity. It observed: "We heard from all sides that corruption has, in recent years, spread even to those levels of administration from which it was conspicuously absent in the past. We wish we could confidently and without reservation assert that at the political level, Ministers, Legislators, party officials were free from this malady. The general impressions are unfair and exaggerated. But the very fact that such impressionis are there causes damage to the social fabric."

The Committee recommended that the President may constitute, on the advice of the Prime Minister, a national panel from which three persons may be chosen from time to time to set up ad hoc committees for inquiring into the allegations against a minister. At least one of the three persons should have held, or should be holding, a high judicial office. If a formal allegation is made by any ten Members of Parliament or of a State Legislature in writing addressed to the Prime Minister or the Chief Minister, through the Speakers of the Lower House or Chairman of the Upper House, as the case may be, he should consider himself obliged, by convention, to refer the allegations for immediate investigation by such a committee.

It was further suggested that the ad hoc committee, constituted from among the persons on the national panel, should first ascertain whether there is a prima facie case against the minister. The Committee should have the power to direct the Central Bureau of Investigation, in suitable cases, to investigate and report. If the Committee wishes to make any inquiries otherwise than through the Central Bureau of Investigation, it should be given all necessary facilities to do so. On the completion of inquiries, the committee should consider the available material and advise on further action, if any, to be taken by the government. It may advise that a regular case may be registered for investigation with a view to prosecuting the minister concerned or that a Commission or Inquiry may be appointed.

The above-mentioned procedure, for action on the complaint of ten or more Members of Parliament or the State Legislature, should, in the opinion of the Santhanam Committee, be in addition to the responsibility of the Prime Minister/Chief Minister of a State to take note of allegations made in the press or which otherwise came to his notice. The Prime Minister/Chief Minister should be free to refer such allegations to the proposed ad hoc committee.

The ministers have also a responsibility to maintain a reputation of integrity and propriety. The Santhanam Committee suggested that where a prima facie case does not in the opinion of the Prime Minister/Chief Minister, exist, the minister against whom allegations are made should, as a rule, institute legal proceedings for criminal defamation and he should be given legitimate assistance by the government. The Committee added that in cases where the ministers are unwilling to take legal action, the Prime Minister/Chief Minister "should consider themselves obliged by convention, unless there is irrefutable proof of the integrity of the Minister concerned, to advise the President or the Governor, as the case may be, to withdraw his pleasure." That would mean that the minister will have to go out of office unless he himself resigns.

Following the recommendations of the Santhanam Committee, the Central Government has evolved a set procedure in regard to complaints of corruption against Ministers. This procedure is broadly as follows:

> If it appears that a complaint against a Minister in the Central Government calls for further inquiry, the Union Home Minister should take it up and with the help of such information as he may be able to obtain through the sources available to him, satisfy himself and the Prime Minister whether a prima facie case exists. If so, the Minister concerned will normally be asked to step down. In certain cases this itself may suffice. If the nature of the case calls for further action, this may be taken in accordance with the circumstances of the case through a suitable agency. There may be cases in which it would be necessary to institute a regular inquiry in some form or the other.

A similar procedure has been evolved for dealing with complaints of corruption against State Ministers and Chief Ministers. The Chief Minister of a State has responsibility in respect of State Ministers corresponding to the responsibility of the Union Home Minister and the Prime Minister in respect of ministers of the Central Government. At the Chief Ministers' conference convened by the Union Home Minister at Bhubaneshwar on 7 January 1964, it was decided that the Union Home Minister should look into allegations of corruption against State Chief Ministers.

In more recent times, there has been a trend towards the constitution of Special Commissions of inquiry to examine complaints of corruption against the ministers, particularly those belonging to the predecessor government. Janata government had appointed a number of commissions against the former Prime Minister, Ministers and a large number of officers for alleged misuse of power, misappropriation of funds etc. In the past several of the State governments appointed ad hoc Commissions of inquiry to go into the allegations of corruption and impropriety against the State Ministers of the preceding government of a different party complexion (e.g.

Punjab, Jammu & Kashmir, Orissa, Bihar, Kerala Tamil Nadu, Karnataka). Some of the findings of such Commissions in brief are:

(i) A quasi-judicial inquiry was conducted in 1956 by Mr. Justice S.K. Das, judge of the Supreme Court against Shri K.D. Malviya, Minister in the Union Cabinet and held him guilty. (ii) Pratap Singh Kairon was held guilty by the Das Commission of allowing his sons and relatives to exploit his influence and powers during the time he was Chief Minister of the undivided Punjab. (iii) Bakshi Gulam Mohammed who was Chief Minister of Jammu & Kashmir for a period of ten years, was found guilty of "gross misconduct" by a Commission of inquiry headed by Mr. N. Rajgopala Ayyengar, a former Supreme Court Judge. The Commission held that "the amount of improper benefits or undue financial advantage obtained by Bakshi and the members of his family totals over Rs.54 lakhs". (iv) Biju Patnaik, as also his deputy, Biren Mitra who succeeded him as Chief Minister of Orissa, earned the strictures of the Commission of Inquiry headed by Mr. Justice H.R. Khanna of the Delhi High Court, for improprieties and abuse of power in matters of administration of the State". The concerns with which their family members were associated flourished immeasurably under their official patronage. (v) the late Raja Kamakshya Narain Singh of Ramgarh set a record in 1952 by winning from four Assembly Constituencies. And with such influence he also "grossly abused" his position in the Bihar Cabinet and was indicted by the Madholkar Commission for "personal corruption". (vi) Mahamaya Prasad Sinha headed a United Front government in Bihar for a brief period of 1967-68. The Madholkar Commission criticized the Chief Minister for sacrificing "public interest on the altar of political expediency" in appointing the late Raja Ramgarh, a big mine-owner, as the minister for Mines and Geology. (vii) "A bidding example to budding politicians" was one of the flowing birthday tributes paid to Mahesh Prasad Sinha, a few years ago, when he was minister in the Bihar ministry. But a Commission of Inquiry held him guilty, in one case, of accepting a bribe of Rs. 1,75,000 from a contractor. (viii) K.B. Sahay, former Chief Minister of Bihar, was found by the Aiyar Commission of Inquiry to have had investments exceeding a lakh of rupees over his income. In the

State Assembly, he had once expressed his plight of having to maintain a family of over 20 members on his monthly salary of Rs.820 and, therefore, maintained that his sons and relations had all the right to engage themselves in business to earn their livelihood. (ix) It is alleged that M. Karunanidhi, former Chief Minister of Tamil Nadu has favoured some parties on consideration of money. (x) There are allegations of corruption and misuse of public money against Shri Devraj Urs, Chief Minister of Karnataka. The Central Government appointed a Commission headed by a retired Supreme Court Judge. Grover Commission in its report has found the Chief Minister of Karnataka and others guilty of charges. The Centre had discovered that it has no powers to take any action against the Chief Minister and hence it has referred the Grover Commission report to Devraj Urs ministry itself to implement it. (xi) Shah Commission headed by former Chief Justice of the Supreme Court was appointed to look into the charges of committing atrocities during Emergency and for misuse of state machinery by those in power for personal gains. The Commission received 46,261 complaints, of which 8,432 were not covered by the terms of reference. Of the remaining complaints, 2,342 were inquired into by the Commission's officials, 6,716 were referred to State Governments and Central ministries for inquiry and intimation of the findings to the Commission, and 28,771 were sent to State governments/ministries for inquiry and disposal. Nearly 75 per cent of the complaints thus went to Central ministries and State governments. The Commission submitted three reports to the government. (xii) The one-man Vaidialingam Commission in its report submitted to the Govt. in January 1980 has indicted the son and daughter-in-law of former Prime Minister Morarji Desai for having functioned as an extraconstitutional authority and pressurized governmental machinery for self-aggrandisement. The Commission also held guilty the wife of former Prime Minister Charan Singh for interference in governmental machinery and for accepting from educated young people of fairly large amounts of money on the promise of providing them jobs.

Of the three commissions appointed by the Janata government under the Commissions of Inquiry Act, 1952, the Shah Commission of Inquiry submitted its first and second interim reports on 11 March 1978 and 26 April 1978 respectively and the third and final report on 6 August 1978. All the three reports have been placed on the table of both the Houses with memoranda of action taken thereon. The officials found guilty by the Commission are to be prosecuted in the Special Courts. Remedial and follow-up action on the constitutional, legislative, administrative and miscellaneous issues arising from the above reports, has been completed. The Special Cell which was set up in the C.B.I. has registered 19 FIRs up to 20 Febuary 1979 against persons who appeared to have committed criminal offences. In one case relating to alleged misuse of government machinery for preparation of designs of election posters for election campaign, charge sheet was filed against Shri V.C. Shukla, former Minister of Information and Broadcasting and others on 7 Febuary 1979. After the new government took over the case has been withdrawn by the C.B.I. from the court as no offence could be established. In four cases (in three of which the former Prime Minister is involved), after completion of investigation, sanction of the Government under Section 197 Cr.P.C. has been sought. The Reddy Commission of Inquiry on the Nagarwala episode submitted its report on 23 October 1978 and did not hold any one guilty. The Gupta Commission of Inquiry on Maruti Affairs submitted its report in May 1979.

The Special Courts Bill

The Special Courts Bill, 1978 which provides for the trial of offences committed by persons holding high political and public offices during the Emergency was referred by the President to the Supreme Court for its advisory opinion under Article 143 of the Constitution on the validity of the Bill. The Supreme Court which gave its opinion in December, 1978, considered the Bill to be within the Parliament's legislative competence but pointed out certain infirmities on its provisions. After removing the infirmities the Bill was introduced and passed by Lok Sabha on 9 March 1979. After its approval by Rajya Sabha it has been brought on the statute book and the Special Courts were established in June 1979. Two courts were accordingly set up. Both the courts have since declared themselves as unconstitutional.

Replying to the debate on the demands for grants of the Union Ministry of Home Affairs, the Minister for Home Affairs stated on 23 November 1966 in the Lok Sabha that where there were numerous cases of wild, fantastic and baseless allegations against ministers, it was not necessary to send all of them for inquiry. The Prime Minister would, however, look into them and, on the basis of personal inquiry dispose them of. If a formal inquiry was considered necessary, it would have to be by an independent, impartial agency.

The belief that corruption prevails at the highest political level in government is obviously very much damaging to the citizen's confidence in administration and to his expectations of receiving an effective redress for his grievances. Recognizing the importance of this problem, the Administrative Reforms Commission feels that "there has to be an institution in which the average citizen will have faith and confidence and through which he will be able to secure quick and inexpensive justice. The Reforms Commission is of the view that the problem of corruption in high places cannot be tackled by the existing machinery, and that the creation of an independent machinery of the Ombudsman-type is a basic necessity to meet the problem. This will also save the country lot of expenditure on appointment of Commissions on political considerations. We revert to this challenging issue in Chapter VIII.

CHAPTER V

Role of Judiciary and Administrative Tribunals

The Preamble to the Indian Constitution enjoins the promotion of social justice and the directive principles of state policy provide the guidelines for the establishment of a welfare state. The phenomenal increase in the activities of the state in the past thirty years has resulted in a large number of enactments which confer extensive powers on the administrative authorities. This has given rise to the problem of controlling the actions of the state to ensure that the rights of individal citizens are safeguarded against arbitrary administrative action. According to the Law Commission, it is all the more necessary to provide such a protection to the citizen because the political party which has been in power at the Centre and in most of the States "wields an almost unlimited influence throughout the country", and tends to "trample ruthlessly upon the rights of the individvals with aid of a stream-roller majority".[1] After the Fourth General Election the position changed significantly and the one-party dominance was lost in several States. The results of the Fourth General Election were in a way a note of warning by the citizens against the growing encroachment on their individual rights. After the Fifth General Election, the tendency to wield arbitrary authority on the part of the majority political party in power at the Centre reappeared. The repeal of the Preventive Detention Act in 1970 by the Fourth Lok Sabha, after the split in the ruling Congress party, and its re-enactment with a different title of Maintenance of Internal Security Act and the addition of a new Section 16A and the Defence and Internal Security of

[1]Government of India, *Fourteenth Report of the Law Commission on Reform of Judicial Administration*, 1958, p. 673.

India Rules after the promulgation of Emergency in June 1975, suspension of the right to move the Courts to enforce Fundamental Rights conferred by Articles 14, 19, 21 and 22 of the Constitution are the glaring examples of the exercise of the power[2] without much regard for the wishes of the large body of the people.

But the question of protection of the citizens' rights has larger dimensions than arbitrariness on the part of the political party in power. The enormous increase in legislation in the wake of the acceptance of wide developmental and welfare responsibilities by the Government has led to vesting in the administrative authorities wide discretionary powers. A sizeable proportion of citizens' grievances relate to this discretionary area. The Courts can only regulate the exercise of discretion, within the framework of law, but they cannot go into the merits of discretionary decisions. Administrative Tribunals, which have come up in a large number in recent years have the advantages of speed, inexpensiveness and simplicity of procedures.

COURTS AS CHANNELS OF REDRESS

The Constitution of India provides safeguards against arbitrary administrative actions. Part 3 of the Constitution enumerates

[2]This problem has been summed up by the Spens Committee in Britain as follows:

"First, there is a growing feeling that the citizen is no longer having the protection of an objective law from the capricious exercise of arbitrary power; secondly, there is a feeling that a system which makes inadequate provision for review of administrative decisions enshrines and sanctions errors; thirdly, there is a firm belief that fairness and justice should be a part as mueh of the administrative processas of the judicial process."

Some years later, Franks Committee gave shape to these principles. The important recommendation of this Committee was that there should be a general council of tribunals which could keep a close watch on the functioning of all tribunals for the purpose of ensuring that they served not merely as instruments for executing official policy, but also as a means of safeguarding interests of the citizens. On the basis of this recommendation the British Government set up a Council of Tribunals in 1958. (*Report of the Inns of Court Conservative and Unionist Society:* Chairman, Right Hon'ble Sir Patrick Spens, 1955.)

certain fundamental rights of the individual citizen which cannot be transgressed by legislative or administrative action. Under Articles 32[3] and 226[4] of the Constitution the Supreme Court and High Courts are empowered to strike down any legislation or administrative order which violates the fundamental rights. The powers of the High Courts under Article 226 are even wider than the powers of the Supreme Court under Article 32. The Supreme Court can interfere only if there has been an infringement of fundamental rights whereas the High Courts can not only interfere for the restoration of fundamental rights but "for any other purpose"[5]. Article 226 is a real protection to the citizen against the arbitrary decisions of the administration. Article 227[6] gives the power of superintendence to the High Courts over all Courts and Tribunals within the country. This Article has been invoked frequently by an aggrieved person against the decisions of the tribunals. But Article 227 confers the power of superintendence over the High Courts and tribunals and does not give them appellate powers to decide a

[3]Article 32 of the Constitution gives a right to any person to approach the Supreme Court for relief against the breach of any of his fundamental rights. Article 32(2) provides, "The Supreme Court shall have power to issue directions or orders or writs, including writs in the nature of habeas corpus, mandamus, prohibition, quo warranto and certiorari, whichever may be appropriate for the enforcement of any of the rights conferred by this Part.

[4]Under the provisions of Article 226 of the Constitution, a person can approach the High Court to enforce his right, whether fundamental or otherwise. Article 226(1) reads, "Notwithstanding anything in article 32, every High Court shall have power, throughout the territories in relation to which it exercises jurisdiction to issue to any person or authority, including in appropriate cases any Government, within those territories, directions, orders or writs, including writs in the nature of habeas corpus, mandamus, prohibition, quo warranto and certiorari, or any of them, for the enforcement of any of the rights conferred by Part III and for any other purpose".

[5]Here "any other purpose" means a purpose for which any of the writs could, according to well-established principles, issue Durga Das Basu, *Commentary on the Constitution of India.*

[6]Under Article 227 of the Constitution the High Courts have powers to entertain revisions from orders of law courts. Article 227 reads, "Every High Court shall have superintendence over all courts and tribunals throughout the territories in relation to which it exercises jurisdiction."

case on merits.

The power of judicial review of the laws enacted by the legislature and the authority to interpret and declare the law valid or otherwise vest in the courts.[7] Within the broad framework of the laws passed by the legislature, the courts can fix scope and limits of administrative discretion, condition of its exercise and decide a plea of mala fides in exercising it. No doubt the court cannot go into the merits or propriety of an administrative decision but it can concern itself with the question of power, procedure and satisfaction of requisite conditions precedent to making of an administrative decision. Though not directly yet indirectly it can review the administrative act and can pass appropriate order or direction to enforce the right of an aggrieved person. The intervention of the courts in citizens' grievances is circumscribed by certain limitations. At present, only the following types of cases can go to a court of law:

1. where an authority has acted in contravention of the power given under a statute,
2. where decision is irregular in disregard to the prescribed rules of natural justice,
3. where the action is alleged to be mala fide, or
4. where the action is inconsistent with the provisions of the Constitution or law or is in excess of powers delegated to the administrative authority.

The court can intervene on the ground of abuse of power or disregard of the provisions of the law. But it cannot interfere with the exercise of discretion by the administrative authority so long as the discretion is exercised within the limits of statute and is not used for any mala fide purpose. Certain enactments place governmental action outside the jurisdiction

[7]The lower courts are of two kinds—with Criminal jurisdiction and Civil jurisdiction. Cases relating to civil matters go to civil courts and those of criminal matters go to criminal courts. The appeal against the judgments of civil and criminal courts can be made to the Session Courts presided over by a District and Sessions Judge. Thereafter, there are High Courts located in each State. In the case of writs a person can go directly to the High Court or the Supreme Court under Articles 32, 136, 226 and 227 of the Constitution of India.

of the courts. Several of the laws provide no right of appeal or revision even to higher administrative authorities; others confer right of appeal or revision, but these lie with high administrative authority only and not to any judicial authority. There are 199 Acts where certain Sections of the Acts bar the jurisdiction of courts for review and the appellate authority is an agency of the government. Some of these Acts are Indian Electricity Act, 1910 (No. 9 of 1910), Indian Telegraph Act, 1885 (No. 13 of 1885), Land Acquisition Act, 1894 (No. 1 of 1894), the Industries Development and Regulation Act, 1951 (No. 65 of 1951), the Foreign Exchange Regulation Act, 1947 (No. 7 of 1947), and the Imports and Exports (Control) Act, 1947 (No. 18 of 1947). For instance, Sections 110 to 110-F of the Motor Vehicle Act provide compensation to be decided by a tribunal. Even if a driver has been acquitted by a court of law the Claims Tribunal can still adjudge the claims compensation payable to an injured person. The compensation can be claimed not only from the driver but also against the owner and such a compensation if fixed by a tribunal will be barred from the jurisdiction of civil courts under Section 110-F of the Motor Vehicle Act. Where a tribunal awarded certain amount of compensation as the victim has become permanently disabled, or a girl has become disfigured affecting her future happiness, it is not open to the insurance company or the High Court to question the quantum of compensation fixed by the tribunal.

The very fact that certain matters are not justiciable may lead to arbitrariness. In many fields of governmental activity, powers involving exercise of wide discretion rest with executive authorities. The exercise of discretion is fraught with the danger of its being abused or misused. In such cases, the only remedy left with the citizen is to invoke the extraordinary jurisdiction of the High Courts under Article 226 of the Constitution or of the Supreme Court under Articles 32 and 136[8]

[8]Article 136 gives powers to the Supreme Court to hear appeal against the decision or order of any tribunal in the territory of India. The Article reads; "(1) Notwithstanding anything in this Chapter, the Supreme Court may, in its discretion, grant special leave to appeal from any judgment, decree, determination, sentence or order in any cause or matter passed or made by any court or tribunal in the terri-

of the Constitution. But the scope for redress under these provisions is very limited. Article 226 provides an extraordinary remedy against administrative authorities and tribunals. It does not, of course, affect the decision of a tribunal on a controversial point of law, provided the tribunal acts within the jurisdiction and does so in conformity with the forms of law. It is only the incorrect application of law that may attract the adoption of these Articles. Thus, the court can correct the jurisdictional defects to avoid any injustice to the citizen. The High Courts have no jurisdiction to decide issue on merits. They can quash the decision of the tribunal but cannot themselves provide a redress.

The High Courts can correct an error of law and can prevent grave and manifest injustice to any person, but they cannot investigate a complaint involving a grievance against maladministration or an allegation of administrative corruption. Article 227 gives the High Courts powers of superintendence over all courts and tribunals within the limits of appellate territorial jurisdiction. The Article has been invoked by the aggrieved litigants against the decision of Labour Tribunals and other tribunals which decide the rights between one individual and another or between an individual and the state. In a case Supreme Court held: "The only question which could be considered by the court is whether the authority vested with the powers has paid attention to or taken into account circumstances, events or matters wholly extraneous to the purpose for which the power was vested, or whether the proceedings have been initiated mala fide for satisfying a private or personal grudge of the authority". The principle has been stated quite succinctly by the Supreme Court in Pratap Singh vs. State of Punjab as follows:

> The court is not an appellate forum where the correctness of an order of Governmental could be canvassed and, indeed, it has no jurisdiction to substitute its own view for the entirety of power jurisdiction, and discretion is vested by law in Government.[9]

---

tory of India. (2) Nothing in clause (1) shall apply to any judgment, determination, sentence or order passed or made by any court or tribunal constituted by or under any law relating to the Armed Forces".

[9]Partap Singh *vs.* State of Punjab, (*All India Reporter*, 1964, Supreme Court 72),

Even if the aggrieved person has a remedy in a court of law, it loses its effect owing to the inevitable delay invoked in the course of litigation. The arrears in the High Courts are mounting up and the justice is being delayed. There are cases which are pending in the courts for more than 15 to 20 years.

In brief, justice through courts today is generally both expensive and dilatory, whereas the individual wishes to seek, and appreciates, quick and inexpensive justice. In discharging their constitutional functions of holding the scales of justice even between the state and the citizen the courts can intervene to set right administrative actions on grounds of illegality, jurisdictional error, error of law or the fact of record, or failure to follow prescribed procedures of rules of natural justice.

ADMINISTRATIVE TRIBUNALS

Administrative tribunals have been evolved as a device to ensure justice to the citizens in view of the enormous expansion in the activities of modern government touching upon the life of the citizens. In the changed environmental context the administration must "satisfy the general body of citizens that it is proceeding with reasonable regard to balance between the public interest which it promotes and the private interest which it disturbs".[10] In several areas, such as excise and customs, sales tax, income tax, acquisition of land, control of rent, transport control and regulation, agrarian reforms, matters connected with social security measures and the like, the government's activities affect the citizens directly and closely and it is here that every one expects that justice must not only be done but seem to be done manifestly and openly. With the growth in the number of laws, the scope of the rule-making authority (delegated legislation) has increased substantially, necessitating, in turn, the adoption of new devices for protecting the citizens against inroads on their rights by government departments and agencies. There is a common feeling that the constitutional protection of the citizens' rights is of a restricted nature and deserves to be supplemented. As we have seen,

[10]Report of the Committee on Administrative Tribunals and Enquiries, op. cit., p. 5.

the rule of the courts in providing redress is limited to points of law, procedural irregularities and rules of natural justice. The departmental channels of redress suffer from inherent limitations of their own. The system of administrative tribunals is designed to maintain an essential balance between individual rights and public welfare.

Types of Tribunals

In India, the first Tribunal, the Income-Tax Appellate Tribunal was set up in January 1941 in pursuance of the recommendations of the Income-Tax Inquiry Committee Report of 1936. The more important tribunals today are:

1. The Railway Rates Tribunal,
2. The Tribunals established under the Motor Vehicles Act,
3. The Tribunals established for the Land Acquisition Act (Act 1 of 1894),
4. Companies Tribunal,
5. Election Tribunal,
6. Income-Tax Appellate Tribunal,
7. Industrial Tribunals,
8. Employees State Insurance Tribunals.

In addition to the tribunals, there exist in India, a large number of administrative authorities enjoying quasi-judicial powers. These include the Press and Registration Appellate Board, the Copyright Board, the Central Board of Indirect Taxes under the Customs Act, 1962, the Board of Direct Taxes, etc. Some executive authorities have also been given quasi-judicial functions, like Chief Settlement Commissioner, the Settlement Commissioners, the Settlement Officers under the Displaced persons (Compensation and Rehabilitation) Act 1954, the Appellate Assistant Commissioners under the Income Tax Act, 1961 etc.

In 1957, an attempt was made by the Ministry of Law, Government of India, to undertake an examination of the Central and State Acts which provide for the setting up of tribunals (other than ordinary courts of law) or of administrative agencies. The analysis revealed that there were about 3,875 administrative tribunals and administrative bodies with semi-judicial functions operating in India. Of them, 187 administrative bodies were functioning under Central Acts and the remaining 2,686 under the States laws.

The tribunals and authorities functioning under various enactments of Central and State Legislatures often decide rights between individuals or between individuals and the state. Some matters are handled by tribunals or authorities as judicial or quasi-judicial proceedings, while others are dealt with administratively. In the former case, there is a certain measure of safety and a certain amount of satisfaction to the individuals concerned. However, when matters are dealt with administratively by the authorities concerned, there is not that feeling of satisfaction because more often than not the administrative authorities or agencies are themselves interested in the proceedings they conduct. Even the existence of hierarchy of higher authorities to whom the matter can be taken up in appeal does not give satisfaction to the aggrieved party so long as the matter is dealt with on the administrative side, because it is felt that an administrative authority is likely to have an unconscious bias in favour of the administration.

The difference in a court and a tribunal is that an administrative tribunal performs quasi-judicial functions whereas the functions performed by a court are entirely judicial. Quasi-judicial functions are the functions of a law court which an administrative authority performs. A tribunal has to apply law and is to follow judicial methods. The difference between judicial and quasi-judicial decisions is that "in the case of judicial authorities their orders can only be either judicial or administrative and cannot possibly be quasi-judicial. Since other authorities are not judicial if they are to be passed judicially; they can be only quasi-judicial."[11]

Merits of tribunal system

The salient features of an administrative tribunal are:

1. It is established by the executive in accordance with the statutory provision.
2. It acts judicially and performs quasi-judicial functions.

[11]Basant Singh vs. Janak Singh, *All India Reporter*, A 11, pp. 447-48.

3. Its proceedings are judicial and in certain procedural matters it has powers of a civil court.
4. It is not wedded to the technicalities of the rules of procedure and evidence prescribed by the Code of Civil Procedure and the Evidence Act.
5. It decides non-conventional type of disputes in aid of the programmes of the welfare state in accordance with the rules of natural justice.
6. It does not satisfy the institutional conditions, although it has the trappings of a court of law.

Tribunals normally follow a simplified court procedure and their members function in more independent manner than those of other semi-judicial administrative authorities. Administrative tribunals adjudicate upon disputes between the citizens and the administrative agencies more inexpensively, efficiently and rapidly than the ordinary courts and are equipped with greater technical knowledge. They may pay greater heed to the social interests involved and shown less solicitude for private property rights. They may make a conscious effort to carry forward the social policy embodied in legislation. The tribunals provide a relief to the ordinary courts. Their proceedings are informal and simple. For the large part, the persons affected are generally debarred from engaging lawyers to represent them. The fact that tribunals have technical or specialised knowledge of dispute matters enables them to go into not only questions of law but also fact. Though the tribunals like the courts cannot intervene in the rightful exercise of discretion, their capacity to identify the element of arbitrariness is much greater than of the courts, and in this regard they have an edge over both the judicial machinery and the departmental channels for redress of grievances. The Administrative Reforms Commission Study Team on Administrative Tribunals has summed up the advantages as follows:

(i) The very existence of an administrative tribunal for exercising appellate powers over orders of the departmental heads is itself an effective control over the executive.

(ii) In writ applications jurisdiction of High Court is confined to defects in the procedure of conducting enquiry; it is chiefly concerned to find out if the rules of natural justice have been properly observed, better justice is expected from a Tribunal dealing with both questions of law and fact.

(iii) Impartial approach is more likely to be made by a Tribunal than by a departmental agency.

In India, special emphasis has been placed on legal qualifications for the appointment of members of the tribunals to enable them to interpret rules properly. There also exists a provision for taking the help of assessors having knowledge and experience in the fields other than law. In some cases, the proceedings of the tribunals are open to the public and lawyers can also appeal, but this is not the normal practice. They have the powers of court in regard to summoning of witnesses, investigations, and examining on oath.

Limitations

The decisions of the tribunals are not excluded from the purview of the Supreme Court. Article 136 of the Constitution authorises the Supreme Court to sit in judgment over the decision of any tribunal. Certain Acts constituting a tribunal can bar the jurisdiction of the court under Article 226 of the Constitution if administrative remedies have not been exhausted. Notwithstanding the bar, the administrative action comes under review of a court indirectly while interpreting the law or deciding the question of its vires. A person can always move the High Court that the statute is ultra vires, the lagislative power of the legislature are unconstitutional. A decision of a tribunal can be challenged on the plea of denial of constitutional right of equal protection of laws, mala fide intentions or wrongful action of authority. Though not directly, yet indirectly, the court can review the administrative action and can pass an order for enforcement of the right of an aggrieved person. The Supreme Court has power under Article 136 to entertain appeals against the orders passed by any tribunal in India other than those relating to the Armed Forces. However, the Supreme Court under this Article interferes only if the cause involves some question of law of public importance. The power of the Supreme Court under this Article is limited to the extent that the Court can grant special leaves to appeal in cases involving questions of law of public importance.

The working of the administrative tribunals in India has not been without certain innate weakness and operational deficiencies. In the first place, the fact that many of the members of the tribunals are retired judges who look up to the government for extension of their tenure or any similar assignments opens the way to their being influenced by the administrators, ministers, and political leaders belonging to the party in power. Again, the rules and procedure of tribunals do not provide for the publication of their proceedings. Nor are the proceedings open to the public and the press. In the absence of the publication of the proceedings, it is not possible for the administrative authorities to improve their decision making process. Secret proceedings do not inspire the public confidence. Thirdly, the quality of investigation into questions of fact is very poor. The tribunals often rely on unsworn written statements not supported by verbal testimony given on oath and subject to cross-examination. The tribunals are often lacking in power of compelling attendance of witnesses and calling for documents. Fourthly, the right of appeal from the decisions of the tribunals is very much limited and in some cases it is not at all available. Judicial review too is of very much limited character. The chances of miscarriage of justice are thus increased in a way.

Operationally, the administrative tribunals have not shown a satisfactory record in the disposal of citizens' grievances. For instance, in the case of the Income-Tax Appellate Tribunal[12], the number of cases pending have shown a significant increase.

The present system of Income-tax Appellate Tribunal is not working satisfactorily. Cases of improper, incorrect or arbitrary assessment or adjudication often arise. The entire

[12]In the case of Income Tax Department, almost every citizen earning an income above a particular ceiling is taxable. In the scheme of things, the Income Tax Act provides for various authorities. There are Income Tax Officers against whose orders appeal lies with the Appellate Assistant Commissioners. Thereafter, the appeal lies with the Income Tax Appellate Tribunals and the rules provide for a reference to the High Courts and the Supreme Court. In certain cases, an appeal lies with the Central Board of Direct Taxes.

The Supreme Court and the High Courts have, however, laid down the following principles on which the Income Tax Officers are required

hierarchy of appeals etc., lies within the Department and has no judicial control over them. The superior officers generally support the junior officers and the person concerned feels aggrieved that he has been denied justice. People have little confidence in the impartiality of these officers as they belong to the respective Departments.

The Law Commission has commented adversely on the Income-tax Appellate Tribunal as follows: "The Tribunal is constituted, the final fact-finding authority for four taxes, income tax, wealth tax, expenditure tax and gift tax and it is also proposed to make it the final fact-finding authority under the Estate Duty Act. We are constrained to observe that men of the requisite calibre and independence are not being recruited for discharging so heavy a responsibility as that of the final fact-finding authority under the new pattern of taxation. There are many complaints that the disposal of appeals by the Appellate Tribunal is very unsatisfactory for a variety of reasons. Often, the judicial and independent approach which is necessary in the final fact-finding authority, is not displayed by the Tribunal. In several cases, the determination of complicated questions of fact and law is done in a very perfunctory manner. Very often, the tribunal does not clearly record its findings of facts or its reasons for arriving at its findings. In a number of cases, factual or legal contentions raised by the parties are not dealt with at all, resulting in applications for rectification being made subsequently to the tribunal for considering the points omitted to be dealt with in the original order of the Tribunal."

As regards the composition of the tribunals, the main deficiency noticeable is that the tribunals are set up by the departments which are responsible for executing particular policies. Thus, they tend to support the policy and programmes of the departments instead of doing justice. They do not have much of a detached and impartial outlook as they are the limbs of the administration. The members of the tribunals do not in several cases possess judicial training and experience. Nor do

---

to work—"(1) there should be a reasonable opportunity given to the persons concerned, (2) The order should be speaking order; and (3) The Income Tax Officers are entitled to make private enquiries but before they make use of the results of such enquiry they must give the assessee an opportunity showing cause against the material gathered."

the tribunals observe any uniform procedure or maintain a consistency in decisions.

For removing the current deficiencies, the Study Team on Administrative Tribunals of the Administrative Reforms Commission has recommended that the Chairman of the Tribunals should invariably be serving or retired members of the judiciary who should be appointed by the appropriate authorities in consultation with the Chief Justice of Supreme Court or the High Courts as the case may be. They should be appointed for a period of five years at a time. The other members, the Study Team feels, should be fairly senior officers—one from the administration side and the other a technical expert. For instance, in the case of proposed tribunals for excise and customs, the Study Team has suggested that the second member should be not below the rank of a Collector of Customs and the third member be analogous to that of the Chief Chemist of the Central Revenue, Central Laboratory. In the case of sales tax, the Study Team recommended that the second and third members should be not below the rank of a Deputy Commissioner of Commercial Taxes and a Chartered Accountant, respectively.

The ARC Study Team on Administrative Tribunals has urged that the independence and impartiality of the Tribunals needs to be fully assured. The members of the tribunals should not be considered for any other office under the government after their term of office is over so that they do not look forward to any further favour from the government in shape of jobs, etc. In view of the usefulness of the administrative tribunals as a channel of redress of the citizen's grievances, the Study Team has recommended that the system of administrative tribunals should be extended to cover several new areas, such as state excise. customs and central excise duties, sales tax, insurance, transport control and regulations, etc. The main justification given by them for the proposed expansion is that a review of administrative decisions by an agency outside the administrative apparatus will bring the required relief to the citizen. The Study Team adds that the working of the tribunals should be watched carefully before the principle is made applicable to departments other than those recommended by it.

AN OVERVIEW

The system of administratitive tribunals has been only a qualified success. The former Union Minister, late Mr. K.M. Munshi, observed that "inspite of the indispensability of administrative tribunals in a modern welfare state, the problem in a democratic state is how to invest the justice dispensed by the tribunals with impartiality, certainty and predicability."[13] "Unless there is a balance", as the Franks Committee said, "between the public interest that is promoted and the private interest that is disturbed the tribunals can become engines of oppression".[14]

The Law Commission drew attention to the perfunctory manner in which the cases were dealt with by the tribunals. There is considerable delay in disposing of the appeals and very often it is said that they, the tribunals, spare very little time for the appellate work with which alone they are concerned. Very often the members of the tribunals, attend the sittings at any time they choose, thereby not conforming to regular office hours, for the disposal of the work. A Bench of two members of the tribunal hears the appeals, but in practice the contribution to the decision of the case by one of the members is often not appreciable.

The expectation that the Tribunals will be able to provide inexpensive and impartial justice and hold the balance between the citizen and the administration has not been fulfilled in any significant measure. In view of the dismal success with the institution of administrative tribunals, the wider question of adopting in India a system of administrative law on the French pattern is obviously not much relevant. The Law Commission of India has rejected the French system of administrative law mainly on the ground that it would oust the jurisdiction of the ordinary courts and thereby offend against the supremacy of the rule of law. The Commission feels that the basic purposes can be equally achieved if the quasi-judicial decisions of

[13]Paper read by Shri K.M. Munshi at a Seminar organized by the Indian Law Institute in December 1957, New Delhi, *The Hindustan Times* 15 December 1957, p. 12.

[14]B.K.R. Kabadi, "What will the Lokpal Do?" *Public Administration*, Vol. 6, No. 2, February 1968, p. 3.

tribunals are reviewed on appeal by an independent body presided over by a person qualified to be a High Court Judge. The tribunal must function with openness, fairness and impartiality as laid down by the Franks Committee. It is also important that the tribunals delivering administrative judgments should conform to the principles of natural justice and should act with openness, fairness and impartiality.[15] In regard to purely administrative decisions, the Commission thinks that it would be enough if the authorities giving a decision are required to state the reasons since it would then be possible to test the validity of the decision through the machinery of the appropriate writs.

The foregoing analysis would show that the institution of administrative tribunals even if extended, is likely to be beset with certain constraints and limitations. Tribunals, can be effective in redressing citizens grievances within the framework of rules and regulations. But they cannot intervene in the exercise of discretion per se and prevent in a significant manner arbitrariness in administrative decisions or help to alleviate hardship to the citizens arising from procedural rigidities. Tribunals have been set up only in a few areas of economic administration and cannot possibly be extended to cover the entire gamut of administration. People's grievances have a larger dimension. It has, therefore, been urged in some quarters that it is necessary to set up an independent agency like the Ombudsman which would hold the scale even between the citizens and government in the matter of application of policies laid down by legislature for the promotion of the common good.

[15]A Sub-Committee of the Special Consultative Group of Members of Parliament made the following recommendations on the functioning of administrative tribunals: (i) reform of the existing tribunals to ensure open, fair and impartial decision in the quickest and the cheapest manner; (ii) standardization of procedure; (iii) extension of the tribunals system to other departments; (iv) establishment of General Tribunals and a Council of Tribunal; (v) legislation on administrative procedure and formulating a Code of Administrative Procedure for Tribunals like the Civil or Criminal Procedure Codes.

CHAPTER VI

Legislative and Other Channels of Redress

In India, the role of the legislature in ventilating the grievances of citizens has been growing in recent years. The establishment of the parliamentary form of democracy has given a fillip to the aspirations of the people. But the Indian bureaucracy is a gigantic organization which moves at a snail's pace. As it is accountable to the government and the legislature, it is to the ministers and legislators that the people look up increasingly for relief. The legislative channels of redress are several—questions, special discussions, adjournment debates, legislative committees, and the like. As the main role of the legislature is the formulation and review of policies and a general supervison of the implementation of policies and programmes, the citizens' complaints can figure in legislative discussions only within this broad framework. Notwithstanding a crowded programme of legislation at the Centre, the Indian Parliament has served as a useful forum for discussion of complaints affecting a large body of citizens or groups of citizens. In this process, individual complaints also figure as typical instances of maladministration, inadequacy of a particular policy or programme or failure in implementation.

At the State level, as we have noted earlier, the citizens are resorting in an increased measure to intervention by the State legislators in speedy redress of complaints. The normal practice is for a Member of Parliament or State legislature to take up the complaint with the concerned ministry or department. tA the Centre, special instructions have been issued to indicate what type of communications should be addressed to the minister and what kind should be sent to the secretary of the ministry or the department. Such letters are given special attention in the departments, because it is realized that if the

Member is dissatisfied with the answer he receives, he can always ask a question.[1] This method is used considerably and the replies are sent to the Member either by the minister himself or by a senior secretary.[2]

PARLIAMENT QUESTIONS

Question time is the occasion for many major statements of government policy. Opposition frames questions[3] which are designed to highlight the shortcomings of the government in the conduct of its general policy and follow them with a quick series of supplementaries in order to make a concerted attack

[1]Members of Parliament in the Commonwealth countries like Britain, New Zealand, Australia, Canada, etc., serve as an important channel of airing grievances. In Great Britain, if the grievance is genuine the Member of Parliament may write to the concerned officer of the department if he knows him. Otherwise he will write to the minister concerned. Such a letter is highly respected in departmental circles. It begins a process of careful investigation and consideration which is every bit as scrupulous as the process gone through in preparing answers to questions asked in the House itself.

[2]Recently, there has been a criticism from Members of Parliament that their letters are replied by the private secretaries to ministers and not by the ministers themselves. The Prime Minister has issued instructions that mere acknowledgements could be issued by the private secretaries but the main replies to the letters should be by the ministers themselves.

[3]The questions are of three types: Starred, Unstarred and Short Notice questions. Starred and Unstarred Questions require a clear ten days' notice from a Member of Parliament whereas Short Notice Questions can be put within 24 hours, provided the matter is of grave importance and the minister agrees to answer. A member is entitled to ask three Starred Questions per day, i.e., questions which are to be answered orally and which can therefore lead to supplementary questions. The number of Starred Questions on the order paper each day is about 50, but in practice only about 10 or 12 of them can be at the utmost answered orally each day, depending upon the number of supplementaries which crop up. Under the Lok Sabha rules the first hour of every sitting of the House is set apart for answering members' questions. A member can also ask a number of Unstarred Questions, i.e. questions which do not require an oral reply. In view of the limited time available, Starred Questions which cannot be answered on a particular day for want of time are treated as Unstarred Questions and the answers are then laid on the table of the House.

on the government's policy.[4] Even the members of the ruling party, who belong to a dissentient group or who are keen to help the government in a constructive manner, come forward with questions to seek information on the working of a particular policy or programme or the reasons for the delay in the bringing forward of a new policy measure. The question hour is also a device for ventilating community grievances. These grievances may relate to national or state issues or even matters of local importance. A wide variety of issues exercise the minds of legislators. According to Moriss-Jones, "the opportunities for the ventilation of grievances are several but there is no doubt that the most important is Question Time, the liveliest part of the parliamentary day. Not all the Questions put can be said to ventilate grievances and hopes; a large number, very properly, are designed to evoke statements of general policy from Ministers. Nevertheless, the proportion of ventilation Questions is quite high."[5]

Questions pertaining to individual cases are ordinarily not admitted. It has been laid down that information in respect of such cases may be obtained by the legislators directly from the ministers concerned. During the thirteenth session of the Third Lok Sabha, a notice of a question given by a member (H.V. Kamath) seeking information about an Indian doctor (Dr. S.R. Ghosh) residing in London was disallowed on the ground that it related to an individual and was of no public importance.[6]

However, as individual grievances reflect upon the manner in which a policy is being implemented inadequately or ineffectively, Members of Parliament or State Legislatures do try to raise individual grievances as a part of the policy issue. Obviously, the legislature to which the administration is accountable, has a right to discuss matters of maladministration, injustice and widespread grievances. The asking of the

[4]Questions are the most important methods of controlling and influencing the government. They turn a "search light" upon every corner of the public service and are a safeguard against neglect or arbitrary conduct.

[5]W.H. Morris-Jones, *Parliament in India*, London, Longmans, Green and Co., 1957, p. 317.

[6]Lok Sabha Secretariat, File No. 76-Q/56-D. Vol. I, p. 107.

question is an indication that the attempt to persuade the department concerned has failed and the member feels obliged to seek publicity for his correspondent's grievance in order that the minister may move into action. Normally, the reply to a question is not a surprise to the member, as the officials of the department or ministry concerned are already seized of the matter and the reply is mostly on the lines already indicated in the correspondence between the minister and the member. In recent years, Parliament has been throwing up increasingly more work on ministries and departments by way of questions.

A sample survey of the questions relating to departments of Agriculture showed that some of these questions related to individual grievances but about 81 per cent of them were about community grievances, like supply of sugar, ban on vanaspati, release of quota, decontrol of rice, etc.

The volume of Parliamentary questions has grown significantly in more recent times. Questions relating to day-to-day administration are generally not allowed, nor are questions concerning individual grievances as already stated. All the same, the question hour is marked by animation in as much as it serves as a major vehicle of ventilation of grievances of public importance. Even though the "question time" is a suitable forum for raising issues of comparatively simple type of cases, controversial matters of detail cannot be disposed of satisfactorily in a single answer and any attempt to probe the issues in depth by means of supplementary questions only helps to heighten the atmosphere of controversy. So far as community grievances go, the question hour is fully utilized by the members of the Opposition, particularly in State Legislatures with fluid party complexion. It has been urged in some quarters that relations between the legislators and the people are so weak that the real grievances and legitimate pressing demands go often unheard. It also happens that a great deal of noise is made out of ill-founded rumour or on behalf of the organized and articulate interest groups. Prof. Morris-Jones points out that this view contains "a little truth, but not enough. For one thing, the Opposition ready to take up a grievance is a mixed blessing, it is not always the most worthy cause that looks good for political investment. Moreover, these criticisms overlook the fact that the absence of a strong opposition can be and in India is associated with a lively internal organization of the major party through which many complaints and demands can find their way upwards."[7]

Special discussions

No discussion is allowed during the question time. However, if a member is not satisfied with the answers given and desires further elucidation of a policy issue of factual position relating to a matter of public importance he may raise a short discussion for half an hour on giving three days notice. A special discussion is rewarding for focussing the attention on a matter of public importance but it is not useful for dealing with complaints against maladministration in individual cases. It is effective only if it arouses the interest of the press. Special discussions on individual grievances which do not have sufficient dramatic interest for the Press do not help to secure redress. Further, nor many cases of individual grievances can be ventilated through such discussions. Besides, a discussion in Parliament is likely to be affected by political considerations.

Adjournment debates

A member may direct attention to a matter of public importance through a motion of adjournment.[8] An adjournment motion carries with it a tinge of censure against the government as a whole and is not easily admitted in the House. Further, there are restrictions on the moving of an adjournment motion. For instance, it must relate to a specific matter of recent occurrence, it must not raise discussion on a matter which has already been discussed in the session, and the like.

[7]W.H. Morris-Jones, op. cit., p. 320.

[8]In Great Britain, it was after the Second World War that the normal hour for the ending of public business was fixed at 10 O'clock, and that it was provided that half an hour should always be left for a debate on adjournment motions. In the House of Commons adjournment debates normally take place late at night when the House is tired and thinly attended except on Fridays.

Committee on Petitions

The submission of petitions to the House is another method of calling its attention to public grievances. A petition can be presented to the House by a member of the Legislature or/and to its Committee on Petitions by any one by forwarding it to the secretary of the House.[9] By a liberal interpretation of the rules, the Committee on Petitions has been looking into cases of individual grievances included in representations which as petitions would have been inadmissible.[10] The Committee goes through the specific complaint made in the petition and suggests measures for redress after due examination of the facts gathered either by the secretariat or through the ministry and if necessary by giving a personal hearing to the parties concerned. The Petitions Committee of the Lok Sabha had up to March 1969 considered 106 petitions on matters of general public interest and 4,697 representations, which could not be treated as petitions under the rules. The Committee could further secure redress (partial or complete) only in respect of 1205 of the representations, which shows that in about 75 per cent of representations the Committee could not be of any help.

It will be of interest to mention here a typical instance of the way the Committee handles a case. Shri M.P. Bhargava, M.P., presented a petition to the Rajya Sabha on 3 December 1966, signed by Shri Mahant Udhavapuri, Patron, Jiv Rakshak

[9]Under Article 356 of the Constitution, every person is entitled to submit a petition to Committee on Petitions in any language used in the country. This Committee is an independent body and it includes representatives from all parties. It is entitled to summon witnesses of officials, examine departmental records and examine the relief to be given. The petitions cannot be entertained on matters falling within the cognizance of the Courts of law, quasijudicial authorities, statutory tribunals, Courts of Enquiry, Authority or Commission.

[10]Rule 307 of the Rules of Procedure of the Lok Sabha requires the Committee to report to the House on the specific complaints made in a petition. The Fourth Report of the Committee on Petitions to the Third Lok Sabha indicated that 7 petitions and 109 representations and letters inadmissible as petitions had been disposed of. In New Zealand, there are two Public Petition Committees. One Committee considers, on their merits, petitions classified by the Clerk of the House as falling within subjects A to L, and other Committee takes subjects M to Z.

Navayuvak Sangh, Agra, as well as by over one lakh other petitioners from the District of Agra against the "proposed establishment of the Cattle Slaughter House" at Hazratpur in Etmadpur Tehsil, Agra district, by the Government of India, Ministry of Defence. The petitioners had represented to the Committee that the slaughter house should not be allowed to be established at Hazratpur as it would hurt the feelings of the vegetarian residents of the nearby localities, particularly the pilgrims coming from Tundla, Firozabad, Agra and other places situated in the holy land of Brijbhoomi. The Committee on Petitions considered the petition in six sittings. The Committee heard four representatives of Jiv Rakshak Navayuvak Sangh (Youngmen's Association for Protection of Animal Life) and examined three officials of two ministries of the Government of India. The Committee paid a visit to the site of the proposed slaughter house at Hazratpur. The Committee was given to understand that only sheep and goat and *not* cows would be slaughtered at the proposed slaughter house. The Committee, after a detailed examination of the case, came to the conclusion that since the government had given an assurance that cows would not be slaughtered, it should not in any way injure the feelings of the residents or the pilgrims visiting Brijbhoomi.

The primary function of the Committee on Petitions is to entertain petitions on public grievances and only incidentally has it come to look into individual grievances. According to Administrative Reforms Commission, "Parliament, through its Committee on Petitions, has provided another forum for the citizens to secure redress against an act of injustice but this procedure is available only in a limited category and number of cases." The Committee meets only occasionally and there is no continuity in its functions. The public would like to have an institution to which they can go at any time with complaints of maladministration. Further, the members of the Committee are drawn from various political parties including the opposition parties. Political considerations are naturally bound to come up when the Committee attempts to discuss cases of alleged maladministration. Again, a large committee consisting of fifteen members obviously cannot function as an efficient instrument for dealing with individual complaints of abuse of power or maladministration. It does not and can not itself directly investigate the complaints and it has to depend upon the investigations conducted by the departments concerned. The complainant is, therefore, likely to feel that he has had not the benefit of what he considers to be an impartial direct investigation by an outside agency having full access to the departmental records.

Assurances Committee

The Union Parliament as well as the State Legislatures also have Assurances Committees which are assigned the responsibility of scrutinizing. Though the Assurances Committee is not directly concerned with the citizens' grievances it plays, at times, an important part in securing redress where the government has given an assurance on the floor of the House to provide relief to a particular group or community of citizens. It will be of interest to mention here an important case of redress of the citizens' grievances by the Assurances Committee of the Lok Sabha. During the course of discussion on the Delhi Premises (Requisition and Eviction) Amendment Bill, 1950, Shri N.V. Gadgil, had given, on the 29 September 1951, an assurance in Parliament, promising the regularization of unauthorized structures built before 15 August 1950 by the refugees from West Pakistan in Delhi city on government land. The Union government informed the Assurances Committee in 1955 that the assurances had been implemented. But the facts of the case were otherwise. The aggrieved refugees from West Pakistan made a number of representations and the matter was taken up on the floor of the House a number of times. The government appointed in July 1960 a five-man committee under the Chairmanship of Shri Anil K. Chanda to inquire into the matter. The report of this Committee, which was given on 31 March 1962, however, remained in the cold storage. The matter came up again before the Assurances Committee in 1968 as a result of public pressure. The Committee examined a number of witnesses, both officials and non-officials. It also made on-the-spot visits. The Assurance Committee reported that it was "unhappy over the perfunctory manner in which the whole affair regarding the treatment of the Chanda Committee

Report had been handled right from the beginning to the end.[11]

The Committee strongly recommended that "the Government should reconsider the whole matter keeping in view the humane aspect of the problem and do their best to implement the solemn assurances which had been given on the floor of the House by the late Shri N.V. Gadgil as far as possible and explore all avenues as to how best these affected persons could be resettled".[12] Following such an active interest taken by the Assurances Committee, the government initiated the necessary steps to redress the grievances. There has also been set up a Parliamentary Committee on the Welfare of Scheduled Castes and Scheduled Tribes which looks after the interests of Scheduled Castes and backward classes.

A mail bag of an important Member of Parliament from Lok Sabha for a particular day was once scrutinized by the author in order to have an idea of the type of mail that he gets. It contained 54 letters and periodicals. The letters included the following:

Complaints on minor issues from the citizens of the constituency (without first referring to normal channels)	12
Complaints of hardship and harassment (after exhausting the normal remedies)	4
Complaints against a minister—1, abuse of discretionary powers—3	
Report from government departments justifying the rejection of petitions forwarded earlier by the M.P.	3
Total	19
Proportion of daily mail	35 per cent

At times, grievances are discussed in detail across the table. For instance, in one of the meetings of the consultative committee of the department of Social Welfare when the minister concerned insisted that refuse was carried in trolleys by scaven-

[11]Second Report of the Committee on Government Assurances (Fourth Lok Sabha), p. 8.

[12]*Ibid.*, p. 20.

gers, a member pointed out that in a number of villages in Punjab the scavengers had still to carry the refuse on their head and no trolleys had been provided for the purpose. The minister promised to look into the matter personally. He programmed a personal visit to that area and asked the member concerned also to accompany. During the course of his tour, the minister saw for himself how the scavengers were carrying refuse early in the morning. He expeditiously took up the matter with the State government and gave a subsidy for the purchase of trolleys.

Consultative Committees

Consultative Committees of Members of Parliament, attached to various Central ministries, also serve as a channel airing of citizens' grievances and securing their redress. The meetings of consultative committees generally take place in the intra-session period and are presided over by the concerned ministers. The discussions are generally on policy matters but there is no bar to dicussing individual cases. In fact, it is in broad framework of grievances which come to the knowledge of the Members of Parliament that policies are reviewed. An advance notice is required to be given by the members of the items they would like to be discussed. Official briefs are prepared and circulated to the members well in advance. The concerned officials are also present in order to assist the minister during discussions.

Party standing committees

After the Fifth General Elections, the Congress government at the Centre set up standing committees of the members of its parliamentary party for eaeh major ministry or a group of departments. During the Parliament session, at least one or two meetings are convened by the respective party standing committees where the difficulties of their constituencies, their general grievances and the party matters are discussed. Such meetings are useful as it is here that a minister concerned is able to help the individuals and groups of citizens through his party members who take up their grievances. Some of the other political parties too have set up groups of Members of Parliament for some of the major Central ministries and departments but these groups do not cover the entire gamut of the Central administration.

CONCLUSION

The Indian experience with the legislative channels of redress has not been much different from that of other Commonwealth countries. While the legislative channels have been quite effective in the matter of community grievances, the question time, adjournment motions and legislative committees have been of limited usefulness for the redress of individual complaints. In Great Britain, some individual cases taken up by Members of Parliament (e.g. Crichel Down case and Sachsen-hausen case, etc.) have sparked controversy and heated discussions leading to some basic reforms. However, in these instances the individual complaints represented a cross-section of the then prevailing state of affairs in an area of administrative activity and came to assume public importance. In Great Britain, since 1945 no minister seems to have made any meaningful concession in replying to questions. Ministers fully briefed by expert civil servants and with the skill of accomplished Parliamentarians are especially facile at saying very little at great length "in a bland and confidential manner", to quote Sir Ivor Jennings. The legislator is a partisan politician. If he belongs to the opposition, he may be ineffective in many instances. The experience in New Zealand, as pointed out by Donald C. Rowat, is that a citizen who seeks to redress by political means, either by parliamentary petition or complaint through the local member and the responsible Minister, has little prospect of having the decision changed. For obvious reasons the Minister will in most cases adhere to his own decision or stand behind his department's decision".[13]

[13]Take for instance, the case of one Mr. H.R. Standford, an Indian Army Officer who was accused of fraud in connection with the advance he took for the purchase of a motor car required to be used in the discharge of his duties. This case engaged the attention of successive Secretaries of State of War for nearly 26 years and was discussed in the House of Commons a number of times. He was court-martialled and

In Federal Republic of Germany, a Commission, constituted in 1968, recommended strengthening of the institution of Parliament instead of creating a new institution of Ombudsman. The Commission felt that the Parliament should have the petitions of citizens investigated through its committees and provide redress. The important measures suggested by the Commission were: setting up of petition committees; reinforcing the information services of the government; analysis of the petitions received with a view to identifying their underlying causes, in particular inadequacies in laws and administrative regulations; closer contacts between Parliament, the press, radio and television for giving publicity to grievances; on-the-spot study and hearing of the parties by the Petition Committees, etc.

In India, as well as abroad there is a lack of appreciation on the part of the citizens generally about the limitations which constrain a Member of Parliament in ventilating public grievances and obtaining relief. The main difficulty in this regard arises from the fact that a minister is likely to take a rigid stand, or make it a point of prestige, irrespective of the merits or demerits of a particular complaint. If the political party in power has a thin majority, it cannot afford to allow its members to come forward with embarrassing questions. On the other hand, if its majority is overwhelming, it would like to enforce party discipline to keep up its image and therefore its members have to follow the party mandate, even though they may know full well that what the government is doing is wrong or that the stand taken up by the administration is unjustified.

An interesting example of the rigidity of government's approach was thrown up during the discussions in Parliament in 1970. In 1969, Mr. X, a Vice-Principal of a State Government Handicapped School at Agra had been selected by the Union Public Service Commission for the post of a Principal of a Centrally run school of Deaf and Dumb at Hyderabad. When

---

for 26 years he had no right of appeal to a Civil Court. He demanded an independent inquiry and protested his innocence. The government's reply was that setting up of a Special Court of Inquiry was costly and troublesome and could become a precedent.

the Central Government contacted the State Government for relieving him, the State government refused to do so on the plea that a vigilance case against him was under investigation. It is gathered that the then State Chief Minister was not happy with Mr. X. In spite of intervention by some Members of Parliament, he was not relieved to take up his new assignment. The matter came up in Parliament also and the members insisted that Mr. X be appointed provisionally pending enquiry. Mr. X was even prepared to resign from the post of the Vice-Principal. The Union Minister for Social Welfare, however, refused to oblige. In the meantime, the Union Public Service Commission had been asked to find another suitable candidate. After some time, the government in the State was changed and the case against Mr. X was dropped as a result of political influence. Some Members of Parliament again pressed the Central Minister for Social Welfare to appoint Mr. X on the post for which he had been selected. But the request was not acceded to.

Further the legislative channels do not admit of discussion on matters of detail which are at times vital to the redress of a public complaint. The present devices by which the legislature exercises its control over administration are not very much effective. The Indian politics have in recent years tended to become, by and large, politics of patronage, particularly, at the state level, and in this context the main interest of the party in power as well as of the opposition parties lies in extending their own influence and authority. This is attempted through maintaining and widening their hold on local political leaders, by dispensing patronage. The problems of making the administration more responsive to the citizens' needs and more accountable to the legislature and of increasing the legislature's interest in redress of public complaints are of a much larger dimension. It is only through the creation of powerful social infrastructure (i.e., a network of voluntary organizations and articulate interest groups extending over the entire community) that the Indian bureaucracy and political institutions can be made more responsive to the citizens' legitimate demands and justified complaints.

PANCHAYATI RAJ INSTITUTIONS

In the countryside, a number of developmental and welfare functions have been developed on the three-tier popular bodies (panchayati raj institutions) at the village, block/taluk and district level. The village panchayats have been allotted functions such as sanitation, conservancy, street lighting, roads, water tanks, handicrafts, registration of births and deaths, education, village defence, protection of forests and cattle. The "panchayat samitis" are responsible for the preparation and implementation of the development plans for the block/taluk, and they operate programmes of education, health, sanitation and communication. They also exercise supervision over "gram panchayats". The "zila parishads" are in some States only a coordinating and supervisory body; in some others, they have, in addition, specific executive functions and in the States of Maharashtra and Gujarat they are responsible for the entire gamut of developmental activity in the district.

The popular body at the village level, namely, the panchayat, does look into individual grievances and is sympathetic to the people's difficulties. The attention devoted to individual complaints decreases and the share of community grievances increases, as we go up to the panchayat samitis at the block/taluk level and the zila parishad at the district level. The panchayati raj institutions, however, are ridden with parochialism and internal strife.[14] The competition for sharing the economic gains has led to bitter rivalries and functionalism in many of the panchayats and panchayat samitis. In such circumstances, the panchayati raj institutions do not provide an appropriate framework for the consideration and redress of the citizens' complaints. Even the community grievances are taken up by these institutions on the basis of parochial considerations or in the light of factional politics.

There is, however, another aspect of the panchayati raj

[14]In a study of village panchayats conducted by Dr. N.R. Inamdar the reasons given by the respondents for want of sympathy on the part of members of the panchayats towards the complaints of the villagers were "partiality to kith and kin and caste-people, personal rivalry, groupism, and selfishness", N.R. Inamdar, *Functioning of Village Panchayats*, Bombay, Popular Prakashan, 1970, p. 171.

PANCHAYATI RAJ SYSTEM

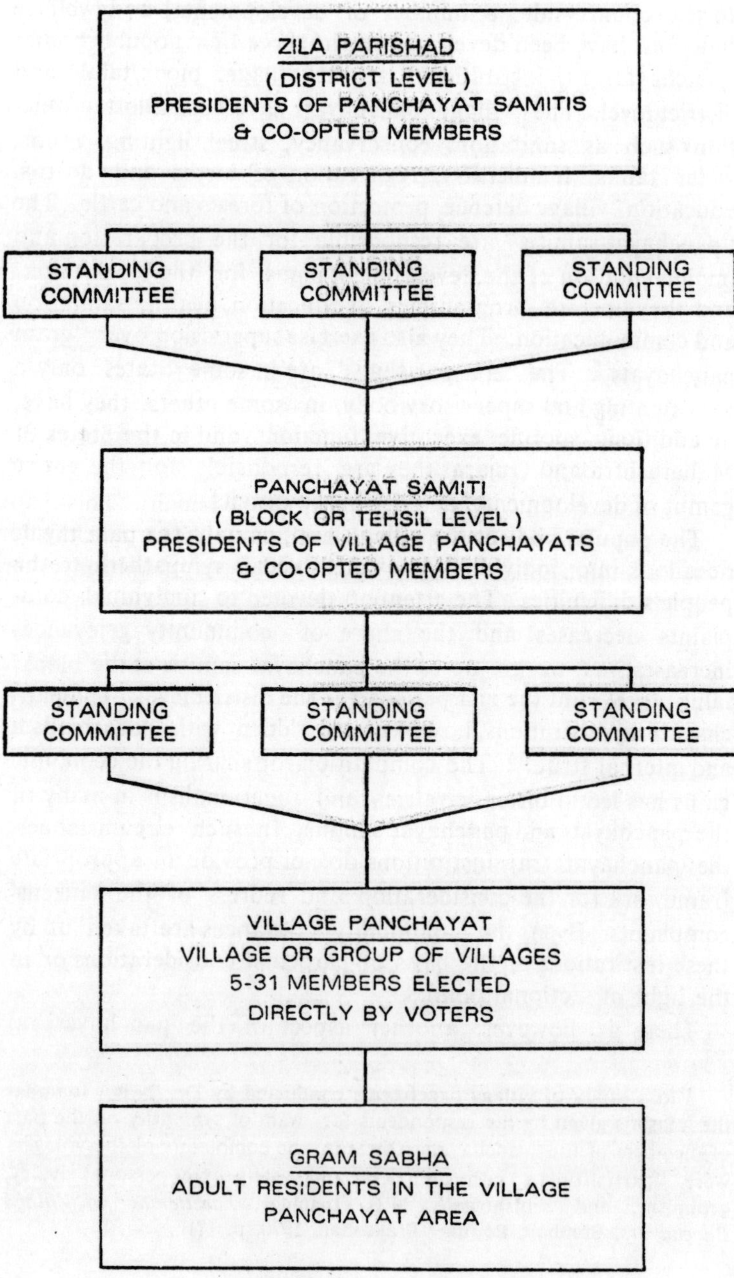

institutions which has a bearing on the redress of public complaints. As we have already noted in Chapter 3, the intervention of elected representatives, including the members and heads of panchayati raj bodies, is increasingly being sought by the citizens for securing relief. Here again, the support which the citizen receives from non-official members and office-holders of panchayati raj institutions is prompted by considerations of caste, community, group and personal loyalties, and, at times, even by graft. Intervention of this kind by panchayati raj leaders may not be conducive to the larger interest but it does in many instances serve to bring relief to the citizens. The position is not different even in the States of Gujarat and Maharashtra where all development functions have been entrusted to the zila parishad.

A study conducted by the Department of Political Science, University of Rajasthan, of the working of the panchayati raj institutions in Gujarat has commended the setting up of a "Panchayat Pal" (a panchayati raj Ombudsman). This institution may consist of a single individual or may take the form of an independent administrative board (multi-membered Ombudsman) and should look into complaints and grievances concerning misuse of power, corruption, etc. It has been emphasized that the need for the creation of the panchayati raj Ombudsman is urgent in view of the growing malpractices that are being committed by these institutions and the vast administrative and financial power structure created at the local levels in rural areas.

CITIZENS' ASSOCIATIONS AND OTHER VOLUNTARY ORGANIZATIONS

Citizens' associations and other voluntary organizations represent the Community effort at attaining certain common goals. In the democratic set up of the country, voluntary organizations constitute the fourth estate, the other three being the government, the public sector undertakings and private sector. People's organizations have a key role to play not only in the developmental effort but also in ensuring the effectiveness of the administrative infrastructure. Their contribution to the prevention and redress of citizens' grievances can be manifold.

They can perform a useful function in regard to the following:

1. Provision of information and advice to the citizens in the making of applications and complaints.
2. Educating the citizens in regard to their duties to the state and advising them about what can be and what should not be expected of administration.
3. Lending support to the citizens' genuine demands and complaints.
4. Bringing to bear influence on the government departments and agencies for improvement of policies, programmes and procedures in the interest of the citizens' welfare and satisfaction.
5. Promotion of high standards of public morality.

Since Independence, a wide net work of voluntary organizations has developed in India. Voluntary bodies have, however, mostly come up in the fields of social and labour welfare, education, community development and cooperation. Citizens' organizations and consumer councils, which are meant to provide information and assistance to the people in their dealings with the government agencies have not developed to the same extent, though a large number of advisory bodies have been constituted by the Government in recent years to associate the people with the formulation and execution of government policies. As a part of the Second/Third Five Year Plans, the government launched a special programme for mobilising public cooperation. The initial effort in this regard, however, got whittled down with the passage of time and the public cooperation programme has hardly been a success. There has been all the same a growing awareness in the recent years that the problem of raising of standards of integrity in administration cannot be isolated from that of moral awakening and social enlightenment among the people, and further that the active support of the people is essential for combating the evils of maladministration.

TWO NOVEL EXPERIMENTS

The credit for experimenting with the idea of active involvement of the people in the efforts of government to raise the standards of public service ethics goes to Mr. Gulzari Lal Nanda, who was the Union Minister for Home Affairs during 1963-66.

Following the findings of the Santhanam Committee on Prevention of Corruption, Mr. Gulzari Lal Nanda, gave a solemn undertaking to the nation on 30 November 1963 that he would eradicate corruption in the sphere of the Central administration within a period of 2 years, and further that if he failed to produce any substantial results in this regard he would quit office.

Sanyukta Sadachar Samiti

As a part of his overall approach to raise social and moral standards in general and involve the people in the fight against corruption and other malpratices, the Home Minister sponsord the formation of Sanyukta Sadachar Samiti at the national, state, district and sub-district levels. The Samiti which was constituted on the 30 April 1964 had its main objective the creation of a social and moral climate which would foster moral values and ethical living and discourage anti-social attitudes and corrupt practices; and with this end in view, to launch an intensive and widespread campaign in the country for moral awakening and social enlightenment. Another objective of the Samiti was to assist in the redress of people's grievances relating to all forms of corruption and in the setting up of suitable machinery for the purpose. The Samiti entertained complaints against officials of the Central administration and of corporations and of institutions administered or controlled by it, in matters relating to corruption, corrupt practices, delay, denial of justice and abuse of power.

During the first month of its formation, the grievances section of the Samiti received 2,200 complaints. For such complainants who did not like that their names should be known to the bureaucracy, the Home Minister maintained a confidential register at his residence. The complaints received were scrutinized by a group of public men of standing, headed by a retired Chief Justice of the Punjab High Court. The services of an officer of the rank of Deputy Inspector-General or police were made available to the Samiti. He heard complaints against the police and also looked into cases of profiteering, hoarding and other inter-connected problems that were brought to his notice. The Home Minister personally dealt with at least five cases daily.

The Sanyukta Sadachar Samiti also organized a series of public meetings, seminars etc., to mobilize public support for the campaign against corruption. As a result of these conferences and meetings a number of suggestions emerged for improving standards of integrity in government, such as amendment of the election laws to keep down the election expenses, non-association of persons of doubtful character with advisory bodies set up by the government, elimination of delay, declaration of assets by officials drawing pay of Rs. 500 and above, ceiling on urban property which may be held by an individual, measures to combat the menace of black money and hoardings, etc.

The experiment with the Sanyukta Sadachar Samiti caught up the imagination of the people in its early days. The fact that the Union Home Minister was actively supporting the efforts of the Samiti in checking corrupt practices helped to inspire confidence of the people. It did also help to make the civil servants with questionable integrity somewhat restrained in their dealings with the public and to generate a general awareness of the importance of high standards of integrity and fair-play. In the matter of redress of the citizens' grievances, the Samiti did play quite a useful role in securing redress. The intervention by the Samiti and the personal interest taken by the Union Home Minister did help to lend, to a certain extent, a sense of urgency to the processing of the citizens' applications and complaints.

The momentum of the experiment, however, could not be maintained for long. The management of the Sanyukta Sadachar Samiti was mostly in the hands of Sadhus (mendicants) and a few retired officials and in some cases their integrity was not unimpeachable. The activities of the Samiti were financed by a meagre membership fee of Rs.5 and donations. As the Samiti's main role was to expose corrupt practices and get redress, it soon incurred the ill-will of the vested interests.

The intervention by the Union Home Minister did not find favour in the higher echelons of the civil service. Within a year, the Samiti began to incur a loss and had not even the funds to pay the staff or meeting running expenses. Litigation started among the members of the management of the Samiti and it had eventually to close down in 1966. A new association named, Nav Jeevan Sangh, was set up in place of the Samiti with a narrow scope of activities.[15]

Standing voluntary help committees in Railways

The second experiment with the mobilization of the people's support and cooperation in combating corrupt practices and redressing citizens' grievances was also sponsord by Mr. Gulzari Lal Nanda who took over as the Union Minister of Railways in February 1969. Under his sponsorship, an Eleven-Point Programme was formulated, providing passenger amenities like provision of additional water coolers, retiring rooms, cleanliness in compartments, etc., observing "No Complaint Weeks", speeding up movement of goods-traffic, safety of passengers, staff welfare, etc. To give effect to the Eleven-Point Programme a Special Programme Implementation Cell (P.I. Cell) was set up in the Ministry of Railways. The cell consists of two wings an official wing and a non-official wing. On the official side, an Officer on Special Duty has been appointed as the head of the team for effecting implementation of the programme. While the detailed responsibility for implementation of the programme continues to be that of the concerned zonal Railways, the Cell has a nucleus staff for the discharge of its functions.

The non-official side of the Cell comprises a standing Voluntary Help Committee of eight members. It functions in an advisory capacity. The non-official wing maintains a list of the voluntary organizations who have offered to assist in the working of the Railways.[16] The services of the persons nominated

[15]Shri Gulzari Lal Nanda who was the Union Home Minister resigned in November 1966 following his inability to deal with the movement against cow slaughter launched by the Sadhus and there were differences between him and the Home Secretary. For a detailed description to the events leading to Shri Nanda's resignation, please see C.P. Bhambhari, *Bureaucracy and Politics in India*, Delhi, Vikas Publication, 1971, pp. 236-51.

[16]As numerous complaints of corruption and public grievances were received against the officials, the then Railway Minister made a Eleven-

by these organizations are utilized in various fields from time to time. The Rashtriya Lok Sena which is a voluntary registered society, has been of great help to the non-official wing in regulating and checking of complaints. The representatives of voluntary organizations meet occasionally and discuss various suggestions and views for implementation of the programme. The non-official wing has also a separate panel of advisors and consultants in specialized fields.

Two recognized unions of the Railway workers, namely, All-India Railwaymen's Federation and National Federation of Indian Railwaymen, are also represented on the National Voluntary Help Committee. Voluntary help committees have also been set up at the zonal, divisional area and station levels. In all, 216 such committees have been constituted at the station level.

The official wing is responsible for maintaining liaison between the Standing Voluntary Help Committee and the Railway administration on all aspects of the Eleven-Point Programme. The observations and suggestions received from members of the voluntary help committees and other agencies are transmitted for review by panels appointed for the purpose before the proposals are put up to the Union Minister for Railways. After the Minister approves the proposals, these are transmitted to the official machinery for implementation. The complaints received are sent to the various departments of the Railway administration for comments and necessary action. Follow-up action is taken by the official wing of Programme Implementation Cell. After the action is completed by the respective zonal Railways, a report is submitted to the Standing Voluntary Help Committee. The Implementation Cell conducted during the months of August and September 1970, 716 inspections covering 834 reservation counters in order to check harassment to the public.

As a result of the efforts made by the Implementation Cell, the average time taken for disposing of complaints came down from 37.9 days in 1968-69 to 36.7 days in 1969-70 and to 35.8

Point Programme to eradicate corruption and to clean the general administration of Railways. This programme was implemented with the help of voluntary organizations.

days in the first six months of 1970-71. In the case of other inquiries, the average time for disposal was reduced from 12.73 days in 1968-69 and 13.2 days in 1969-70 to 12.6 days in the first six months of 1970-71.

Citizens' advice bureaux

In several countries of the West, there exist citizens' advice bureaux. The main purpose of these bureaux is to make available to the individual citizens accurate information and skilled advice on many of the personal problems that arise in daily life, to explain legislation, to help the citizen to benefit from and to use wisely the services provided for him by the state, and in general to provide counsel to men and women in the many complexities which beset them in an increasingly complex world.

In the U.K., the institution of the Citizens' Advice Bureau is over 25 years old and there are today over 400 bureaux, established nearly in all the states and major towns. They are staffed, for the most part, by volunteers but they usually have a panel of consultants from whom they can seek guidance on special subjects. They also have a national committee which deals with Central administration. The citizens' advice bureaux maintain a close liaison with government departments and also advise the latter when their actions cause friction or unfairness to the citizens.

Another important citizens' organization which operates in the U.K. is John Hilton Bureau. Its primary purpose is to advise readers of national newspapers on social and personal problems. Its headquarters are in Cambridge where it employs about forty persons, many of whom possess professional qualifications as barristers, solicitors, civil servants, army paymasters, trade union secretaries' etc., or have had practical experience of social work. The Bureau is consulted by approximately 200,000 persons a year on a large number of subjects covering such matters as pensions, insurance, housing, foster parents, education, taxation, police and prisons. As a result of its efforts to help in inquiries, the Bureau is in frequent contact with government departments and has acquired a large store of knowledge concerning the kind of administrative action which gives rise to problems in individual cases.

It must, however, be stated that the citizens' bureaux in the U.K. are more concerned with giving information and advice to the people than with investigating allegations or maladministration or injustice. This is because they have no power to look into government documents, inspect administrative activities or to influence the administration.

In India, the institution of citizens' advice bureau has not much developed. A start in this direction has, however been made, in recent years. A number of citizens' advice bureaux have come up in Delhi to give free advice to the citizens on social and economic matters as well as on their dealings with the administration. The bureaux are an independent, non-sectarian and non-political organizations which are run by volunteers who have the knowledge, capacity and aptitude to give free advice to the citizens. The activities of the various citizens' bureaux are coordinated by a headquarters' organization, known as Nagrik Sabha Kendra (Council of Citizens' Bureaux).

In addition, there have also come up institutions like the lawyers' Rifle Service, and voluntary organizations engaged in social welfare activities of various kinds. For instance, All-India Citizens' Welfare Council looks after the interests of the people through a number of branches all over the country. They also help the citizens in removing their grievances by imparting necessary information and advice free of charge. Again, Bharat Dalit Sewak Sangh is engaged in the uplift of the Harijans (backward classes engaged in scavenging work). Some other important voluntary organizations worth mentioning are the All India Harijan Sevak Sangh, Depressed Classes League, Indian Red Cross Society, Ramakrishna Mission, Indian Council for Child Welfare, Bhartiya Adamjati Sevak Sangh and All India Backward Classes Federation.

Consumer councils and advisory committees

Since the advent of five-yearly national plans of development, the governments at the Centre and the States have set up a large number of advisory bodies to associate the effected interests with the activities of the various government departments and agencies. These advisory bodies do not deal with general complaints only. The scope of their activities is much wider, extending to policy formulation, programme planning, programme implementation and review. We have already noted the existence of the Users' Committees in the Railways and the Posts & Telegraphs Department. These committees mostly deal with the citizens' complaints. But other advisory bodies, such as the development council for individual industries, Export Promotion Advisory Council, Central Industries Advisory Councils, Regional Port Advisory Committees, Tripartite Labour Machinery, Tribe Advisory Councils, Scheduled Tribes Advisory Bodies in several States, etc., perform a useful function in the matter of associating the citizens with the administration. These advisory bodies are composed of representatives of different interest groups. For instance, the Export and Import Advisory Council on Trade includes four Members of Parliament, Secretary, Ministry of Commerce, Minister and Deputy Minister of Commerce, representatives of public sector trading organizations, Chairmen of Commodity Boards, representatives of Reserve Bank of India and Export Credit and Guarantee Corporation and several other officials and non-official members. Similarly, the Board of Trade, which has the Minister of Foreign Trade as its Chairman, consists of economists, non-officials representing trade interests, and senior officers of government departments concerned with various economic departments. The Board is advisory in nature; it advises government on all important matters connected with internal and international economic, commercial and industrial developments having a bearing on the development of export trade. The Board undertakes detailed studies of specific problems through expert sub-committees.

The role of the advisory bodies in articulating and redressing the citizens' complaints is largely of a limited character. They mostly take up pressing matters affecting one or more categories of interested groups and individual cases are only considered to illustrate the common difficulties. Nor is the opinion favourable for the use of the advisory bodies for the redress of individual complaints. For instance, the Administrative Reforms Commission recommended that discussions with the non-official members of the Advisory Council on Trade should be held periodically by the government regarding the policy and the procedure for the allotment of foreign exchange to the industries and the principles to be followed. But the Commission was not in favour of using the Council as a forum for various interests to air their individual grievances.

In the context of the rising prices, the government have sponsored the establishment of consumers' associations and councils. They have even opened a number of restaurants, fair price shops, super markets, etc. A central consumers' organization, known as the "Consumers Council of India" has been set up under the sponsorship of the Central Planning Commission. The main object of this Council is to protect the consumers from exploitations of various kinds, such as rise in prices, adulteration, deception of weights and measures, etc. It includes representatives of the Ministries of Foreign Trade, Home, Health, Finance, Information and Broadcasting, Food and Agriculture, Community Development and Cooperation and institutions such as Indian Standard Institution, All India Women's Conference, National Council of Applied Economic Research, Central Social Welfare Board, etc.

ROLE OF POLITICAL PARTIES

Political parties in India have taken quite active interest in ventilating the grievances of socially or economically backward groups, such as unskilled agricultural workers, tenant farmers, industrial workers, scheduled castes and tribes and the like. Some of the political parties have even supported civil disobedience movements for the uplift of the poorer sections of the society. "There are two aspects of these opposition movements that have concerned the Government. They disrupt law and order by their demonstrations and civil-disobedience movements against high irrigation taxes, high prices, food shortages, and so on; and until recently they have been unwilling to encourage peasant participation in Government programmes to increase food production and improve village conditions . . . the government often alternates between unresponsiveness to the demands of large but peaceful groups and total concession to groups that press their demands violently. Indeed, since 1947, some of the major concessions made by the Government have been to mass movements, violent or non-violent."[17] However, the political parties till recently did not show much concern in the creation of the machinery for the redress of the grievances of individual citizens. In their election manifestoes, for mid-term elections of 1971 for Parliament, the Congress (O), Swatantra, Jana Sangh and Praja Socialist Party supported the proposal for the setting up of an independent agency of the Ombudsman type. When all these parties formed a combined Party, they repeated this in their Election Manifesto and have since introduced a Bill in the Lok Sabha.

In order to reduce the public grievances the Janata Party promised through their Election Manifesto, 1977 to adopt the following:

1. Lift the emergency;
2. Restore the fundamental freedoms that have been suspended by Presidential Order;
3. Repeal MISA, release all political detenues, and review all other unjust laws;
4. Enact laws to ensure that no political or social organization is banned without independent judicial enquiry;
5. Seek to rescind the 42nd Amendment;
6. Amend Article 352 of the Constitution to prevent its abuse in the interest of an individual or group;
7. Move to amend Article 356 to ensure that the power to impose President's Rule in the States is not misused to benefit the ruling party or any favoured faction within it;
8. Introduce electoral reforms after a careful consideration of suggestions made by various committees including the Tarkunde Committee and, in particular, consider proposals for recall of errand legislators and for reducing election costs, as well as for reducing voting age from 21 to 18;
9. Repeal the amendment to the Representation of the People Act which redefines corrupt practices and places electoral offences by certain individuals beyond the scrutiny of the courts;
10. Re-establish the rule of law;

[17]Myron Weiner, *The Politics of Scarcity*, Bombay, Asia Publishing House, 1963, pp. 5 and 116.

11. Restore the authority of judiciary and safeguard the independence and integrity of the Bar;
12. Ensure that all individuals, including those who hold high office, are equal before law;
13. Assure the right to peaceful and non-violent protest;
14. Abolish censorship and all harassment to newspapers, journals, publishers and printing presses;
15. Safeguard the freedom of the press by repealing the Prevention of Publication of Objectionable Matters Act, and restore the immunity that the Press previously enjoyed in reporting legislative proceedings;
16. Ensure that All-India Radio, Doordarshan and the Films Division are converted into genuinely autonomous bodies that are politically objective and free from governmental interference;
17. Ensure that news agencies are completely independent of the government and are not given the right to monoply;
18. Delete property from the list of Fundamental Rights and, instead, affirm the right to work;
19. Ensure that Government employees are not victimized, are freed of political pressure, and are not compelled to execute illegal orders and unlawful actions. Their right to access to Courts will be restored.
20. An end to destitution within ten years;
21. Narrowing down of rural-urban disparities and a new rural-urban nexus;
22. Emphasis on wage goods production for mass consumption;
23. Education reform with middle schooling for all within 12 years;
24. Eradication of illiteracy;
25. Safe drinking water for all;
26. Stress on community and preventive health, and measures towards group health insurance;
27. A new village movement;
28. Low-cost building and mass public housing;
29. A comprehensive scheme of social insurance;
30. Family planning as part of a larger population policy package, without coercion;
31. A new deal for the scheduled castes and tribes with special

machinery to guarantee their rights and interests;
32. A Civil Rights Commission;
33. Automatic machinery for combating corruption;
34. Women's rights and youth welfare;
35. Legal aid and inexpensive justice.

Janata Party promised immediate and firm steps to rid public life of the corruption that has crept into it at all levels. The party felt that unless those who hold office at the highest levels, including ministers, legislators and bureaucrats, set an example in probity and honesty, it will be impossible to restore integrity in public life. The Party promised that every one of its officers and cadres would adhere to the highest norms of integrity and would give effect to the recommendations of the Santhanam Committee on corruption in the administration and public life. It also promised to enact the long-pending Lokpal and Lokayukta Bill and would bring the Prime Minister and Chief Ministers within its purview. Unfortunately, most of these promises remained on paper and the government was defeated in the mid-term poll of January, 1980.

By and large the citizens' associations and other voluntary organizations have not developed in numbers and strength to make a dent on the attitudes of the administration towards the citizens in the matter of speedy processing of their applications and the redress of their genuine complaints. While the union government has, time and again, declared its intentions to strengthen the voluntary social infrastructure and has even supported its declarations by financial support and other measures it has not shown any real concern to help improve the efficient functioning of the voluntary bodies. It has hesitated in fostering the growth of voluntary organizations by adopting a bolder and more vigorous policy. In the context of the present stage of political and social conditions in India, it is difficult to conceive that the administration can be made more responsible and responsive to the people unless the social infrastructure outside the government is adequately reinforced to make its weight felt. It is a question of building into the entire socio-political system a number of checks and balances so that each of its part subserves fully the total public interest. This point is dealt with in some detail in the next chapter, which contains an overview of the problems of public grievances and of the machinery for their redress in the wider perspective of the present stage of economic, social and political development of the country and the formidable challenges of the next twenty years.

CHAPTER VII

Ombudsman—Comparative Experience Abroad

CONTEMPORARY IMPORTANCE

In an earlier chapter a reference was made to the proposals of the Administrative Reforms Commission for the constitution of the Ombudsman-type institution of Lokpal and Lokayukta. Before discussing these proposals in detail, it will be appropriate to examine the role and functions of Ombudsman as obtaining in the West, particularly in the Scandinavian countries, and the success attained by this institution.

Broadly speaking, the Ombudsman is an officer of Parliament, who investigates complaints of citizens of unfair treatment meted out to them by government departments, and suggests remedy thereof if he finds that a complaint is justified. The institution of Ombudsman originated in Sweden in 1809. It, however, took over a century to spread to other countries—Finland in 1919, Denmark in 1955, West Germany in 1957, and Norway in 1961. A modified version of the Ombudsman, that is, the office of the Parliamentary Commissioner was established in New Zealand in 1962 and in the United Kingdom in 1967. New Zealand Act of 1875 extended the jurisdiction of Ombudsman and two additional Ombudsmen were appointed in 1975. The new New Zealand Statute provided the model for the establishment of Ombudsmen in Australia, Western Australia appointed an Ombudsman in 1971, South Australia in 1972, Victoria in 1973, Queensland in 1974, and New South Wales in 1975. Australia still does not have an Ombudsman at federal level. Developments in United States began two years earlier than in Australia. Hawaii was the first State to set up an Ombudsman in 1969, Nebraska appointed in 1971, Iowa in 1972 and Alaska in 1975, West Germany has had an Ombudsman of the Armed Forces since 1957. There has been no further development at federal level but in 1974 one of the ten States, Rhineland-Pfalz, set up an Ombudsman. In Italy an Ombudsman was appointed for the region of Tuscany in 1975, in Israel an Ombudsman was appointed at the national level in 1971 and two of the principal cities in Israel, Jerusalem and Haifa also have an Ombudsman. Switzerland has as yet no Ombudsman at the federal level but Zurich has an Ombudsman for city affairs since 1971. Tanzania set up a collegiate form of Ombudsman in 1966, Guyana in 1967, Mauritius in 1970, Fiji in 1972, Zambia in 1973. In Canada eight out of ten provinces had set up an Ombudsman. The office of Mediateur in France was set up by a law of land in January 1973 which is well-developed system of administrative justice provided more effective redress for the citizens against public.

The institution of Ombudsman has been evolved to counteract the adverse impact, on the citizens' legitimate rights and claims, of the increase in the size and activities of bureaucratic organizations resulting from the substantial extension in the functions of the state. In the early days of development of democracy, the concept of Liberty, Equality and Fraternity gave it a philosophical content. The second stage of the growth of democracy saw the adoption of the rule of law and the division of powers among the legislature, the executive and the judiciary. The executive then was concerned mainly with the defence of the state, expansion of its territories and maintenance of law and order and economic infrastructure in the laissez-faire economy.

The concept of democracy has since developed a step further to incorporate the ideal of a welfare state. The eradication of disease, poverty, idleness, squalor, and illiteracy have come to be commonly regarded as responsibilities of the state. The recognition of economic justice and equality of opportunity as state functions has led to a general acceptance of the state as planner, promoter, and regulator of social and economic development. Liberal individualism has given way to benevolent collectivism. In the bargain, however, the executive has in many ways overtaken both the legislature and the judiciary. The control functions of the last two have been constrained by the complexity and size of the administrative machinery.

The welfare state has put into the hands of civil servants enormous and ubiquitous powers over the daily life of the people. The average individual by the middle of the twentieth century in the West had begun to find the state intervention more and more irritating, unnecessary, and stifling. The Parliament and the courts could offer not much relief. Delay, negligence, discourtesy, arbitrary decision and uncompensated damage against life, liberty, and property seemed to go unchecked under the pretext of executive necessity and administrative discretion. The dominance of bureaucracy in the welfare state in the present century seems to have no less potential for mischief and tyranny than that of the feudalism of earlier centuries. The French and the German in this context have developed a distinct jurisprudence of administrative justice and have set up separate courts. The Americans have codified the elementary principles of justice and fair-play in the administrative process by the Administrative Procedure Act. The East European countries have developed similar codes, specialized courts, tribunals, and prosecutors to oversee administrative decisions.

In recent times, the most popular and the most talked about machinery in the West has perhaps been that of the Ombudsman, which is perceived as the father figure for the aggrieved citizens and which takes up the cudgels against the government, matching power with power. It exposes the administrative process and machinery which may be harsh, unreasonable, unfair and oppressive, to an objective review by an independent institution.

The concept of Ombudsman is essentially that of an institution which is independent of the executive, the legislature and the judiciary. It is freely accessible to the individual citizen who is aggrieved by administrative action or omission. If the citizen approaches the Ombudsman with a genuine complaint, the latter takes up the responsibility of fully investigating the case himself without any expense or onus of proof on the complainant. This is of great advantage to the citizen. It is here that this prompt remedy steels a march over the delaying type of judicial proceedings of the courts. The courts do not take any initiative in collecting information and facts, but merely decide upon whatever facts either party is able to adduce. The Ombudsman is primarily the people's investigator, defender and guide.

In the matter of the citizen-administration relations, the emphasis in the western countries has shifted from inflicting penalty on the civil servants to exacting a redress for the citizen.[1] The Ombudsman, by issuing instructions, warnings, and admonitions which may extend to even those government servants who may not be directly involved, and also by suggesting modification of procedures, rules and even policy, tries to bring about administrative improvement so that the particular instance of malpractice may not recur. In the Scandinavian countries, where the institution of Ombudsman has flourished, over the years a certain corpus of administrative jurisprudence has been evolved as a result of "Ombudsman law" which provides guidelines for the ethical and professional conduct of public servants. "The office of the Ombudsman is acclaimed as an important element and it offers very definite advantages: for the ordinary citizen he is a tribune to which one may turn with one's complaint without the need of lawyer, for the public servant who has been unjustifiedly criticized he offers rehabilitation. In a modern welfare State with an expanding administration and growing latitude given to it, the Ombudsman has a healthy preventive influence on officials who might tend to be high-handed, arrogant, negligent or forgetful of the limits of their powers. He is in a position, moreover, to assist in briniging about consistency in the interpretation and application

[1]In ancient China, the system of censuring the officials for their lapses existed from time immemorial. The performance of individuals was watched at every stage by the special officers appointed by the kings. In case of delays, the clerical functionaries, who were immediately responsible, were subject to beating with the bamboo to a maximum of 40 blows, according to the number of instances; and their supervising officials were subject to 30 blows. For errors, the functionaries might receive a maximum of 50 blows and again the punishment for their overseers was reduced by one degree, to 40 blows. In all cases, the senior official of the agency was himself likely to be fined a maximum of three months' salary. More serious offences, involving wilful evasion of the law, were dealt with more severely according to the particular circumstance. Charles O. Bucker, *The Censorial System of Ming China*, Stanford University Press, 1966, p. 145.

of legislation and to suggest improvements in deficient laws."[2]

The institution of Ombudsman is not new to the world. It has a resemblance to the Roman "Tribune of the People" and the "Censors" in China in 206 B.C. In Sweden, the institution of Ombudsman was created as a part of the Constitution of 1809 to supervise the observance of statutes and regulations by the courts, public officials and employees and to prosecute them, if necessary. The need for the establishment of this institution arose from the absence of control over the large body of civil servants by the ministers.[3] In 1951, a Military Ombudsman was also appointed in Sweden. A new form of Organization was passed in 1975 by the Parliament. According to new system, there are four institutions in Sweden today to supervise the administration. One of the Ombudsmen is elected by Parliament to hold the office of Chief Ombudsman and Administrative Director of the Ombudsman's office.

The Finland Ombudsman was appointed in 1919 by the Parliament as a counterpart of the Chancellor of Justice appointed by the executive. The institution of Ombudsman in Denmark was set up in 1955 by an amendment of the Danish Constitution, which authorised the Folketing (Parliament) to appoint one or two individuals to control the civil and military administration of the state. It was felt that the existing safeguards against mistakes, negligence or direct abuse of power by the civil servants and the available remedies like the access to the courts by the citizens or the right of administrative appeal were not sufficient.

In West Germany, the office of Military Ombudsman was

[2]Blix Hans, "The Ombudsman: What He is and What He is not" in *Public Administration*, Kanpur, July 1965, pp. 307-379.

[3]In Sweden, in 1809, when the new Constitution was under discussion, its Parliament wanted its own officer to supervise and prosecute civil servants who contravened the law. This was considered necessary due to the peculiar governmental structure in Sweden as ministers chosen by the Prime Minister in Sweden need not be members of parliament. They do not head the administrative departments. Nor are the officials answerable to the ministers. Ombudsman rightly fits in at such a place. "The Citizen and Administration" in *The Whyatt Report* (Chairman: Justice Whyatt, Report of International Commission of Jurists (British Section), Stevens, 1961, p. 94.

created in 1957 in order to have parliamentary control over the army and to safeguard the basic rights of the recruits.

The office of the Ombudsman in Norway, which was set up in 1961, is modelled on the pattern of the Danish Ombudsman. Since 1969 Norwegian Ombudsman was given the right to investigate complaints against certain local government services as well.

There are in Scandinavian countries some variations in the arrangements for protecting the citizens against the arbitrary decisions of administrative authorities. Sweden and Finland have a system of administrative courts, but Denmark and Norway do not have this type of judiciary.

Among the Commonwealth countries, New Zealand has been the first to appoint an Ombudsman. Known as the Parliamentary Commissioner, the institution of Ombudsman was created in New Zealand in 1962 by a special statue, the proposal having found a mention in the manifesto of the National Party in 1960.

The Ombudsman Act of 1962 was replaced by a new Act on 26 June 1975. The revised statute consolidates and amends the original Act in several respects, e.g. the requirement that clients pay a two-dollar fee when complaint is dropped, creation of multiple Ombudsmen to handle the increased workload caused by the extension of Ombudsmen jurisdiction into local government matters which became effective from 1 April 1976. On 10 October 1975, Sir Guy Powles was designated Chief Ombudsman and two additional Ombudsmen were appointed. The idea was to increase three times the size of the staff and open regional offices in Auckland and Christ Church under the charge of two Ombudsmen. Except that the Chief Ombudsman coordinates the work, all Ombudsmen have equal powers and jurisdiction. The Chief Ombudsman is stationed at Wellington and will be incharge of complaints against Central Government organizations and departments. In his Report of 1975, Sir Guy Powels has a word of praise for troika of Ombudsmen. According to the Report,

> The deliberate choice for the extended jurisdiction of a collegiate system of Ombudsman—each one exercising full jurisdiction, and being equal, and having the division of their functions settled almost wholly

by agreement is a better solution than attempting to quild a hierarchical structure with authority stemming from the Chief Ombudsman down through successive layers. The collegiate system has worked well in Sweden, and there is no reason why it should not work well here. There will be ample scope for the Ombudsmen to develop their individual approaches while keeping within a coordinated and cooperating framework.

This system is a definite improvement over Swedish system. In Sweden the Ombudsmen are all housed in the same building in Stockholm and have common staff whereas in New Zealand the three Ombudsmen work independently in different cities, each one exercises full jurisdiction and being equal have the division of their functions setteled by agreement.

Another important provision in the Ombudsmen Act 1975 (Section 13(5)) which did not exist in the earlier enactment is "The Prime Minister may, with the consent of the Chief Ombudsman, refer to an Ombudsman for investigation and report any matter, other than a matter concerning a judicial proceeding, which the Prime Minister considers should be investigated by an Ombudsman. Where a matter is referred to an Ombudsman pursuant to this Sub-section, he shall notwithstanding anything to the contrary in this Act forthwith investigate the matter and report thereon to the Prime Minister, and may thereafter make such report to Parliament on the matter as he thinks fit. Nothing in Section 22 of this Act shall apply in respect of any investigation or report made under this Sub-section." This affects the autonomy of Ombudsman to some extent. In this case he only exercises the powers of an Inquiry Committee as protection granted under Section 22 to those under investigation are suspended.

In the United Kingdom, the main initiative for the creation of a Parliamentary Commissioner came from the Whyatt Report in 1961. The then British government rejected the proposal on the ground that the appointment of an Ombudsman would conflict with the doctrine of ministerial responsibility. However, when the Labour government came into power, it brought before the House of Commons a Bill in July 1966, and simultaneously announced the appointment of Sir Edmund Compton, the retired Comptroller and Auditor General, as the United

Kingdom's first Parliamentary Commissioner.[4] The Bill was approved in principle by Parliament on 18 October 1966 and it was referred to a Standing Committee for detailed study. The new Parliamentary Commissioner was granted funds for an office and staff on the next day, i.e. 19 October 1966. The Standing Committee reported back in November 1966, proposing some amendments and the Bill was passed by Parliament, with further amendments in March 1967. Under the National Health Service Reorganization Act 1972, a Health Service Commissioner has been established to examine complaints against hospital authorities. Under Acts of 1974 and 1975, local Commissioners for Administration were set up for England, Wales and Scotland. Sir Idwal Pugh is holding a dual charge of the Parliamentary Commissioner and Health Service Commissioner.

Among other countries, Canada has been considering the appointment of an Ombudsman since 1965. Two Canadian Provinces, Alberta[5] and New Brunswick were the first to establish an Ombudsman in 1967. Quebec followed in 1968 and in 1969 Nova Scotia and Manitoba also appointed an Ombudsman. Saskatchewan appointed an Ombudsman in 1973 and Ontario and Newfoundland in 1975.

In the U.S A., proposals of different kinds have been coming up before the U.S. federal government since 1963. About one-third of the States in the U.S.A. have had under consideration in recent years one or the other type of a Bill on the Ombudsman. Hawaii has enacted legislation in 1969 providing for the

[4]It was after a long public debate and a number of government and professional reports that the Labour Party in 1964 Election manifesto included a scheme of Ombudsman within their promised legislation programme. On 3 November 1964, the Queen of England in her speech before the British Parliament promised the appointment of an Ombudsman to investigate and redress individual's grievances.

[5]In January 1967, the Government of Alberta Put in an advertisement in newspapers all over Canada, inviting applications for 'Ombudsman, Commissioner of Legislature' at a salary of $ 20,000 per annum. The qualifications prescribed were "a substantial record of formal education and related experience, preferably in law and social science." Alberta's Ombudsman Bill was given final approval on 30 March 1967 and on 7 April 1967, it was announced that the new Ombudsman, chosen from among 230 applicants would be the retiring head of the Federal Royal Canadian Mounted Police, who was to take office in September 1967.

appointment of an Ombudsman followed by three other States in U.S.A. This nomenclature has become so popular in U.S.A. that this name is even being given to the person handling customer's problems in a San Francisco department store. The Public Protector appointed in May 1966 by the Executive of Nassau county was popularly called an Ombudsman.[6] Several complaints officers at the Federal and local levels have also used this term. The president of the State Bar of Michigan has appointed an "Ombudsman Committee" of seventeen past presidents to hear complaints from members of the bar against its own officers. The State University of New York at Stony Brook has appointed faculty members as Ombudsman to receive student appeals.[7] It has been pointed out that the Ombudsman idea has some value in promoting due process of law in private institutions, but the indiscriminate use of the term may rob it of its essential meaning.

The American Assembly devoted its entire Thirty-Second Session, held in 1967, to a discussion on the Ombudsman.[8] Its report on the subject recognizes that in any large and complex government, there is a real need for mechanisms devoted solely

[6]On anonymous complaints, Judge Greason, the Ombudsman for Nassau county, has adopted the following procedure:

Anonymous complaints cannot be pursued in the usual manner, but they are not ignored. No departmental response to an anonymous complaint is required by the county Ombudsman. The substance of the grievance is directed to the department concerned for whatever action may be deemed appropriate. Justification for consideration of this type of complaint lies in the possible disclosure of a general situation requiring improvement.

[7]In February, Congressman Reuss gave shape to his Ombudsman Bill at the Central level by temporarily appointing a personal assistant as an 'Ombudsman' for his Milwaukee constituency. Professors Gellhorn, Anderson and Donald C. Rowat were appointed as consultants. The assistant held office at six postal stations as also the central office. During a four-month period he received nearly 500 complaints and enquiries for some action or the other. Most of these were telephonic or personal calls, and a few by mail. Out of these complaints, 40 per cent related to state or local government. A large number of complaints were about administrative delay.

[8]The Assembly was established by Dwight D. Eisenhower at Columbia University in 1950. It holds non-partisan meetings and publishes books to illuminate issues of United States policy.

to receiving, examining and channelling citizens' complaints and securing their expeditious and impartial redress. This report describes the Ombudsman as "an independent, high-level officer who receives complaints, who pursues inquiries into the matters involved, and who makes recommendation for suitable action. He may also investigate on his own motion. He makes periodic public reports. His remedial weapons are persuasion, criticism and publicity. He cannot, as a matter of law, reverse administrative action.[9]

Some thought has also been given to the transplantation of the institution of Ombudsman to the American scene. Professor Walter Gellhorn has even prepared a set of rules for the model Ombudsman.[10] Chairman of the Conference of United Nations Representatives, William Morey (who formerly served on the political science faculties at Columbia University and the College of the City of New York), was so much inspired by the concept of Ombudsman that he suggested the creation of a "Global Ombudsman". Morey designated the institution as a "High Commissioner for Human Rights" and envisaged the appointment of the functionary on the occasion of the twentieth anniversary of the Universal Declaration of Human Rights in 1969. The High Commissioner could give advice and assistance in the form of fact-finding or quiet diplomatic mediation, offer expert aid and services in creating institutions for securing human rights or in giving effect to various United Nations

[9]Report of the Thirty-second American Assembly, New York Columbia University, October 1967, p. 8.

[10]According to section 11 of the Model Ombudsman, action on complaints by the Ombudsman has to be as under:

(a) The Ombudsman may receive a complaint from any source concerning an administrative act. He shall conduct a suitable investigation into the things complained of unless he believes that—(i) the complainant has available to him another remedy or channel of complaint which he could reasonably be expected to use; (ii) the grievance pertains to a matter outside the Ombudsman's power; (iii) the complainant's interest is insufficiently related to the subject matter; (iv) the complaint is trivial, frivolous, vexatious, or not made in good faith; (v) other complaints are more worthy of attention; (vi) the Ombudsman's resources are insufficient for adequate investigation; or (vii) the complaint has been too long delayed to justify present examination on its merit.

human rights treaties, and inquire into complaints about human rights violations.

Among the developing countries, provision for the creation of the institution of the Ombudsman has been incorporated in the constitutions of Guyana and Mauritius. The Permanent Commission of Enquiry in Tanzania, which was set up in 1965, is modelled on the pattern of the Ombudsman.[11] In some other countries, there have come up organizations which partake in some respects the institutions of the Ombudsman, e.g., the Presidential Complaint Committee in Philippines which was appointed by President Magasaysay immediately after his election in 1953.

FUNCTIONS AND POWERS

(1) *Wider role of general supervision of administration*

The common duty enjoined on the Ombudsman in all the countries, where this institution exists, is the protection of rights and liberties of the citizens. In investigating the citizens' complaints and suggesting their redress, he also pinpoints the faults in the administration and thereby helps improve administrative procedures. Apart from these common characteristics, there are significant differences in the powers and jurisdiction of the Ombudsman in various countries.

In the Scandinavian countries, the role of the Ombudsman is not confined only to the redress of the citizens' grievances but it also includes the general supervision of the civil administration. In Denmark, Norway, Sweden, and Finland, his functions cover as well a general surveillance of the functioning of the administration. In Sweden and Finland, the Ombudsman is required to undertake a tour of inspections and visit institu-

[11]The Permanent Commission of Enquiry in Tanzania inquires into the conduct of persons holding office under the corporate bodies, public authorities or boards, corporations, the civil, judicial, local government and police service commissions, trade unions and the women's organizations. It has no jurisdiction in regard to the President, the head of the executive for Zanzibar and the Armed Forces. The Permanent Commission of Enquiries can, however, investigate complaints against ministers and the police.

tions (like prisons) to satisfy himself that there is no default or negligence in the discharge of official duties.[12]

In case an official is guilty of abuse, error, or neglect in the performance of his duties, the Ombudsmen in Sweden and Finland have the powers to institute proceedings against him. In Sweden, in cases of misuse of public property, the Ombudsman can even suggest that the official or the magistrate concerned should make restitution as an alternative to prosecution. The Ombudsman in Denmark can, in the same circumstances demand that criminal or disciplinary proceedings be initiated; while in Norway and New Zealand, he may only recommend this procedure.

It is interesting to note that when the Ombudsman was first appointed in 1809 in Sweden, the objective was not to provide a means for the redress of citizens' grievances but to institute proceedings in the courts against those who in the execution of their official duties had, through partiality, favouritism, or other causes, committed any unlawful act or neglected to perform their official duties properly. It is only by a process of transformation that the Ombudsman's functions in Sweden as a prosecutor have become unimportant and he has assumed the role of a forum for the ventilation of citizens' grievances. He may administer a reprimand and include the case in his report to the Parliament. He may also decide not to take any further action. Of course, it is only in a very few cases that Ombudsman had instituted proceedings before the court.

In Denmark, the Ombudsman stands on the sidelines of

[12]Accompanied by a small staff, the Swedish Ombudsman will, after giving 48 hours' notice, arrive at a district government headquarters and then discuss difficult administrative problems, if any, and will take out 20 to 30 files at random for examination. He will look into the files to satisfy himself that the complaints have been thoroughly investigated and that officials have given reasons for their decisions and that the decisions are not wrong. He lays great stress on officials letting the citizens know the reasons for the decisions. After completing the examination of the files, he inspects the prisons, the asylum, children's schools and other such institutions in the locality. If, as a result of these inspections, he finds officials guilty of maladministration, he will take action against the persons responsible in the same way as when he receives complaints of maladministration from the members of the public.

government to observe, to appraise and to censure. Where there is a prima facie case of an actual breach of law by a public official, he may, in appropriate cases, instruct the public prosecutor to start criminal proceedings, or he may recommend the plaintiff for legal aid in the pursuit of civil remedies.

But the essense of his influence arises from the interest which the Danish Press habitually takes in his work. Thus, a grievance which after investigation is found to be well-grounded becomes a public issue. The Danish Ombudsman can order prosecution against a civil servant for maladministration but in the event of a civil servant demanding that the matter be referred to a committee under the Civil Services Act, the Ombudsman has to discontinue his investigation in that case. The observation of a Swedish Ombudsman has a flexible approach and sometimes uses persuasion rather than criticising an action.

The Norwegian Ombudsman has limitations to his powers. Unfortunately, he has complete lack of executive authority. He has no power to nullify any administrative decision; he has no resources out of which to compensate any aggrieved party; no civil servant can be disciplined by him.

In New Zealand, the ombudsman is regarded as having been established not only for the purposes of checking administrative abuses and of writing off wrongs but also for actually reviewing administrative decisions and securing changes. The scope of the Ombudsman in New Zealand is wider than that of the original institutions of this name in other countries such as Denmark, Norway, Sweden, etc.

(2) *Government agencies, within Ombudsman's purview*

The jurisdiction of Swedish and Finnish Ombudsman is more extensive than that of their Danish, Norwegian and New Zealand counterparts. The judicial authorities come under the supervision of the Ombudsman in Sweden and Finland but not in Demark, Norway or New Zealand.

In Sweden, the Ombudsman is fully competent to investigate cases of corruption against the judges of Supreme Court and subsidiary courts. It not only hears complaints against judges and civil servants but also against clergy of the Lutheran Church.[13] The Swedish Ombudsman's jurisdiction over the judges has not affected the independence of the latter. Some judges were prosecuted and fined for delay. In exercising his powers, the Ombudsman has to make a distinction between complaints against decisions and complaints against the conduct of persons who come within his jurisdiction. For instance, the Ombudsman does not concern himself with the judicial decisions, whether given in the ordinary courts or in the administrative courts, and in case there are erroneous decisions, these can be remedied by the ordinary process of appeal. On the other hand, if a judge or a civil servant through negligence—intentionally or otherwise—acts beyond his duties prescribed by the statute or instructions, he is answerable to the Ombudsman.

For a long time, Finland was the only country in which the Ombudsman supervised local government authorities, but Sweden and Denmark have extended the jurisdiction of the Ombudsman to local government in 1957 and 1961 respectively. In Norway and New Zealand, the local authorities do not come under the jurisdiction of the Ombudsman.

In Sweden and Norway, there is one Ombudsman to supervise the civil administration and the judiciary, and another to supervise the military authorities. In Finland and Denmark, supervision of both civil and military authorities is entrusted to a single Ombudsman. However, Section 11(5) of the New Zealand Act does not permit investigation of matters pertaining to military affairs by the Ombudsman. This has been criticised by the Ombudsman in New Zealand who would like his jurisdiction to be extended to include matters relating to armed forces as well.

In New Zealand, practically all the government departments and agencies come under the purview of New Zealand Ombudsman except for special statutory corporations which are not engaged in state administration. For example, the New Zealand Broadcasting Corporation and the National Airways Corporation are outside the jurisdiction of the Ombudsman. But all central departments and 22 organisations and statutory

[13]The clergy of Lutheran Church is regarded as civil servant in Sweden.

corporations, including the railways, the departments of foreign affairs and defence and public utility departments are included. The armed forces are not excluded but personnel matters are.

In the case of the United Kingdom's Parliamentary Commissioner, only specified departments and all authorities, including the Ministry of Defence but not the Armed Services are subject to his jurisdiction. The Act lists the government departments which are to be subject to investigation by the Commissioner in matters within his scope. It also provides for an amendment of the list through an order-in-Council, from time to time, in accordance with the changes in the structure of the government machinery. The U.K. Parliamentary Commissioner has no jurisdiction over the national health service, hospitals, local government departments except those listed in the second schedule[14] of the Act and there is a catalogue of specific exclusions in the third schedule[15] of the Act. Although hospitals are under the jurisdiction of the central government, these are specifically excluded because other parts of the national health service are under the jurisdiction of local authorities and it was thought that the health service must be treated as a whole. A reorganization of the health service was under consideration and the Labour government announced in 1969 that it saw a good case for the Health Commissioner to investigate complaints throughout the health service. It also announced that in principle it accepted the case for an Ombudsman system for local government. In the case of police also, there is a considerable public demand for improved redress machinery. In 1962, a minority of the Royal Commission on Police recommended that there was a need for a complaints procedure of the Ombudsman type which would be impartial in the eyes of the citizens. The present position is that the complaints against the police are investigated by police officers.

[14]Second schedule of the U.K. Parliamentary Commissioner Act lists 44 departments. It includes Ministry of Agriculture, Fisheries and Food, Charity Commission, Civil Service Commission, Commonwealth Office, Crown Estate Office, Customs and Excise, Ministry of Defence, Department of Economic Affairs, Ministry of Health, and Lord Chancellor's Department.

[15]There are 11 items in this Schedule of the Act which are not subject to the investigation of Parliamentary Commissioner.

Accordingly, the above recommendations were implemented by the new enactments of 1973, 1974 and 1975 respectively by having separate Commissioners for Health and local governments. The exclusion of complaints against the police from the Parliamentary Commissioners's jurisdiction was partially remedied by the new Police Act of 1976 which provided for three-man tribunal consisting of two laymen and the Chief officer of the police force concerned, to hear complaints against the police.

(3) *Limitations regarding types of decisions*

In Norway, Sweden and New Zealand, ministers are excluded from the jurisdiction of the Ombudsman. The Swedish ministers are not, either collectively or individually, directly responsible for the individual acts of civil servants employed outside their relatively small ministries and do not come under the purview of the Ombudsman.[16] The jurisdiction of the Ombudsman in New Zealand extends to matters of administration, but matters concerning policy are excluded. The provisions of the statute do not authorize the Ombudsman to inquire into the decisions of ministers themselves, but any recommendation made to a minister by a department or agency, even if the minister has already acted upon it, may be inquired into and, if necessary, reported upon by the Ombudsman.

In Finland, the ministers are, in contrast to the position in Sweden, subject to surveillance by the Ombudsman. The Danish Ombudsman's jurisdiction covers ministers, as also others in the service of the government. Normally, a citizen aggrieved by an administrative decision or by the conduct of an official may lodge a complaint with the Danish Ombudsman, but under an amendment in 1959 of the Ombudsman Act, 1954, the complainant must exhaust all remedies, such as approaching the higher authorities, etc., before complaining to

[16]This is, however, not of much consequence because in Sweden the ministers are concerned only with matters of policy and are not collectively or individually responsible for the administration of government departments or the acts of civil servants. This freedom of the civil servants from the control of the ministers has made it all the more necessary to have a separate institution for supervising administrative acts.

the Ombudsman. This reduces the nature of complaints with the Ombudsman and also discourages premature complaints.[17] As mentioned earlier, the Ombudsman in Finland can also prosecute even the judges and the Chancellor of Justice. All Cabinet agenda are seen by Ombudsman, but since 1923, he has never attended cabinet meetings. The Ombudsman must have parliamentary consent before prosecuting a minister. He can go to the floor of Parliament and indict a minister. In 1952, two Cabinet ministers were indicted for misuse of public funds to help private business. He publicly rebuked a minister on another occasion.

In the U.K., several items are excluded from the jurisdiction of Parliamentary Commissioner, having in view considerations of national or public interest, e.g., the exercise of powers to preserve the safety of the state; matters which ministers certify as affecting relations with other countries; and the exercise of powers in relation to investigating crime or determining whether a matter shall go to courts. The Parliamentary Commissioner also cannot look into appointments by the Crown or by ministers. He will be excluded from investigating actions of departments in personnel matters. Purely commercial relations of departments with customers or suppliers do not come within his purview. The Commissioner will not look into the exercise of the prerogative or mercy or personal decisions of the Sovereign is conferring honours and privileges.[18]

[17]Exhaustion of remedies is the general rule, but the Norwegian Ombudsman can deal with the complaint straightaway if he finds certain reasons to do so. This enables the Ombudsman to come into the picture before the matter becomes final and administrative attitudes harden.

[18]The Parliamentary Commissioner in his first report pointed out certain anomalies in his powers. He cannot investigate cases against police force except for the Metropolitan Police which is not listed in Schedule 2 of the Act. It was suggested that the Parliamentary Commissioner should examine cases against magistrates since they are appointed by Lord Chancellor and the office of Lord Chancellor comes under the jurisdiction of the Parliamentary Commissioner. But the Commissioner did not like to investigate complaints against the decisions of magistrates' courts in civil procedures as the actions of the courts are outside the jurisdiction of the Parliamentary Commissioner. Similarly, he refused to investigate complaints of ratepayers. Another anomaly which the Parliamentary Commissioner pointed out was that claims for service disability pension which relate to service before 4 August 1914

The Parliamentary Commissioner of the U.K. has been given extensive power to obtain evidence from civil servants and also from ministers. In fact, the Parliamentary Commissioner Act went a good deal further than the original report of 'Justice' and it is important to note an important departure from that report. The Whyatt Report recommended that a minister could apply a veto in extreme circumstances, for example, on security grounds. This suggestion was discarded, and under the Act no minister has power to refuse to allow an investigation to be made into his department by the Parliamentary Commissioner.

(4) *Exercise of discretionary powers*

The discretionary powers of the Ombudsman vary in different countries where this institution has been established. In Sweden, as also in Finland, the Ombudsman has no specific right to criticise the wisdom of a decision and he rarely does so, but in Denmark he has been given the right to do so if he considers the decision to be arbitrary or unreasonable. The Danish Ombudsman can investigate also cases of misbehaviour, inefficiency or negligence.[19] He will not, however, take up a complaint against a discretion exercised by an administrative authority merely because he would or might have exercised

---

or between 31 August 1921 and 3 September 1939, are the responsibility of the Ministry of Defence, while those arising out of service between 1914 and 1921 and since 1939 known as war pensions fall under the Ministry of Social Security. The Commissioner was not able to examine the cases coming under the Ministry of Defence as the latter was excluded from his jurisdiction by paragraph 10(c) of Schedule 3 of the Act. Further paragraph 10(c) of Schedule 3 of the Act excludes from his jurisdiction not only such public service matters as are not covered by paragraph 10(a) or (b), e.g. teachers' pensions, but also the whole range of appointments by minister to public and non-public bodies.

[19]Donald C. Rowat, op. cit., p. 400. The importance of differences in the investigation of discretionary powers by the Ombudsman, need not, however, be exaggerated, because the Denish Ombudsman has used this power sparingly, while the Swedish Ombudsman has usually managed to intervene on grounds of illegality where a decision was patently unreasonable.

the discretion differently if he had been sitting in the chair of that authority. It is only in an exceptional case of abuse of discretionary power, resulting in an arbitrary or unreasonable decision—the discretion thus losing its real character—that the Ombudsman intervenes. Such occasions for interference have, however, been very few.

In Norway, he has no power to deal with complaints against discretionary decisions unless it appears that the discretion has been so abused as not to amount to a genuine exercise of discretion, or the discretion exercised is "clearly unreasonable." In New Zealand and the U.K., the Ombudsman has power to investigate cases only where discretionary power has been exercised for an improper purpose or on irrelevant grounds. The Parliamentary Commissioner in the U.K. cannot criticise the policy, or to examine a decision on the exercise of discretionary powers of the minister, unless it appears to him that the decision has been affected by a fault in the administration. A difficulty in the interpretation of his role to look into discretionary decision arose in the very first few months of his functioning. The Commissioner in his first report indicated that though he could look into the quality of procedures governing the administrative decision, he could not look into the quality of decision itself. This may mean that if there has been no delay and a regular procedure has been followed, the administrative discretion exercised with corrupt or improper motive cannot be looked into by the Commissioner. A view has been taken in some quarters that under such an interpretation of the role of the U.K. Parliamentary Commissioner, there is very little that he can do to provide effective redress.

New Zealand, Denmark and Sweden have a novel feature. If the complaint discloses the existence of law or practice which in the Ombudsman's opinion is "unreasonable, unjust, oppressive or improperly discriminatory", he can make a recommendation that the law or the practice itself should be amended. If the recommendation is not given effect to within a reasonable time, he will communicate his recommendation and consequent happenings to the complainant and make a report of the circumstances of the case to the Prime Minister.

SANCTIONS BEHIND THE OMBUDSMAN

(1) *Pre-eminence of Ombudsman*

The institution of the Ombudsman, if it is to operate effectively, must be independent of all the three branches of government, namely the executive, the legislature and the judiciary. It must be protected against interference of all kinds, which means that the Ombudsman should be a person of pre-eminence and he must enjoy the confidence both of the government and the opposition as well as high status in the machinery of the government.

Keeping in view the nature of functions of the Ombudsman, it is generally considered that he should necessarily have legal background with some experience of administration. In the Scandinavian countries, legal education is a condition precedent to the appointment of a person as Ombudsman. Generally, lawyers, judges, law teachers have heen appointed as the Ombudsman. In Sweden, he is selected from amongst jurists of high reputation. In New Zealand, the first Ombudsman has been an active legal practitioner, administrator and a diplomat. As against this, the first Ombudsman appointed in England is a civil servant of over 30 years' standing, with no experience of legal practice or teaching.

In Denmark and Sweden, the Ombudsman gets the salary of a judge of the Supreme Court. In addition, he may be granted a personal allowance. The expenditure of his office is charged to the budget of Parliament. The salaries and pensions of the Norwegian Ombudsman and his Deputy are fixed by Parliament. In New Zealand, his salary is NZ £3500 per annum. The Finnish Ombudsman gets the same salary as the Chief Judge of the Supreme Administrative Court. In the U.K., his salary is £8,600 a year which is less than that of a High Court Judge. He is entitled to pension.

(2) *Appointment and recall*

For inspiring the confidence among the masses, it is necessary to have an independent person as an Ombudsman who can investigate complaints and pronounce views thereon, which, if not accepted by the administrative authorities, can be brought to the notice of the Parliament. It is important that the Ombudsman should enjoy confidence of the legislature (both of the party in power and the opposition parties), as otherwise his efficacy would be very much vitiated. In order to achieve this objective, the Ombudsman is mostly appointed either by Parliament or in consultation with the members of the Opposition.

In all the Scandinavian countries, the Ombudsman is selected by Parliament, usually after each general election with a tenure conterminous with the term of the national legislature. There is a slight variation in the case of Sweden in as much as that a Board of 48 persons elected by both the Houses of Parliament appoints the Ombudsman.[20]

In the U.K. and New Zealand, the appointment of the Ombudsman is formally made by the Head of the State, i.e., by the Queen [21] and the Governor-General respectively, on the advice of the Prime Minister, in the case of U.K. and on the recommendation of the House of the Representatives in the case of New Zealand. In Guyana and Mauritius, the Ombudsman is appointed by the Government in consultation with the opposition leaders.

The tenure of the Ombudsman in the Scandinavian countries is normally four years which (as already mentioned) is conterminous with that of the national Parliament. The term of the Parliamentary Commissioner in New Zealand is three to four years. No time limit has been fixed for the tenure of the U.K. Parliamentary Commissioner. But he must vacate office at the age of 65.

The initial term of the Ombudsman is renewable in most of

[20]An interesting suggestion mooted in Norway was that the Ombudsman should always be elected from the opposition in the Parliament. But the government rejected this suggestion with the counter argument that the Ombudsman was not going to engage himself in political questions and that the essential idea behind the institution was to create an organ to protect and safeguard the rights and interests of the individual citizen.

[21]It is interesting to note that the government of the U.K. appointed the first Parliamentary Commissioner in anticipation of the passage of the Bill.

the countries. In New Zealand, Denmark, Sweden, Norway, and Finland the same person can be appointed for successive terms. The recommendations for the appointment in New Zealand, are made in the first or second session of every Parliament, and this means that the Ombudsman has a three or a maximum of four years' term, but the term is renewable. The reason for renewing his term after the new Parliament comes into being is that the Ombudsman is in a very powerful position to embarrass the government by criticising it and thus may lose the confidence of the ruling party.

If at any time it is felt that the Ombudsman in Denmark and Norway does not enjoy the confidence of Parliament, it may dismiss him and elect a new Ombudsman in his place. Every year, a parliamentary committee reviews the working of the Ombudsman in Sweden and it may recommend to Parliament his dismissal if it feels that he does not deserve the confidence of Parliament and should be relieved of his office before the expiry of his term. However, no person has so far been dismissed from office, though extensions of term have been refused in some cases. In Norway, the Ombudsman can be removed from office by a two-thirds majority vote of Parliament. In Finland, though Parliament elects him, Parliament cannot dismiss him during his term of office. It can show its displeasure only by not re-electing him for the next term and this right has been exercised at times.

In the U.K., the Parliamentary Commissioner can be removed by the Queen in consequence of addresses from both Houses of Parliament. The Ombudsman in New Zealand may at any time be removed or suspended from his office by the Governor-Generel upon an address from the Parliament for disability, bankruptcy, negligence, or misconduct.

It is obviously essential that the Ombudsman should be independent of political affiliations. In all the Scandinavian countries, the Ombudsman cannot be a member of Parliament. In Denmark he cannot hold office in a public or private firm, enterprises or institutions except with the consent of a Special Parliamenatry Committee which has been given the power to decide on this question. A similar position obtains in Sweden and its Ombudsman cannot without the approval of the Prime Minister hold any office of trust or profit or engage in any trade for reward outside his duties of office.

In all the countries which have the institution of the Ombudsman, Parliament can determine the jurisdiction of the Ombudsman but cannot issue any instructions to him as to which cases he should investigate. The Danish Ombudsman Act expressly states that the Ombudsman shall carry out his task independently of the Folketing (Parliament).

(3) *Reporting to Parliament*

A common feature of the institution of Ombudsman in the Scandinavian and some other countries is that he submits annually a report to the Parliament on his activities in the preceding year. In the report, he includes his decisions on important cases, calls attention to the shortcomings, if any, in the administrative bodies, or to any loopholes in the law which require legislation or amendment. The names of the civil servants complained against are very rarely mentioned in the reports of the Ombudsman.

In all the countries, however, the Ombudsman has power to make recommendations to the department concerned before reporting to Parliament. This latter power is of some consequence, for no department wants to get undue and adverse publicity, or to be discussed in Parliament. Because of this ultimate sanction, Ombudsman's suggestions and recommendations are given due weight and are invariably accepted by the administration.

In Norway and Finland, the annual and special reports of the Ombudsman are first handled by one of the Parliamentary Committees and are thereafter discussed in Parliament. In Denmark, if after making an investigation, the Ombudsman comes to the conclusion that a minister or a former minister should be held responsible under civil or criminal law for his official conduct, he submits a recommendation to that effect to the Parliamentary Committee dealing with the Ombudsman's office. In New Zealand before reporting to Parliament, the Ombudsman has to refer the matter to the Prime Minister. In England, he has to refer the same to the minister concerned. If the recommendation of the Ombudsman is not given effect to within a reasonable time he will communicate his recommendation and consequent happenings to the complainant and make a report of the circumstances of the case to the Prime Minister and Parliament.

(4) *Publicity and relations with the press*

In all the countries, publicity in the Press and an enlightened and vigilant public opinion are major sanctions behind the Ombudsman's recommendations. No department wants to get an adverse press or public criticism by refusing to accept what the Ombudsman wants, unless it is absolutely necessary or inevitable.

The independence of the institution in Sweden is further safeguarded by keeping the door open to the Press. Publicity is given to the Ombudsman's criticism of the administration and the admonitions issued by him to the administrative authorities. Every day at 11 a.m. a representative of the Swedish Press Bureau calls at the Ombudsman's office to examine the complaints and the decisions of the previous day. The pressman selects those cases which are of general interest and circulates the information to the national newspapers. If a case is merely of local interest, he sends information only to the provincial newspapers. On some occasions the press report contains criticism of even the Ombudsman's handling of the case if there appears to have been unnecessary delay in his office. The wide and continuous publicity resulting from the system of daily visits by a representative of the Press Bureau in many ways provides a more effective weapon than prosecution and it is much feared and respected by civil servants.

In Finland, it is not uncommon for the Press to expose violation of the rules, and the Ombudsman may, if he thinks it necessary, follow up the case officially. A register is kept at the office of Ombudsman of all matters brought to his knowledge, of the documents submitted and the action taken by him.

VIABILITY AND EFFECTIVENESS

(1) *Complaint procedure*

The Scandinavian countries provide that the Ombudsman can

not only receive complaints, but can also start investigations of his own.[22] There is no suo-moto power to investigate with the Parliamentary Commissioner of the U.K. The complaints must reach him through the members of the House of Commons. He cannot entertain complaints directly from the citizen. The New Zealand Ombudsman can act suo-moto as well as on a reference by a Parliamentary Committee.

In all the Scandinavian countries, the complainant must be one who is personally affected by the administrative action complained of. This is a safeguard against entirely querulous complaints, from self-appointed persons. The complaint should, as far as possible, be submitted in writing and accompanied by the complainant's evidence. Any citizen has a right to call on the Ombudsman or write to him, his complaint, and it will be investigated. Anonymous letters are disregarded. The Ombudsman has discretion to refuse to pursue a case where he thinks there are no sufficient grounds for the complaint or where he considers that it does not fall within his jurisdiction. He acts only if the complainant claims to have sustained injustice in connection with the action taken by a government authority in exercise of its administrative functions. The complainant can personally come to explain his case. He is allowed to comment on the statement of the department given on the complaint.

In New Zealand, the petitioner can either go to the Ombudsman or to the Committee on Petitions. The Committee will refer the Petition to the Ombudsman and ask him to report. The Committee can refer a point or points from a petition.

No fee is to be paid in Scandinavian countries for filing a complaint. But in New Zealand, a fee of £1 is charged in

[22]The complaints when received are indexed department-wise. The Ombudsman then allots the complaints to his officers. When the relevant information is obtained, the first question to be decided is whether the complaint is within the jurisdiction of the Ombudsman. Then the case is referred to the concerned department for report. If the case is important, relevant files are also called for. In some cases, the Ombudsman sends the comments of the department to the complainant for further comments, if any, and then these comments, are returned back to the department for further observation before the case is finally disposed of by the Ombudsman.

order to discourage frivolous complaints. The fee can be waived by the Ombudsman if he so desires.

The investigations are conducted in private and the procedure is intended to be informal as far as possible. This investigating function of the Ombudsman is facilitated by the principle of "document publicity" which is unique in Sweden and by which any citizen can, subject to certain minimum restrictions, examine any file in a government office without assigning any reason. Similarly, the closed investigation files in the office of Ombudsman can also be examined by any citizen.

If the Ombudsman decides not to make an investigation, he will inform accordingly the complainant. In the U.K., the Parliamentary Commissioner[23] sends his findings to the Member of Parliament through whom the complaint was made.

No body needs to employ a lawyer or any other help for submitting a complaint to the Ombudsman. The Parliamentary Commissioner in the U.K. is, however, empowered to decide whether the parties can be legally represented, but legal representation is expected to be an exception and not the rule. The Ombudsman may, however, recommend that a complainant be granted free legal aid where he intends to bring an action against a state authority or person acting or having acted in the service of state in respect of alleged errors or negligence.

A complaint has to be filed before the Ombudsman in Norway, Denmark, New Zealand, and the U.K. within one year after the action complained of took place, though the Ombudsman has an option to take up a case on his own initiative even after the lapse of the time limit. Finland and Sweden have not fixed any time limit in this regard.

Ombudsman in Scandinavian countries can inspect any document he wants and every person and government servant is obliged to supply him with such information or produce such documents or records as he may require for the performance

[23]In his last report, Sir Edmund considered a request made to him by Members of parliament that they should be present at an interview between a complainant and a member of his staff. The Commissioner has laid down that any complainant may be represented either by friend or an adviser, and he has no objection to the Member of Parliament being present.

of his duties.

In New Zealand, excepting very special cases, the Ombudsman can have access to departmental records, and can summon and examine persons on oath.[24] The Parliamentary Commissioner in the U.K. has been given extensive power to obtain evidence and to examine documents. These powers extend to obtaining evidence from civil servants, and also from ministers.[25]

In Scandinavian countries, the Ombudsman is in the same position as the courts with regard to securing oral testimony from public servants. The Norwegian Ombudsman may also demand that evidence be taken by the courts, in which case the public is not admitted to the court sittings. He is not to divulge any information he obtains in his official capacity and must observe such secrecy even after retirement from office. His staff is also under the same obligation. Trade and business secrets must in no case be made public.

Before making any report or recommendation injurious to any department, organization or individual, the Ombudsman in Scandinavian countries gives the person complained against an opportunity to comment on the complainant. If necessary, the Ombudsman holds interviews with the complainant the civil servant concerned and other persons, if any, who may be able to give relevant information. This interview takes place in an

[24] Government documents cannot be withheld from him on ground of secrecy unless the disclosure is certified by the Attorney-General to be prejudicial to security, defence, international relation, police detection, Cabinet or Cabinet Committee's deliberations or proceedings.

[25] The Parliamentary Commissioner Act has gone a step further than the recommendations of Whyatt Report. The Whyatt Report recommended that internal minutes within a ministry in the U.K. should be regarded as confidential and the Parliamentary Commissioner should not be entitled to see these Minutes. The Parliamentary Commissioner Act gives the Parliamentary Commissioner full power to see all documents, including internal departmental Minutes. Further, the Whyatt Report upheld the doctrine of Crown privilege and recommended that a minister could have the power to object to the production of any document on the ground that it was contrary to the public interest that the document should be disclosed. The Act expressly states that Crown privilege shall not apply and that no minister can raise this objection to the production of documents.

informal atmosphere and it has not so far been found necessary to use the Ombudsman's powers to summon witnesses. During the investigation in Denmark, civil servants are given full opportunity to defend themselves. As a special protection, the civil servant complained against may at any time demand that the matter be referred to a disciplinary investigation under the procedure of the Civil Service Act. The Ombudsman will then discontinue his investigation and transmit the case to the appropriate administrative authority, stating what had happened and enclosing the information obtained. However, no civil servant has so far exercised this right.

In the event of refusal to comment upon the complaint the Parliamentary Commissioner in the U.K. can refer the matter to the High Court for consideration as if it were a contempt of that court.

2. Magnitude of complaints

On the whole, the number of complaints received by the Ombudsman in Sweden, Finland, Denmark, Norway, and New Zealand have been generally between 1,500 and 2,000 a year. Between 75 to 90 per cent of complaints were either dismissed or did not call for any action after investigation.[26] The proportion for such complaints was as follows:—

Sweden	79 per cent
Finland	84 per cent
Denmark	94 per cent
Norway	84 per cent
New Zealand	79 per cent

The comparative figures of complaints and their disposal in some of these countries in 1975 was as shown in Table 1.

[26]The Ombudsman does not reject a case merely because there is a judicial remedy. One of the cases the Danish Ombudsman examined was about the quality of the coffee served in a Danish prison. His investigation revealed that the contractor supplying the coffee was the brother-in-law of the prison governor. Matters were straightened by the Ombudsman and the prisoners got a good quality of coffee thereafter.

TABLE 1

Number of complaints and their disposal by Ombudsmen in 1975

	Sweden	*Denmark*	*France*	U. K. *PCA*	*Health Service Commissioner*
Total number of complaints	3,602	2,009	3,150	928	610
Rejected for lack of jurisdiction	1,309(36.34%)	1,098(54.65%)	967(30.70%)	595(64.12%)	377(61.80%)
Investigated but no action taken	1,245(34.56%)	684(34.05%)	664(21.08%)	154(16.59%)	61(10%)
Action taken	648(17.99%)	233(11.60%)	410(13.02%)	90(9.70%)	67(10.98%)

The annual report of Danish Ombudsman contains 35 to 40 cases at length. In 1975, 1889 cases were disposed of, out of which 1098 were rejected. Out of 797 cases formally investigated, 233 resulted in critical comments and in various types of recommendations.

Out of 8,458 cases received by the New Zealand Ombudsman from 1 October 1962 to 31 March 1975, only 4,773 (56 per cent) were found fit to be investigated and 3,685 (44 per cent) cases were rejected as lying outside his jurisdiction. Only 10 per cent complaints were found to be justified. Not only cases of malfeasence but those of misfeasence or non-feasence have been taken up by the Ombudsman in New Zealand.[27]

The average number of cases investigated in a typical year by the Swedish Ombudsman is 2,293, out of which 1,893 originate from complaints. About 72 per cent cases result in recjection or no action, 23 per cent cases result in warnings and admonitions and hardly 5 per cent in prosecution.

In Norway, the total complaints received in 1976 were 1,379 out of which 52 per cent cases were investigated. During the first eight years of the office from 1963 to 1970 the Ombudsman made a criticism or recommendation in 547 cases out of a total of 2,351 complaints which he investigated. This is proportion of 23.3 per cent. Two-thirds of the complaints received were not accepted either because they lay outside the Ombudsman's competence, or were barred by limitation, or right to redress to a higher administrative authority was available or were groundless.[28]

The U.K. Parliamentary Commissioner received 8,500 complaints since 1967 through Members of Parliament. About 5,000 were not accepted for investigation and about 3,500

[27]Sound principles of administrative jurisprudence like clarity of order, well reasoned-decisions, and equity of pre-emption have been developed by the New Zealand Parliamentary Commissioner.

[28]A number of refused cases are, however, passed on to the competent authority. In many cases of an inquiring nature, the Ombudsman tries to give advice where possible, short of performing the work of a regular legal consultant. Quite a large number of complaints concern administrative decisions and many of these relate to procedure. In some cases, there were grounds for criticism; in some. redress was given by the administration concerned.

were investigated. During the same period about 8,000 complaints were sent direct by the public. At the end of the year 1976, 505 complaints out of a total of 815 submitted through Members of Parliament had to be rejected. Similary in 1977, 528 complaints were rejected. Of these, 151 were rejected—nearly 33 per cent—on grounds of lack of jurisdiction. Over one-third of the cases related to departments which were not covered by the provisions of the U.K. Parliamentary Commissioner Act, 1967. About 17 per cent did not involve administrative functions and 13 per cent were excluded because there was a right of appeal to a tribunal.[29] It is found that about 63 per cent of complaints do not fall within his purview either because the department to which they relate do not fall within his purview or because there is no administrative function involved in the complaint or there is a right of appeal provided to a tribunal; maladministration has been found in 16 per cent of cases actually investigated and action taken by the Ombudsman.

(3) *Office organization and staff*

In the matter of selection of his staff, the Ombudsman in Scandinavian countries enjoys a good deal of independence. The number, salaries and pensions of members of the staff are generally fixed by Parliament in the same manner as prescribed in Parliament's rules or procedure for its own officials. However, in the selection of the members of staff or in dispensing with their services, the Ombudsman has unfettered power. In Denmark, the staff normally consists of ten officers, five of which are legally qualified. The staff there does not change when the Ombudsman changes.

In Finland, the Ombudsman has only two full-time and six part-time assistants. In Norway, the staff of the Ombudsman is appointed by the Parliamentary Committee on the recom-

[29]The remaining rejected cases related to personnel matters in respect of the civil service and armed services which are outside the scope of the U.K. Parlimentary Commissioner Act. Only in some of the cases investigated, the Commissioner found an element of maladministration of a culpable nature. Most of the cases concerned errors and delays attributable to pressure of work.

mendation of the Ombudsman and their salaries are fixed in the same manner as in the case of Parliament's staff.

In New Zealand, however, the staff of the Ombudsman will be such as is approved by the Prime Minister and neither he nor his staff come under the Public Service Act. The peculiar feature of the British practice is that the Parliamentary Commissioner in the U.K. is not a lawyer. Even his staff of some fifty officials does not include a qualified lawyer either.[30]

(4) *Attainment of objectives*

On the whole, it is seen that more than 50 per cent of the complaints are dismissed in Scandinavian countries for various reasons without investigation. A number of cases are dismissed on the ground that the complaints relate to persons or matters outside the jurisdiction of Ombudsman, e.g., court judgements, municipal administrations, or private affairs. As far as possible, these complaints are referred to the competent authority or the complainants are advised about the authorities to which they should apply. It is only about 10 per cent of the cases investigated that the Ombudsman has found it necessary to find fault or put forward recommendations of one kind or another to the authorities concerned. As a special point, it may be mentioned that in some cases a civil servant instead of exercising his discretion in each individual case, as he should do, follows a uniform rule established in practice. In such cases, the Ombudsman has questioned the decision and recommended reconsideration.

In Denmark, as a result of the investigation, it is usually found that there is no basis for criticism of the civil servant. Complaints are made in such cases because the administrative officers had not indicated the reasons for their decisions. By giving complainant an explanation, it has been possible for the Danish Ombudsman to set his mind at rest. By and large, the Scandinavian experience with the institution of Ombudsman

[30]It is not because of a famine of trained lawyers that no lawyer has been appointed on the staff of the Ombudsman in England but because the Ombudsman wanted to have people who know their way around government and could get to the root of the matter. Therefore, people with experience in public administration had been appointed.

does not show that its adoption has resulted in a loss of efficiency or diminished the sense of responsibility of the civil servants to the Minister.

The limitations[31] of the British Parliamentary Commissioner have been severely criticized by the British Press.[32] However, the working of this new British institution, even within limitations, shows that it can help the citizen a lot.[33] As mentioned earlier, the U.K. Parliamentary Commissioner, who started his work on 1 April 1967, had by the end of October 1967 received 816 complaints through Members of Parliament. Of these, 405 cases were outside his jurisdiction, of the remaining 411, 125 were completed and the results reported to the Members of Parliament concerned. Among the latter, there were only 10 instances of maladministration. The quick action by the Parliamentary Commissioner has created a good impact on the general public and those in authority. For instance, one pensioner, Mr. Frederick Blake of Wimborne Dorsite, had been struggling with the ministry and its predecessor, the Ministry of Pensions for several years. When he was called in 1942, he had to sell his grocery business for only £50. Subsequently, he did not have sufficient capital to start it again, and he, therefore, claimed an additional pension on the ground that his standard of living had been lowered. When his case was referred to the Parliamentary Commissioner, he was awarded pension arrears of £540, and a weekly pension of £4-14 Sh. He could also, as a result of further inquiries, receive some additional arrears. In his communication, sent to Sir Richard Glyn, the concerned Member of Parliament, Sir Edmund wrote: "The Ministry has now centralised the work of awarding allowances for lowered standards of occupation, so it may be hoped

[31]Local government, the police, the magistracy and matters in the public service are excluded from his jurisdiction.

[32]*The Times* (London), in an editorial dated 2 February 1967, wondered whether the British Parliamentary Commissioner was "Ombudsman" or "Ombudsmouse".

[33]In an interview with the author, Lord Hailsham, Lord Chancellor of the U.K. (who was in India in January 1971 for the Fourth Commonwealth Law Conference) expressed that the institution of Parliamentary Commissioner has immensely improved and is doing very good work for the public.

that similar mistakes will not recur. I find that there has been maladministration in the Ministry of Social Security in handling this case, but I think their proposals for correcting it are entirely satisfactory."[34]

The Parliamentary Commissioner of the U.K. is not as effective and as useful as Ombudsman in the Scandinavian countries. This is due to the restrictive nature of the Parliamentary enactment. In regard to the Parliamentary Commissioner in the U.K., the general criticism is that there is too much investigation but the net result is too little. In New Zealand, the Ombudsman finds maladministration in about 15 per cent of the cases; same is the position in Denmark. In Britain, the Commissioner's corresponding figure, as given in his annual reports, was 10 per cent in 1967 and 1968. It was 16 per cent in 1969, but in 1969 things were not normal. Out of the 48 cases of maladministration in 1969, 26, i.e. over half, were related to Inland Revenue and consisted mainly of "errors and delays attributed to pressure of work of the tax offices who were severely overburdened.[35]

The Commissioner's productivity ratio is thus 10 per cent. This modest figure gives an impression that the standards of public administration in Britain are quite high. But there is also a criticism that it is excessively wasteful to hold a hundred investigations in order to remedy ten grievances. In the 90 per cent rejected cases, the Commissioner explained to the administration that the official action was right, though it was not understood by the complainant and a sense of injustice resulted. This is equally a valuable service, since it is as much desirable to remove genuine grievances where the action is right as where it is wrong. The Ombudsman also acts as a public relations officer who justifies the actions of administration to those who are most aggrieved at them. This shows that the public service should look on the Ombudsman as a friend rather than an enemy. According to H.W.R. Wade, "He is a lightening conductor for bonafide grievances and will keep the departments out of many political storms in the long run."

[34]*The Guardian*, London, 13 September 1967.

[35]Parliamentary Commissioner for Administration, *Annual Report*, 1969, para 9.

THE SACHSEN-HAUSEN CASE

The case of the Sachsen-hausen prisoners is of great interest as it involved the foreign secretary personally and provoked a controversy about ministerial responsibility. Out of the funds paid over by Germany to Britain, the Foreign Office was responsible for dealing with claims for compensation made by victims of Nazi persecution. The government rejected claims from twelve British prisoners who had been held at Sachsenhausen camp on the ground that they had not been held in the concentration camp proper and had not suffered those conditions. They had to struggle a lot to establish the genuineness of their claim. The Foreign Officer's final refusal came within the Parliament Commissioner's time limit of twelve months when he began work on 1 April 1967. The Commissioner upheld the complaint and reported that Foreign Office had decided in the first place "on partial and largely irrelevant information" and maintained their decision "in disregard of additional information and evidence."[36] Finally, the compensation was paid. The foreign secretary (then Mr. George Brown) told the House of Commons that though he did not agree with the findings of maladministration but he felt that the commissioner's report had to be acted upon. He felt that by paying compensation he was "probably being unfair to quite a number of gallant men who have suffered very badly but who were outside the compensation scheme". On the doctrine of ministerial responsibility, the foreign secretary felt that the officials concerned should not be held responsible and that the whole reponsibility should be that of the minister in this case. In a later report, the Select Committee criticised the above statement of the foreign secretary and rejected his point about unfairness and also recorded dissatisfaction with the evidence given to them by the Foreign Office.

[36]Parliamentary Commissioner for Administration, *Third Report*, 1967-68, para 6.

CHAPTER VIII

Lokpal and Lokayuktas—Indian Ombudsman

NEED FOR INDEPENDENT REDRESS MACHINERY

In the foregoing chapter, we discussed at length the functions and role of the Ombudsman in the Scandinavian countries, the United Kingdom and New Zealand, the limitations circumscribing his jurisdiction and the usefulness and viability of the institution. The need for this important institution is much more pronounced in the under developed countries of Asia. The institution of Ombudsman or the Parliamentary Commissioner is gaining increasing recognition as a powerful instrument for redressing the citizen's complaints arising from the callousness of the administrative machinery or the transgression by it of the individual's rights. This institution is also useful in focussing attention on the improvement of administrative procedure through continuous criticism of the working of the bureaucratic system as revealed in the enquiries instituted by the Ombudsman on the citizen's complaints or even on his own where he has the powers to do so. This helps to stimulate government departments to give attention to underlying purposes and policies and not merely to decide each case as it arises. The Ombudsman can push a department towards clarifying vague statutory standards and filling the gaps in law; he can protect parties against undue delay by digging into causes of delay. In brief, such a functionary can combine two major tasks of investigating complaints in specific cases and making sustained enquiries into possible ways to strengthen administrative procedure.

In the underdeveloped countries, the case for the Ombudsman is even stronger. "The pressure for rapid development implies that individual rights and the fine points of fair legal procedure are more likely to be disregarded in the interests of speed, efficiency and the broader public interest. Also, the bureaucrats in many former colonies have inherited from their colonial masters an attitude of superiority rather than service, an insolence of office which often leads to arbitrariness."[1] In the present times, with the activities of Government of under developed countries expanding at a fast pace, the exercise of discretion by administrative authorities cannot be done away with nor can it be rigidly regulated by instructions, orders, or resolutions. The need for ensuring the rectitude of the administrative machinery in this vast discretionary field is not only obvious but paramount. Where the citizen can establish the genuineness of his case, it is plainly the duty of the state to set right the wrong done to him. The need for giving this approach a concrete form arises from the fact that parliamentary supervision by itself cannot fully ensure to the citizen the rectitude over the entire area covered by administrative discretion. Nor have the various administrative tiers and hierarchies proved adequate for the purpose. An assumption of unquestionable superiority of the administration, a feeling of the sanctity of authority and neglect or indifference on the part of a superior authority may prevent a citizen from obtaining justice even at the final stage of the administrative system. It is in these circumstances or in instances where he is unable, for some compelling reasons, to seek other remedies open to him, that an independent institution for redress of grievances must be provided within the democratic system of government. It has to be an intstitution in which the average citizen will have faith and confidence and through which he will be able to secure quick and inexpensive justice.

In view of the shortcomings of the traditional protections against administrative arbitrariness, the office of the Ombudsman, in the words of the Whyatt Report, has a number of desirable characteristics, which argue for its adoption:

> First, there is the principle of impartial investigation. If a citizen makes a complaint against the conduct of a civil servant, the matter is investi-

[1]Donald C. Rowat, "Recent Development in Ombudsmanship. A review article", *Canadian Public Administration.* Vol. 10, March 1967, pp. 45-46.

gated and reported upon by the Ombudsman, who is an impartial authority entirely independent of the Administration. Secondly, the impartial authority acts on behalf of Parliament although he is also protecting the interests of the individual complainant. Thirdly, the investigation is conducted openly. Fourthly, the method of submitting complaints and the investigation of complaints is very informal.[2]

The main advantages of the Ombudsman in under-developed countries were summed up as follows by the U.N. Seminar on Judicial and Other Remedies against the Abuse of Administrative Authority.

1. The Ombudsman is not only an instrument of Parliament for supervising the administration, but also a protector of the rights of the individual. The institution not only affords a fulfilment of the sense of justice and fair play inherent in every individual, but also provides supervision on behalf of the people of the day-to-day activities of their government even if the government is elected by the people at specified periods.
2. There is the principle of impartial investigation by an authority entirely independent of the administration.
3. An investigation can be started by the Ombudsman not only on a complaint by an individual but also on his own intiative as a result of information he might acquire from inspections, press reports or other sources. Courts, on the other hand, are seized of case only upon complaint of the interested parties.
4. The investigation of the Ombudsman is conducted informally. In investigating complaints, the Ombudsman has free access to all the files of the administration and he can demand explanations from the officials or authorities concerned. Administrative tribunals and courts, on the other hand are bound by formal rules in hearing cases and have more limited powers of inspection.
5. The Ombudsman has considerable flexibility in the form of action which he can take in a given case. Various forms of action are open to him. If after investigation he finds that an official has handled a case wrongly or unjustly or made an erroneous or improper decision, the Ombudsman can

[2]*Whyatt Report*, pp. 67-72.

recommend that proceedings be instituted against such an official or he may administer a reprimand and include the case in his report to Parliament. His intervention may also take the form of persuasion instead of a critical report.[3]

The need for an Ombudsman in a country like India arises from several reasons. With the taking up by the government of developmental and welfare responsibilities of a vast magnitude, the points of contact between the administration and the citizens have multiplied substantially in recent years. The size of the administrative machinery has proliferated. The innumerable economic controls, which have been adopted for ensuring that development proceeds in accordance with the objectives and priorities of the five year plans, have tended to regulate economic activity and citizens life in several respects. As an accumulative results of all these developments, the magnitude of the citizens' grievances against administration has increased a good deal.

In India, the main argument for the Ombudsman derives from the shift from a laissez-faire to a welfare state. There has been a tremendous growth in the range and complexity of discretion to the executive. Millions of administrative decisions are made each year, and if some of these decisions are arbitrary or unjustified, there is no easy way for the ordinary citizen to gain redress. The need for an Ombudsman is greater in India than in the U.K. The position regarding the United Kingdom was summarized in 1961, by Lord Shawcross in the following words:

> The general standards of administration in this country (U.K.) are high, probably indeed higher than in any other. But with the existence of a great bureaucracy there are inevitably occasions, not insignificant in number, when through error or indifference, injustice is done—or appears to be done. The man of substance can deal with these situations. . . . But too often the little man, the ordinary humble citizen, is incapable of asserting himself. . . .[4]

[3] *Report of U.N. Seminar on Judicial and Other Remedies against the Abuse of Administrative Authority*, Stockholm, Sweden, (12 to 25 June 1962), pp. 15-16.

[4] Whyatt Report, p. xiii of the Preface.

(The Rt. Hon. Lord Shawcross was the Chairman of 'Justice' which sponsored this report.)

The need for an independent agency to look into the citizens' complaints against administration is apparent from the review in the preceding chapters of the nature and magnitude of citizens complaints and the inadequacies of the existing machinery for their redress. The necessity of having an independent machinery for redress of grievances is highlighted by the recent trend towards political instability in several of the States of India.

The machinery for redress of the citizen's grievances at present available at the Centre and in the States is not only singularly indequate but also not much effective. Parliament's watch over the administration, in particular in the latter's relationship with the citizens, is too broad in character and seriously constrained by several limitations. It is only once in a while that Parliament takes up the cudgels for the citizens directly or through its committees. The right to complain to one's Member of Parliament does not meet the problem, because of the cumbersome process involved in getting redress. Moreover, while Parliament does exercise general control of administration, particularly in matters of wide public interest, it is doubtful whether it can play a really effective role in affording redress to individuals in specific cases. The work of Parliament in modern times has become increasingly complex, and in some countries, legislators do not have the time and the means to examine individual complaints and see if any abuse has been committed by civil servants.

The overall position, in India, as of today is that the courts can provide redress only in a limited way and the redress machinery, which is an integral part of executive branch of the government, cannot have an objective and impartial look at the complaints in every case. Eighty-six Acts provide for final decision by departments in which no appeal has been provided for, or if it is provided for, the appellate authority is the government itself. It is true that these decisions are subject to judicial review by virtue of Articles 33 and 226 of the Constitution. But Article 226 which provides for the power of issue of writs can be exercised by courts only to correct errors of jurisdiction or acts contrary to law or violation of the Constitution, or errors apparent on the face of the record. Besides, the process of litigation is costly; often beyond the means of ordinary citizen. Apart from cost, there are many other factors that tend to delay redress of grievances. The number of appeals is so large that even if the court in first instance decides in favour of the plaintiff the implementation of the decision can be avoided for any number of years. Such complaints are often heard in respect of decisions of industrial disputes' tribunals.

As noted earlier, a number of attempts, though not adequate enough, have been made in the past 20 years to evolve measures and machinery to meet the problem of grievances. An O & M division was set up in 1954 at the Centre for improving the speed of disposal of government business. The Union Department of Administrative Reforms set up in 1964 (with which the O & M division was amalgamated) has carried out several "composite" organizational studies, touching inter alia upon modification of procedure to remove the citizens' difficulties. O & M units have come up in many Ministries and in almost all State secretariats. Other important developments have been the setting up of complaint cells, anti-corruption units, vigilance commissions at the Centre and in the States, special police establishment (to enquire into cases of corruption) and the Central Commissioner of Public Grievances. The emphasis in more recent times has been on combating corruption, improvement of the redress machinery at the district level and the search for more viable alternatives. As regards corruption, the Vigilance Commissioner today cannot take notice of allegations against government employees earning less than Rs. 1,000 a month. This means, that cases of "speed money" which usually occur at lower levels, escape the net.

The ineffectiveness of the departmantal machinery for looking into the citizens' complaints was significantly highlighted by the commissioner of public grievances in his report given in October 1966. His main findindgs, which are even valid today, were as follows: (i) The existing government machinery is not adequate to deal with complaints from the public (ii) The expectation of the government that in each ministry an independent person unconnected with the original government decision which give rise to the complaint would bring to bear upon the grievances a corrective, has not been fulfilled. A complaint is generally examined by the same person against whose decision (or the decision in which he had a hand) it is made. (iii) If senior officers of the level of Joint Secretaries cannot be spared for looking into complaints in each Ministry/Department, the institution of complaints officer should be scrapped.

The creation of the Ombudsman institution at the Central and State levels in India would bring in its wake several advantages. We shall discuss this aspect in detail in a subsequent section of the chapter. At this stage, it needs to be emphasised the fact that the citizen has a reasonable opportunity of presenting his case before an authority which is in a different hierarchy from the authority which passes the order and which is independent and impartial, would in itself be a source of satisfaction to him even if the result of investigation is unfavourable.

Another important consideration which is relevant to the establishment of the Ombudsman institutions in India is that the indirect effects of such a machinery are likely to be much more pronounced than the direct benefits accruing from the redress of complaints. The very existence of an Ombudsman would act as a powerful preventive influence to ensure speedy and impartial decisions in matters affecting the citizens at large.[5] This point is examined at some length later.

BIRTH OF THE IDEA

In India, the idea of an independent authority for looking into citizens' grievances really originated as a part of the search for solutions to the growing corrupt practices in the fifties. In 1952, there was animated discussion in Parliament on the various facets of the problem of corruption in government at the time of consideration of the Prevention of Corruption (Second Amendment) Bill, the Criminal Law Amendment Bill, and the Commissions of Inquiry Bill. The problem evoked considerable

[5]According to T.E. Utley there can be little doubt that the Ombudsman has in some degree a psycho-therapeutic function in relation to habitual malcontents. The incurable lunatic with a persecution mania will no doubt not be mollified by the knowledge that his case has been competently examined, but many complaints against the civil services, in Denmark as elsewhere, arise from misunderstanding, which a minor investigation and a few words of independent, authoritative and courteous explanation can dispel."

interest on several subsequent occasions, e.g., during the consideration of the Resolution moved in 1954 for the establishment of a Commission of Enquiry to examine the administrative set up and procedures of work of the Government of India, the Prevention of Corruption (amendment) Bill in 1955, etc. The demand of an independent agency to enquire into complaints of corruption prevalent at the higher levels (which was the forerunner to the proposal for Ombudsman-type of institution in India) was for the first time made formally and authoritatively by the then Chairman of the University Grants Commission and former Minister of Finance, Shri C.D. Deshmukh. Delivering a lecture in Madras on 11 July 1959, he observed: "An uneasy public hears of nepotism, high-handedness, gerrymandering, feathering of nests through progeny, and a dozen other sins of omission and commission, and yet is helpless for lack of precise data, facts and figures, evidence and proof." He had asked for the establishment of a "high-level, impartial, standing judicial tribunal to investigate and report on complaints or lying of information" and further promised that if such a tribunal was set up, "I shall be happy to make a beginning by lodging half a dozen reports myself." Later on, in his private correspondence with Pt. Jawaharlal Nehru, the then Prime Minister of India, Shri Deshmukh claimed to be in possession of evidence that improprieties have been committed by members of the government, including the Ministers of the Cabinet rank. He was willing to divulge the information only before an independent judicial tribunal, if one was set up for the purpose.[6]

During the last ten years or so, public opinion and Parliamentary debate has been focussed increasingly on the desirability of setting up of effective machinery to look into the grievances of individuals against the administration. The importance of such machinery was urged by Third All India Law Conference held on 12-14 August 1962. The question of

[6]Pt. Nehru opposed the formation of such a tribunal, at a Press Conference on 8 January 1960, and also in Parliament, on the grounds that such a tribunal would be repugnant to democratic practice and would create an atmosphere of distrust and mutual accusation. He suggested the appointment of a judge for looking into the allegations made by Dr. Deshmukh.

appointing a Parliamentary Commissioner figured in the Lok Sabha on 3 April 1963, during the debate on the Demands for Grants of the Ministry of Law. Dr. L.M. Singhvi, stressing the need for the setting up of an Ombudsman institution, justified it on the following grounds:

> That the institution of Ombudsman would enable the citizen to effectively ventilate his grievances; that the question hour in Parliament and writing letters to Ministers are no substitute for it; that the availabie judicial remedy is not adequate as the courts are hide-bound by limitations of procedure and technicalities; that through it Parliament would effectively function in individual cases; and that it would ensure independen: impartial justice in matters of administrative excesses in individual cases.

In reply to the debate, the Minister for Law, inter alia, stated:

> There are various points of view to be considered and all that can be said is that this matter should be kept under consideration. . . . And Parliament may discuss it from time to time. In this country, to make it effective a constitutional provision should be made, as for the office of the Election Commissioner, or the office of the Comptroller and Auditor-General. So, there are many things which have to be considered. All that I can say is that my view on the legal side of the matter is that we have to amend the Constitution to set up any such office and define its functions and possibly even the procedure which it has to follow.

Shri P.B. Gajendragadkar, the then Chief Justice of India, in his analysis of the "Role of Administration in a Democratic Welfare State" on 15 July 1963, commended for careful examination the idea of an independent authority for the redress of public grievances. In October, 1963, the Madras Provincial Bar Association supported the creation of the institution of Ombudsman for India. Following up on the idea of the Ombudsman type machinery for redress of citizens' grievances, moved by him in Parliament in 1963, Dr. L.M. Singhvi moved a resolution in Parliament on the 3 Aprll 1964 for setting up an Ombudsman-type mechanism. The resolution sought to express the opinion of the House that:

> An officer of Parliament to be known as the People's Procurator (Lok Ayukta), broadly analogous to the institution of Ombudsman in Sweden, Denmark and New Zealand, be appointed, under suitable legislation, for the purpose of providing effective and impartial investigation machinery for public grievances, for eradicating corruption at all levels,

for redressing administrative wrongs and excesses, for securing the liberties of citizens, and generally for strengthening the basic foundations of Parliamentary democracy as a system of Government.

The above resolution was not adopted by the Parliament as the government had not by then made up its mind about setting up an independent institution of the type envisaged.

In September 1963, the Administrative Reforms Committee of Rajashtan recommended the appointment of an Ombudsman to look into the complaints against high state officials and Ministers. It was proposed that an Ombudsman should be appointed by the President on the advice of the Chief Justice of India; he should possess the status of the Chief Justice of the High Court, be responsible to the State Legislature, and should submit an annual report to it. He should be removable only by a two-thirds majority vote of the legislature and should hold office for a period of three years. His functions would be to keep a watch over executive actions and investigate cases in which action taken by Government agencies was either illegal, unjust, or arbitrary.

Addressing the All India Congress Committee on the working of the 'Kamraj Plan'[7] at Jaipur on 3 November 1963, the late Prime Minister, Pt. Jawaharlal Nehru, welcomed the idea of an Ombudsman who should have the authority to deal with the charges against the Prime Minister and command respect and confidence from all. In December 1963, while accepting the recommendation of the Committee on Prevention of Corruption[8] for the setting up of the Central Vigilance

[7]K. Kamaraj was the then President of the Indian National Congress. On his advice, the then Prime Minister, Pt. Jawaharlal Nehru asked some Central Ministers and State Chief Ministers to resign their posts to enable them to devote full time for the party work. This came to be known as 'Kamraj Plan'.

[8]The Committee on Prevention of Corrpution (popularly known as the Santhanam Committee) was set up in 1962 by the Government of India in the Ministry of Home Affairs. The Committee gave its final report to the Government on 31 March 1964. The Committee recommended the creation of a Directorate General of Complaints and Redress as part of the Central Vigilance Commission. The Government of India did not accept this recommendation as they felt that corruption and maintenance of integrity in the public services was quite a big

Commission, the Government also promised to examine further the question of evolving a machinery for dealing with the grievances of the citizens against the administration.

The appointment of an independent officer of Parliament known as Ombudsman, which could deal with the public grievances, for eradicating corruption at all levels, for redressing administrative wrongs and excesses, for securing the liberties of citizens, and generally for strengthening the basic foundations of Parliamentary democracy as a system of Government was urged again in a Private Member's Resolution by Dr. L.M. Singhvi in Lok Sabha in April 1964. Dr. Singhvi moved a second time a resolution in the Lok Sabha for setting up an Ombudsman-type of institution. The resolution read as follows:

> An officer of Parliament to be known as the People's Procurator (Lok Ayukta), broadly analogous to the institution of Ombudsman in Sweden, Denmark and New Zealand, be appointed under suitable legislation, for the purpose of providing effective and impartial investigation machinery for public grievances, for eradicating corruption at all levels, for redressing administrative wrongs and excesses, for securing the liberties of citizens, and generally for strengthening the basic foundations of Parliamentary democracy as a system of Government.

The Lok Sabha discussed the Resolution on the 3 April and 22 April 1964. During the course of the debate, all sections of the House expressed support to the proposal. However, the Resolution was withdrawn by Dr. Singhvi on an assurance given by the Minister of State for Home Affairs that the Government would get the entire matter investigated in full detail.

In pursuance of a demand made in Parliament, the Government of India constituted a Special Consultative Group of Members of Parliament in early 1965 on administrative reforms. At its fourth meeting held on 8-9 June 1965, the Group appointed three sub-committees with specific reference to public grievances, namely (i) sub-committee on controls, with Home Minister as its Chairman and Shri S.L. Saraf, M.P. as its Convener, (ii) sub-committee on administrative tribunals and

---

problem and the Central Vigilance Commission should not be burdened with additional responsibility.

machinery for redress of grievances at Centre (Chairman, Minister in the Ministry of Home Affairs; Convener: Shri B.K.P. Sinha), and (iii) sub-committee on district administration—removal of citizens' grievances—with Deputy Home Minister as its Chairman and Shri S.N. Chaturvedi as its Convener.

The sub-committee on controls was asked to explore the possibilities of better administration of controls, particularly those relating to the grant of permits and quota or licences. Normally, the persons who fail to get licences, permits, etc. complain that the controls are not being administered impartially. The sub-committee examined the scope and feasibility of entrusting regulatory controls to an independent judicial body. It was felt that such a body would help to reinforce the citizens faith in impartiality of the administration and also help remove the disadvantages which the ordinary citizens suffer under the existing system of controls. The group agreed that the decision-making authority should be free from all influences and pressures. The current practice is that after the licensing committee has supported an application, its decision is screened by a review committee. Personal hearing is also granted in case of individual grievances. The sub-committee favoured the idea of strengthening the review committee, rather than appointing a High Court Judge at the State level and a Supreme Court Judge at the Centre to function as an impartial body for the purpose.

The sub-committee on administrative tribunals and machinery for redress of grievances at the Centre examined in detail the implications of introducing the French system of administrative law and administrative tribunals and of an Ombudsman-cum-Parliamentary Commissioner. It came to the conclusion that grievances of citizens against the administration could be of two types: (i) Grievances arising out of exercise of discretion not conforming to the wishes of the applicant even though the discretion is lawful and unbiased, and (ii) grievances arising out of maladministration like exercise of discretion with bias, negligence, delay, harassment, extortion, discourtesy, etc. The sub-committee felt that these two broad types needed different kinds of machineries of redress. Grievances of the first type could be profitably looked into by an appellate authority, tribunal or a court, while the second type of complaints would need to be redressed through an independent prosecutor like the Procurator in the Eastern European countries, Ombudsman in the Scandinavian countries, or Parliamentary Commissioner in New Zealand. The sub-committee was further of the view that in order to inspire public confidence, the machinery for either type should be manifestly independent of the executive.

The sub-committee thought that the concepts of administrative tribunals and Ombudsman were complementary and not exclusive of each other. Both these institutions co-existed in the Scandinavian countries. The sub-committee agreed that administrative tribunals even in their beset form would not obviate the need of an Ombudsman and that studies of Ombudsman and Administrative tribunals should be taken up simultaneously, preferably by the same committee. The sub-committee added that for carrying out a thorough study of administrative tribunals and Ombudsman in foreign countries, a committee consisting of administrators, jurists, Members of Parliament and others should be appointed by government. The reports of these sub-committee were considered by the special consultative group of Members of Parliament on Administrative Reforms. But it took wider view of the problem and favoured the setting up of a high-powered enquiry commission on administrative reforms, which should also look into the question of machinery for redress of citizens' grievances. It even formulated the terms of reference for the proposed Administrative Reforms Commission. The demand for such a Commission was also voiced in Parliament and in the Press during 1963-65.

The (all India) Administrative Reforms Commission (A.R C.) was appointed in January 1966 to make recommendations on the reorganisation of the public administration system of the country, with a view to making it a fit instrument for carrying out the social and economic policies of the Government and achieving social and economie goals as well as for making the administration more responsive to the people. The Commission's detailed terms of reference covered 10 major areas. The tenth being "Problems of redress of citizens' grievances". Listed under this heading were two sets of problems: (i) the adequacy of the existing arrangements for the redress of grievances; and (ii) need for introduction of any new machinery or special institution for redress of grievances. The A.R.C. constituted a study team on 25 June 1966 to look into the problems of redress of citizens' grievances with Shri Charu Choudhary Director Incharge of Research, Indian Law Institute, as its Chairman. On the basis of the report of the study team, given towards the end of August 1966, the Administrative Reforms Commission submitted an interim report on the subject to the government on 20 October 1966.

A.R.C. PROPOSALS FOR LOKPAL AND LOKAYUKTA

The major recommendation of the Commission related to setting up of two Ombudsmen-type of institutions, viz., "The Lok Pal and Lokayukta". Under the A.R.C. scheme the Lok Pal (Protector of the People) was expected to deal with the complaints against the Ministers and the secretaries of government posted at the Centre and in the States. Further there was to be appointed a Lokayukta[9] (commissioner of the people) in each State and one for the Centre to look into the complaints against public officials other than ministers and secretaries to the government.

The A.R.C. noted that in recent years there has been an increasing regulation of the citizen's life. In the past, the citizen was affected by the activities of a comparatively small number of state functionaries and in respect of only a small sector of his daily life. Today, he is exposed at numerous points to the impact of the multifarious activities of the administration ranging over a vast field, and in the process the citizens' grievances have multiplied. The spread of education and growing political enlightenment has brought about, in the average citizen, a greater awareness of his own rights and needs and has changed his attitude of resignation to the fate. Thus, the main issue before the Commission was how to provide the citizen with an institution to which he can have easy access for the

[9]The title "Lokayukta" was first used by Dr. L.M. Singhvi in a Resolution on the subject moved by him in Lok Sabha in 1964. Dr. Singhvi used it as equivalent to the "People's Procurator".

redress of his grievances. If the citizen has a feeling of grievance, whatever be its nature, the state must try to satisfy him, after due investigation, that the grievance is untenable, in which case no action is called for, or false, in which case he must answer for having made a baseless accusation. In the context of change environment, the administration's attitude of complacency or taking the citizen for granted has to yeild place to the exploration of ways and means to remove genuine discontent amongst the people and to promote a sense of satisfaction with, and recognition of, the merits of the actions taken by administration in pursuance of state policies.

The Commission went into: (i) the adequacy of the existing arrangements for the redress of grievances, and (ii) the need for introduction of any new machinery or special institution for redress of grievances. The urgency and dimension of this problem were impressed upon the Commission by the large volume of both official and non-official opinion, particularly by the Ministers of Central and State governments. The Commission also took "note of the oft-expressed public outcry against the prevalence of corruption, the existence of wide-spread inefficiency and the unresponsiveness of administration to popular needs." The Commission came to the conclusion that "the answer to this outcry lies not in expressions or reiteration of Government's general satisfaction with the administration's achievements or its attempts generally to justify itself but in the provision of a machinery which will examine such complaints and sift the genuine from the false or the untenable so that administration's failure and achievements can be publicly viewed in their correct perspective." The Commission felt that the "problems brooked no delay. An urgent routine of this problem would strengthen the hands of the Government in administering the laws of the land, its policies, 'without fear or favour, affection or ill-will' and enable it to gain public faith and confidence without which social and economic progress would be impossible."

The main arguments advanced by the Administrative Reforms Commission for the creation of Ombudsman-type of redressal machinery were as follows:

1. The establishment of the Ombudsman-type of machinery will

help to arrest deterioration in the people's faith and confidence in the administration and the political executives by providing independent, impartial and effective channels for redress of citizens' grievances. Such faith and fair amount of satisfaction with the administration are of utmost importance for the success of Indian democracy.

2. The institution of the Ombudsman would not only serve as an impartial forum of enquiry against acts of maladministration and corruption, but also ensure speedy and cheap remedy to the aggrieved. Writ petitions and other judicial proceedings are costly and cumbersome. Justice delayed is justice denied, and the cost of it is ruinous.
3. The new machinery, by investigating complaints, would help correct the current exaggerated notions of corruption, inefficiency and lack of fair play in higher quarters in Government. Allegations without enquiries are distorting the image of administration and political executives. An independent machinery will help to redress the citizens' genuine complaints, to sort out the unjustified complaints and to protect the public officials in the right exercise of discretion.
4. The very existence of the institution would act as a deterrent to acts of maladministration. The new machinery is vital to all other reforms which the Commission may recommend, in as much as it would establish a built-in mechanism to make the administration continuously responsive to the citizens' genuine difficulties and needs. It will release new forces and pressures for reform.

The A.R.C. was of the view that parliamentary supervision by itself could not fully ensure to the citizen that rectitude over the entire area covered by administrative discretion. Never had the various administrative tiers and hierarchies proved adequate for the purpose: "A tendency to uphold the man on the spot, a casual approach to one's own responsibilities, an assumption of unquestionable superiority of the administration, a feeling of the sanctity of authority and neglect or indifference on the part of a superior authority may prevent a citizen from obtaining justice even at the final stage of the administrative system." It is in these circumstances or in instances, where he is unable for some compelling reasons, to seek other remedies open to him, that an institution for redress of grievances must be provided within the democratic system of government. It has to be an institution in which the average citizen will have faith and confidence and through which he will be able to secure guided and inexpensive justice.

The Commission concluded: "We therefore visualise an Ombudsman-type of institution not only as justified by the study of the past, but also as a safeguard for the future. Nor do we consider that such an institution would be, in any way, a burden or imposition on the administrative machinery; on the other hand, we are confident that it will exercise a protective role in regard to it. If the standards of conduct of the services are in fact as high as they are claimed to be, the functioning of such a machinery will confirm this fact against the prevailing unfavourable impressions that unfortunately exist; if facts prove otherwise, it will provide a corrective which in due course of time is bound to influence the psychological attitude of the services as a whole. Its influence is bound to pervade the different strata of the administrative machinery and thereby bring all-round improvement in its outlook and efficiency."

As mentioned earlier, the Lokpal will, under the A.R.C. Scheme, enquire into complaints against administrative acts of Ministers and secretaries to government at the Centre and in the States. Lokayukta to be appointed in each State and one at the Centre will look into complaints against the administrative acts of other authorities. The Lokpal will be appointed by the President of India on the advice of the Prime Minister, Chief Justice of India and the Leader of the Opposition in the Lok Sabha (if there is no such leader, a person will be duly elected for this purpose by the Opposition in the Lok Sabha in such a manner as the Speaker may direct). The Lokpal will not hold any office of profit, nor can he continue as a Member of Parliament or State Legislature if he is already elected. He will hold office for a period of five years and can also be reappointed. The Lokpal shall not be removed from his office except by an order of the President, passed after an address, by each House of Parliament (supported by a majority of the total membership of that House and by a majority of not less than two-thirds of the Members of that House present and voting), has been presented to the President in the same session for such removal on the ground of proved misbehaviour or incapacity. The Lokpal will have the same statues, salary and allowances and conditions of service as the Chief Justice of India. If the Lokpal is satisfied on the action taken on his recommendations, he will close the case but where he is not so satisfied and he considers that the case so deserves, he may make a special report upon the case to the Lok Sabha or the Legislative Assembly of the State concerned, as the case may be. He will also lay before Parliament or the legislature of the State concerned annual reports on the performance of his functions.

The Lokpal may investigate any action taken with the approval of a minister or secretary in case a written complaint is made to him, or when an information comes to his knowledge, that a particular action has resulted in favour being unduly shown to any person or in injustice in consequence of maladministration. He will no doubt afford an opportunity to the Minister or Secretary to explain their conduct. The Lokpal may require any minister or officer or any other person (who in his opinion is able to furnish information or produce documents relevant to the investigation) to furnish such information or produce such documents.

The A.R.C. also appended to its report to the government, a draft Bill on the subject. The idea behind proposing this draft Bill was to enable the government to take prompt and speedy action to set up the institutions of Lokpal and Lokayukta.

THE LOKPAL AND LOKAYUKTAS BILL, 1969

The report of the Administrative Reforms Commission on "Problems of Redress of Citizens' Grievances" was, as already stated, given in October, 1966. The government made a number of announcements in Parliament and outside that they proposed to introduce legislation in this regard and that they had accepted the recommendations of the A.R.C. in regard to the Lokpal and Lokayuktas. There was a feeling in some quarters at that time that the report of the A.R.C. as well as the government announcements were motivated by the General Elections of 1967. The Government, however, did not introduce any legislative measures prior to the fourth General Elections.

The General Elections reduced the majority of the Congress Party in the Lok Sabha from 361 to 283.

The Congress Party also failed to gain majority in the States of West Bengal, Kerala, Punjab, Tamil Nadu, Orissa. In Uttar Pradesh, Bihar, and Madhya Pradesh, the Congress ministries were short-lived and subsequently coalition ministries were formed. Haryana had a Congress ministry in the beginning, but due to defections, a non-Congress government had to be formed, though for a very short time. The ministries in Uttar Pradesh and Bihar proved unstable resulting in mid-term elections. The political uncertainties following in the wake of the General Elections diverted the government's attention.

The public opinion, however, did not totally lose sight of the importance of Ombudsman-type of machinery. In November, 1967, a private member's Bill on Lokpal and Lokayukta was introduced in the Lok Sabha by Shri P.K. Deo, M.P. This Bill was mostly the reproduction of the recommendations of the A R.C. The Bill involved certain financial commitments which were required to be recommended by the President, before its consideration by Parliament. But the President declined to give his consent. Such consent was, however, not required for the publication of the Bill for elucidating public opinion. The sponsor of the Bill, therefore, moved on 1 December 1967 that the Bill be circulated for public opinion. The Government was defeated on a snap vote, and with the majority of two votes the Lok Sabha gave its approval. This was the first time in the history of Indian Parliament that the ruling Congress Party was defeated on a substantive motion. This Bill was, however, withdrawn as the Government of India made the following announcement in the Lok Sabha:

> Government have now decided to set up a statutory machinery to enquire into complaints alleging corruption or injustice arising out of maladministration. The machinery will be headed by a Lokpal who will have authority to enquire into the allegations arising out of administrative acts of Central Ministers and Secretaries. The Lokpal will also coordinate the working of two other functionaries of the status of Lokayuktas. The first will primarily go into allegations of corruption and the second into other allegations made against Central Government servants lower in rank than Secretaries. A Bill on the subject will be

introduced in Parliament during the present session.[10]

Following an announcement, the Government introduced the "Lokpal and Lokayuktas' Bill, 1968" on 9 May 1968. The Bill was sent to the Joint Select Committee of Parliament which gave its report on 21 March 1969.

The Joint Select Committee made quite a few changes, some of which can be considered quite significant. The changes made by the Committee are mentioned further below at appropriate places in the discussion on the main provisions of the Bill. The Bill as revised by the Joint Select Committee was considered in the Lok Sabha and passed by it on 20 August 1969. However, as the Bill having originated from the Lok Sabha and was pending with the Rajya Sabha, it lapsed with the dissolution of the Lok Sabha on the 27 December 1970. The Bill was reintroduced in the Lok Sabha.[11]

It is to be specially noted that the "Lokpal and Lokayukta Bill, 1969" provided for Ombudsman-type of machinery only for the Centre. The scope of the Bill did not extend to ministers and public officials of states which were also covered under the A.R.C.'s proposals. The main reasons for this change was the intransigence of some of the State Governments in accepting the A.R.C.'s proposals. It is understood that of the then 17 states, 7 states[12] did not agree with the recommendations of the Commission and 5 states did not send any reply to the communications[13] addressed by the Central government. Of the Union Territories, two[14] did not agree with the proposals of the A.R.C.

Some of the main objections raised by the States were as follows :

[10]Address delivered by Dr. Zakir Hussain, President of India, to the *Joint Session of both the Houses of Parliament* on 12 February 1968, p. 7.

[11] Clause 107(5) of the Constitution of India reads:.

"A Bill which is pending in the House of the People, or which having been passed by the House of the People is pending in the Council of States, shall subject to the provision of Article 108, lapse on a dissolution of the House of the People."

[12]Andhra Pradesh, Haryana, Kerala, Mysore, Nagaland, West Bengal and Jammu & Kashmir.

[13]Maharashtra, Madhya Pradesh, Orissa, Punjab and Rajasthan.

[14]Himachal Pradesh and Pondicherry.

1. Complaints against ministers should be looked into by a panel consisting of President, Prime Minister, Governor, Chief Minister and Speaker of the Legislative Assembly. Clubbing of government servants and ministers for the purpose of these enquiries would not be desirable and would not work.
2. The setting up of the institution of Lokpal to enquire into the conduct of ministers in their public capacity will clearly involve serious encroachment on the powers of the legislature and of the electorate.
3. It is not clear whether the institution of Lokpal can be created without an amendment of the Constitution. Ministers in a State are appointed by the Governor and their constitutional function really is that of aiding and advising the Governor, vide Article 163(1). The advice tendered by a minister to the Governor cannot be enquired into by any Court (Article 163(3)) and it is doubtful whether a mere act of Parliament can make him answerable to any Central authority for any action taken by him which is legally in the nature of advice given to the Governor of the State.
4. The Constitution of India in its present form does not admit of an institution of this type, independent at once of the judiciary, the executive and the legislature. There is no justification either for the Constitution being amended for the purpose.
5. The institution of Lokpal will result in the curtailment of the power of the States which would be unwarranted and unacceptable.
6. The setting up of the proposed institutions will provide an easy means to persons who, for political or other motives, desire to indulge in character assassination of the politicians in office.
7. The number of "complaints" against ministers and officials is likely to be very large and the disposal of the cases will be delayed, or a large number of functionaries will have to deal with these complaints. This will involve the setting up of a parallel machinery for the existing administrative agencies which will entail avoidable expenditure and will also be impossible to justify in principle.
8. In the case of the elected representatives of the people in

the States, it should be the State Legislature rather than the Central Government or Parliament, that should deal with corruption charges. Vesting this authority in a Central body would lessen the control of State Government over its own officials. Such an authority would obviously be in a position to impose the will of the Centre on the States and thus make inroads into the autonomy of the States.

It deserves to be noted that the loss of power by the Congress Party in several States after the general elections of 1967 had reduced its influence in Union-State relations. After the general elections of 1967, the demand for greater State autonomy has been on the increase. It is understandable that the governments of the states which had different party complexion than of the ruling party at the Centre did not favour the proposal for the Lokpal, who is to be appointed by the President on the advice of the Prime Minister of India and will have the power to investigate into complaints against State ministers.

Under the provisions of the Bill of 1969, there was to be a Lokpal and one or more Lokayuktas working under him to look into complaints against the Central administration. The Bill did not include even an enabling provision for the appointment of Lokayuktas in the States.

FUNCTIONS AND POWERS

At this stage, it will be of interest to examine briefly, the functions and powers of the proposed institutions of Lokpal and Lokayuktas as provided for in the Bill of 1969. It is relevant to discuss these proposals in detail in view of the introduction of a Bill in Parliament by the Janata Party so that a comparative study could be made.

Appointment and status

As already mentioned, the Bill of 1969 provides for the appointment of a Lokpal and one or more Lokayuktas, their jurisdiction being limited to the public officials directly under the Central government or in organizations owned or controlled by it.

The Lokpal will be appointed by the President in consultation with the Cheif Justice of India and the leader of the Opposition in the Lok Sabha. If there is no such leader, the Prime Minister has to consult a person elected by the members of the Opposition in such a manner as the Speaker may direct. The Lokayuktas will be appointed by the President in consultation with the Lokpal. Both the Lokpal and the Lokayuktas will hold office for five years (without any age limit).[15]

Further, the provision in clause 5(1)(c) of the Bill that "the Lokpal or a Lokayukta, shall notwithstanding the expiry of his term, continue to hold office until his successor enters upon his office" was deleted on the recommendations of the Joint Select Committee. The Committee felt that such a provision might be misused by delaying the appointment of a successor and thereby enabling a particular Lokpal or a Lokayukta to continue in office beyond his tenure.

The Joint Select Committee further recommended that the consultation of the Lokpal in the case of first appointment of Lokayukta may be dispensed with. Under the proposed legislation, it will not be possible to remove the Lokpal except after an inquiry by an acting or retired judge of the Supreme Court, and only on an address by each House of Parliament, presented to the President in the same session, supported by a majority of the total membership of that House and a majority of not less than two-thirds of the members of that House present and voting.[16] The procedure proposed for removal of Lokayuktas is the same as that for the Lokpal.

The Lokpal will enjoy the status of the Chief Justice of India and the Lokayuktas that of a judge of the Supreme Court. The Lokpal will get a salary of Rs.5,000 and a Lokayukta

[15]Though the Bill is silent on any further extension of term of appointment by another 5 years, the Joint Select Committee suggested restriction of this period to only one term. The Committee felt that the provision made in proviso 5(1) of the Bill "but shall be eligible for re-appointment for not more than one term" might be misused. As such, these words have been deleted from the Bill passed by the Lok Sabha.

[16]In a note of dissent, Shri P.K. Deo, M.P., felt that a similar procedure as in the case of removal of the judge of Supreme Court should be followed for the removal of Lokpal and Lokayuktas on the grounds of misbehaviour or incapacity, etc.

Rs. 4,000 per month, provided that if the Lokpal or a Lokayukta at the time of his appointment is in receipt of a pension (other than a disability or wound pension) in respect of any previous service under the government, his salary will be reduced by the amount of that pension.

Functions and jurisdiction

The proposed functions of the Lokpal under the Bill of 1969 are to be confined to investigation of citizens' complaints against the public servants of the Central Government and to making recommendations for their redress. The Bill provides that the Lokayuktas will investigate actions taken by public servants except the actions of the ministers and secretaries, which will be investigated exclusively by the Lokpal.[17] The Lokpal can also investigate, for reasons to be recorded in writing, any action which may otherwise be investigated by a Lokayukta. However, the Lokpal and Lokayukta will have no powers to annul or modify an administrative action complained against. They can only recommend that the competent authority should remedy injustice and take corrective measures within a specified period.

The Bill divides the public complaints into two parts: (a) allegations, and (b) grievances. Allegations against a public servant cover (i) abuse of position by an official so as to obtain any gain or favour to himself or to any other person or to cause undue harm or hardship to any other person, (ii) discharge of functions as public servant with personal interest or improper or corrupt motives, or (iii) corruption, lack of integrity or improper conduct as such public servant. A grievance has been defined as a claim by a person that he sustained injustice in consequence of maladministration. The latter, according to the Bill, means action taken or purporting to have been taken in the exercise of administrative functions in any case : (i) where such action or the administrative procedure

[17]In a note of dissent, Shri M. Ruthnaswamy, Member of Parliament, objected to bringing the ministers within the jurisdiction of the Lokpal on the ground that (a) the minister is a political public servant and that (b) he is subject to political checks and controls of his constituency, legislature, the Prime Minister and the Council of Ministers.

or practice governing such action is unreasonable, unjust, oppressive, or improperly discriminatory, or (ii) where there has been negligence or undue delay in taking such action, or the administrative procedure or practice governing such action involves undue delay.

Under the Bill, the judiciary and the armed forces are to be outside the purview of the Indian Ombudsman. The jurisdiction of the Lokpal and Lokayuktas will extend to allegations or grievances against all public servants as defined in the Bill. The definition of "public servant" includes ministers and officers of Central government (including those of union territories) and the employees of corporations and companies owned or controlled by the Central government, the employees of the local authorities in the territories, and societies controlled by the Central government which are notified in the Official Gazette. However, only allegations against the employees of such local authorities, corporations, companies or societies will be investigated by Lokpal and Lokayuktas; grievances in case of these organizations are excluded from the jurisdiction of Lokpal and Lokayuktas.

If, after investigation relating to a grievance, the Lokpal or Lokayukta is satisfied that injustice has been perpetrated to the complainant or any other person, he shall, by a report in writing, recommend to the public servant and the competent authority[18] concerned that such injustice shall be remedied in such manner and within such time as may be specified in the report. The competent authority shall, within one month of the expiry of the specified term, intimate to the Lokpal (or a Lokayukta as the case may be) the action taken for compliance with the report. If, after investigation involving an allegation, the Lokpal or Lokayukta is satisfied that such allegation can be substantiated wholly or partly, he shall report his findings to the competent authority, and the concerned authority shall, within three months, intimate to the Lokpal or Lokayukta the action taken or proposed to be taken. If the Lokpal or a Lokayukta is satisfied with the action taken (or proposed to be taken) in

[18]"Competent authority", in relation to a public servant, means; (i) in the case of a minister or secretary, the Prime Minister, (ii) in the case of any other public servant, such authority as may be prescribed.

relation to a grievance or an allegation, he shall close the case. If not, he may report to the President. Such a report, with an explanatory memorandum, shall be laid by the President before each House of Parliament.

On the suggestion of the Joint Select Committee, a new clause has been added to enable the Lokpal or the Lokayukta to concentrate on really important cases when the work becomes unmanageable. Under the revised Bill, the Central government will have the power to exclude by notification, on the recommendation of the Lokpal, complaints against public servants carrying a minimum monthly salary of one thousand rupees or more (exclusive of allowances). Such a notification will have to be placed before each House of Parliament and if both the Houses agree that the notification should not be made, the notification in that case will have effect only in modified form or will have no effect, as the case may be.

A point which deserves to be mentioned is that the Prime Minister does not come within the purview of the Lokpal. The Joint Select Committee in its report desired that clause 2(b) be amended to make it clear that the Prime Minister is excluded from the scope of the Bill.[19]

[19] According to clause (c) (I) read with clause 2(H) of the Bill of the Lokpal and Lokayuktas, 1969, when introduced brought the Prime Minister's Office within the definition. But in the Joint Committee, government moved an amendment and excluded the Prime Minister from the scope of the Bill. In his note of dissent, Shri C.C. Desai, a member of the committee, argued that "when the office of the Deputy Prime Minister can be subjected to the jurisdiction of the Lokpal, there is no reason and there is no logic why the office of the Prime Minister should not be subjected likewise." When the Lok Sabha took up the Bill for consideration on 13 August 1969, a demand for including the Prime Minister under the purview of the powers of the proposed "Lokpal" was made by Mr. P.K. Deo, a member of the Swatantra Party. This was despite a long explanation by the Minister of State for Home Affairs, Shri Vidya Charan Shukla, who moved the Bill, pointing out that it would be inappropriate to equate the Prime Minister with other ministers. If a minister was to resign because of any adverse remarks by the "Lokpal" only he went out of office, but if the Prime Minister were to go, the whole government would have to resign. Mr. Shukla added that the change of government was the exclusive right of the Lok Sabha and the right could not be shared by any other

In order to improve the utility of the new institutions to provide for their smooth functioning and to ensure that they contribute to the effectiveness of the administration rather than detract from it, certain types of grievances have been excluded from the jurisdiction of the Lokpal and Lokayuktas. These mainly are:

1. complaint involving a grievance or an allegation inquired into by, or referred for inquiry to, a commission under the Commissions of Inquiry Act;
2. matters relating to foreign affairs, action taken under the Extradition Act or the Foreigners Act or dealings with international organization etc.;
3. matters connected with the investigation of crime, passports and travel documents;
4. exercise of discretion whether a matter should go to a court or not;
5. matters relating to commercial transactions and contracts except where harassment or gross delay are alleged in meeting contractual obligations;
6. personnel matters except those relating to pension, etc.;
7. matters relating to grant of honours and awards:
8. matters relating to the judges.

Besides policy decisions and cases in which discretion has been properly exercised, cases where the remedy lies before any tribunal or court of law have been excluded from the jurisdiction of Lokpal and Lokayuktas. However, they have been given the discretion to conduct an investigation in cases which could have gone before a tribunal or a court, if they were satisfied that the complainant could not or cannot, for sufficient cause, have recourse to such remedy.

The new functionaries can refuse to investigate or cease to investigate any complaint of grievance or allegation where, in their opinion, such complaint or allegation is frivolous, vexatious, malafide and unsubstantiated.

The A.R.C., in a subsequent report, made an additional

---

authority. Mr. P.K. Deo, in his note of dissent, also urged that Governors, Lieutenant Governors and the Chief Commissioners should be brought in the scope of the Bill.

recommendation to reinforce the role of the Lokpal in the matter of ensuring high standards of integrity at the level of ministers. It proposed that the initial and annual statements of their financial assets and liabilities to be furnished by the ministers under the "code of conduct" should be made available to the Lokpal. If any minister fails to furnish such a statement, the fact should be mentioned by the Lokpal in his annual report to Parliament. The Commission recommended that provision to this effect may be made in the Lokpal Bill which is now before Parliament.

Shri H.V. Kamath, a member of the A.R.C., has expressed dissent with the new via media role envisaged for the Lokpal in this report. His 13-page note of dissent says that requirement proposed on the part of ministers to send statements of their assets and liabilities, besides the Prime Minister, to the Lokpal, though helpful to a certain extent, will not have the desired effect unless Parliament is seized of the matter. Kamath would have the Lokpal empowered to bring to the notice of Parliament not only the failure of a minister to send him the statement, but also cases where he is satisfied that the statement is not quite correct or adequate. He demands that all ministers, including the Prime Minister, should furnish such statements to the Lokpal.[20]

Independent character of the institution

The Bill of 1969 contains several provisions for ensuring the independent character of the institutions of the Lokpal and Lokayuktas. On appointment, these functionaries are to resign from the membership of Parliament or State Legislature if they are members and delink themselves from political parties if they belong to any of them. If they are connected with business (except ownership) or any office of trust or profit, they have to terminate that connection. On ceasing to hold office, they will be ineligible for further employment under the Government of India except that

[20]At present, ministers and civil servants have to submit their annual financial statements to Chief Minister in the States and the Prime Minister at the Centre. Apparently, these statements have not enabled Chief Ministers or the Prime Minister to deal with corruption, if any, among those who submitted their financial statement.

a Lokayukta can be appointed as Lokpal. The procedure for removal of Lokayuktas will be the same as that for the Lokpal. Under the Bill, the Lokpal and Lokayuktas will be for all purposes independent of the executive, the legislature and the judiciary. Lokpal will be required to submit every year a consolidated report on the performance of his functions to the President, who will lay a copy of the report before each House of Parliament.[21]

The Lokpal and Lokayuktas Bill, 1969 spells out the procedures to be followed for receipt and redress of the citizens' complaints. As already mentioned, in case of a grievance, the knowledge of the impugned action, and not occurrence, should not be more than one year old. This time-limit is relaxable in hard cases. In case of allegations, occurrence itself should not be more than five years old. Unlike U.K., the Lokpal and Lokayukta can receive a complaint directly from the citizen and no fee has been prescribed for the filing of a complaint.

On receipt of a complaint from a person claiming to have suffered an injustice through an administrative act, the Lokpal will scrutinize it and come to a conclusion as to whether he has jurisdiction to deal with it and if so, whether the case is worth investigation. If his conclusion is in the negative on either of these points, he should reject the complaint and inform the complainant accordingly. If he decides to take up the investigation, he will, in the first instance, communicate the complaint to the administration and invite the administration's comments thereon. At this stage, it may be possible for the administration to rectify, on its own, any faulty decision made by it or it may seek to establish the correctness or justice of the action taken. The Lokpal, on receipt of the administration's comments, will decide whether the complaint is actionable; if it is not actionable, he will inform the complainant that he has

[21]Though it is not mentioned in detail in the Bill, the A.R.C. recommended that besides giving a summary of the cases disposed of by him, he may indicate the need for amending any law in order to remove occasions for unintended hardship experienced as a result of the administration of the existing law. The identity of the complainant and the complainee is not to be disclosed in these reports. The substance of the defence adduced by the complainee is to accompany any adverse comment made in the report against him.

decided not to take any further action. If, on the completion of cases which he investigates, he is satisfied that there is no cause for grievance, he would inform the complainant accordingly and close the case. If, however, he considered that an injustice had been done to the complainant, he would suggest to the administration a possible remedial action.

The Lokpal would enquire into allegations on a complaint.[22] The Lokpal will have powers of a court with regard to calling of witnesses, documents, etc. However, it is expected that the exercise of the powers as a court will be unnecessary and that the Lokpal's procedure will be as informal as possible. The investigation by the Lokpal will be conducted in private. Nothing relating to the investigations will be published or caused to be published by him till the enquiry is completed and his findings are communicated to the complainant, or to the legislature. Publication of any matter pending before the Lokpal or decided by him save to the extent that it is included in the ad hoc or annual report or is permitted by the Lokpal shall be an offence under the relevant law. In regard to information available with government or subordinate authorities, he will have access to whatever information, document, etc., he requires and no privilege will be claimed for any such information or document except in matters affecting the security of the state or foreign relations. The public authorities can, however, while giving confidential information, request the Lokpal and Lokayuktas not to disclose it in their reports and publications.

The proposed Bill of 1969 also contains several provisions for smooth functioning of the new institutions. If any person without lawful excuse obstructs the Lokpal in the performance of his functions or is guilty of any act or omission in relation to an investigation, which, had the investigation been proceeding in a court of law, would have constituted contempt of

[22]In addition to making investigations on the basis of complaints received by him, the Lokpal might also suo motu investigate administrative acts of the types referred to in the chapter which come to his notice otherwise than through a complaint of an adversely affected person. Though the Administrative Reforms Commission has explicitly made this recommendation, this power has not been expressly and clearly conferred in the Bill.

court, the Lokpal may certify the offence to the Supreme Court. If a person making a complaint of maladministration involving undue favour being shown or to the accrual of a personal benefit makes a false statement before the Lokpal knowing it to be such, he shall be deemed to be guilty of an act constituting contempt of court. When an offence is certified, as above, the Supreme Court may enquire into the matter and dispose it of as if it related to a charge of contempt of the Supreme Court.

DIFFERENCE BETWEEN GOVERNMENT'S PROPOSALS AND A.R.C. SCHEME

The proposals embodied in the Lokpal and Lokayuktas Bill of 1969 differ in several respects from the scheme proposed by the A.R.C. In most matters, the provisions in the Bill represented an improvement; on a few, they lag behind the recommendations of the A.R.C. The main changes proposed in the lapsed Bill over the A.R.C. scheme are as follows:

1. The A.R.C. scheme provides one more term for the Lokpal after he completes his first five years. But the government Bill has not made any provision for reappointment. As already explained, this has been done on the recommendations of the Joint Select Committee who did not want the Lokpal to carry favours in order to get further extensions. Similarly, the A.R.C. scheme is silent about the continuance on an officiating basis of a Lokayukta in the absence of Lokpal. But the Bill includes such a provision, which is liable to be misused by allowing a Lokayukta to continue indefinitely and by delaying the appointment of a Lokpal.

2. As pointed out earlier. a new clause has been added in the Bill according to which the Central government may, on the recommendation of the Lokpal, exclude complaints involving grievances or allegations against the government servants drawing a pay of more than Rs.1,000 from the jurisdiction of the Lokpal or Lokayukta. There is no such provision in the A.R.C. scheme.

3. Under the A.R.C. scheme the jurisdiction of the Lokpal was to be confined to complaints against ministers and secretaries to government; and of complaints against other public officials at the Centre were for the Lokayukta to investi-

gate. Under the Bill of 1969, Lokpal will have the overall responsibility for all types of public complaints, though complaints against ministers and secretaries will be investigated by him personally. Under the government's proposals, there can be one or more Lokayuktas at the Centre; the A.R.C. scheme, however, contemplated only one Lokayukta for looking into complaints against Central government employees other than secretaries. The Central Lokayuktas will function under the overall guidance of the Lokpal.

4. The A.R.C. scheme clearly invests the Ombudsman with the power to investigate suo motu even without the receipt of a complaint, but this power is not provided for in the Bill.

5. Under the Bill of 1969, as we have already seen, public complaints have been divided into two parts, namely, allegations and grievances. The jurisdiction of Lokpal, as proposed by the Bill of 1969, would not extend to local bodies and public undertakings in the matter of grievances though they will cover allegations against their officials. The underlying idea of this provision seems to be that Lokpal should be able to look into complaints concerning corrupt practices. Allegations of this ype against the officials of the autonomous public sector undertakings at present come under the Central Vigilance Commission which is proposed to be abolished both under the A.R.C. scheme as well as the Bill of 1969.

6. A new provision of the Bill is that matters which have already been gone into by a Commission of inquiry should not be subjected to another investigation by the Lokpal or Lokayukta. Further, the Lokpal will not normally be able to act if a complainant has an alternative legal remedy.

7. The A R.C. scheme provides that the Lokpal would be able to examine complaints against administrative actions which took place within the 12 months preceding the lodging of the complaint. The Bill of 1969 has liberalized this provision to provide that the period of 12 months should be counted not from the date of the action, but from the date of the knowledge of such action by the complainant. The Bill also clearly specifies that the time limit for allegations of corruption will be five years from the date of occurrence. In the case of grievances a provision has been made for the relaxation of time in really

hard cases.[23]

8. The Lokpal and Lokayukta Bill of 1969 clearly provides that any letter written to the Lokpal or a Lokayukta by a person in police custody, or in a jail or in any asylum or other receptable for insane persons, shall be forwarded to the addressee unopened and without delay by the police officer or other person in charge of such jail, asylum or other receptable. This is a very important provision on which the A.R.C. scheme is silent.

9. An additional provision made in the lapsed Bill is that the identity of the complainant and the public servant concerned should not be disclosed to the public or the press at any time. This is in order to maintain the morale in the public services.

10. A special feature of the Bill is that the Lokpal/Lokayukta will, in case of grievances, recommend also the manner in which an injustice should be remedied. Further, the recommendations will be sent not only to the public servants reported against but the competent authorities also.

11. The Bill also contains some provisions for ensuring proper and timely action of the mandates of the Lokpal. It has been laid down that the competent authority, to whom a report is sent, shall within one month of the expiry of the time specified in the report, intimate or cause to be intimated to the Lokpal or, as the case may be, the Lokayutka, of the action taken in compliance with the report.

12. In order to safeguard the public servants who cannot defend themselves before Parliament, a provision has been made that in case an adverse comment against any person or department or organization has been made in any annual or special report, such report shall also contain the substance of the defence adduced by the person complained against and the comments made by or on behalf of the department or organization affected. The Bill also provides that the substance of cases which are of general public academic or professional interest, may be made available by the Lokpal in such a manner as he deems appropriate.

13. The President is empowered to confer on Lokpal or Lokayukta, as the case may be, such additional functions in

[23]This is in conformity with the S. 6 (3) of the U.K. Act.

relation to the redress of grievances and eradication of corruption or investigation of any other important matter as may be specified in the order. Though the A.R.C. scheme is silent on this, the new provision in the Bill will enable the President to transfer to the new functionaries various quasi-administrative consultancy and supervisory functions which are at present discharged by the Central Vigilance Commission and the Commissioner for Public Grievances. This will also enable the Government to refer important cases to the Lokpal for investigation and report. However, Professor Rowat has given a note of caution in this respect. A different view is, however, taken by some eminent authorities who have made a special study of the Ombudsman institutions. It has been pointed out that the government should not have the power to interfere with the work of Lokpal by giving him additional powers or directions as is provided in the Bill. It should only be the Parliament or parliamentary committee which should have the right to give directions.

The Lokpal and Lokayukta Bill, however, falls short of the A.R.C. scheme on certain important issues. The main differences here are:

1. As noted earlier, the Bill does not extend to the public servants in the States. Under the A.R.C. proposals the jurisdiction of the Lokpal would extend to ministers and secretaries to the government both at the Centre and in the States. There was to be a Lokayukta at the Centre and one also in each state, the latter being appointed by the Governor on the recommendations of the Chief Minister, who would obviously consult the leader of the Opposition and the Chief Justice of the High Court in this matter, before making his recommendation. However, the Bill of 1969 provides only for the appointment of a Central Lokpal and Central Lokayuktas. It does not even have an enabling provision for its extension to the States.[24]

[24]This mutatis mutandis appointment of the Lokayukta in the States is implied in the following recommendations of the A.R.C. in its report on "Problems of Redress of Citizens' Grievances":

"We, therefore, consider that his powers, functions and procedures may be prescribed mutatis mutandis with those which we have laid down for the Lokpal."

2. The A.R.C. scheme provides that the reports, annual or special, of the Lokpal and Lokayukta shall be made to the Lok Sabha or the Legislative Assembly of the State concerned as the case may be. Whereas the Bill of 1969 lays down that the Lokpal or the Lokayukta will submit his annual or special report to the President who will lay it before the Parliament.

3. Under the A.R.C. scheme, complaints could be registered with Lokpal and Lokayukta by any person, but under the Bill of 1969 public servants are debarred from making "allegations". Under both, the A.R.C. scheme and the Bill of 1969, it is not open to a public employee to take up a complaint concerning his conditions of service or any other similar matter to the Lokpal.

DEVELOPMENTS IN STATES

Some modified versions of the Ombudsman-type of institutions have been introduced in some States, such as Madhya Pradesh, Uttar Pradesh, Bihar, Maharashtra and Rajasthan. The Uttar Pradesh Public Men Inquiries Act, 1967 provides for investigation of complaints against certain top level public functionaries namely, ministers, deputy ministers, parliamentary secretaries, members of the legislature, Adhyakshas (President) and Upadhyakshas (Vice President) of Zila Parishads, Nagar Pramukhs (Mayor) and Upnagar Pramukhs (Deputy Mayor) of Nagarmahapalikas (Town Municipalities), and Presidents, Chairman and Vice-chairman of district cooperative federations, banks or unions, and of State-level apex institutions. The scheme provides that any person may make a complaint of misconduct against a present or past holder of any of the offices mentioned above, to the governor for inquiry. He will be required to file an affidavit in support of the complaint and to deposit a security of Rs.1,000. The governor will then request the Chief Justice of the High Court for nominating a judge for preliminary scrutiny. The Governor may also, of his own, refer any accusation for preliminary scrutiny as aforesaid. The judge in the case of a minister, parliamentary secretary, nagar pramukh or upnagar pramukh will be a serving High Court Judge or a retired Supreme Court Judge, while that in the case of others, will be from amongst serving district judges.

The U.P. Public Men Inquiries Act, 1967 was converted into U.P. Lokayukta and Uplokayukta Act, 1975 and was enforced from 12 July 1977. The Janata government in Uttar Pradesh, committed to give to the people a clean, efficient and responsive administration, took a series of steps to eliminate corruption. A vigorous drive was launched in the State to eliminate graft from the administration, especially at points of public contact. A major event in pursuance of government policy to cleanse the administration and public life was the appointment of Shri Bishambhar Dayal a retired Chief Justice of Madhya Pradesh High Court, as the State's Lokayukta under the U.P. Lokayukta and Uplokayukta Act, 1975 who would probe into the complaints of corruption against top officers and persons holding high public office including ministers, secretaries to government, legislators and presidents of local bodies.

In Madhya Pradesh, an Ordinance, entitled "The M.P. Enquiry Commissioner (Public Men and Public Servants) Ordinance" was promulgated in 1968. But the Ordinance did not receive the approval of the Assembly when it was convened and therefore the Ordinance lapsed. However, the salient feature of this Ordinance was that for conducting of investigation an Inquiry Commissioner of the status of a Supreme Court Judge was to be appointed by the Governor for a period of five years.

In its report submitted in January 1968, the Administrative Reorganisation Committee, appointed by the Government of Maharashtra in 1962, recommended the appointment of an Ombudsman for Maharashtra. The Maharashtra Lokayukta and Uplokayukta Act was brought on the Statute Book in 1971. The Lokayukta looks into the complaints against State Ministers and secretaries to government and the Deputy Lokayukta (Uplokayukta) deals with grievances against other public officials. With this difference, the powers of these functionaries are similar to those proposed for the Lokpal and Lokayuktas at the Centre under the Bill of 1969. The State Ombudsman is to be appointed by the Governor on the advice of the Chief Justice of the High Court and the leader of the Opposition in the Legislative Assembly and his emoluments and other service conditions are to be similar to that of a Chief Justice of a High Court and of a High Court Judge respectively. The jurisdiction of the Ombudsman of Maharashtra extends to all the administrative agencies of the State Government. Though the Act created an impressive authority to deal with maladministration and graft complaints, it proved to be a thoroughly hypocritical measure. The powers vested in this authority by one section of the Act are so sharply eroded by other provisions and the number of listed and unlisted "sacred cows" is so large that the sum total of the entire exercise under the Act worked out to an easily distinguishable naught.

Experience has created an impression that the main purpose of the government in creating this institution of only Lokayukta and Uplokayukta was to play to the gallery. The only encouraging result produced so far by this measure is that it has amply demonstrated an insatiable desire in all classes of people to assist the authorities in putting down corruption and maladministration, although the provisions of the Act, cumbersome procedures and the costburden are a damper on this desire.

The farce, that the Act is, has been unmasked completely by the two highly qualified hands holding the posts—the Lokayukta and Uplokayukta. Mr. Sohrab Peshotan Kotwal was Chief Justice of the Bombay High Court for six years and the Uplokayukta, Mr. L.M. Nadkarni, an I.C.S. was a former Chief Secretary to the government of Maharashtra. Both are of the unanimous view that the limitations placed on their jurisdiction under the Act "are stringent and numerous and drastically affected their functions". They have further said that various provisions of the Act gave almost complete immunity to the police from their jurisdiction. In their words, "it is rather difficult to see in which case of corruption, the Lokayukta and the Uplokayukta have jurisdiction at all". They have no doubt, that in its present form, the Act would not achieve "the very useful and laudable objective" for which it had been framed.

The working of the Act so far gives the impression that the government has not been serious about it. In 1971, Maharashtra was the first State to make an Act to appoint a Lokayukta and an Uplokayukta. It took the government more than ten months to find an incumbant for the post of Lokayukta and another ten months after that to appoint Uplokayukta. The Lokayukta and Uplokayukta submitted their first annual report to the Governor as required under the Act on 17 November 1973. Their unanimous report pointed out faults in the Act and recommended modifications to make it "meaningful". The report was presented to the State Legislature only on 16 December 1974. The suggestion made to put some life in the institution of Lokayukta and Uplokayukta in the report and repeated by the Lokayukta in a letter to the government on 11 March 1974 made it clear that they cannot work independently unless the Act was radically amended to remove the unreasonable drag.

Under the Act, no investigation of a complaint can even be initiated unless the "competent authority" named by the government is formed. While in the case of the Uplokayukta various "competent authorities" were named on 18 July 1973, although he was appointed on 1 October 1973, the "competent authorities" for the Lokayukta were listed only on 5 November 1973, more than a year after his appointment. In both cases, it turned out to be the proverbial "cart before the horse" management. The Act was so casually framed that it did not cover any of the five municipal corporations in the State.

The "achievements" of the Lokayukta and Uplokayukta in the first year were just ridiculous; of course, neither of them could be blamed for the sordid situation. They received 903 complaints and disposed of 594. The manner of disposal was: default 43, vague 78, anonymous and pseudonymous-134, withdrawn 10, want of jurisdiction 311, settled to the mutual satisfaction of the parties 18. It shows that 52 per cent of the complaints were dropped for want of jurisdiction.

The Lokayukta and the Uplokayukta are of the view that of the complaints disposed of on the ground of "no jurisdiction" quite a substantial portion had, prima facie, substance, in the complaint and these were not taken up on technical grounds, want of jurisdiction or some other remedy was theoretically open to the complainant.

Right from the day of his appointment, the Lokayukta had authority to go into complaints against ministers and secretaries to the government because the "competent authority" for them had been defined in the Act itself: it is the Chief Minister. But here too, the Lokayukta realised his helplessness. He says, "my experience in this respect has not been happy. In important cases, especially against a Minister, the investigations had either not been held or had been inordinately delayed." He has listed five cases to illustrate the point.

A complaint against a minister was received by the Lokayukta on 17 November 1972. He personally handed over the papers to the Director of State Anti-Corruption Bureau (ACB), on 29 November 1972. Reminders were sent to the ACB on I5 January, 11 April and 24 July 1973. Their reply was: "inquiries in the matter are still incomplete. Final report will be forwarded to you as soon as the inquiries are complete."

It is understood that after the first annual report was submitted by Lokayukta and Uplokayukta to the Governor on 17 November 1973 the Director, ACB, woke up and sent a report expressing his unsolicited opinion that the minister was not guilty. According to the compentent sources, the list of certain names on the Director, A.C.B., files which he should have secured from the concerned department is materially different from the official list on the records of the concerned department. The name of the minister is not in the list on the A.C.B. file but it figures prominently in the files of the concerned department.

If a complainant says that he sustained injustice or undue hardship as a consequence of maladministration, it is classified as a "grievance". If the complainant has not sustained any injury himself, his complaint is taken as an "allegation". Anybody can make an allegation but only the aggrieved person can lodge a grievance.

The Act lays down that the Lokayukta and Uplokayukta shall not investigate any complaint involving a grievance against public servants belonging to any local authority, any government company in which the government has 51 per cent or more of the paid-up capital and its subsidiaries, any society covered by the Registration of Societies Act of 1860 which is subject to the control of the government. All employees in these four types of organizations are "sacred cows" under the Act.

Again the Lokayukta and Uplokayukta cannot entertain any complaint where the complainant has or had another remedy open to seek justice or if the complaint relates to an action taken for purposes of investigating crime or protecting the security of the state, or an action taken in the exercise of powers in relation to determining whether a matter shall go to a court of law or not. Or an action taken in matters which arise out of the terms of contract governing purely commercial relations of the administration with customers or suppliers, or action taken in respect of appointments, removals, pay, discipline, superannuation or other matters relating to the conditions of service of public servants or where it relates to grant of honours and awards.

And the top joke of the Act is that the term "action" includes "failure to act". In view of this, inaction or wrong action by a government department on an issue is also "action taken" and no complaint relating to that can even be entertained by the Lokayukta and Uplokayukta.

The exemption relating to cases of action and inaction given almost complete immunity to the police and the departments which give contracts—public works department, excise, all leases and licences, including those for forests from the jurisdiction of the Lokayukta and Uplokayukta The report has pointed out that in the matter of corruption, the jurisdiction of the Lokayukta and Uplokayukta is so hedged in by limitations that it becomes practically ineffective.

The Act says that no complaint for which another remedy is available would be entertained by the Lokayukta and the Uplokayukta. Every case of corruption could be theoretically fitted in within the provisions of the Prevention of Corruption Act. The person complained against can always find some ground, however, weak it might be, to go to a court of law with a petition that the Lokayukta or the Uplokayukta had no jurisdiction to entertain the complaint against him because another remedy was available to the complainant. This provision would always be handy to cause the fourth dimension of defence-delay.

All these sum up to produce an interesting situation: A complainant files a complaint at a police station regarding an offence which disclosed, prima facie, that an offence had been committed, but the concerned police officer, after recording this complaint does absolutely nothing for a year or more and the complainant goes to the Lokayukta and complains that no one was taking cognizance of his complaint, the Lokayukta cannot investigate the complaint, because action, which in this case was inaction, had already been "in operation". Even after recording the statements of witnesses from which it would appear that a prima facie case listed for prosecution, if the police officer did not launch prosecution, the Lokayukta can do nothing because it is action taken in exercise of powers in relation to determining whether or not a matter shall go to a court of law.

In another case, a citizen complains to the police that a certain public servant had demanded a bribe from him and the police officer had simply declined to do anything, the Lokayukta cannot interfere because action or inaction for investigation had started. If such a citizen, after waiting for a considerable time, goes to the Lokayukta, the Lokayukta would have no right to summon the police officer to explain his conduct. This makes it clear that it would be difficult for the Lokayukta or Uplokayukta to proceed to investigate any complaint against police officers or relating to charges of corruption against public servants.

The Government of Kerala set up in December 1969, a machinery to probe into the corruption charges against ministers and M.L.A.s including the former ministers. Under the scheme any person can send a petition listing the charges to the Chief Secretary of the State. The petition must be accompanied by a deposit of Rs.500. The charges are first referred to a sitting or retired judge for deciding whether there is any prima facie case. If a prima facie case exists, the complaint will be referred to an Inquiry Commission set up under the Commission of Inquiries Act. The above arrangements are in the nature of an interim measure and will continue to function till the permanent machinery on the lines of Lokayukta is evolved for the purpose.

The Bihar Assembly adopted in July 1970, a special resolution for the creation of the post of a Lokayukta to inquire into the charges against ministers and others. The Bill was brought on the Statue Book in 1973. The Bihar enactment provi ed that the State Governor shall appoint the Lokayukta after consulting the Chief Justice of Patna High Court and the leader of the Opposition in the State Assembly. The Lokayukta will investigate any complaint involving allegations or grievances resulting from any action taken by or with the general or specific approval of a minister or a secretary or any other public servant. Certain areas, such as cases relating to Extradition Act, security of state etc., have been exempted from his jurisdiction. The Lokayukta can be removed from his office by the Governor only on the ground of misbehaviour or incapacity on the basis of an enquiry by a person of the rank of a Chief Justice of High Court or a Judge of the Supreme Court. There has been lot of controversy as the Chief Minister of the State refused to take note of the discrepencies pointed out by the State Ombudsman in Bihar.

A new dimension of the establishment of the Ombudsman-type of machinery in India concerns the citizens' grievances against administration in the rural areas. The heads of the village panchayat (village council), the panchayat samiti (the popular body at the block/taluk level) and the zila parishad (the district level representative body) already function as important channels of redress of citizens' grievances. The effectiveness, however, is circumscribed by pressure of different kinds and their direct involvement in many cases in local administration. One of the studies conducted on panchayati raj institution by the Indian Institute of Public Administration on behalf of the Administrative Reforms Commission, has emphasized the need for the appointment of a local Ombudsman. The study observes:

> In view of the State control having been weakened because of the political pulls from below, and the malpractices that are being committed in the wake of the vast administrative and financial power structure created at the local level, a Commission or "Panchayatpal" on the lines of Lokpal at the Centre and Lokayukta at the State level as envisaged convincingly by the A.R.C. is recommended with all the weight at the command of the author. Such Panchayatpal (Panchayati Raj Ombudsman) or Commission should deal with complaints, grievances and enquiries on definite formalized requests in regard to misuse of powers and corruption etc. Such a body should have multi-judicial capacity to

deal with such cases.[25]

RECENT DEVELOPMENTS

Janata government's proposals on the Lokpal Bill, 1977

Janata government, based on their commitment in the election manifesto, introduced the Lokpal Bill in the Lok Sabha on 28 July 1977. The salient features of the Bill are:

1. The Lokpal will be a standing commission of inquiry whose machinery any citizen can set in motion against the "public men".
2. The definition of "public men" in the Bill covers members of the Union Council of Ministers, Members of Parliament, Chief Ministers of States, Members of Legislative Assemblies of the Union Territories, the Executive Council of the Delhi Administration and Mayors of Municipal Corporations in any Union Territory.
3. The present Bill confines its scope solely to allegations of misconduct against public men and the allegations of misconduct against public servants; grievances by citizens in respect of injustice or undue hardship in consequence of maladministration as distinct from corruption are not within the scope of this Bill.
4. The Lokpal will be appointed by the President after consultation with the Chief Justice of India, the Chairman of the Rajya Sabha and the Speaker of the Lok Sabha.
5. He will hold office for a five-year term. On retirement he will be ineligible for further state employment or to hold any other office of trust or profit.
6. The Lokpal will be free to secure the services of any officer or investigating agency and also any other person or agency for his investigations.
7. Special Lokpals can be appointed for expeditious disposal of cases.
8. The President is empowered to confer on the Lokpal such

[25]D.N. Pathak, *State Control of Panchayati Raj Institutions in Gujarat, An Area Report*, Department of Political Science, Rajasthan University, 1967, p. 30.

additional functions in relation to the eradication of corruption. He can also refer to him any specific allegations of misconduct for inquiry.

9. Lokpal can delegate some of his functions such as the verification of complaints and the holding of an inquiry to his officers, employees or agencies. But he cannot delegate such powers in case of summary dismissal of complaints or the submission of the final report.

10. Any person can make a complaint to the Lokpal within five years of the commission of misconduct and after depositing a sum of Rs.1,000. The Lokpal can waive both these conditions.

11. No matter which the Lokpal is competent to inquire into under the Bill can be referred to a Commission of Inquiry except with his consent.

12. The Lokpal is debarred from inquiring into any matter concerning a person "if he has any bias in respect of such matter or persons". Any dispute on this point will be decided by the Chief Justice of India.

13. The conduct of a person other than a public man can be investigated only in so far as it is necessary for the inquiry into the allegations against the public man.

14. The inquiry will be in two stages. At this stage frivolous or vexatious complaints will be rejected. Detailed investigation starts at the second stage when a copy of the complaint will be forwarded to the "competent authority" under whom the public man functions and to public man himself. The Bill enjoins the Lokpal to afford an opportunity to represent his case but no such right is conferred expressly on the complainant.

15. The inquiry will normally be held in camera and the Lokpal is given unfettered power to conduct it by such procedure as he considers appropriate. He will enjoy the powers of a civil court while trying a suit, such as summoning witnesses and requisitioning records, besides the power to order search and seizure of documents.

16. The decision of the Lokpal will be conveyed to the "competent authority" for example, the Prime Minister vis-a-vis his colleagues in the Council of Ministers and the Chief Ministers.

17. The "competent authority" is bound to communicate to

the Lokpal within three months of the report, the action taken or proposed to be taken. The case is closed if the Lokpal is satisfied with the action. If not, he reports accordingly to the President and informs the complainant.

18. Lokpal will submit an annual report to the President who is obliged to lay all such reports before Parliament together with an explanatory memorandum.

19. As regards the Prime Minister himself, the notice of the formal inquiry as well as the Lokpal's final report are required to be placed before his colleagues in the Council of Ministers.

Differences from the previous proposals

Lokpal is essentially a parliamentary institution whose only sanction is parliamentary action and the public opinion but cannot be made penal offences. He is not empowered to pronounce sentence and inflict suitable punishment.

Unlike the Lokpal and Lokayukta Bill of 1971 this Bill does not cover the public servants. Unless the Bill clearly includes the public servants, it will not be possible for Lokpal to do full justice. The public grievances in respect of sheer maladministration are also excluded from the Lokpal's jurisdiction. Shri Bhupesh Gupta in his note of dissent appended to the Joint Committee Report suggested an investigation to "unrevel the mystery behind the exclusion of public servants". The Lokpal can inquire into the allegations of "misconduct" against a public man but the definition of misconduct has not been properly defined even though it includes conferment of improper benefit or favouritism as well by allowing directly or indirectly, the public man's position to be taken advantage of by any of his relatives or associates.

Two specific categories of cases are sought to be excluded from the Lokpal's province of inquiry: those alleging public misconduct that occurred more than five years ago, and those that already form the subject matter of the current spate of special investigations under the Commission of Inquiry Act. These two conditions might well produce strange and even unintended results as it may involve only those responsible within the five year period.

A levy of fee of Rs.1,000 may be out of the reach of an

ordinary citizen and may discourage many to lodge a complaint even though the Lokpal has a discretion to waive the above condition.

According to the 1971 proposal, the Lokpal was to be appointed by the President in consultation with the Chief Justice, Prime Minister, and the leader of the Opposition. The new proposal excludes the leader of the Opposition. It will be a healthy practice if the leader of Opposition is also involved in the selection of the Lokpal.

Joint Committee Report

The present proposal introduced in the Lok Sabha by Janata Government is in a battered form. The very sanctity of the institution which is supposed to be the defender of the people is lost. The powers of Lokpal have been further curtailed by the Joint Committee which presented its Report to the Parliament on 20 July 1978. As already stated the present form of the Lokpal cannot look into the public grievances against administration, government servants are not within his purview, he has no suo muto powers of investigation, complaints against the Legislators should first be scrutinized by the Presiding Officers of the respective Houses of Parliament. Even some members suggested that the Union Territories with their own legislatures and government should not be under the purview of the Lokpal. In other words this institution has been reduced to a Permanent Commission of Inquiry against political officers. The Joint Committee excluded the Chief Ministers from the purview of the Lokpal but later the Home Minister gave notice in the Parliament that Chief Ministers should also be included in the Bill.

According to the Bill the Lokpal will enjoy the powers of a civil court while trying a suit, such as summoning witnesses and requisitioning of records, besides power to order search for and seizure of documents but will not be a court for punishing the contempts even if he is subjected to most uncharitable attacks in Press and elsewhere. Mr. R.D. Gattani, a member of the Joint Committee, has rightly put it that "there can be actual interruption in his work by say sounding of conches or cymbals or by uttering nonsense in loud tone making him impossible to work."

The original Bill provides that the Lokpal will send his decisions to the "competent authority" for example, the Prime Minister vis-a-vis his colleagues in the Council of Ministers and vice versa. The Joint Committee suggested Speaker as the "competent authority" in the case of Prime Minister and Deputy Speaker in the case of Speaker. The Joint Committee is silent in the case of Chairman, of Rajya Sabha. For the Speaker to take action against the Prime Minister will be embarrassing and as one of the members of the Joint Committee, Mr. B.C. Kamble, has put it: "His office as Speaker of House of People and his office as 'competent authority' may come into conflict when he is required to take some action. The office of the Speaker cannot be criticised at all. Whereas the office of the 'competent authority' assumed by the Speaker cannot be allowed to be immune from criticism." It would have been more appropriate to make President of India as the competent authority in the case of the Prime Minister and the Speaker. However, the Home Minister has given notice to the Parliament to the effect that in the case of Prime Minister the competent authority will be the Lok Sabha and not the Speaker as approved by the Joint Committee.

The most important amendment suggested by the Joint Committee is in respect of the Members of Parliament. Any complaint against them should first be scrutinized by the Presiding Officers of the Houses who will send it to the Lokpal provided they are satisfied about its genuineness, provided again that no publicity is given about such an inquiry which should be held in camera and "whoever contravenes the provisions of Sub-section (1) shall be punished with imprisonment for a term which may extend to six months or with fine, or with both". There appears to be no strong reason why Members of Parliament should be included within the scope of this Bill since M.P.s hardly enjoy any power of authority to be misused. If, however, there are secluded cases like that of Tulmohan Ram, the law has enough powers to deal with them. Having included M.P.s in the Bill, it will not be proper to give them any special treatment over the other "public men". When the

Lokpal examines a case any adverse publicity can equally damage the reputation of any individual then why special provision for M.P.s alone. An impression is being created that the Joint Committee has favoured their colleagues which has got to be avoided, as Mr. Ram Jethmalani has put it in the note of dissent, "it creates a misleading impression in the public mind that Members of Legislatures being collectively the law-making authority are unwilling to subject themselves to the wholesome restraints of the Act". In any case the provisions of the original Bill are not likely to deter a legislator from doing his duty to his electorate or to the Parliament.

The Joint Committee also suggested removing the Chief Ministers from the scope of this Bill on the ground that "the Chief Ministers were primarily answerable to their respective Legislatures and not to Parliament" and that the States should be asked to enact their own legislations. So far, only the States of Orissa, Maharashtra, Bihar, Rajasthan, Karnataka and U.P. have enacted legislations for the appointment of their Lokayuktas. The experience of Maharashtra and Bihar have shown that they are not getting enough cooperation from the State machinery. The office of Lokayukta cannot be effective unless it is directly under the control of Lokpal. Even otherwise, the Commission of Inquiry Act provides for an inquiry against the Chief Ministers of the States by the Central Government. The recent decision of the Supreme Court in the case of Commission of Inquiry against the Chief Minister of Karnataka has further strengthened the case of inclusion of Chief Ministers in the purview of Lokpal Bill.

Some other changes suggested by the Joint Committee like defining the term "misconduct", incorporating a table of "competent authorities" in the Bill, etc., are not very relevant. Various Commissions of Inquiry have already defined the misconduct and in regard to competent authority the appointing authority should invariably be the competent authority. In the case of the Speaker it should not be the Deputy Speaker but the President of India. Some changes suggested by the Committee are equally good such as consulting the leaders of various parties and groups in the respective Houses of Parliament in regard to the appointment of the Lokpal, mode of appointment of officers and staff required by the Lokpal, provision of deterrent punishment in order to check on the filing of frivolous or false complaints, etc. But in a country like India where millions are poor, the provision of Rs.1000 as deposit will certainly discourage many genuine complaints being brought before the Lokpal and in view of the provision for deterrent punishment for false complaints there is hardly any justification for the deposit of Rs.1000. The Lokpal and the Lokayuktas should be freely accessible to the common man. There should not be any intermediary between the Lok (public) and the Lokpal/Lokayukta. There should not be any fee or security deposit to start with. This may provide unnecessary hurdle for the citizen and appear to attach a price-tag to the services of the new institution. The term "public men" also needs to be changed as Shri Ram Jethmalani has put it, "its feminine gender 'public women' has a connotation of an entirely different kind".

Having changed the main objective of the A.R.C. recommendation restricting the scope of "public men" excluding the public servants, public grievances and their redress, etc., and further changes suggested by the Joint Committee, a confusion has been created and it is not certain whether the government will be in a position to get through the Bill even in this "battered" form. The citizen in India feels greatly concerned with delay, favouritism, corruption and inefficiency in administration, whether it be at State or Central level The awakening in public has reached new heights after the emergency. The Press, the Legislatures and other platforms are furiously at war with the acts of omission and commission. In particular the opposition parties and members have been insistent on Commissions being appointed to inquire into allegations against ministers. While the institution of Ombudsman in the West is grievances-oriented, the scheme of the Bill is being overshadowed more and more with the concept of an anti-corruption machinery. Not that such a machinery is not needed but the fear is that this may leave the grievances angle uncared for. It is after all public grievances that need immediate succour.

The Bill apart, the idea of Lokpal has to be understood by the people of India in all its implications. The commonest argument against the institution of an Ombudsman is that for a big country like India with more than 600 million people and with the Central, State and local governments criss-crossing the various layers of administration, it will be impossible for a single person or a body of persons to look adequately into all the grievances against administration. The argument lost some of its force when for the first time a comparatively well administered country like the U.K. adopted the scheme. The beauty about the institution is not what it is able to act upon but what it is able to prevent from happening. The very presence of the Lokpal and Lokayukta will keep the bureaucracy on its toes. The knowledge that there is someone legally empowered to look into public grievances will compel the concerned officials to keep themselves on the straight path. The saying that an "ounce of prevention is worth a pound of cure" applies well to the overall influence which such an institution will have an official conduct and attitude. There are about one crore persons employed in the government and the public sectors all over the country. The need for vigilance and readiness to step in to correct administrative failures is greater in India than in small countries like Denmark, Sweden, New Zealand and even the U.K. If such an institution is adopted by the states and local governments, there is a likelihood of an immediate toning up of administration at all levels.

The conduct of ministers and high officers must be above suspicion, as well as outside the reach of malicious and false attacks and allegations. Allegations are often reckless, exaggerated and false. A whispering campaign may snowball into a politically motivated demand for the resignation of even an innocent and conscientious Minister. Lokpal will prove to be a protective devise against false and malicious allegations.

The success and usefulness of the institution of Lokpal and Lokayukta depends upon the kind of persons appointed to these offices. They must be of unimpeachable integrity and character. Their courage must be such as to take decisions regardless of personal consequences. They must have been persons who commanded public confidence and respect. They must have had administrative experience. Besides, they must have had experience of having moved among the poor and the helpless without hate and of communing with powerful and exhalted without fear. Lokpal, in particular has to be a man of great stature. The first appointment to this post is of special importance. The image of the office is the one created by the first occupant. An unsuitable occupant may undermine the institution. The Parliament, the Judiciary and the Executive must let Lokpal and Lokayuktas investigate into complaints without any interference. Prestige consciousness should not be allowed to impede the path of Lokpal and Lokayuktas.

In view of the above the government should review the whole issue and if they still want to have the Lokpal in the present form at least they should simultaneously appoint two Lokayuktas under the Lokpal one dealing with grievances and the other dealing with allegations against the administrative machinery. The second Lokayukta will replace the Central Vigilance Commissioner. A similar network of Lokayuktas should be appointed in all the States directly under the Lokpal on the lines of High Courts even if it means amendment of the Constitution. The present investigating staff and accommodation of one of the Commissions of Inquiry can be an immediate gap arrangement for the office of the Lokpal. The institution will be an expression of the highest homage which any government can pay to the cause of good public administration. This is a great experiment as no country of such size and complexity as ours has so far attempted this experiment. Let us give the institution the cooperation it needs and the dignity it deserves. If the common man is to remain the ultimate unit of democracy, the degree of success of the institution of the Lokpal will be the measure of our democratic spirit and commitment.

CHAPTER IX

The Case for an Indian Ombudsman

SOME BASIC ISSUES

The Administrative Reforms Commission's proprosals for the establishment of the Lokpal and Lokayuktas have aroused not only some considerable interest but also opposition from several quarters. It is contended that the creation of Ombudsman-type of institutions will be a transgression of the Constitution of the country; it will curtail autonomy of States and create new tensions in Union-State relations. The new institutions will cut across the supremacy of the Parliament and the doctrine of ministerial responsibility to legislature, and denigrate the judiciary. It has even been said that the Ombudsman will be a new star chamber with a different Indian title instead of a Nordic name. The titles Lokpal and Lokayuktas are not only flambouyant but also dangerously pretentious, much reminiscent of the benevolent despots. An Ombudsman will not be like a Supreme Court or a High Court Judge and soon after the Ombudsman, we will have to have an Ombudsman for the Ombudsman. Further, there is a risk of the Ombudsman being overwhelmed by the weight of his work and not being able to fulfil all the expectations of those who go to him. Some of this criticism reflects a measure of difficulty in fitting the Ombudsman-type of institutions into the constitutional and political framework of the country but a good deal of it appears to be due to lack of correct appreciation of the nature and purposes of the new machinery and the resistance of the interests which will be affected by its creation. The discussion of the basic issues involved, which follows, relates mostly to the proposals as made by the Administrative Reforms Commission, and not much to the provisions of the Lokpal and Lokayukta Bill.

Lokpal and the States

It has been urged that unless we are prepared to throw the whole Indian Constitution lock, stock and barrel overboard, an Ombudsman cannot fit in the Indian Constitution. The constitutional difficulties arise mainly in regard to two aspects: (1) The extension of the jurisdiction of the Lokpal as proposed by the Administrative Reforms Commission over the secretaries to government and Ministers in the States; and (2) the curtailment of the supremacy of Parliament and the State Legislatures. As regards this first aspect, the difficulty arises because the executive powers in relation to state matters vest in States. The Administrative Reforms Commission duly noted that Norway, Sweden, Denmark, New Zealand, and the United Kingdom have centralized administrations whereas India is a federation based on a division of functions between the Union and the States. It deserves to be mentioned that the United Front governments of West Bengal and some other States objected to the institution of the Lokpal on the ground of transgression of State autonomy. These State governments, which were controlled by parties or coalitions opposed to the party in power at the Centre, were apprehensive that the new institution might be used as an instrument of political vendetta. Even if there be no such intention on the part of the ruling party at the Centre and even if the character of the new Institutions will safeguard against any such intention being put into effect, the suspicion that it may be so used can be politically damaging. It will put new strains on the delicate balance of Union-State relations. As already noted, the Lokpal and Lokayukta Bill, 1969, did not cover the States and the new legislation which was introduced by Janata Government even though covers the political heads of the states such as Chief Ministers, Members of Legislative Assemblies, etc. is also not likely to succeed.

The Administrative Reforms Commission was of the view that such difficulties could be resolved by the amendment of the Constitution, if necessary, and consequently they need not constitute an insurmountable obstacle in bringing into force the proposed system. This school of thought holds that a constitutional amendment is not necessary for extending the scope of the Ombudsman's activities to the States. The Union government has already at times conducted enquiries into the corrupt practices indulged in by State ministers etc., under the provision of Commissions of Inquiries Act, 1952, which is a Central Act. Accordingly, a law proposed by the Union Parliament should suffice. Another approach to overcome the constitutional difficulties which has been suggested, is the enactment of enabling laws, parallel to the Central law by the States.[1] A point has also been made that the Lokayuktas for the States should be appointed by the President for ensuring their objective and independent functioning. The appointment of the Lokayuktas in the States by the State Governor on the recommendations of the Chief Minister, even if the latter consults the leaders of the Opposition and the Chief Justice of the State, is not likely to inspire public confidence, nor ensure effective independce in their working. Another danger is that a new government which does not like this institution may have it abolished as has happened in the case of Karnataka where the Lokayukta has been asked to resign and his office has been abolished by the new government which took over in January 1980.

As the Administrative Reforms Commission has observed in its report on State administration, the extension of the jurisdiction of the Lokpal to the States will help to meet this problem by bringing into existence a standing machinery for the purpose. A Lokpal appointed in consultation with the Chief Justice of India and the leader of the Opposition in the Lok Sabha could ensure confidence in the new institution and help curb the emergence of undesirable features of public life.

Parliamentary supremacy over administration

As regards the objections relating to the sovereignty of Parliament, it has been pointed out that Parliament's control over administration has necessarily to be of a general character. "We do not mean that parliaments have, or pretend to have,

[1]Donald C. Rowat's letter, dated 9 March 1967, to Shri Morarji Desai, the then Chairman, Administrative Reforms Commission, Government of India. Professor Rowat also suggested that this difficulty might be surmounted if the States were to pass enabling laws parallel to the federal law. He also apprehended that the State-appointed Ombudsman would not be independent enough.

or ought to have, the powers of continuous intervention in administration and positive participation in the operation of the law. They do not, in fact, do more than act as the judge and the corrector of the Cabinet and its administrative assistants. We could show, further, that it is almost impossible to do more than this."[2] In view of the broad character of the surveillance of Parliament over the administration, the new Ombudsman-type of institution should help to serve as powerful instrument and agency for Parliament. In India, we have already a few constitutional authorities like the Union Public Service Commission and the Comptroller and Auditor General who assist the Parliament in exercising effective control over administration. The new Ombudsman institutions should be able to provide authoritative material to Parliament to act upon and save its time and effort, thereby enabling it to concentrate on more important work of the House. At present the reports of the Comptroller and Auditor General, help to feed Parliament's Public Accounts Committee. If necessary, the Lokpal may also be fitted in through a Committee of Parliament so that his recommendations, even when they are against the minister or administration, are assured of a fair deal. He need not in any way encroach upon the Parliament's authority, nor on the jurisdiction of the Petition Committee which only calls for reports from departments.

An allied objection which has been raised is about the conflict this institution will have with the legislators who have traditionally performed personal services for citizens wronged by the government. To deprive them of this function, would be to deny them a potential vote-winning device. It would also tend to reduce the contacts between the legislators and their constituencies and eliminate an important source of information the legislators have come to rely upon in their search for methods of improving administrative efficiency. It is true that the normal habits of the people is to turn to their legislators with complaints about administration and to the minister concerned through them. However, it is not likely that all such complaints may go to Ombudsman only. Even if an Ombudsman

[2]Herman Finer, *The Theory and Practice of Modern Government*, 2 volumes, London, 1932.

received everyone of the complaints against administration, the legislators would still continue to have many opportunities to build electoral support through case work.

Allegations against ministers and doctrine of ministerial responsibility

Connected with the problem of Parliamentary supremacy are two important interrelated issues: (a) the investigation by the Lokpal into the allegations against ministers; and (b) the validity of the enquiries by the Lokpal and Lokayuktas against civil servants in the context of doctrine of ministerial responsibility for all actions of the civil servants, and the difficulties likely to be experienced by the Lokpal in fixing responsibility for certain administrative decisions or actions in such a situation.

As regards the first issue, the Administrative Reforms Commission considered carefully the question whether ministerial decisions should come within the purview of the Ombudsman or not, and came to the conclusion that these decisions should be included within the jurisdiction of the Ombudsman. For this, the Commission has advanced the following reasons:

1. Having regard to the manner in which our democracy has been functioning, both at the Centre and the States, cases of injustice at the ministerial level must be dealt with.
2. It is only at the level of Minister or the Secretary, subject to his instructions and directions that many of the important orders of Government affecting the citizen acquire finality. At lower levels, correctives through appeals, representations and personal access to various authorities are available, but at the level of the Minister or his Secretary there is a finality from which, only in very rare cases, there is any escape.
3. If the institution could deal effectively and expeditiously with matters at the source of authority, it would have an exemplary effect on other officials and other levels of official hierarchy and thereby it would induce a rise in the general level of efficiency, propriety and justice.

The Administrative Reforms Commission conceded that it is open to Parliament or State legislature to deal with a minister when he goes wrong, or to deal with an officer (under him and for whom he is answerable) who commits a wrongful act or is guilty of a culpable omission. But these channels are not, in the nature of things, easily accessible to the common man, and the time at their disposal, their procedures, their conventions and practices do not make for quick, speedy or effective action in a large number of cases. The Administrative Reforms Commission concluded that the appointment of the Ombudsman cannot be regarded as a breach of the spirit of the Constitution. In recent years, in a number of cases, commissions under the Commissions of Inquiry Act have been appointed to inquire into ministerial conduct.

Against the proposed jurisdiction of the Lokpal in the matter of ministerial decisions, it has also been contended that even when commissions are appointed to investigate into the conduct of ministers, it is the Parliament or legislature which becomes seized of the matter and is the final authority which takes action or to which action is reported. Again, no court can inquire into the question as to what advice has been tendered by the ministers to the head of the state. An investigation into the advice tendered by the minister or by an outside authority would, therefore, be against the spirit of the Constitution. It also deserves notice that under the Indian system, the ministers, speaking technically are only advisers to the President or the Governor, who in theory, is responsible for all the executive action of the Government. No minister has any authority to pass executive orders. All enforceable orders are issued under the signature of the executive officers in the name of the Head of the state though they act in accordance with the direction of the minister. Politically, it is thus possible to argue that if the Prime Minister advises the President on the recommendations of another functionary, i.e. the Lokpal, rather than on his own judgement, it would dilute the responsibility of his colleagues to him and weaken his authority over them.

The Administrative Reforms Commission, taking due cognizance of this criticism, pointed out in its report that there is not much substance in the political argument. The Prime Minister's hands would be strengthened rather than weakened by the new institution. Firstly, recommendations of such an authority will save him from the unpleasant duty of investigating against his own colleagues. Secondly, it will be possible for him to deal with the matter without the glare of publicity which often vitiates the atmosphere and affects the judgement of the general public. Thirdly, it would enable him to avoid internal pressures which often help to shield the delinquent. What applies to the Prime Minister of the Indian Union applies mutatis mutandis to the Chief Minister of a State.

As regards the doctrine of ministerial responsibility for the acts of civil servants, such responsibility is obviously there under the Cabinet govenment. In theory, a minister is responsible for all the decisions of the civil servants working in the department under his charge even though decisions may have been made by the lowest official. However, in practice, ministers have been called upon to resign only in case there has been a gross failure in policy or its impropriety, implementation, or negligence on the part of a minister. While all administrative actions are taken on behalf of the President and all orders are issued under the signature of civil servants (and not ministers), the minister concerned or the government as a whole remains responsible for redressing the injustice which may have been done to the citizens in the exercise of the executive powers. Some of the executive orders affecting the citizens may have been issued by the civil servants under the powers vested in them by a statute; other orders may have been passed by them under delegated powers.

The Administrative Reforms Commission seems to recognize this in the wording of its report, "an administrative act for which a Minister or a Secretary to Government is finally responsible" and the "action taken by *or with the approval of* a Minister or Secretary". But the affected citizen will obviously have to lodge a complaint with the Lokpal or the Lokayukta, as the case may be, against the officer who has issued the relevant executive order. It would be for the Lokpal and Lokayukta to look into the *papers* and to allocate internal responsibility within the governmental system for a particular administrative decision and to fix the responsibility for the mala fide decisions on the part of the officers. Under the proposals contained in the Lokpal/Lokayukta Bill of 1969, the Lokayukta at the Centre would be working under the overall supervision of the Lokpal. Though the Lokpal will mostly look after the complaints against ministers and secretaries, he would also guide the Lokayuktas. This integrated scheme of the functioning of the Lokpal and Lokayukta is obviously an improvement over the Administrative Reform Commission's proposals.[3]

The fears that the new institution would affect the functioning of the judiciary are unfounded. According to the Administrative Reforms Commission, the Indian system already provides for the functioning of the judiciary and administrative tribunals and for a hierarchy of appeals against the orders of subordinate authorities to superior authorities. The Ombudsman system is not envisaged as coming into clash with these institutions. The scope of action available to the courts is too narrow and limited to meet adequately the needs of the public.

On the whole, it can, therefore, be said that the institution of Ombudsman, if adopted in India, will in no way compromise the principle of Parliamentary system. On the other hand, it would help strengthen the same. The Ombudsman will be a representative of Parliament, will act on its behalf and report to it, and thus Parliament will be able to function much more effectively as a controller of the executive than at present. Even if we leave aside the experience of the Scandinavian countries with the Ombudsman institution on the ground that their governmental system is different from ours, the experience of United Kingdom and Canada shows that the Ombudsman idea is not incompatible with the Parliamentary system.

The question of viability

The proposed institutions of the Lokpal and the Lokayukta have also come in for some good criticism on grounds of their unsuitability to Indian conditions and their non-viability. It is said that, as compared to the political and social standards

[3]Some eminent authorities on the subject, however, feel differently. The most unusual aspect of the proposal is the recommendation that there should be Ombudsmen at two levels. "I must admit that I am somewhat confused as to the dividing line between the two in the handling of complaints." (Letter dated 6 March 1967 from Professor Donald C. Rowat to Shri Morarji Desai, the then Chairman, Administrative Reforms Commission).

in the Scandinavian and other countries where the Ombudsman machinery has been adopted, there is in India a lack of sense of duty or dedication to public service and a lack of resistance to conform one's own behaviour to the accepted norms of honesty and probity in public life. Illiteracy reigns supreme in India and enlightened public opinion necessary to make the Ombudsman institution work is virtually lacking. In addition, there is also in evidence a persistent tendency in all walks of life to subordinate national interests to personal or party interests which reflects an inordinate love of office. The cumulative effect of all this is to create conditions vastly different from those obtaining in the countries of the West. The desirability or otherwise of setting up the Ombudsman machinery in India will, therefore, have to be judged in the context of these conditions as a whole.

Besides, these Scandinavian countries have all achieved a very high standard of living and their citizens have not much to complain about. The small number of complaints which have gone to the Ombudsman in these countries are prompted not so much by the distress of persons seeking redress as by a desire to assert their rights—rights of the members of economically advanced societies. It has, therefore, been easy for the Ombudsman in these countries (with limited staff) to manage the complaints received by him. In fact, the Ombudsman in New Zealand "considers himself a little under-employed as yet". In India, the people have as yet a long way to go to attain a reasonably decent standard of living. The hardships which are inevitable in traversing that way and the suffering presently undergone due to the insufficiency of resources have produced a social atmosphere whch is surcharged with complaint-mindedness. Will it be possible for an Ombudsman in India to cope up with the large number of complaints with which he will be flooded? And if he fails to do so, will it not lead to a worsening of the situation? Will it not, therefore, be better to concentrate upon production which ultimately will remove the basic cause of complaints, viz. distress caused by the low standard of living? These are obviously some important considerations which deserve attention.

Geographically, India is a very vast country and bears no comparison with small countries like Sweden, New Zealand, etc. In the U.S.A., the sheer size of that country is a matter of concern to its people in considering the establishment of the Ombudsman institution. In India, with more than 680 million people and with the Central, State and local governments criss-crossing the various sectors, it may not be feasible for a single person or a body of persons to look adequately into all the grievances against administration. This argument is obviously based on the ground that the Ombudsman can function effectively only in countries with small population such as Sweden (7 millions), Denmark (4.5 millions), New Zealand (2.25 millions), Britain (over 50 millions).

In the Scandinavian countries, with their small size and high public morality, the functioning of the Ombudsman does not present much difficulty. In India, the Central government employees are about 20 lakhs and the State government employees nearly number 75 lakhs. With such a vast body of personnel, coupled with a vast amount of legislative output, there are bound to be a large number of authorities and officials vested with discretionary powers. It would be a difficult task for the Indian Ombudsman to supervise the work of such a vast number in the matter of citizens' complaints. In other countries the number of staff that assists the Ombudsman is limited to 10 or 12 persons.

Critics of the Ombudsman idea have therefore dismissed its proposed application on the national level in India as unrealistic and impractical. They contend that the Indian Ombudsman would either soon become immobilized beneath an avalanche of complaints from the country's huge population and the vastness of governmental machinery or it would have to expand its staff so greatly that it would become merely another bureaucracy bogged down in red tape.[4]

The Administrative Reforms Commission also examined this aspect but felt that the vastness of the country and its population need not deter us from establishing an Ombudsman in India. In order to reduce the volume of complaints, the Commission was of the view that the Ombudsman should

[4]Justice P.B. Mukherjee of the Calcutta High Court even fears that India will soon need a super-Ombudsman to supervise the work of first-generation Ombudsmen.

function only in respect of those matters for which such remedies are not available or where, in some cases, it might not be reasonable to expect a citizen to take recourse to legal proceedings. This would substantially reduce the number of complaints eligible for investigation and thus enable the Ombudsman to devote his attention and energies only to those cases in which prima facie the need for redressing an act of injustice or maladministration exists. The institution of Ombudsman need not be overwhelmed by the number of complaints it might be receiving. Over a period of years, when the public becomes accustomed to the working of the system, it would realize the futility of approaching it with cases which do not need its attention or in which the complaints are not genuine. Again, by a suitable division of functions between the Ombudsman and other functionaries to deal with citizens' grievances, it should be possible to distribute the work load in such a manner as would enable each functionary to do justice to the complaints it received. There is some force in the argument that the Ombudsman may not prove useful in dealing with the complaints of a vast population. But the way out of this difficulty is not to throw the baby along with the bath water but to adapt the institution with necessary changes to suit the genius of our country. We have noted earlier the differences in the role of the Ombudsman in various countries. Our ingenuity will be in making suitable adaptations in the context of our particular circumstances. One can even think of a number of Ombudsmen each specializing in certain kinds of complaints or taking care of territorial subdivisions but coming together to consider hard cases. For big countries, Professor Donald Rowat has suggested a Commission of three Ombudsmen "who would handle less important cases individually and most important cases collectively. The Commission should consist of a judge, an administrator and a public man."

Some opponents of the Ombudsman have opposed the proposal on the ground that it would subject the governmental agencies to constant interference, thereby decreasing efficiency and smooth operation. It is feared that the new institution may engender among the civil servants a tendency towards timidity and hesitation in the exercise of discretion and taking of responsibility. Under constant threat of investigation officials may be forced to rely more and more on precedent and red tape and the public services might develop a kind of "hardening of the arteries" which would be damaging to delegation and flexibility.

As regards the argument that Ombudsman would dampen the initiative of the civil servant to take initiative, the experience of other countries shows that there need not be any fear on this count. As to the charge that an attempt to exercise regulatory check on the actions of the executive will lead to a serious and widespread slowing down of governmental action, this should not and need not be the result of the functioning of the Ombudsman. The directive or instrument of instructions issued by Parliament to the Ombudsman may provide that in discharging his obligations the Ombudsman will act with sympathetic understanding and in such a manner that conscientious officers are not scared into adopting an over-cautious attitude and thus developing a habit of seeking support for their decisions from higher authorities. The Ombudsman in New Zealand and Scandinavian countries has come to be accepted by the administration and there is no hostility, apathy or antipathy against him.

CASE FOR AN OMBUDSMAN

Inevitability of the institution

By and large, India has failed so far to adopt her administrative system to the new challenge of development, democracy, and socialism. There are nearly a crore of persons employed in the public sector all over the country who come in contact with millions of people every day. The dissatisfaction of the people with administration cannot but increase unless the administrative machinery is geared effectively for the expanding developmental and welfare tasks. In addition, it will be necessary to provide effective machinery for redress of citizens' grievances. Even with the best of the administrative system the citizens' grievances are likely to multiply because of the advance of processes of democracy and socialism. The redress machinery needs to be conceived not as an indicator of the failures of administration but in the wider perspective of the increased need for the citizen's satisfaction and protection of his rights in the context of a phenomenal growth in the state activity. In the U.K., the Ombudsman has been established even when the administration is said to maintain high standards of integrity and impartiality. The Ombudsman can therefore be regarded as the manifestation of the society's respect for rule of law, social justice, equality before the law, and democratic ideals.

The importance of the Ombudsman-type of machinery in a modern welfare state has been very well brought out in the following observations of the Norwegian Committee on Administrative Procedures:

> [Our] recommendations are not based upon any assumption or allegation on the part of the Committee that the Norwegian administrative system is a bad one or that the civil servants are incompetent. The Committee states, on the contrary, that our administration may bear comparison with any other system of administration. This is also true of the guarantees and safeguards. The reasons behind the proposal to strengthen the means of control are much more far-reaching and go deeper. They have their origin in the characteristic development of the modern welfare state. It seems unavoidable at the stage of economic and technical development which, regardless of politics, has been achieved in all modern societies, that ever larger and broader powers shall be bestowed upon the administrative authorities. This is the background against which the Norwegian proposals and the many efforts in other countries to introduce reforms in the same field must be considered.

In creating the Ombudsman-type of institutions in India we can profitably draw upon the traditional values. In olden days when societies began to govern themselves, and the problems were simple and not many, the kings themselves undertook the function of hearing complaints either in their durbars or on their inspection rounds; and redressed the people's grievances on the spot. One of the Mughal emperors, Jahangir, had put a chain outside his palace which was attached to a bell inside his bedroom. His instructions were that in case there were complaints against officials or individuals, the citizens were at liberty to draw his attention any time of the day or night by pulling the chain. The king, on hearing the bell, would come out to listen to the complainant personally. The legend goes that one night a donkey which was not properly fed by its master was brought by some sympathizer and it pulled the chain. The king came out immediately and sent for its owner.

The Indian social system continues to be, by and large, authoritarian and paternalistic. An Ombudsman, as the protector of the people's rights, once appointed, should be able to build on the societal values and win the confidence and respect of the people.

Ombudsman as citizens' defender

In the area of citizens' grievances, the new institutions of Lokpal and Lokayukta should be able to provide a real service to the people.

A court or tribunal may find itself helpless when there is, in a technical sense, non-compliance by an administrative agency with the rules. But the Ombudsman may go beyond the formal requirements and see if there has, in substance, been injustice irrespective of the formal observance of the rules. A major source of grievance is the large quantum of discretionary powers, not properly defined and articulated, excercised by administrators. Not unoften it is seen that the discretion is exercised only in name with reason and justice. If the discretion is patently exercised the wrong way, the Ombudsman will be able to question it. However, if an officer knows that each and every of his decision relating to the citizens will be subject to a review by the Ombudsman, he will undoubtedly be averse to showing favours and delaying matters.

The Lokpal can also perform an important public relations role. He can act to bridge the gulf between the people and the administration. If the reasons for the rejection of his complaint are explained to the citizen, he would often feel satisfied that after all the administration had not acted in an arbitrary fashion. A number of grievances continue to linger because the concerned departments do not explain the reasons for rejection of their cases.[5]

In New Zealand and Scandinavian countries, the very

[5]The Swedish Ombudsman has, in fact, made a suggestion that a legal obligation may be placed on the administration to give reasons so that the number of complaints coming to him may be reduced.

existence of the Ombudsman is reported to have brought satisfaction to the citizens even where no gain or redress for a complaint could be achieved. The Swedish Parliamentary Committee on the effectiveness of the public control officer called the Justice Ombudsman (JO) commented in 1939 that "The less cause the JO has to intervene with his official authority the more surely is the objective of his office attained." Thus the usefulness of the new institution will lie much more in what it prevents from happening than in the grievance it redresses. In India "Ombudsman will keep bureaucracy on toes".

Ombudsman as protector of officials

A large number of complaints are likely to be found to be devoid of any substance and to the extent the Ombudsman says so, the public will be assured that there is nothing fundamentally wrong with the administration. A better relationship would get established between the people and the administration After all, a standing suspicion in the public mind against the impartiality, objectivity, or rationality in administrative actions does no good to anybody. The Ombudsman can help remove such suspicions and doubts in the public mind through his investigations.

Often for the wrongs and corruption of a few, the entire hierarchy is held in suspicion, if not in disgrace. This distorted image is bound to be corrected when complaints are proved baseless. The New Zealand Ombudsman brings out this aspect of his work in the following words:

> It would be incorrect to look upon my office as being 'anti-administration'. The Ombudsman is not concerned to try to find fault if no fault exists, and it has proved necessary to advise a few complainants, in quite forceful terms, that they should cease groundless attacks on departments or officials. In so far as thorough and independent investigation of allegations of malpractice establishes that those allegations are unfounded, the office acts as a valuable shelf to the administration, while at the same time members of the public can be assured that any such allegations, if reasonably supported by evidence or inference, will be carefully investigated. In fact, up to the present time, no such allegations have been found to be justified.

The Administrative Reforms Commission was of the view that the informal character of inquiries by the Ombudsman would save the public servant from exposure to public gaze during the course of an inquiry. A public inquiry often has the effect of condemning the government servant in the public eye before he is really found guilty or innocent, as the case may be. The Commission seems to be justified in taking an optimistic view of the usefulness of the institution in the Indian context. The new institution will thus be a protection for, and a source of strength rather than a discouragement to, an honest official.

Lokpal as preserver of standards in high places

Ministers and high officers must be above suspicion, as well as outside the reach of malicious and baseless attacks and allegations. Allegations are often reckless, exaggerated, and false. A whispering campaign may snowball into a politically motivated demand for the resignation of even an innocent and conscientious minister. The Indian Ombudsman will prove to be a protective device against false and malacious allegations. The inquiries will be held in camera and it is only when some substance is found in the allegations made that these will be mentioned in the report to Parliament, indicating also the action, if any, taken by the government.

It is true that the effectiveness of the Lokpal/Lokayuktas will be significantly conditioned by the values and standards of public conduct which the politicians are prepared to accept irrespective of party and personal loyalties and which the public are prepared to impose on the body politics. However, even within the environmental constraints the Lokpal and Lokayuktas will furnish a standing and purposeful machinery to look impartially into allegations of corruption and impropriety in high places. It has been contended that Administrative Reforms Commission's original proposal of the Lokpal looking into complaints against ministers and secretaries, both at the Centre and the States, will cut across Union-State boundaries and may intensify tensions in Union-State relations. But it cannot be denied that the institution of the Lokpal will help ensure probity in high public offices and check maladministration. In the larger interest of the nation, the future of Indian democracy and the purity of administration such a step will be in the right direction.

Role in administrative improvement

The Ombudsman in India will not merely redress the grievances; he would also indirectly help to bring about improvement in administrative procedures and practices for the benefit of the general public and assist in increasing public confidence in the administration. If the Lokpal considers, as a result of his study of one or more cases, that an amendment of the law would be justified, he will make appropriate recommendations. The Ombudsman, as an independent external control agency, is likely to be more effective than any other control mechanism which the Indian bureaucracy can provide.

How the Swedish Ombudsman goes about his task has been succinctly described by a writer as follows:

> The telephone rings. He picks up the receiver and listens, sometimes tugging at his moustaches or chewing on his cigar, his forehead puckered in thought. The instrument continues to make noises. Then, he hangs up, and softly swears. He frequently looks at his intercom, which he knows will blow up with life within 15 or 20 minutes. And he is right to the second. A man, shuffling his feet, knocks tentatively on the door, is admitted. Papers are read, questions asked, and the man withdraws. The big man takes his side, gets into a jeep, and is gone. Suddenly, somewhere in town, in some government office, there is tension; all alert, all eyes. All are asked to go out. Files are taken out, read and replaced; some of them sealed and taken away, an officer questioned separately, assistant separately. Some time in the evening, an officer is dismissed; he is no more required.

SUGGESTIONS FOR IMPROVEMENT

Lokpal and anti-corruption macninery

The recommendations of the Administrative Reforms Commission and the government's proposals as contained in the Bill of 1969 and Janata government's Bill of 1977 lack realism in the matter of providing effective machinery for dealing with the complaints of corruption. One of its study teams as well as the Administrative Reforms Commission itself have recommended that the Lokpal and Lokayuktas when appointed, should look after the work at present being done by the Vigilance Commissioner at the Centre. Even the lapsed Bill contains a proposal for abolishing Central Vigilance Commission[6] and transferring its functions to the proposed institution of Lokpal and Lokayuktas. It is worth noting that the institution of Ombudsman in the West is grievances-oriented whereas the Indian schemes are being over-shadowed more and more by the concept of an anti-corruption machinery.[7] It is feared that this may leave the grievances angle inadequately attended. It is after all public grievances that need remedying.

At the same time, the charges of corruption, nepotism and maladministration are made so frequently and with such intensity that there is need for a protective edifice against these evils inherent in administration.

Recent inquiries into the cases of corruption against the former Prime Minister, Chief Ministers, ministers, officials and individuals lend support to the view that corruption flourishes and not much has been done to check it. It is necessary to evaluate the work of Vigilance Commissioners and do some heart searching and find out why they have not been able to function effectively.[8]

The Santhanam Committee on corruption did not favour the creation of a permanent body to deal with corruption charges against ministers. It felt that such a body would very likely be suffocated by the heat of political controversy, which was bound to be let off by an inquiry into the conduct of a minister in office. But the Administrative Reforms Commission has taken the view that a private inquiry by the Lokpal would really strengthen the hands of the Prime Minister or Chief Minister,

[6]The Central Vigilance Commission was set up in 1964 on the recommendations of Santhanam Committee to ensure that complaints of corruption or lack of integrity on the part of government servants are given prompt and effective attention and to become an effective deterrent to any attempt at suppressing action in cases of corruption brought to light.

[7]In Scandinavian countries the need for an Ombudsman did not arise because of the need to combat extensive administrative corruption. Vices such as red tape, delay, rigid and unimaginative administration are the main concern of the Ombudsman in those countries. The famous Crichel Down case in Great Britain some years ago was an instructive example of oppressive administrative action.

[8]The then President V.V. Giri's address to the Conference of Vigilance Commissioners, *The Hindustan Times*, 10 October 1970, p. 1.

who would be spared of the unpleasant duty of investigating into the conduct of his colleagues.

The question of the investigation of complaints of corruption by the Lokpal and Lokayuktas needs to be viewed from a pragmatic angle. In the Punjab State, when grievance officers in districts were appointed they were flooded with all sorts of complaints and grievances. Dr. Radhakrishnan, the then President of India, started durbar in order to receive complaints in Rashtrapati Bhawan. But soon he had to abandon the idea as he was receiving complaints mostly of corruption.

In a note of dissent appended to the Joint Select Committee Report, it has been suggested that allegations of corruption should be excluded from the scheme of the Bill, as that would increase the work-load of Lokpal. This work should remain with the Vigilance Commissioners who have had already experience of more than five years and have developed suitable techniques for inquiring into charges of corruption. It is contended that the number of complaints will be so much that it will not be possible for the new institutions to function smoothly. For the first month when the Sadachar Samiti was set up, it received 2,200 complaints of corruption and public grievances. The number of complaints received by the Public Grievances Section of the Union Ministry of Home Affairs during the years 1966-69 was 4,393. The total number of complaints, relating to public grievances and corruption was 12,27,691 in 1975-76, as reported by the various ministries, departments and offices. From these figures a rough idea can be formed of the magnitude of likely complaints.

Corruption and maladministration are closely interrelated and it is therefore desirable that there should be a unified machinery for the redress of complaints in both these areas. It is all the same necessary that this machinery is viable enough for dealing effectively both with the "grievances" and "allegations". From this perspective it would be appropriate to separate, in the office of the Lokpal, the grievance functions from the anti-corruption functions by having two functionaries. These two sets of complaints need different procedures, approach, and emphasis. If both are mixed up, the anti-corruption functions may completely overwhelm the grievances functions. There should, therefore, be two Lokayuktas under the proposed

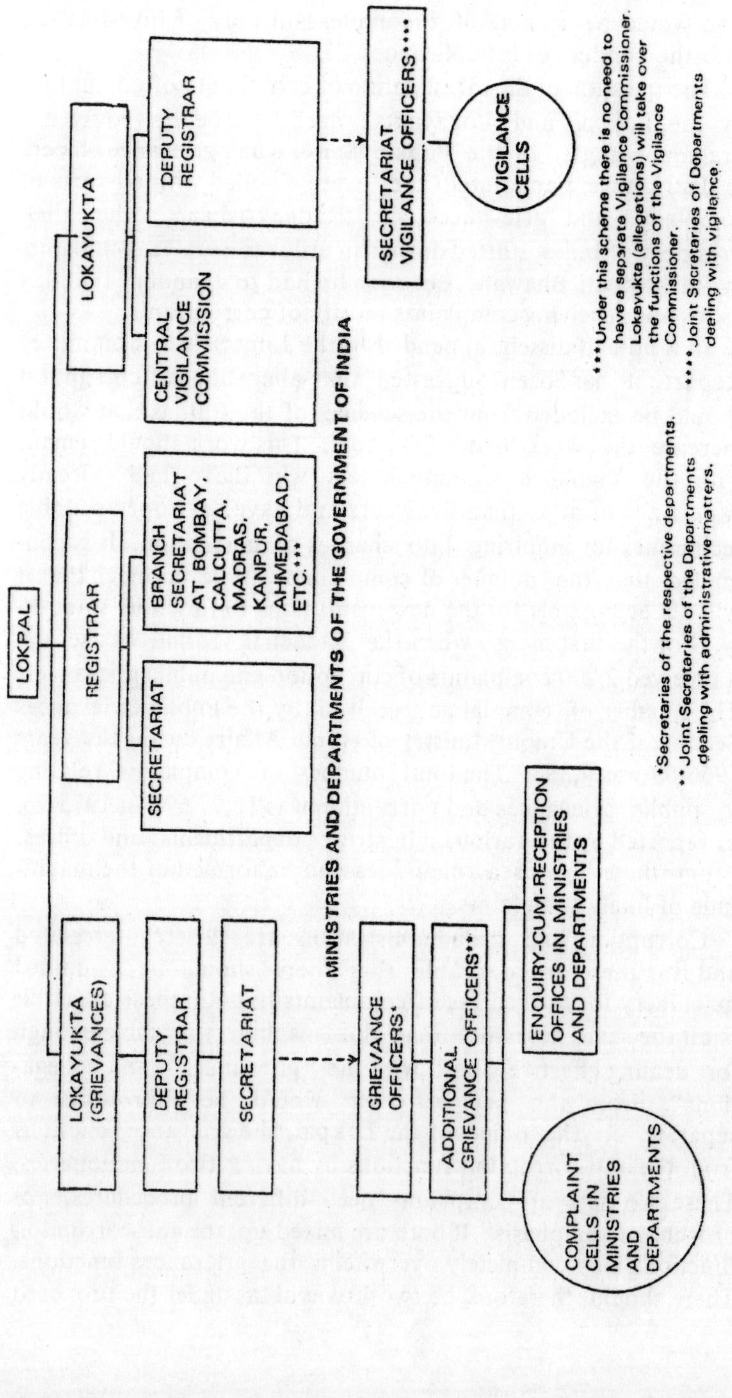
LOKPAL
LOKAYUKTA (GRIEVANCES)
REGISTRAR
LOKAYUKTA
DEPUTY REGISTRAR
SECRETARIAT
SECRETARIAT
BRANCH SECRETARIAT AT BOMBAY, CALCUTTA, MADRAS, KANPUR, AHMEDABAD, ETC.***
CENTRAL VIGILANCE COMMISSION
DEPUTY REGISTRAR
MINISTRIES AND DEPARTMENTS OF THE GOVERNMENT OF INDIA
GRIEVANCE OFFICERS*
ADDITIONAL GRIEVANCE OFFICERS**
ENQUIRY-CUM-RECEPTION OFFICES IN MINISTRIES AND DEPARTMENTS
COMPLAINT CELLS IN MINISTRIES AND DEPARTMENTS
SECRETARIAT VIGILANCE OFFICERS****
VIGILANCE CELLS
*Secretaries of the respective departments.
** Joint Secretaries of the Departments dealing with administrative matters.
*** Under this scheme there is no need to have a separate Vigilance Commissioner. Lokayukta (allegations) will take over the functions of the Vigilance Commissioner.
**** Joint Secretaries of Departments dealing with vigilance.

Lokpal, one dealing with "grievances" and the other dealing with "allegations". It is also necessary that the Central Vigilance Commission should not be abolished and that it should continue to perform the present function under the Lokayukta dealing with allegations.[9] It may, however, not be necessary to continue the Central Vigilance Commissioner. The Commission should function directly under the control of the Lokayukta (allegations) through its secretary. If the Lokpal comes across a case which arouses his suspicion he may, after taking the necessary action to redress the grievance, pass on the case to the Vigilance Commission which will deal with its corruption aspect. No details have been worked out so far of the different categories of the staff which will be needed for the office of the Lokpal. This organization will obviously require branch offices in the metropolitan cities of India. It will also have to maintain links with the departmental machinery for the redress of complaints. It is suggested that the proposed organization of the Lokpal should be structured as shown in the chart.

Increasing institutional effectiveness

As we have already seen, neither the Bill of 1969 nor the Janata government's Bill contain the recommendations made by the Administrative Reforms Commission that the Lokpal should have wider powers of investigation suo moto with a view to enabling him to discharge his duties in a positive manner.[10]

As stated in an earlier chapter, the Ombudsman in other countries do enjoy such powers[11] and some of them initiated

[9]The present Vigilance Commission has several handicaps. It is directly under the Department of Personnel and the Chairman is appointed by the government. It has neither sufficient power nor status nor jurisdiction, and can neither touch nor protect the head of the administration.

[10]Ombudsman should, however, have freedom to act without receiving any complaint if his suspicion about official affairs has been aroused by other means. All the countries included in this study have conferred that authority. Nowhere has it been used over-aggressively. Power to proceed in the absence of a complaint has been exercised by the external critics chiefly to inquire into problems of general public concern as distinct from individually focussed conflicts.

[11]Similar powers have been provided in: (a) Alberta's Ombudsman

investigations on the basis of reports published in the newspapers. In Denmark during the years 1960-64, out of 5,745 cases instituted about 60 were started on Ombudsman's own initiative. Unless such powers are conferred in India, a department in which maladministration is rampant may escape the notice of the Lokpal and Lokayukta if the citizens do not come forward with complaints.

Clause 12(1) of the 1969 Bill and the Janata's proposals unduly circumscribe the contents of the reports to the President of the Lokpal and the Lokayuktas, by specifying that the report under the clause can be sent only if they are satisfied that the action investigated by them has resulted in injustice or undue hardship to the complainant or any other person. They have no power to send a report to the President if no injustice has actually occurred. This will mean that the educative and preventive aspect of the work of Lokpal as found in other countries cannot be performed in India under statutory power.[12] This is a major lacuna in the proposed scheme of the Ombudsman-type machinery and needs to be removed.

The Janata government's Bill, in its present form does not provide for the direct responsibility of the Lokpal or the Lokayuktas to Parliament. Their consolidated annual report presented to the President will, however, be laid before Parliament.[13] Their

---

Act 1967 (Section 11), (b) Hawaii's Ombudsman Act, 1967 (Section 7(b), (c) Mr. Long's Ombudsman Bill introduced in the U.S.A. clause 4(b), and (d), the Canadian Parliamentary Commission Bill [clause 7(1)].

[12]In the U.K., the Parliamentary Commission is authorized to send a report of the results of the investigation to the principal office of the department concerned. Clause 11 of the Bill proposed for Canada envisages wide discretion for the Canadian Ombudsman in his report to the National Legislature.

[13]This is similar to S.12(8) of the Lokpal and Lokayuktas Bill of 1969. Mr. Sumar Guha in his note of dissent to the report of the Joint Select Committee suggested that the annual reports received by the President should be laid before the Parliament within two months. H.H. Maharaja Pratap Keshari Deo proposed that the appointment of a Standing Committee of both the Houses of Parliament to be known as the "Joint Committee for Petitions and Public Grievances" may be entrusted with the task of implementing the reports of the Lokpal and Lokayuktas, as it would not be possible for Parliament to look into voluminous reports dealing with the grievances and complaints of a country with 600 and odd million population.

special reports will also be so laid. It has been urged in some quarters that the Lokpal should submit his reports directly to Parliament. But this may affect the doctrine of accountability of the Cabinet to Parliament. The reports of the Comptroller and Auditor General of India and the Union Public Service Commission are sent to Parliament through the government and a similar practice in the case of Lokpal should be followed.

An important feature of the Administrative Reforms Commission's scheme and government proposal is that the recommendation of the Lokpal and Lokayuktas will be of an advisory character, i.e. the administration will not be obliged to accept them as a matter of course. A similar position obtains in the U.K. and New Zealand. But the practice in some Scandinavian countries is different. In some of the Scandinavian countries, for instance Denmark, the Parliamentary Commissioner acts as a supervisor of administration and not in an advisory capacity. The advisory character of the institutions of the Lokpal and Lokayukta appear to be in keeping with the Indian political and administrative climate. It, however, needs to be emphasized that the government should develop a convention to accept invariably the recommendations of the Lokpal and Lokayuktas. This will help building its image and increase its influence with the people.

The Joint Select Committee recommended that the government should be authorized to exclude from the purview of the Union Public Service Commission matters considered by the Lokpal and Lokayuktas. It therefore deleted the relevant provision on this point included in the 1969 Bill as introduced by the government. In a note of dissent, Mr. A.D. Mani observed, "How is it possible for the government officer deprived of the benefit of an intricate procedure, to regard the adverse report of a Lokpal or Lokayukta as the final word on the subject? Judges are likely to err and it is for this reason that under the existing procedure, even the findings of the Inquiry officers are not regarded as final and cases are referred to the Union Public Service Commission for decision." In the past there have been cases in which the Union Public Service Commission differed with the findings of judicial inquiries. The Union Public Service Commission is a body set up by the Constitution and nothing should be done to weaken its proposition as the protector of the rights of government servants. The Lokpal and Lokayuktas therefore should not have the last word so far as the disciplinary proceedings against the officials are concerned. The proper procedure should be followed in the interest of justice.

Appointment and tenure of Lokpal

The appointment of the Lokpal in consultation with the Chief Justice of India and the leader of the Opposition will help ensure objectivity in selecting the best man. But, from the point of view of wider acceptability it would be more appropriate if some better device of arriving at a consensus is adopted. The appointment of Indian Ombudsman should not be allowed to be influenced by regional, political, or personal considerations. Some have suggested that a national committee of the Chief Justice of India, the Chief Justices of the High Courts, the Speakers and Chairmen of the two Houses of Parliament and State Legislatures, leaders of the various political parties in the legislatures and nominees of the Central and State governments should draw up panels for the Lokpal and the Lokayuktas and the appointment of these functionaries should be made by the Prime Minister only from this panel on the advice of the Chief Justice of India. However, such a large committees with diverse membership may not be able to arrive at a unanimous decision. There already exists in India a well established convention of unanimity of recommendations of Parliamentary Committees, such as the Public Accounts Committee, Estimates Committee, Committee on Public Sector Undertakings, etc. A Lokpal who is appointed on the recommendations of the Parliamentary Committee will enjoy wide confidence and will be more effective in his role.[14] It is, therefore, suggested that a Parliamentary

[14]H.H. Maharaja Pratap Keshari Deo in his note of dissent to the report of Joint Select Committee suggested that a sub-committee consisting of the Prime Minister, the Chief Justice and the leader of the Opposition or if there be no such leader, a person elected on their behalf by the members of the Opposition, should consider names for the selection of the Lokpal and make specific recommendations to the President for his appointment. Some other members of the Joint Select Committee

Committee, specially set up for this purpose, should make the selection of the Lokpal in consultation with the Prime Minister and the Chief Justice of India. The proposed restriction on the tenure of the Lokpal to one term of five years only and the ban on his employment thereafter under the Central and State governments are likely to discourage the young talented persons from offering themselves for this important office. The scope of selection will thus become mostly limited to the old or retired persons. The original 1969 Bill rightly allowed renewal of the tenure of the Lokpal for a second term of five years. It would be desirable to restore the original provision. Another equally good alternative will be to allow the incumbents to carry on till the age of retirement which is normally fixed at 62 years for the judges of Supreme Court.[15] (For the Parliamentary Commissioner in the U.K. the retirement age is 65 years.)

Procedural improvements

The Lokpal Bill provides for the Lokpal the powers and procedure of court. According to the lapsed Bill any proceedings before the Lokpal or a Lokayukta shall be deemed to be a judicial proceeding within the meaning of Section 193 of the Indian Penal Code. A formal court procedure will undermine the very purpose of the institution. Under the proposed procedure the citizen will be allowed to appear through a lawyer if he so chooses. The petitioner who makes an oral complaint will have to reduce it to writing later on. The institution in Sweden is known for its informal procedure, though this is not so in Denmark and Finland.

The inquiries of the Lokpal and Lokayuktas should mostly be confidential, informal, inexpensive and speedy. Their func-

felt that the Chief Justice's advice should be binding for appointment of Lokpal and Lokayuktas.

[15]The 1969 Bill as it was introduced in the Lok Sabha provided for the re-appointment of Lokpal for another five years. But this was not agreed to by the Joint Select Committee. Mr. Sham Sunder Narain Tankha, suggested in his note of dissent that the initial term of office of the Lokpal be fixed at 6 or 7 years, instead of 5 years, in order to avail of his experience for the maximum period possible. (*Report of the Joint Select Committee*, op. cit., p. xxxi.)

tion should mainly be to establish whether a prima facie case exists or not. Unless specially required, they should not take up the functions of a Commission of Inquiry which are formal, expensive and give more or less a conclusive finding. Instead of smothering the Lokpal and Lokayuktas by such inquiries, Commissioners of Inquiry may be appointed on the advice of the Lokpal and Lokayuktas.

In view of the need for inexpensive and quick redress, there should be a ban on cases being brought before the Lokpal and Lokayuktas through lawyers. The lawyers exploit the situation in such a way that the simple cases are made complicated and the procedural delays are created. In exceptional cases where a complainant is physically not in a position to present his case, a representative or a lawyer may be allowed to appear on his behalf with the special permission of the Lokayukta.[16]

In India, the tendency to levy false or malicious charges against a civil servant who refuses to accept an irregular request of a citizen is not uncommon. It is, therefore, important that the identity of the public servant complained against should not be publicly divulged by the Lokpal and Lokayuktas. Even though Janata government's proposals restrict the scope of inquiry to political heads, it should be emphasized that the Lokpal and Lokayuktas should confine themselves to exposing the administrative lapses, and should not do anything which will bring the individual civil servant into disrepute. The doctrine of anonymity of civil servants deserves to be preserved if demoralization is not to overtake them. In recent years the tendency to name civil servants in the legislatures has been on the increase. Obviously, it would be damaging to the civil service morale if the consolidated report of the Lokpal and Lokayuktas were to refer to the civil servants complained against by their names. A mention of their designation would suffice.

The institutions of the Lokpal and Lokayuktas need to be adequately protected in the matter of completion of their in-

[16]The procedure already exists in the case of Central government servants. According to Rule 15 of Government of India (Classification of Appeal) Rules, a government servant cannot produce a lawyer for defending himself before a departmental Inquiry Commissioner. He can at the most be represented by another government servant if the Commissioner so permits.

vestigations. The Bill forbids the challenging of the proceedings taken by the Lokpal and Lokayuktas except on the ground of jurisdiction. The provision may, however, prove inadequate in preventing challenge at every interlocutory stage. It will not be difficult for a clever lawyer to make out some plausible ground of non-jurisdiction at interlocutory stages of investigation pending before the Lokpal and Lokayuktas, secure admission before the High Court under article 226 and obtain stay of further proceedings. It is, therefore, essential to introduce suitable safeguards to meet such an obstacle in the investigations of the Lokpal and Lokayuktas.

Extension of jurisdiction to Members of Parliament

A demand was made in the Joint Select Committee that Members of Parliament should be included under Clause 2(k) of the 1969 Bill in the category of public servants and brought within the jurisdiction of the Lokpal. Janata Government's proposal does not include M.P.s within the purview of Lokpal. It was argued by some members of Joint Select Committee that "Members of Parliament enjoy many privileges denied to the public and it would look strange, if Members of Parliament who discharge many public responsibilities and who are in a position to influence Ministers and Government generally, are kept out of the orbit of the Bill." This view, however, is marked by short-sightedness and lacks a correct appreciation of the position. Members of Parliament have the responsibility of overseeing administrative actions and reporting to Parliament. The legislators are not expected to take administrative action and if their conduct is included they will be judging their own cases when the consolidated report of the Lokpal and Lokayuktas is discussed in Parliament. The supporters of the idea of bringing Members of Parliament within the purview of Lokpal also suggest that the Members of Parliament complained against may abstain from participating in the discussions for Parliament on the report of the Lokpal. This view, however, is unrealistic in the context of present party politics. The party considerations may be so strong that the report is bound to be discussed with sharp political undertones. For tackling the misconduct of the legislators, special machinery needs to be carved out from within the legislatures. The least the Lokpal and the Lokayuktas are involved in the affairs of the legislators, the safer would be their political neutrality which is vital to their successful functioning.

Indian Ombudsman and ordinary citizens

The Ombudsman machinery will need to be oriented towards the poor and the weak. The Lokpal and the Lokayuktas should be freely accessible to the common man. There should be no intermediacy of the legislators or Members of Parliament between the Lok (the public) and the Lokpal/Lokayuktas. A deposit of Rs.1000 by the complainant according to the latest Bill has been suggested to prevent the filing of frivolous complaints. But in a poor country like India this may act as a constraint on free access to the Lokpal. It may, therefore, be provided that the fee prescribed should be automatically waived in all cases where the citizens' complaint is channeled through a state legislator or a Member of Parliament or where the Lokpal or Lokayukta is satisfied about the genuineness of the complaint.

Another salutary provision which needs to be added is that the Lokpal or the Lokayukta should frequently hold their sittings all over the country so that the Ombudsman's machinery is easily accessible to the ordinary citizens.[17] This will also help infuse confidence in the minds of the people and save them from the inconvenience and hardship which may be caused being required to visit the capital. An unseemly feature of the grievances machinery at the state headquarters is that the citizens have to travel long distances to present their case. The lessons of this experience should be utilised by the Lokpal and Lokayuktas.

CONDITIONS OF SUCCESS

The new institutions of Lokpal and Lokayukta require for theirs uccessful working certain basic conditions. These require-

[17]Even in the case of Supreme Court of India, there is a provision that the Court shall sit in Delhi or in such other place or places, as the Chief Justice of India may, with the approval of the President from time to time appoint.

ments, however, need not held up setting up of the new institutions. The very establishment of the institution would help improve the wider framework of their operation.

In the first place, there has to be a basic soundness about the administrative machinery before the institution of Lokpal or Ombudsman can succeed. There is a need for right type of people not only at the top but also in the lower echelons of administration. There should be men of integrity, and should inspire confidence in the public. It has been said that the institution of Ombudsman succeeds most where it is needed least and it succeeds least where it is needed most. It hardly needs to be emphasized that the institution can never be a substitute for a good and just administration; nor can it help much to discipline an administration which has very low standards of integrity and fair play. It is, therefore, necessary that, along with the establishment of the new institution, the political party in power at the Centre should initiate a special drive for general improvement of political and administrative standards.

It will be a matter of self-denying ordinance for the government to subject itself voluntarily to the risk of getting its seamy side of administration exposed to the world at large and place itself in the dock before an independent authority. The creation of the Ombudsman machinery will thus call for a special effort and a high-level commitment on the part of the government to raising the standards of administration as well as the social and political norms.

The inauguration of the new institution of the Lokpal and the Lokayukta will need to be supplemented by a special public relations campaign to explain to the political leadership, the officials and the citizens the implications of the Ombudsman machinery. Nobody could have dreamt of a Lokpal or a Parliamentary Commissioner proving a success in the British India to get redress for the great killing of 'Jallianwala' to such a functionary.[18] No Ombudsman would have functioned effectively during Emergency. The successful functioning of the

[18]Jallianwala Bagh (Garden) is in Amritsar (State of Punjab). It was on the 13 April 1919, that ghastly Jallianwala Bagh massacre took place when thousands of unarmed persons were killed and thousands wounded as a result of firing under orders of the British General Dyer.

Ombudsman institutions will need a clear understanding among the political parties to keep above party politics. The new institution must be helped to operate effectively irrespective of the fate and vicissitudes of political parties. Parliament, the Judiciary and the Executive must let it investigate the complaints without any interference and should not impede its working by refusing overtly or covertly the facilities needed for collecting information and assessing it without fear or favour.

It will also be necessary to impress upon the public officials that they should consider the recommendations of the Lokpal and Lokayuktas with respect and accept them unless there are reasons to the contrary which are positively in the larger public interest and can be explained to Parliament. Even though only recommendatory, the findings of the Lokpal and Lokayuktas should have the same status as the rulings of the Supreme Court.

The faith of the people in the Lokpal and Lokayuktas as well as the success of these functionaries will depend considerably on the quality and character of men who are appointed. The persons selected for the offices of the Lokpal and Lokayuktas must be of unimpeachable character. They must command the confidence of the citizens and public servants. They should be learned in the philosophies and the techniques of law, administration and human conduct. They must have an experience of moving amongst the poor and the helpless without hate, and of communing with the powerful and the exalted without fear.

In the preceding section some suggestions have been made for improving the scheme of the institutions of the Lokpal and Lokayuktas, as set out in the Janata government's Bill and Bill of 1969. A major difficulty in the implementation of this scheme, when adopted by Parliament, will relate to the operational viability of the new institution. It is important to emphasize that the proposed institution of Lokpal and Lokayuktas will succeed only if they are not flooded with complaints of all kinds. It goes without saying that it will not be possible for the new institution to take up every complaint falling within their jurisdiction. It will therefore be necessary to lay down criteria for acceptance of complaints for investigation.

Under the provisions of the Bill of 1969, all complaints

where a remedy is available before any tribunal or court of law are excluded, but the Lokpal/Lokayukta can entertain a complaint of this category if he is satisfied that the complainant could not or cannot for sufficient cause have recourse to the judicial or semi-judicial channels. A point of view can be taken that it should be necessary for the complainant to exhaust all available administrative remedies before he approaches the Lokpal or Lokayukta. The lapsed Bill and Joint Select Committee report are silent on this point. If a rigid stand is taken on the question of exhausting all other administrative remedies, the utility of the Ombudsman institution is likely to be curtailed considerably. On the other hand, if no such safeguard is provided for, the Lokpal and Lokayukta will be submerged under hundreds of thousands of complaints. Levying of compulsory fee for admission of a complaint is also not likely to serve much useful purpose; and it will be necessary to relax this condition so that the Ombudsman machinery does not become oppressive for the poor and backward sections of the society.

One compromise solution would be to prescribe that the available administrative remedies will have to be exhausted before a complaint can be accepted, but to give at the same time the necessary authority to the Lokpal/Lokayukta to waive this requirement where he is satisfied that the complainant cannot, for sufficient cause, have recourse to these remedies. Such an approach, though somewhat flexible, will be of limited utility only in view of the protracted delays which take place in securing even a simple reply from the departmental redress machinery. Further it is open to a citizen to resubmit his complaint to successive higher levels of the administrative hierarchy. For instance, a complaint for the non-issue of a permit for the supply of fertilizers may be taken up successively at the levels of the Block Development Officer, District Agricultural Officer, District Collector, Director of Agriculture, State Agriculture Commissioner and State Minister for Agriculture. It will, therefore, be necessary to specify in operational terms the implications of existing administrative remedies. It will be useful to lay down, for different types of complaints, the number or level of administrative remedies which must be gone through and the minimum time (for each particular stage or for all stages together) which must lapse after an application has been made to the departmental channels of redress. It will not serve any useful purpose to prescribe a uniform requirement for all kinds of complaints; but too many yardsticks are also likely to confuse the citizens. This is an area where a considerable amount of operational spade-work will be necessary before a realistic solution can be found. The success of the Ombudsman-type of institution will depend to a significant measure on the finding of the right answers to the myriad problems of their inter-relationship with the departmental redress machinery.

Even after the establishment of the institution of Lokpal and Lokayukta, it will be necessary for the administration to play a major role in redressing the grievances and providing departmental remedies on an extended and more effective basis. The responsibility of government departments to deal adequately with public grievances must squarely be faced by them in the first instance. The Ombudsman institution serve as the ultimate, and not as the initial remedy for an aggrieved citizen. We have already noted the limitations and weaknesses of the existing departmental redress machinery. The final answer to the problem of citizens' grievances lies not in machinery for their redress but in making the administrative system more efficient and responsive in terms of the citizens' needs.

Furthermore, the utility of the new institution will remain limited unless the States are pursuaded to participate in the experiment. The central Ombudsman will not be able to give relief to the majority of the common citizens who have dealings mostly with the State agencies. The central institution is likely to provide "redress services" largely to the more fortunate classes of society, e.g. industrialists, traders, etc., while the citizens in the villages will remain untouched and unrequitted. This may widen the gap between the denizens of the metropolitan cities and the villagers. Accordingly, the Ombudsman-type of institution will need to be established not only at the entre but also in the States.

Action in this direction has already been initiated by a few States. The governments in these states have assigned to the Lokayuktas the responsibility for enquiring into complaints against state ministers and secretaries. This obviously is a departure from the scheme recommended by the Administrative

Reforms Commission. Karnataka, Bihar and U.P. stand on a different footing than states like Kerala and West Bengal. Even if the state Lokayukta is appointed by the Governor on the recommendations of the Chief Minister and in consultation with the leaders of the Opposition and the Chief Justice of the High Court, it is doubtful whether he will be effective in his role in the context of coalition governments in some States. The other possibility is also there, though it is not likely to occur. We may provide a useful and stable solution to the current trend towards the appointment of inquiry commissions to look into the charges of curruption against the ministers of an outgoing government by its successor.

The establishment of the institutions of the Lokpal and Lokayukta will undoubtedly be a big step forward in improving the machinery for redress of public grievances. The usefulness of the new institutions will depend not only on their character, jurisdiction and powers but equally on the toning up of the wider framework within which they operate. The Ombudsman device is not a panacea for all administrative ills nor a substitute for good and efficient administration. Professor Rowat brings out this point beautifully as follows:

> The age-old problem of the individual is far too complex to be solved by one simple scheme. We need a whole variety of controls over administrative action, and the Ombudsman scheme must be accompanied by a number of other reforms that are needed to plug the gap in our systems of control. Otherwise, the scheme may fail because we are trying to make it do too much. We must remember that in Nordic countries the scheme only supplements a battery of other effective controls and New Zealand is adding this scheme to an already well-developed parliamentary grievance system.
>
> On the other hand the danger in setting up a network of controls is that if the administration is surrounded with too many controls it will be unable to move. This is the danger in extending court review too far or in judicializing the administrative process too much. What we need is a fence along the administrative road, not a gate to cross it. The great virtue of the Ombudsman scheme is that the weapons are publicity and persuasion rather than cumbersome controls—it is in the category of the fence rather than the gate.

CHAPTER X

Summary and Conclusion

The problem of the citizens' grievances has become accentuated in the past 65 years as a result of several political, economic and social developments and a general deterioration in standards of administrative efficiency and integrity. Politically, the establishment of a parliamentary democracy, based on adult franchise, has created among the people an increasing awareness of the rights and their claims on the government. The one-party dominance in the politics of the country till the fourth General Election of 1967 helped reinforce the overbearing attitude and callousness on the part of administration inherited from the British rule. It is true that the Indian National Congress addressed itself to the stupendous task of stepping up the economic growth and living standards by embarking upon plans of economic and social development. But the monopoly of power which it enjoyed made it, for the most part, indifferent and irresponsive to the demands and the difficulties of the common people. The one-party dominance in States disappeared with the General Election of 1967, and evaporated even at the Centre after the split of the Indian National Congress in December 1969. The mid-term General Elections of March 1971 and January 1980 brought back the Congress government of Mrs. Indira Gandhi with an overwhelming majority in Parliament. The trend was reversed for a short period in the Elections of 1977 when the Opposition parties joined together and with overwhelming majority, threw out the one-party rule.

Again, there has not been adequate emphasis on achievement of results in the field and the lag between the promise and performance in five-year plan schemes and projects has helped increase the dissatisfaction and frustration of the people. The gains of economic development have not been distributed evenly and economic unrest and social discontent have increased. The political life has been contaminated by the evils of corruption and patronage. In a polity where the people are the eventual masters, where the spread of education, growing influence of modern civilization and developmental thrust are giving a spiralling push to the people's expectations but where the rate of capital formation is low and the increasing state intervention in daily life is making the people more and more dependent upon the government, the people's dissatisfaction with the administration is likely to grow substantially.

While the people's demands on administration have increased, the administrative system, despite its expansion and reinforcement in serveral directions, does not still have the capability to meet those damands adequately. Since the advent of planning, there has been quite a measure of experimentation with new organizational forms, such as the community development organization, agriculture extension services, small scale industries institutes, the government company and the board-type of management for promotional activities. A significant O & M effort has been underway, directed at streamlining of procedures and improvement of efficiency. A Central O & M division was created in 1954 and a Committee on Plan Projects was set up in 1956 in the National Planning Commission. In 1964, a Management and Development Administration division was constituted as the main arm of this Committee to promote the use of modern tools of management and to undertake studies on problems particular to development administration at the district level. This division has, however, since been abolished.

A full-fledged Department of Administrative Reforms[1] came

[1] "Until 1966 reforms were incremental in nature and did not directly affect the bureaucracy's power or position. Administrative reform leadership was also scattered throughout the government organization with the result that an integrated programme of objectives, priorities, evaluation and feedback could not be developed. The situation improved after the Department of Administrative Reforms was set up in 1964, showing that the institutionalization of administrative reform is a necessary condition for its success." V.V. Moharir, "Administrative Reforms in India", in *Development and Change*, Institute of Social Studies, The Hague, Volume II—1970-71, No. 2, p. 96.

up at the Centre in March 1964 and it has carried out or sponsored several detailed studies, many of a composite character, on administrative reorganization in selected areas of administrative activity. Some of these studies were carried out by working groups or study teams which included the representatives of the concerned interest groups. These studies have made a useful contribution in the matter of streamlining the procedures, fixation of time limits for disposal of citizens' applications and other measures for prevention of delays. In most of the States, there have also come up O & M units or small administrative reforms departments. But their role in procedural improvments and reduction of delays has rather been limited.

All-India Administrative Reforms Commission laboured hard for four-and-a-half years to produce 20 reports of its own, supplemented by reports of 34 study teams, working groups and task forces. Most of the reports of the Administrative Reforms Commission were kept pending by the government. The overall impact of the commission on administrative reforms and improvement had hardly been significant during this period. An analysis of the work of the Commission also bears out that "intra-bureaucratic politics have quite an influence on the formulation of reform proposals and that an entrenched bureaucracy can frustrate major administrative reforms unless the latter are supported by the political executive".

The effect of all the reform efforts in terms of improving administrative capability has been very little till the beginning of 1977. With the phenomenal increase in the developmental and welfare responsibilities of the government the proliferation of the administrative machinery and in the absence of any long-term strategy of administrative change, there has been a general decline in the standards of administrative effectiveness. No wonder, therefore, that the citizens' dissatisfaction and complaints have mounted up. It is inconceivable that, even with a renewed and more dynamic attempt at reforms, the Indian administrative system will be able to cope fully with all the demands of the citizens. It is, therefore, important that the capability of Indian bureaucracy should be increased to the maximum possible extent in the interest of maintaining social and political stability. This also underscores the importance of adequate and effective redress machinery to look into citizens' complaints and to help control[2] the new stresses and tensions which are likely to emerge in the wake of increasing industrialization and urbanization, population growth and the stepping up of tempo of development.

NATURE OF GRIEVANCES

The citizens, by and large, are highly dissatisfied in regard to the acceptance of their applications and demands as well as the redress of their complaints. The intensity of dissatisfaction has been highlighted by the few studies which already exist and by two special studies conducted as a part of the present research. One of these covered 8 villages in Barabanki district of the State of Uttar Pradesh. The study revealed that the citizens were very sceptical of securing fair decisions from the government machinery on their own, unless they could mobilise influence and support for their requests. It also indicated that the citizens' complaints largely relate to delays in provision of supplies and services, inconvenience and harassment, non-issue of quota and permits and the lack of impartiality in decisions due to political and parochial influences. As large a majority as 80 per cent of respondents felt that there were a substantial amount of corruption among the officials and it was not possible to get things done either without political pull or some kind of graft.

The second field study, which related to Treasuries, pinpointed that the bureaucratic procedures have become an end in themselves and are much more attuned towards the comforts of the bureaucracy than to the citizens' needs and convenience. The tortuous and elaborate procedures cause the citizens con-

[2]For, unless some way of institutionalizing and otherwise coping with demands is devised, the system itself is certain to disintegrate into violence and chaos. Certainly the nature, flow and magnitude of demands will make any kind of development, political or economic, easier or more difficult. Difficulties are certain to increase in the degree to which the bureaucracy fails to manage demands in some systematic way. Joseph La Palombera (ed.), *Bureaucracy and Political Development*, New Jersey, Princeton University Press, 1963, pp. 29-30.

siderable harassment and the illiterate people, particularly those from the rural areas, are the worst sufferers. Interesting light on the dimensions of the problem of citizens' complaints is thrown by the report of the Central Commissioner for Public Grievances submitted to the government in 1966. According to this report, there were, during the quarter ended 30 June 1966, in all 10,889 complaints received *directly* by the Central ministries and departments. Of these, over 60 per cent related to delay. The largest number of grievances (5,356) were against the Department of Rehabilitation (office of the Chief Settlement Commissioner), Posts and Telegraphs came next (2,023) and the Ministry of Home Affairs occupied the third place (1,916).

The efficacy of the departmental redress machinery for providing relief to the citizen can very well be assessed by the sad experience of the Central Commission for Public Grievances in the matter of receiving replies from the Central ministries and departments to the communications addressed by him about the public complaints he was examining. Of the total number of 324 references made by him to the central ministries and departments during the period 7 February 1966 to the 31 August 1966, he got effective replies in 89 cases only. Again, 67 replies took about 1-2 months to come in; 42, 2-3 months; 21, 3-4 months and 6, 4-5 months. At the end of August 1966, 90 replies were still pending—34 with the Department of Rehabilitation and 24 with the Railway Board.

MACHINERY FOR REDRESS OF COMPLAINTS

The administrative machinery for redress of citizens' complaints largely consist of (a) traditional hierarchical channels of redress; (b) inter-departmental special machinery, such as complaint cells, reception-cum-enquiry counters and public relations units; (c) supra-departmental agencies like the district-level complaint committees, units or directorate of grievances attached to the Chief Minister's office in the States and the Central Directorate of Grievances in the Government of India; and (d) procedures of on-the-spot redress by the district collector and ministers. There are also available to the citizens additional channels of redress, such as the courts, administrative tribunals, the legislature and its committees, citizens' associations, voluntary organizations and advisory bodies set up by the government.

Administrative machinery

The present study has revealed that the hierarchical channels of redress, whether at the State level or at the Centre, do not provide any effective means for consideration of the citizens' complaints on an objective and impartial basis. Formal procedures of appeal or review generally do not exist and where they do, there are long delays and ample opportunities for arbitrary decisions and corrupt practices. Very often the complaint against a particular officer is processed by the same officer and even if a senior officer looks into it, he normally supports the stand already taken. The higher officers are too busy to apply their minds afresh to the matter.

The citizens living in the rural areas and having a complaint against one of the local-level agencies of the State administration can lodge a complaint at six or seven successive hierarchical levels—to the sub-district and district officers of the concerned executive department, the district collector, the head of the executive department at its headquarters, to the secretary of the administrative department concerned, to the minister and even to the Chief Minister. The availability of opportunity for appeal to several levels in the administrative hierarchy, however, does not help the citizen in any way. It only adds to inconvenience and expense, raises false hopes and keeps him in suspense for a long period of time.

The special intra-departmental machinery, which has come up in recent years, has not brought relief in any significant manner to the citizens. The general pattern of the special machinery is more or less the same both in the Central ministries and departments and in the States, i.e. the constitution of complaint cells and reception-cum-enquiry offices or public relations units in all major departments having dealings with the citizens. In fact, the special machinery at the State level has been evolved in response to the initiative taken by the Government of India. The complaint cells have been set up, inter alia, with the object of providing for the examination of the complaints by an officer other than the one against whose decisions the complaint has been made. In practice, however, the complaint cells have come to play only a coordinating role and the complaints, by and large, continue to be considered by the same officer or unit in which the decision complained against was taken. Further, complaint cells are not headed by a senior officer as was initially proposed. In terms of the calibre of the staff, this means that they are not well equipped for the functions assigned to them.

A review made by the Central Commissioner of Public Grievances in 1966 showed that complaint cells had been successful only in those cases where they were headed by a complaint officer of the status of Joint Secretary to the Government of India. Unfortunately, there were only two cells of this kind. The Commissioner recommended that if officers of the status of the Joint Secretary could not be spared on full-time or part-time basis, it would be preferable to abolish the cells rather than allow them to continue. Otherwise, the complaint cell is likely to act as a delay-making intervening agency between the citizens and the central ministry or department concerned with his complaints. Though it was compulsory for the complaint cells to investigate a few cases directly, the Commissioner of Grievances found that these instructions had not at all been followed. The Commissioner came to the conclusion that the machinery for redress of citizens' grievances "must have necessary status and the authority to obtain prompt redress of justified grievances and by personal investigation to bring to light cases of delay, abuse, error, inefficiency or negligence so that steps can be taken against their recurrence". But it is doubtful if any internal machinery can ever exercise such influence in the administrative climate as obtaining today.

Reception-cum-enquiry offices or public relations unit perform only ancillary functions, i.e. supply of information to the citizens, receipt of applications and complaints and their transmission to the appropriate quarters, etc. Their activities have a measure of educative value for the citizens but their functioning is rather perfunctory, and, for the most part, the civil servants who cannot fit elsewhere, are posted to the reception cells.

District-level complaint committees constitute another category of special machinery. They have the advantage that the representatives of the citizens, political leaders and public men are also their members, apart from the concerned officials. They consider complaints mostly of the community nature, though the people's representatives who sit on these committees also at times raise individual complaints. The working of the district-level committees shows that the approach of non-officials represented on them is generally narrow and parochial. They show concern mostly for those individual or community grievances the redress of which is likely to advance their personal interests or the interests of their friends and supporters, and they are not very appreciative of the difficulties of the administrative agencies. Some States have coordination committees or public relations committees at the district level who look into community grievances as one of the items of their manifold responsibilities.

Coming to the supra-departmental level, it appears that the growing trend towards 'on-the-spot' redress of grievances by ministers in some of the States is perhaps due to the increased political pressures for winning and retaining support of the people. The emergence of coalition governments in several States with a thin majority had given a push to such a tendency in early seventies. The device of on-the-spot redress has been quite useful in the State of Gujarat where the system is well organized and the citizens are given advance notice and their applications are kept ready, duly processed for the minister's consideration during his visit to the district or sub-district headquarters. In this State, the minister can pass orders on the spot only in cases which fall within the purview of his ministry. In some other States, however, like Haryana and Maharashtra, each minister has been allotted a district and he has the authority to intervene in any important matters even if it falls whithin the portfolio of another minister. However, the tours of the minister are mostly not intimated in advance and no effort is made to look into the complaints and keep a brief ready for the minister. Accordingly the system of on-the-spot redress in such circumstances carries with it the danger of crossing the boundary-line. It creates difficulties of inter-departmental jurisdiction. Ministers are inclined to pass oral orders on the spot and such a manner of disposal does not admit of taking into account all relevant administrative rules and regulations. An order by the minister on-the-spot may not be appropriate and may go against the rights of some other citizen or citizens. Some of the State administrative reforms committees have therefore suggested that the oral orders passed by the ministers during tours should be reduced to writing by the district officer and sent over to the secretary of the department for confirmation by the minister.

In most of the States there has also come up in recent years a special complaint cell or unit attached to the office of the Chief Minister. A couple of States like Punjab and Rajasthan have also experimented with the full-fledged Directorates of Public Grievances. The Complaint Directorate in Rajasthan was, however, wound up in 1966 after three years trial due to financial stringency and the unfavourable attitude of the administrative departments. The Directorate of complaints in the Punjab has since been merged with the Public Relations Directorate. The complaint cells in other States, which are located in the office of the Chief Minister or Chief Secretary, perform mainly two-fold functions. In the first place, they receive complaints from the citizens and transmit them to the relevant authorities—either to the secretariat departments or to the executive agencies. They also fix up interviews with the Chief Minister, and at times with other ministers also. In most of the administrative departments, who have large dealings with the public, the personal office of the minister has an additional staff member to look after the complaints received from the citizens or arrange for the interviews with the minister. For the most part, the complaints received in the office of the ministers and the Chief Ministers are sent down the line unless the minister feels personally interested or he has been approached by some influencial person or members of the State legislature to look into a particular complaint.

A Directorate of Public Grievances was set up at the Centre in 1966 and it still continues to function, though it is no longer headed by a full-time officer. The first Central Commissioner of Public Grievances complained that he did not enjoy adequate powers to investigate the citizens' complaints. Nor did he find the attitude of the Central ministries and departments very helpful. The Central Directorate of Public Grievances today operates mostly as a coordinating agency.

The rush to the State secretariat and the Central secretariat by the citizens has increased phenomenally in recent years. There is a growing feeling among the people also that nothing moves in the administration unless the right influence is brought to bear upon their request or application. This proposition is equally true for the processing of complaints.

The growing politicalization of the process of redress of the citizens' complaints is hardly a salutary feature. One of its direct effect has been that the civil servants too are taking to the mobilization of political support for furthering their career prospects or avoiding disciplinary action when they go wrong.

Courts and administrative tribunals

The courts and administrative tribunals provide other avenues of redress. The jurisdiction of the courts is limited to points of law or violation of considerations of natural justice, prescription of set procedures, arbitrary exercise or abuse of discretion, malafide intentions in decision making, infringement of fundamental rights, action in excess of power, etc. The courts cannot interfere with the exercise of the discretion per se unless this exercise is outside the powers delegated to the administrative authority or impinges upon matters mentioned above. The citizen can also invoke the extraordinary jurisdiction of High Courts under Article 226 of the Constitution (which relates to enforcement of the individual rights—fundamental or otherwise through orders or writs), and of the Supreme Court under Article 32 (concerning enforcement of fundamental rights) as well as under Article 136 of the Constitution (regarding appeal against judgment, decree etc., of any court or tribunal). On the whole, the jurisdiction of the courts to look into the citizens' grievances is so circumscribed that their usefulness in the matter of redress is quite limited. Justice rendered by the courts is very costly and often delayed and the corruption in the lower levels of the judiciary is said to be on the increase.

The institution of administrative tribunal has been evolved to provide for quick, inexpensive adjudication of disputes be-

Since the advent of planning, a network of advisory committees has come up in almost all the programme areas which directly touch upon the daily life of the citizens, such as education, labour welfare, agriculture, price control, industry, rehabilitation. These advisory committees are meant to associate the people's representatives both with formulation of policies and their implementation. Their functioning shows that they are mostly concerned about sectional interests. Individual grievances hardly attract their attention except by way of illustrating failures in implementation or the inadequacy of a particular policy.

Citizens's associations and other voluntary organizations have multiplied during the past 65 years. Voluntary organizations are mostly engaged in providing information and advice and service of one kind or another. They have been unable to command any significant influence with the government agencies; nor have they been able to affiliate themselves into strong central organizations. Experiments of associating the voluntary organizations with the fight against corruption and redress of citizens' grievances have hardly been much of success. Consumers' bodies have developed only to a limited extent in certain areas like Posts & Telegraphs and Railways and the potentialities of this forum have hardly been fully exploited.

ADEQUACY OF REDRESS MACHINERY

The detailed examination of the attempts at improving the redress machinery at the Centre and in the States, made in the earlier chapter, shows that these efforts were largely of an ad hoc character. The various measures which were initiated for streamlining the procedures and improving the redress machinery were not conceived in terms of any overall and comprehensive policy on the subject; nor were they evolved from any integrated perspective. They were lined up in a piecemeal manner, and were prompted by the desire to do something for the redress of complaints, without thinking out the problem in depth and to its logical end. Even though the State governments enjoy a leeway in the matter of administrative reforms and the State administrations touch upon the daily life of the people much more than the Central administration does, their overall approach to the problem of the citizens' grievances and the broad lines of the development of the redress machiney have been characterized by apathy and "ad hocism".[3] The intensity of the grievances is more acute at the State and district levels but this has not led to the finding of any better solutions, except that political intervention in the States for the satisfaction of the citizens' demands, both legitimate and illegitimate, has increased much more than at the Centre.

Another important lacuna in the effort at the redress of citizens' grievances has been the failure on the part of both the government and the administrative inquiry committes and commissions to assess on an empirical basis the nature and dimensions of the problem and to evaluate the success of measures for improving the institutional and procedural arrangements for redress, initiated from time to time. This shows that the government have not been much exercised about the problem of citizens' grievances and have hardly been earnest to find pragmatic solutions. A view generally taken in the government circles is that the problem cannot be tackled effectively unless the efficiency and integrity of the administration is improved substantially. In other words, the answer lies more in preventive than in curative measures. As already noted, the performance of the government, in the matter of raising administrative capability has hardly been creditable.

To summarize the main findings of the present study:

1. There exists at present a high level of dissatisfaction with the administration, particularly in matters of the unhelpful attitude of officials, lack of proper attention by government agencies, delays, inefficiency, corruption and inadequacy of basic services.

[3]For the large part, the approach of the government to the problem of citizens' grievances takes partly the character of "exploitationist time orientation", i.e., ambivalent attitude towards change, with a focus on the present. It also contains in itself an element of "escapist time orientation", i.e., an emphasis on the status quo and indicative attitude towards the change. For a detailed statement of the typology of time, elite-role, and programme orientations and of bureaucratic roles, see, Hahn-Been Lee, "Korea: Time, Change and Administration", Hawaii, East-West Centre Press, 1966, pp. 6-37 (Chapters I and II).

2. The existing machinery for the redress of the citizens' complaints is inadequate in several respects, ineffective for the most part, and fails to inspire the people's confidence in fair-play and impartiality of the administration.

The various attempts at improving the redress machinery, made during the last 65 years or so in India, do not reveal that the government at the Centre or in the States has any clear or positive strategy. The general approach to the problem was one of incremental and unplanned reforms. The experiment has hardly been a success. The major drawbacks are the lack of sustained political support and the absence of strong civil service leadership favourable to reforms. It is true that in their efforts to achieve development goals and outputs, public agencies actually prefer to encourage unplanned change and planned change that avoids major alterations in the system.[4]

As we have already seen, the government's policy in this regard has so far been halting and narrowly conceived. The need of the hour is to formulate a comprehensive policy and delineate the role of different channels of redress from an integrated perspective. In the formulation of a bolder and comprehensive policy the following considerations would need to be borne in mind:

1. It is not necessary to evolve a uniform type of machinery for all administrative agencies, and for the Centre and States. From the system's perspective, the redress machinery must take into account the environment of the administration, the organizational goal of the administrative agency concerned, its resources and its capacity. Empirical investigations and innovating thinking will be necessary for this purpose.

2. The experiment with the complaints cell has been a virtual failure and it has not been possible to provide in practice that the officer who looks into the complaint is different or isolated from those who took the original decision. If the underlying purpose is to be realized, it will be necessary to

[4] Edward W. Weidner, "The Elements of Development Administration" in Edward W. Weidner, *Developing Administration in Asia,* Durham, op. cit., p. 23.

revitalize the institution of the Central Commissioner of Grievances and create a similar body at the State level. The Commissioner of Grievances should be vested with adequate authority. The creation of such an institution should be in addition to the appointment of Lokpal and Lokayukta. In fact, the Directorate of Grievances should be a part of the organization of the Lokpal and Lokayukta. As has been emphasized by the first Central Grievances Commissioner, "Some form of sympathetic, responsible and independent representation is not only desirable, but necessary if the private citizen is to receive proper consideration, at the highest levels within the Ministries."

3. There are generally several levels involved in processing of complaints. There has been a growing recognition in India, in recent years, of the need for reducing the number of levels for consideration, and even some experiments with officer-oriented patterns of work are being tried. It will be worth while to extend this approach to public grievances also, and lay down that the number of levels involved in the consideration of public complaints should not normally exceed two.

4. Further, the machinery for redress needs to be supplemented with an effective information system for informing and educating the citizens. At present, the role of the public relations units and reception-cum-enquiry offices in the redress of public grievances is vague and undefined, and their functioning singularly below the mark.

5. The personnel, who man the redress machinery and the public relation offices, have necessarily to be of high calibre. The present tendency is to syphon off the unwanted or inefficient officers to the public relation units and the complaint cells. Unless the personnel are of requisite quality, redress machinery is going to serve no useful purpose. Equally important is to transfer periodically the personnel who deal with public complaints. The past experience shows that the continuation of the same person in seat of power leads to abuses of various kinds. In the present organizational climate of Indian administration, the selection of the officials for the complaint cells and their transfers should be in the hands of a high-level authority, preferably the directorate of public grievances.

AN OMBUDSMAN FOR INDIA

The failure of the departmental channels of redress, the limited usefulness of the courts and adminitrative tribunals, and the marked increase in the citizens' dissatisfaction with administration have stimulated some new thinking on the problem of citizens' complaints. The idea of independent redress machinery initially originated towards the close of 1950s as a part of the public debate concerning the measures needed to combat the growing corruption at the higher levels in government. In the early sixties the possibility of setting up Ombudsman-type of independent institutions began to attract attention. A proposal for the appointment of an Indian Ombudsman was mooted in Parliament in April 1963, but it assumed a concrete shape only in the report of the Rajasthan Administrative Reforms Committee given to the State government in 1963.

Administrative reforms commission's proposals

A shake up to the government's slovenliness in the matter of public complaints was given in October 1966 by the All-India Administrative Reforms Commission which gave the problem of citizens' grievances the topmost priority. The Commission has found that the answer to this outcry lies not in expressions or reiteration of government's general satisfaction with the administration's achievements or its attempts generally to justify itself but in the provision of a machinery which will examine such complaints and sift the genuine from the false or the untenable so that administration's failures and achievements can be publicly viewed in their correct perspective.

The Commission recommended the creation of Ombudsman type institutions of the Lokpal and the Lokayukta. The Lokpal would look into complaints against ministers and secretaries to government both at the Centre and in the States, and the Lokayukta would enquire into complaints against other civil servants. The complaints could cover acts of maladministration, administrative injustice, favouritism and corruption. The Commission's scheme provides for objectivity in the appointment of the Lokpal and Lokayukta, independence of their functioning, and accountability to Parliament and not to the political executive.

In support of its proposals, the Administrative Reforms Commission pointed out that the proposed institutions of the Lokpal and Lokayukta would be meant to rebuild the people's faith and confidence in administration and the political executives by providing independent, cheap and speedy machinery for redress of citizens' grievances. Such faith and a fair amount of satisfaction with the administration are of utmost importance for the success of democracy in India. The institution of the Ombudsman would serve as an impartial forum of enquiry against acts of maladministration and ensure speedy relief to the aggrieved. The new machinery, by investigating complaints, would also help correct the current exaggerated notions of corruption, inefficiency and lack of fair play in higher quarters in government. Thus it will help to protect the officials against false allegations and malafide complaints. Again, the very existence of the institution will act as a deterrent to acts of maladministration.

The institution of the Ombudsman has been quite a success in the Scandinavian countries and New Zealand and even in the U.K. though its jurisdiction in the latter has been found to be not comprehensive enough. The idea of the Ombudsman is catching up in other parts of the world and Ombudsman-type of institutions have been established more recently in Alberta, New Brunswick, Hawaii, Guyana and Mauritius. According to the report of the A.R.C. the institution of the Ombudsman is "supplement to the Parliamentary control, independent of any political affiliations, outside the normal administrative hierarchy, and free from the formalism, publicity and delays associated with governmental machinery. They work unobstrusively to remove the sense of injustice from the mind of the adversely affected citizen and yet uphold in a very large measure the prestige and authority of the administration, instilling public confidence in its efficiency and faith in its working and introducing a proper perspective of it in the mind of public."

The A.R.C. submitted its proposals for the Indian Ombudsman in a special report given to the government in October 1966—within five or six months after it really got going. The sense of urgency and speed shown by the A.R.C. in making the recommendations was said to have been prompted by the desire to make available to the government a radical measure of reform which could come handy to it in the forthcoming General Election to be held in February 1967. The government, however, took a year to announce its acceptance of the proposals. A Bill on the Lokpal and Lokayukta was introduced in Parliament in May 1968. Though it was passed by the Lok Sabha in August 1969, it could not be taken up for discussion in the Rajya Sabha and lapsed on the dissolution of Lok Sabha towards the end of 1970. The Government, reintroduced the Bill in 1971 but it lapsed on account of low priority given. In July, 1977 the Janata government introduced the Lokpal Bill as a permanent machinery against the actions of the public men but public servants were completely out of its purview.

The delay in acceptance of the A.R.C.'s proposals and the long time taken in their processing into legislation indicates the low priority attached to the problem. It is true that negotiations with the States on the question of the extension of the jurisdiction of the Lokpal to ministers and secretaries to government at the State level had to be completed. Several of States, however, did not agree to the proposal and as a result it was provided that the Lokpal and Lokayukta Bill 1971 would apply only to ministers and officials of the Union government. Had the Government of India been prompt and vigorous in accepting and pushing through the proposals, the final picture might have been different.

The provisions of the Lokpal and Lokayukta Bill differed from the A.R.C.'s proposals in several other respects. The tenure of the Lokpal was reduced from ten to five years. The citizens' complaints were divided into two parts: (a) 'allegations' relating to the abuse or malafide exercise of power and corruption and (b) 'grievances' about maladministration. Some other important differences were the absence of any provision in the Bill conferring upon the Lokpal the power to investigate suo motu and the submission of the reports of the Lokpal to the President and not directly to the Lok Sabha, as proposed by the A.R.C. The jurisdiction of the Lokpal was to extend to ministers and officers of the Central government and the employees of corporations, companies and local authorities.

However, 'allegations' against the latter alone were to be investigated by the Lokpal and Lokayukta and not the 'grievances'. On the recommendations of the Joint Select Committee the Bill was revised to exclude the Prime Minister specifically from the jurisdiction of the Lokpal. Policy decisions, cases of rightful exercise of discretion, cases for which access to a tribunal or the court or a commission of inquiry is available and certain other specified matters have also been excluded.

Suitability and viability of Ombudsman in India

The institution of the Lokpal has come in for criticism on the ground that its establishment will require an amendment of the Constitution if its jurisdiction were to cover both the Centre and the States, and further that it would constitute a transgression of State autonomy. It has also been urged that the Ombudsman institution will undermine the conventional functions of the legislators in the matter of voicing public complaints and securing their redress, and that it will cut across the doctrine of ministerial responsibility for actions of the civil servants. The A.R.C. anticipated most of these objections, and in its interim report expressed the view that the appointment of the Lokpal and Lokayuktas need not call for a Constitutional amendment. The Union government has even currently the powers, under the Commissions of Inquiry Act of 1952 to investigate complaints against State officials. Nor would the appointment of the Lokpal and Lokayuktas erode in any way the ministerial responsibility because the Indian Ombudsman will be only an adviser to the government in the matter of bringing to light acts of maladministration and cases of abuse or malafide exercise of discretion and corruption. The responsibility for redressing the injustice done to the citizens will all the same continue to rest with the concerned minister.

Second criticism levelled against the proposed institution of the Lokpal and Lokayuktas relates to their unsuitability in Indian conditions. It is contended that the Indian Ombudsman will be flooded with complaints in view of the mass illiteracy, woefully inadequate sense of social obligations, low living standards, the increased complexity and large size of the administrative machinery and the enormous number of public employees.

The standard of public morality in India differs from that of the Scandinavian countries. The establishment of the Ombudsman institution in India might even adversely affect the exercise of initiative and responsibility by civil servants.

However, the above arguments can hardly stand scrutiny. It is precisely because of the relatively low standard of probity in public life and in the civil services and the monolithic character of the administrative machinery that the setting up of the institution of the Lokpal and Lokayukta has become a necessity. The Lokpal will be the citizens' defender, protector of officials, the preserver of standards in high places, and a catalyst of administrative improvements. As the citizens' defender he will help the weak and the illiterate to secure redress of their grievances when they are unable to seek other remedies open to them. According to the Whyatt Report "With the existence of great bureaucracy there are inevitably occasions, not insignificant in number, when through error and indifference, injustice is done or appears to be done; the man of substance can deal with this situation, but too often the little man, the ordinary humble citizen, is incapable of asserting himself. The Ombudsman would assist the ordinary humble citizen and would enable him to assert himself. What is more, it would cleanse the Augean stables of our administration and perennially protect and restore the dignity and freedom of man." The fact that he has had a reasonable opportunity of presenting his case before an authority which passes the order, and which is independent and impartial, would in itself be a source of satisfaction to the citizen concerned even where the result of investigation is unfavourable to him.

As the protector of officials, the Indian Ombudsman would defend them against malicious complaints, exaggerated reports and unjustified suspicions.[5] A distressing feature of the current

[5]"It is absolutely essential that whispers should not go round the country about the honesty of persons in high authority, whether ministers, judges, or public administrators, and the most effective way of meeting the challenge of such whispers is to institute a high officer like the Ombudsman who would be authorized to deal with complaints made by citizens and will take steps to publish his decisions in regard to those complaints." P.B. Gajendragadkar, "Role of Administration in a Democratic Welfare State", *Indian Journal of Public Administration*, Vol. IX, No. 4, October-December, 1963.

political scene is brandying of allegations of corruption and impropriety against ministers who have stepped down from power. The establishment of the institution of the Lokpal, provided its jurisdiction extends to State ministers as proposed by the A.R.C. would provide a standing and effective machinery to meet the problem of corruption in high places. This function can even be performed, may be somewhat less effectively, by the Lokayuktas at the State level.

The very existence of the Ombudsman institution would act as a deterrent to acts of maladministration. The new machinery is vital to all other administrative reforms inasmuch as it would establish a built-in-mechanism to make the administration continuously responsive to the citizens' genuine difficulties and needs. It will release new forces and pressures for reform. The creation of Ombudsman-type of institution is likely to have a far reaching effect on the process of administrative reforms. The fact that applications of the citizens which are not properly dealt are likely to find their way to the Ombudsman would in itself act as a catalyst to administrative reforms. When a complaint of the citizen will be inquired into by the Ombudsman apparently for reasons of arbitrary exercise of discretion or its misuse or non-use, it is going to be difficult for the administration to isolate its genuine difficulties (arising from the weaknesses of the administrative system or the bad quality of personnel) from the lack of failure to follow the set procedures or principles of natural justice, etc.

Modifications needed in government proposals

The present study shows that the recommendations of the A.R.C. and the government proposals concerning the Lokpal need to be improved upon in several directions. Firstly, Lokpal should have two Lokayuktas—one for enquiring into grievances and the other into allegations. The Ombudsman machinery should be viable enough in order to deal effectively both with the grievances and allegations not only against the public men but also against government servants. Accordingly, the Central Vigilance Commission should be transferred to organization of the Lokpal and redesignated as the Lokayukta (allegations). There will, thus be two functionaries under the Lokpal—one for dealing with "grievances" and the other to look into complaints of corruption. If both these functions were combined in the same person, the anti-corruption functions are likely to overwhelm the grievances functions. The Lokpal, may however, himself handle all complaints of corruption against ministers and secretaries to government.

Secondly, the Ombudsman should have the powers to investigate suo motu with a view to enabling him to discharge his duties in a positive manner. Thirdly, it is important that the enquiries of the Lokpal should mostly be confidential, informal, inexpensive and speedy. Commissioners of Inquiries may be appointed on the advice of the Lokpal to assist him in the discharge of his duties. Lawyers should not be allowed to appear before the Lokpal. Only in exceptional cases where the complainant is physically not in a position to present his case that a representative or a lawyer may be allowed to appear on his behalf, with the permission of Lokpal or Lokayukta. It is also essential that the identity of the public servants against whom complaints are lodged, should not be publicly divulged by the Lokpal. The institution of Lokpal should be adequately protected in the matter of complaint or investigations. Cases brought before the Lokpal should not be allowed to be taken to the Supreme Court and other High Courts on the plea of the non-jurisdiction of the Lokpal.

For ensuring that the Lokpal is freely accessible to the common man, there should be no intermediary like the legislators, members of Parliament, etc. Again, no fee should be levied normally. However, in order to avoid frivolous complaints, a fee of Rs.10 may be levied on each petition on an experimental basis. This fee may be waived by the Lokpal if he is satisfied about the genuineness of the complaint and the inability of the complainant to pay. Furthermore, the Lokpal should hold sittings frequently all over the country to save the complainants the inconvenience of coming to the Capital all the time.

The creation of the institution of Lokpal will require the strengthening of the internal machinery for the redress of the citizens' grievances. In the first place, it will be necessary to set up a separate directorate of public grievances in each State at supra-departmental level. The Directorate of Public Grievances at the Centre, which at present is headed by a part-time Commissioner, will have to be revitalized. The head of a Grievances Directorate should be a senior officer. In the States the Director should not be below the rank of joint secretary, and the Commissioner of Public Grievances at the Centre should be of the rank of additional secretary to the Government of India. Efforts should be made to see that once these officers are posted to the Directorates they should not go back to the departments of the Government of India or of the State government. They should be given posting in autonomous bodies so that they are able to maintain their independence while working in the Directorates.

Further, the functioning of these directorates will need to be clearly defined. They will have to be vested with authority to investigate a sample of cases directly and to secure the full collaboration of the various departments for purpose of prompt and effective investigation of cases referred by them to the departments. Each Directorate of Public Grievances would need to have a research wing which would analyse the nature and causes of public complaints and make suggestions from time to time for improvement and streamlining of organization and procedures.

The organization of the Lokpal and Lokayukta will need to maintain a close link with the Central Directorate of Public Grievances as well as the complaint cells in various ministries and departments. It should even be possible for the Lokpal to transfer routine cases to the Central Directorate of Grievances for direct disposal by the latter. It might well happen that the individual ministries and departments may take too long to provide the Lokpal or Lakayukta the information which he has sought. This fear is borne out by the sad experience in the matter of the first Commissioner of Public Grievances in 1966. Even through the present scheme provides that the Lokpal and Lokayukta will have the right to call in the official documents, this right may, in practice be nullified if the ministries and departments delay the supply of information. A good strategy on the part of the Lokpal would be to mention such delays in his report to Parliament. He can even write to the Prime Minister personally if he considers that the department is taking too much time in forwarding the information.

For being effective in its functions, the organization of the Lokpal and Lokayukta will require to evolve certain clear guidelines and procedures for their working. The experience of the Scandinavian countries, U.K. and New Zealand shows that the complaints are not likely to be of a large magnitude. The number of complaints received by the Ombudsman in Sweden, Finland, Denmark, Norway and New Zealand have generally been between 1,000 to 1,800 a year. Of these, the cases which deserved relief ranged from 6 to 20 per cent. In India, however, in view of the enormous size of the country and its population, the Lokpal will have to evolve detailed criteria to govern the entertainment of complaints; otherwise, he will be flooded by all sorts of applications. It will be necessary to lay down, for different types of complaints, the number or levels of administrative remedies which must be gone through and the minimum time (for each particular stage or for all stages together) which should lapse after the making of an application to the departmental channels of redress.

No less important would be to improve the political and administrative environment in India. A special public relations committee should be appointed to explain to the public and political parties the implications of Lokpal machinery. The political parties will do well if they keep the institution above party politics. If the institution of the Lokpal has to be successful it is essential that the officials must show the same respect for its recommendations which they give to the court judgments. It will be equally necessary to persuade the States to fall in line with the Centre and appoint Lokayuktas. To limit the Lokpal institution to public men only would not go a long way to create heightened sensitivity among the civil services towards the citizens' difficulties.

SYSTEM PERSPECTIVE

The problem of the citizens' grievances and the machinery for their redress needs to be considered also from the wider perspective to totality of the socio-political system, with administration as one of its parts. From the perspective of general system theory, Indian administration is a partially open social sub-system. It is governed partly by the environmental demands, partly by the system's needs. Within the administrative system, there has to prevail a substantial measure of "security" if the organizational goals have to be achieved and the technical (i.e. productive) and the social parts of the sub-system have to be fitted together for the purposes of administrative effectiveness. The administrative system has all the same to adopt itself to changes in the environment; and if it is to attain effectiveness and to survive, it must also try to influence the environment. The citizens constitute a part of the environment of administration. A progressive increase in the citizens' satisfaction and adequate redress of their complaints is considerably a matter of the growth of the "delivery capacity" of the administrative system.

Socio-political context

The capability of the administrative system depends not only on the efficiency and the inter-relationships of its parts but equally on the patterns of interaction between the administrative system and the other components of the socio-political system. We have noted earlier that the efforts at administrative reforms have not succeeded in raising the level of administrative efficiency and capability. There has been a growing recognition in recent times that administrative development cannot proceed much far unless there is a synchronization and balancing of all categories of development-economic, social, political and administrative development.

The working of the administrative system is considerably influenced by the political environment in which it operates. The present pattern of political development in India is impeding administrative development. The general elections of March, 1977 and mid-term election of 1980 were won by the parties on the basis of an appeal to national issues as separated from local and parochial considerations. However, the Indian political scene, by and large, continues to be dominated by the politics of patronage.[6] The growing political intervention in day-to-day

[6]Indian villages and towns are socially divided not only into caste, linguistic and religious groups but into factions which lean to one party or another or to one or another faction within the major parties. Successful district and State party leaders are skilful in providing

administration, prompted by the politics of patronage, is tending to demoralize the Indian bureaucracy thereby affecting impartiality and fair play.

The civil services were so far accustomed to function within a structured and more or less unambiguous framework. Today, they are increasingly called upon to operate in a climate of increasing social and political uncertainty. This uncertainty is going to increase in the years to come. Accordingly, a solution has to be found to the constraints at present imposed on the development of administrative capability by the political and social factors.

It has been suggested that the responsibilities of bureaucracy in underdeveloped and developing countries should be sliced, to meet the needs of political growth or development. But in countries like India, which are committed to development planning and economic growth, it is difficult to divest the administration of its role as an agent of social and economic change and of its role in nation building. Interrelating the political administrative elements in the development process is important but administrative change and reform cannot await the growth and maturing of the political system if development has to proceed ahead. If the administrative system is not geared adequately to the requirements of stepping up the pace of development, the spiralling citizens' dissatisfaction is likely to threaten the entire edifice of the Indian polity as has been amply proved by the mid-term elections of 1980. Accordingly, the efforts at administrative reform need to be mounted up, from the point of view of the prevention of the grievances at the very source. Simultaneously, attention should be increasingly directed to initiate such social and political reforms as are necessary to facilitate the growth of the administrative capability.

Reorientation of attitudes

A democratic reorientation of the attitudes of the officials

rewards to diverse factions and communities—by giving one local leader a position in the zila parishad, another a position as a Member of Parliament. Myron Weiner, "Mrs. Gandhi and the Electorate", New Delhi, *The Hindustan Times*, 14 January 1971, p. 7.

towards the citizens has become necessary for both the prevention of the citizens complaints and their prompt redress. The prevailing ambivalent attitude of the officials are impeding significantly the heightening of their sensitivity to the citizens' needs and adoption of administrative system to such demands. In the context of increased development and welfare responsibilities of the government and the growing social and political awareness, the officials have come to occupy a "guardian role" in maintaining administrative stability, and in protecting public interest against the inroads of political pressures and intervention by ministers and elected representatives. Quite a few among the senior civil servants are concerned about deterioration in the public standards. The "guardian role" has in a way helped to reinforce the authoritarian style of administration inherited from the British rule. Not that the administrators are not oriented towards public welfare but that their approach to the problems is more in terms of prescriptions of what is good for the citizens rather than finding out what the citizens want.[7] At the same time there is among the public officials a singular lack of sensitivity to the citizens' felt-needs and convenience, an attitude of callousness towards their requests and demands, and absence of any genuine and sustained concern for their welfare.

The government's approach to the problem of citizens grievances too is marked by a philosophy of procrastination, lack of sense of urgency, and "routine" orientation towards improving the existing state of affairs. The tragedy of the situation is that political leadership and senior management in government are cognizant of the growing volume of citizens' grievances and realize that something should be done to arrest and redress

[7]In the absence of a vigorous and respectable tradition of politics, a civil bureaucracy sustained by traditional factors is likely to remain the most important element of government—an elitist bureaucracy initiating change, not always with maximum regard for the aspirations of the public mass, regarding itself as the embodiment of Platonic guardianship, creating its own consensual base." Ralph Braibanti, "The Relevance of Political Science to the Study of Underdeveloped Areas" in Ralph Braibanti and Joseph J. Spengler (eds.) *Tradition, Values, and Socio Economic Development*, Durham, Duke University Press, 1961, p. 170.

them, but they hardly make a concerted endeavour to go to the depth of the problem and initiate adequate measures which are needed.

In the present transition from an agrarian and traditional society to an industrial and modern polity, the citizens' attitude in India towards the government is marked by some inner contradictions. On the one hand the citizen expects the administration to be always helpful to meet all the demands; on the other, he does not feel any compunction in asking for favours and concessions and putting forward unreasonable claims. His sense of social obligations to the state and the people is not commensurate with his demands upon the administration. While he has become increasingly aware of his rights, there has not been any corresponding realization of the duties. There is "a peculiar blend of respect for 'authority' and impatience with 'authorities', of desire for administrative progress and frustration at administrative tactics and style, of 'realism' as to how things get done and bitterness that one cannot get things done, of confidence in the system and cynical appraisal of the system.[8]

Reorientation of the attitudes of the officials towards the citizens is going to be an uphill task. It will require an attack on several fronts, such as in-service training, professionalization recruitment from a wider social base (particularly, from among the rural families), special assignments in rural areas and the like. A mighty educational effort will be needed to develop among the citizens a sense of social obligation and to raise the general standard of public morality. The problem of evolving and adopting suitable methods of attitudinal change has much larger dimension than our present field of enquiry; but unless it is tackled on a priority basis, all other measures to deal with the citizens' grievances will be of limited effectiveness only.

Role of redress machinery

The redress machinery can perform three important functions in attuning the administrative system to the goals set for it by

[8]Samuel J. Eldersveld, V. Jagannadham and, A.P. Barnabas, *The Citizen and the Administration in a Developing Democracy*, p. 159.

the wider socio-political system and to the environmental change. In the first place, it provides a mechanism of compensation for the inadequacies of the administrative system in meeting the citizens' genuine claims and demands and provides relief to the citizens in matters of administrative injustice and maladministration. Secondly, the redress machinery can be of great help in facilitating the adaptation of the administrative system to the environmental demands and challenges. A detailed analysis of public complaints can serve as a useful feedback to help identify the key issues for administrative improvement. Redress of individual grievances is important but equally important is that these grievances should help bring about the needed modifications and change in the system so as to reduce the volume of grievances. The redress machinery needs to be properly reinforced for performing this diagnostic role. These two aspects have already been discussed in detail.

Thirdly, an independent outside redress agency can serve as a useful instrument of control over the bureaucracy. Its very existence will act as a curb on the callousness and insensitivity of the civil servants towards the citizens and help improve the quality of decision on the citizens' applications and complaints.

There has been a growing realization in recent years that bureaucracy cannot be made responsive and responsible unless the outside social controls are effective. The need for special control of the bureaucracy arises from the fact that it is a part of the wider socio-political system. Unless the system is structurally differentiated, well integrated and balanced, neither the system as a whole nor any of its part will be much effective in attaining system or sub-system goals.[9]

[9]Prof. Fred W. Riggs has evolved a comprehensive concept of dynamic balancing for system effectiveness. The concept of balancing covers a balanced governmental system, a balanced elected assembly, a balanced party sytem, a balanced constitutive system, a compensated bureaucracy, an accountable but serious chief executive, a balance between the bureaucracy and constitutive system, and a balance between government and public. If any of these balances is missing the efforts at administrative reform may aggravate the conditions rather than make for imrovement. Fred W. Riggs, *Administrative Reform as a Problem of Dynamic Balancing*, a paper presented to International Round Table on Administrative Reform and Development, Beirut (11-18 April 1970), convened by the National Institute of Administration and Development, Civil Service Board, Republic of Lebanon, p. 23.

The establishment of Ombudsman type of institution of Lokpal and Lokayukta will help impart a measure of balance to the politico-administration system. Though they will prima facie be set up for purposes of securing quick redress for citizens' complaints, their role as a useful yoke to tame the Indian bureaucracy can be of a far-reaching character. The redress machinery, even when reinforced, is likely to function as efficiently or inefficiently as other parts of the administrative system. It is only the establishment of the Ombudsman-type of institution which can provide a fulcrum for raising the administrative capability to progressively higher levels. No doubt, the creation of other controls and balances within the politico-socio system is equally important. All the same, the setting up of the Ombudsman-type of institution will be a step towards creating a balance between the government and the public. Within the executive branch of government, the Directorate of Grievances at the State and Central levels will also provide a balancing factor; and a similar role could be played usefully by the complaint cells in the individual departments provided these are headed by senior officers and properly reactivised.

PREVENTIVE MEASURES

The conclusions of this study also suggest certain preventive measures which may either plug or minimize the public grievances:

1. The range of economic controls to be reduced to the minimum, and operated only to the extent to the time and area necessary.
2. Rigorous enforcement of Rule of Law.
3. Rules and procedures to be made clear-cut, unambiguous and expressed in simple language.
4. Number of decision making levels to be increased and delegation of powers to be adequate.
5. Area of discretionary powers to be reduced to the minimum.
6. Severe punishment to be imposed for:
   (i) non-exercise of powers;
   (ii) evasion of responsibilities;
   (iii) improper exercise and abuse of power;

(iv) discrimination on grounds of caste, community and region.

7. Adequate training to be given to all officers in:
   (i) public relations;
   (ii) methods and procedures.
8. Public to be educated:
   (i) on points of contact;
   (ii) procedures to be adopted in their dealings with Government machinery for their various requirements.
9. Special arrangements to be made to provide all literature pertaining to common laws, rules and procedures, points of contact, etc., in English and the regional language down to the taluk or block level.
10. Political control to be exercised over undue political and administrative interferences in the process of administration.

Besides the following curative measures are also needed:

1. All petitions containing justiciable complaints should be straight away rejected and the parties asked to seek redress in court of law.
2. All petitions, whatever may be the level at which they are received, should be directed to the decision-making levels for disposal without calling for reports unless the decision is to be made at the receiving level.
3. All petitions should be acknowledged and the party intimated of the action taken.
4. All decisions made should be immediately intimated to the petitioners, so that it may avoid further correspondence on the subject and enable the petitioner to go on appeal if he prefers to do so.
5. Exercise of effective supervision and inspection from top to bottom in regard to the disposal of grievances.
6. A systematic method of classification and expeditious disposal of petitions to be enforced.
7. Disciplinary proceedings should be made more simple and action to be taken against erring officials expeditiously.
8. The States may set up more than one Disciplinary Tribunals at convenient centres if the volume of work so requires.

9. High level ad hoc tribunals to be set up, if necessary, to deal with complaints of malpractices at higher levels.
10. The States should immediately appoint Ombudsman-type of institution.

RESPONDING TO FUTURE CHALLENGES

The eightees are going to witness a sizeable increase in the peoples' demands on administration. These demands would, in all probability, outstrip the expanded capacity of administration. Accordingly, the volume of public complaints would mount up. The character of citizens' complaints may also change in as much as the growing psychological insecurity and economic uncertainties would reduce the reserve power of the people to put up with harassment and hardship at the hands of the bureaucracy.

The political and social environment of administration in coming years will be turbulant. Political flux is likely to continue and might even increase. All the same, the pressures on political leadership for attaining results in the fields would intensify. Social ferment and discontent may highten in the wake of increase in industrialization and urbanization, the wider spread of education and the changed aspirations of the new generation. The failure to carry the gains of development to the grass-roots of the society and to distribute them evenly has already created new strains. Even with the efforts underway for reducing inequalities in income and wealth, the thurst of development would throw up new stresses and tensions.

The existing administrative machinery is woefully deficient in the matter both of processing of citizens' applications and the redress of their complaints with speed and justice. The government has initiated several measures to improve the redress machinery but little effort has been directed to make it function effectively. The government's approach to the problem of citizens' grievances has lacked realism, depth and width of perspective. The attitudes of the administrators and political leadership on the matter have largely been ambivalent.

If the future challenges in the field of citizens' grievances have to be met, it would be necessary to augment administrative capability appreciably, to strengthen and streamline the departmental redress machinery, to educate the citizens regarding their social responsibilities and to reorient the attitudes of the officials. The government will have to evolve a comprehensive policy and a dynamic strategy to tackle successfully the mounting volume of citizens' complaints. If the redress machinery has to be effective in its role, it will need to line up depth studies on the nature, magnitude and causes of public grievances, the contribution it is making in providing relief and other connected matters.

Above all, the Ombudsman-type of machinery will need to be established without further delay and be nursed properly. It has great potentiality for rebuilding the confidence of the people in administration, securing justice to the citizens, protecting the officials against malicious allegations and projecting a correct image of administration. It can also serve as a catalyst to administrative reforms and as a useful control instrument to make the Indian bureaucracy responsive to the citizens' needs and difficulties.

भारत राजपत्र

सत्यमेव जयते

का

The Gazette of India

असाधारण

EXTRAORDINARY

भाग–1 खण्ड–1

Part-1 Section I

प्राधिकार से प्रकाषित

PUBLISHED BY AUTHORITY

सं. 76 नई दिल्ली षुकवार अप्रैल 8 2011/चैत्र 18, 1933

No.76 NEW DELHI. FRIDAY, APRIL 8, 2011/ CHAITRA 18, 1933

विधि और न्याय मंत्रालय

(विधायी विभाग)

संकल्प

नई दिल्ली 8, अप्रैल 2011

सं. 1(42)/2004 वि.–1– भारत सरकार लोकपाल विधेयक का प्रारूप तैयार करने के लिए एक संयुक्त प्रारूपण समिति का गठन करती है ।

2. संयुक्त प्रारूपण समिति भारत सरकार कं पॉच नामनिर्देषित मंत्रियों और श्री अन्ना हजारे के (उन्के सहित) पॉच नामनिर्देषितियों से मिलकर बनेगी ।

3. भारत सरकार के पॉच नामनिर्देषिती मंत्री निम्नलिखित है :–

1. श्री प्रणव मुखर्जी, संघ के वित्त मंत्री
2. श्री पी.. चिदंबरम, संघ के गृह मंत्री
3. डा. एम. वीरप्पा पोइली, संघ के विधि और न्याय मंत्री

4. श्री कपिल सिब्बल, संघ के मानव संसाधन विकास मंत्री और संचार एवं सूचना प्रोद्योगिकी मंत्री
5. श्री सलमान खुर्षीद संघ के जल संसाधन मंत्री और अल्पसंख्यक मामले मंत्री

श्री अन्ना हजारे के (उन्के सहित) पॉच नामनिर्द्रेषी निम्नलिखित है ।

1 श्री अन्ना हजारे
डाकघर रेलेगन सिद्दि
तालुक पामेर
जिला अहमदनगर, महाराष्ट!

2. न्यायमूर्ती श्री एन. संतोष हेगडे
94 ए 9 वा क्रास
आर एम वी एक्सटेसंन, सदाषिव नगर
बंगलुर–80

3. श्री शांति भूषण
ज्येष्ठ अधिवक्ता
बी–15, सेक्टर 14, नोएडा

4 प्रषांत भूषण
बी–16, सेक्टर 14, नोएडा

5. श्री अरविन्द केजरीवाल
परिवर्तन एल 403 गिरनार
कोषाम्बी, गाजियाबाद–201 010

5. श्री प्रणव मुखर्जी संयुक्त प्ररूपण समिति के अध्यक्ष होगें
6. श्री शांति भूषण संयुक्त प्ररूपण समिति के सह–अध्यक्ष होगें
7. डा. एम. वीरप्पा मोइली संयुक्त प्ररूपण समिति के संयोजक होगें
8. संयुक्त प्रारूपण समिति अपना कार्य तुरन्त आरम्भ करेगी और प्रस्तावित विधान तैयार करने के लिए अपनी स्वंय की प्रकिया बनाएगी ।
9. संयुक्त प्ररूपण समिति अपना कार्य 30 जून 2011 तक पूरा करेगी

बी0 के0 भसीन, सचिव

MINISTRY OF LAW AND JUSTICE

(Legislative Department)

RESOLUTION

New Delhi, the 8th April, 2011

No.1(42) no W-Leg-I.-The Government of India hereby constitutes a Joint Drafting Committee to prepare a draft of the Lok Pal Bill.

2. The Joint Drafting Committee shall consist of five 'nominee Ministers of the Government of India and five nominees of Shri Anna Hazare (including himself).

3. The five nominee Ministers of the Government of India are as under-

1) Shri Pranab Mukherjee
Union Minister of Finance.

(ii) Shri P. Chidambaram,
Union Minister of Home Affairs.

(iii) Dr. M. Veerappa Moily,
Union Minister of Law and Justice.

iv) Shri Kapil Sibal.
Union Minister of Human Resource Development and Minister of Communication and Information Technology

(v) Shri Salman Khursheed
Union Minister of Water Resources and Minister of Minority Affairs

4. The five nominees of Shri Anna Hazare (including himself) are as under-

(i) Shri Anna Hazara,
At Post-Relegan Siddhi,
Taluk Pamer
Distt.: Ahmednagar, Maharashtra

(ii) Shri Justice N. Santosh Hedge
94 A, 8th Cross, RMV Extension
Sadashiv Nagar, Bangaluru-80

(ii) Shri Shanti Bhushan,
Senior Advocate,
B-15, Sector-14, Noida.

(iv) Shri Prashant Bhushan,
Advocate
B-16, Sector-14, Noida

(v) Shri Arvind Kejriwal
Parivartan,
L403, Girnar, Kaushambi
Ghaziabad-2010

5. The Chairperson of the Joint Drafting Committee shall be Shri Pranab Mukherjee.

6. The Co-Chairperson of the Joint Drafting Committee shall be Shri Shanti Bhushan.

7. The Convener of the Joint Drafting Committee shall be Dr. M. Veerappa Moily.

8. The oint Drafting Committee shall commence its work forth-with and evolve its own procedure to prepare the proposed legislation.

9. The Joint Drafting Committee shall compete its work latest by 30th June, 2011.

V.K. BHASIN, Secy.

BIBLIOGRAPHY

A. BOOKS AND PAMPHLETS

Almond, Gabriel A. and Sidney Verba, *The Civic Culture*, Princeton, Princeton University Press, 1963.

Allen, C.K. *Aspects of Justice*, London, Stevens & Sons, 1958.

Altekar, A.S., *State and Government in Ancient India*, Delhi, Motilal Banarsidass, 1958.

American Academy of Political and Social Science, *The Ombudsman or Citizens' Defender*, Philadelphia, 1968.

American Assembly, *Ombudsman for American Government*, Stanley V. Anderson (ed.) Englewood Cliffs, N.J., Prentice-Hall, 1968.

———, "The Ombudsman": *Report of the Thirty-second American Assembly*, 26-29, October 1967, N.Y., the Assembly, Columbia University, 1967.

Anderson, Stanley V., *Canadian Ombudsman Proposals*, Berkeley, University of California, Institute of Governmental Studies, 1966.

Appleby, Paul H., *Citizens as Sovereigns*, Syracuse, Syracuse University Press, 1962.

———, *Policy in Administration*, Alabama, University of Alabama Press, 1957.

Archibald, Kathlsen and Bagdikian, Ben. *Televised Ombudsman*. Santa Monica, Calif, Rand Corporation, 1968 (p. 3841).

Asaron, Thomas J., *The Control of Police discretion: the Danish Experience*, Springfield III, Charles C. Thomas, 1966.

Basu, Durga Das, *Commentary on the Constitution of India*, 1970.

Barnabas, A.P. *Citizens' Grievances in Development Administration*, New Delhi, Indian Institute of Public Administration, 1966.

———, *The Experiences of Citizens in Getting Water Connection*, New Delhi, Indian Institute of Public Adm nistration, 1965.

Bendix, Reinhard, *Nation-Building and Citizenship: Studies of Our Changing Social Order*, New York, John Wiley & Sons, 1964.

Bensman, Joseph and Bernard Rasenberg, *Mass, Class and Bureaucracy*, Englewood Cliffs, New Jersey, Prentice Hall, 1963.

Bexelius, Alfred, *The Swedish Ombudsman: Special Parliamentary Commissioner for the Judiciary and Civil Administration*, 1810-1860, Stockholm, Royal Ministry for Foreign Affairs, 1961, (mimeo).

Bhan, Peter M. *Bureaucracy in Modern Society*, New York, Random House, 1956.

Cahn, William, *Ombudsman Report*, Mineola, N.Y., Nassau County Board of Supervisors, 1966.

Chapman, B., *The Profession of Government: The Public Service in Europe*, London, George Allen & Unwin, 1959.

Chien Tuan-shang, *The Government and Politics of China*, Cambridge, Mass., 1950.

Clark, Roger Stenson, *A United Nations High Commissioner for Human Rights*, The Hague: Martinus Nijhoff, 1972.

Coombas, David, *The Member of Parliament and the Administration*, London, George Allen & Unwin.

Cowell, Herbert, *History and Constitution in the Courts and Legislative Authorities in India*, Calcutta, Thacker Spink & Co., 1936.

Crozier, Michel, *The Bureaucratic Phenomenon*, Chicago, The University of Chicago Press, 1964.

Danet, Brenda, *Coping with Bureaucracy*, The Research Case Study, American Sociological Association, Denver, Colorado, 1971.

David Baston, *A Framework of Political Analysis*, Prentice-Hall, Englewood Cliffs, 1965.

Desai, N.B., *Report on the Administrative Survey of the Surat District*, The Indian Society of Agricultural Economy, Bombay, 1958.

Dicey, *Introduction to the Study of the Law of the Constitution*, London, Macmillan & Sons, 1959.

Dimock, Marshall E., *Administrative Vitality*, London, Routledge and Kegan Paul, 1955.

Eldersveld, Samual J., Jagannadham V. and Barnabas, A.P., *The Citizen and the Administrator in a Developing Democracy*, Delhi, Indian Institute of Public Administration, 1968.

Embree, A.T., *British Rule in India*, London, George Allen & Unwin, 1962.

Finer, Herman, *The Theory and Practice of Modern Government*, 2 volumes, London, 1932.

Friedmann, W., *Law in a Changing Society*, London, Stevens & Sons, 1959.

Friedmann, K.A., "Canadian Ombudsmen" Cyclostyled paper prepared for the International Ombudsman Conference, Edmonton, Alberta, September, 1976.

Gajendragadkar, P.B., *Role of Administration in a Democratic Welfare State*, Indian Institute of Public Administration, Vol. IX, No. 4, October-December, 1963.

Gellhorn, Walter, *Ombudsman and others: Citizen's Protectors in Nine Countries*, Cambridge, Mass., Harvard University Press, 1966.

———, *When Americans Complain: Governmental Grievances Procedures*, Cambridge, Mass., Harvard University Press, 1966.

Gerth, H.H. and C.W. Mills (eds.), *From Max Weber, Essays in Sociology*, New York, Oxford University Press, 1948.

Gouldner, Alvin, "*Metaphysical Pathos and the Theory of Bureaucracy in Amitai Etzioni, Complex Organizations*, New York, Holt, Rinchart, 1961.

Gregory Roy and Peter Hutchesson, The Parliamentary Ombudsman: *A Study in the Control of Administrative Action*, London, George Allen & Unwin, 1975.

Gwyn, W.B., "A Comparative Study of the Investigative Methods of Ombudsmen", cyclostyled paper prepared for the International Ombudsman Conference, Edmonton, Alberta, September 1976.

Hayak, F.A., *The Constitution of Liberty*, London, Routledge.

Henkow, H. Memorandum on the Institution of the Swedish Procurator of Military Affairs (MO), Stockholm, 1955 (mimeo).

Heady, Ferrel, *Public Administration. A Comparative Perspective*, Prentice-Hall, Inc., Englewood Cliffs, N.J. 1966.

Hiden, Mikael, J.V., *The Ombudsman in Finland: The First Fifty Years*, Translated by Aaron Bell, edited and with a Foreword by Donald C. Rowat, Berkeley, University of California, Institute of Governmental Studies, 1973.

Hill, Larry B., *The Model Ombudsman*, Princeton, New Jersey, Princeton University Press, 1976.

Hurwitz, Stephen, *The Ombudsman*, Copenhagen Det Danske Selskali, 1961.

Indian Institute of Public Administration, Madras Regional Branch, *Redressal of Public Grievances: Report of a Seminar* (August 1968), K. Venkataraman (ed.), Madras, The Branch, 1969.

Indian Law Institute, *The Ombudsman*, The Third All India Law Conference, 12 to 14 August 1962, New Delhi.

Institute for Local Self Government, Berkeley. *The Mexican "Aspare" as a Supplemental Remedy for the Redress of Citizen Grievances in California*, Berkeley, 1967.

Inter-Parliamentary Union, *Parliaments*, London, Cassall, 1966, 2nd ed. (pp. 302-4).

Iqbal Narain, Sushil Kumar, P.C. Mathur and associates, *Panchayati Raj Administration—Old Controls and New Challenges*, New Delhi, Indian Institute of Public Administration, 1970.

Jain, M.P. *The Lokpal: Ombudsman in India*: Institute of Constitutional and Parliamentary Studies, New Delhi, 1970.

Jagannadham, V. and Mukhija, H R., *Citizen Administration and Lokpal*, Delhi, S. Chand, 1969.

Jagannadham, V. and Bakshi, N.S., *Citizen and the Municipal Bureaucracy*—a survey of the Building Department of the Delhi Municipal Corporation, New Delhi, Indian Institute of Public Administration, 1971.

———, *Citizen and the Municipal Bureaucracy*—a study of the Assessment and Collection Department of the Delhi Municipal Corporation, New Delhi, Indian Institute of Public Administration, 1969.

Justice (British Section of the International Commission of Jurists), *The Citizen and the Administration: the Redress of Grievances—A Report*, London, Stevens, 1961, (Director of Research, Sir John Whyatt).

———, *Our Fettered Ombudsman*, 1977.

———, *The Citizen and the Public Agencies: Remedying Grievances*, 1976.

Kagzi, Mangla Chandra Jain, *The Indian Administrative Law*, New Delhi, Metropolitan Book Co., 1969.

Kass, Benny L., *Ombudsman: A Proposal for Demonstration in Washington, D.C.*, Washington D.C., Washington Center for Metropolitan Studies, 1968.

Katz, Seul M., "A Systems Approach to Development Administration", Special Series No. 6, Washington, D.C., *American Society of Public Administration, A Paper in Comparative Public Administration*, 1965.

Kothari, Shantilal, *Relations between Politicians and Administrators at the District Level*, Indian Institute of Public Administration, New Delhi, 1968.

Kersell, John E., *Parliamentary Supervision of Delegated Legislation*. McMaster University, Hamilton, Canada.

LaPalombara, Joseph (ed.), *Bureaucracy and Political Development*, New Jersey, Princeton University Press, 1963.

Landis, *The Administrative Process*, New Haven, Yale University Press, 1951.

Lappzig, Brian and Radice Gibs (eds.), *More Power to the People: Young Fabian Essays on Democracy in Britain*, London, Longmans, 1968.

Laski, Harold J., *Parliamentary Government in England*, London, George Allen & Unwin, 1952.

Llambias, H.J., "The Need for an Ombudsman System in Canada". M.A. Thesis, Carleton University, Ottawa, 1969.

Lyall, Alfred, *The Rise and Expansion of the British Dominion in India*, London, John Murray, 1910.

Lee, Hahn-Been and Samonte, Abelardo G. (eds.), *Administrative Reforms in Asia*. Phillippines, Eastern Regional Organisation for Public Administration, 1970.

———, *Development and Change*, The Hague, Institute of Social Studies, Volume II, 1970-71, No. 2.

———, *Korea: Time, Change, and Administration*, Hawaii, East-West Center Press, 1966.

Lipser, S.M., *Political Man: The Social Bases of Politics*, Garden City, New York Doubleday & Co., Inc., 1960.

Livingstone, John C. and Robert G ; *Thompson, The Consent of the Governed*, New York, Macmillan, 1971.

Maddick, Henry, *Democracy Decentralisation and Development*, Bombay, Asia Publishing House, 1963.

Mann, Dean E., *The Citizen and the Bureaucracy: Complaint Handling Procedures of the Three California Legislatures*, Berkeley, University of California, Institute of Governmental Studies, 1968.

March and Simon, *Organisations*, New York, John Wiley & Sons, Inc., 1958.

Merrtow, Robert, *Social Theory and Social Structure*, Clencoe, III, The Free Press, 1957.

Moharir, V.V., "Administrative Reforms in India", *Development and Change*, Institute of Social Studies, the Hague, Volume IX, 1970-71.

Montairo, John B., *Corruption; control of Maladministration*, Bombay, Manaktalas, 1966 (pp. 189-299).

Morris, Janowitz, *Public Administration and the Public Perspectives Toward Government in a Metropolitan Community*, Ann Arbor, Institute of Public Administration, University of Michigan, 1958.

Morris-Jones, W.H., *Parliament in India*, London, Longmans, Green and Co., 1957.

Nanda, Gulzarilal, *New Tasks for the Railways—Implementation of the Eleven-Point Programme*, New Delhi, Ministry of Railways, 1971.

Nehru, Jawaharlal, "Administration—A Human Problem", (address delivered at the Inaugural meeting of the Institute of Public Administration), *The Indian Journal of Public Administration*, January-March, 1955.

Orr, G.S., *Report on Administrative Justice in New Zealand*, Wellington, Government Printers, 1964.

Os, Audvar, *The Ombudsman in Norway*, Royal Norwegian Ministry of Justice, No. 71, 1963 (mimeo).

Palmor, Norman D., *The Indian Political System*, University of Pennsylvania, Boston, Houghton Mifflin Co., 1961.

Park, Richard L. and Tinker Irene (eds), *Leadership and Political Institutions in India*, Madras, Oxford University Press, 1960.

Pathak, D.N., Shetty, Pravin K. and Iqbal Narain, *State Control of Panchayati Raj Institutions in Gujarat, An Area Report*, Department of Political Science, University of Rajasthan, 1967.

Paul, Burton, *Corporate Public Relations*, New York, Reinhold Publishing Corporation, 1966.

Philadelphia, *Mayor's Ad Hoc Committee on Improvement in Municipal Standards and Practices*, Final Report, 1962, Title VIII. The Continuing Watchdog Function.

Prasada, Mahabir, *Public Grievances Redress System*, 1964 (mimeo).

Presthins, Robert, *The Organisational Society, An Analysis and a Theory*, New York, Alfred A. Knoph, 1962.

Pelz, Donald C. and Barnabas, A.P. *Administering Agricultural Development*, New Delhi, Indian Institute of Public Administration, 1970.

Pye, Lucian W., *Aspects of Political Development*, Boston: Little, Brown & Co., 1966.

Rajeshwar Dayal, *Panchayat Raj in India*, Delhi, Metropolitan Book Co., 1970.

Ralph Braibanti and Joseph Spengler (eds.) *Administration and Economic Development in India*, Duke University Commonwealth-Studies Centre, London, Cambridge University Press, 1963.

Ralph Braibanti, (ed.), *Political and Administrative Development*, Durham, Duke University Press, 1969.

——— (ed.), *Tradition, Values and Socio-Economic Development*, Duke University Commonwealth-Studies Centre, London, Cambridge University Press, 1961.

Ralph Linton, *Study of Man*, New York, D. Appleton Century Co., 1936.

Ramachandran, V.G., *Administrative Law*, New Delhi, Eastern Book Co., 1969.

Riggs, Fred W., and Edward D. Weidner, *Models and Priorities in the Comparative Study of Public Administration*, Chicago, American Society for Public Administration, 1963.

Riggs, Fred W., *Administration in Development Countries—The Theory of Prismatic Society*, Boston, Houghton Mifflin Co., 1964.

———, *Administrative Reforms as a Problem of Dynamic Balancing*, a paper presented to International Round Table on Administrative Reform and Development, Beirut, 1970.

Robson, William A., *The Governors and the Governed*, George Allen & Unwin Ltd., (pp. 22-34).

———, *Justice and Administrative Law*, London, Stevens & Sons, 1951.

———, *The Civil Services in Britain and France*, London, Hogarth Press, 1956.

Rowat, Donald C. (ed.), *The Ombudsman: Citizens' Defender*, (second edition), London, George Allen & Unwin, 1968.

Russell, Bertrand, *New Hopes and a Changing World*, London, George Allen and Unwin Ltd., 1951.

Sawer, Geoffrey, *Ombudsmen*, Melbourne, Melbourne University Press, 1964.

Scott, Stanley (ed.), *Western American Assembly on the Ombudsman*, Berkeley, University of California, Institute of Governmental Studies, 1968.

Silverman, David, *The Theory of Organisation*, Heinemann, London, 1970.

Simon Herburt, A., *Administrative Behaviour: A Study of Decision-Making in Administrative Organization*, New York, Macmillan.

Spangler, Joseph, *Allocation and Development, Economic and Political, Political and Administrative Development*, Duke University Press, 1969.

Stahl, O. Glenn, *Public Personnel Administration*, New York, Harper & Row, 1971.

Stacey, Frank, *The British Ombudsman*, Oxford, Clarendon Press, 1971.

———, *Ombudsman Compared*, Oxford Clarendon Press, 1978.

Strauss, Erich, *The Ruling Servants, Bureaucracy in Russia, France and Britain*? London George Allen & Unwin, 1961, (pp. 288-91).

Thompson, Victor A., *Modern Organisation*, New York, Alfred A. Knopf, 1963.

Utley, T.E., *Occasion for Ombudsman*, London, Christopher Johnson 1961.

Vithal, B.P.R., *Report of Committee of Case Studies, Reorganisation of District Administration in Andhra Pradesh*, 1967.

Wade, H.W.R., *Towards Administrative Justices*, Ann Arbor, University of Michigan Press, 1963, (pp. 95-105).

Wahlke, John C., "Behavioural Analysis of Representative Bodies," in Austin Rammey (ed.) *Essays on the Behavioural Study of the Politics*,

Urbana, University of Michigan Press, 1962.

Weeks, K.M., *Ombudsman Around the World: A Comparative Chart*, Institute of Governmental Studies, University of California, Berkeley, 1973.

Weidner, Edward W. (ed.), *Development Administration in Asia*, Durham, Duke University Press, 1970.

———, *Technical Assistance in Public Administration Overseas, The Case for Development Administration*, Chicago, Public Administration Service, 1964.

Weiner, Myron, *The Politics of Scarcity*, Bombay, Asia Publishing House, 1963.

———, "Mrs. Gandhi and the Electorate", New Delhi, *The Hindustan Times*, 14 January 1971.

William Anderson, Penniman, Clare, Weidner, Edward D., *Government in the Fifty States*, Madison Holt, Rinehart and Winston, Inc., 1960.

Wyner, Alan J., *The Nebraska Ombudsman*: Innovation in State Government, Institute of Governmental Studies, Berkeley, University of California, 1974.

——— (ed.), *Executive Ombudsman in the United States*, Institute of Governmental Studies, Berkeley, University of California, 1973.

Young Conservative and Unionist Organisation, *Law, Liberty and Licence*, London, Conservative Political Centre, 1955, (pp. 16-17).

B. PUBLIC DOCUMENTS

Aberta's Ombudsman Act, 1967.

Andhra Pradesh, Report of the Administrative Reforms Committee (Chairman—K.M. Unninathan, ICS), 1960 (mimeo).

Annual Reports of the Commissioner for Local Administration in Scotland from 1976.

Annual Reports of the Commission for Local Administration in Wales from 1975.

Denmark, Act No. 203 of 11 June 1954, on the Parliamentary Commissioner for Civil and Military Administration.

Denmark, Directives for the Parliamentary Commissioner for Civil and Military Government, issued in pursuance of Act No. 203 of June 1954, Section 3.

Denmark, New Constitution Act of June, 1954, Section 55.

Finland, Constitution of Forms of Government of Finland, 17 July 1917—Articles 37, 46, 47, 48 and 49.

Finland, Regulations for the Solicitor-General of Parliament (Ombudsman), 10 January 1920, No. 2.

Folketingets Ombudsman, English version of part of Annual Report for 1975.

Gujarat, Report of the Sabarkantha Field Project, 1964, (mimeo).

Gujarat, Resolution No. DPS-1064-AES-I, 2 December 1964, General Administration Department, outlining the action for redress of public grievances and appointing seven honorary public men.

Gujarat, Resolution No. CMD-1064-AES-I, 20 July 1964, General Administration Department, the procedure to be followed for disposal of complaints on the spot by the Ministers.

Hawaii's Ombudsman Act, 1967.

India, Displaced Persons (Compensation and Rehabilitation) Act, 1954.

India, The Constiution of India, New Delhi, Ministry of Law.

India, Report of the Railway Corruption Enquiry Committee, 1953-55, Ministry of Railways.

India, Fourteenth Report of the Law Commission on Reform in Judicial Administration, 1958.

India, Report of the Evaluation of the Gram Sahayak Programme, Programme Evaluation Organisation, Planning Commission, 1961.

India, Report of the Evaluation Committee on Panchayati Raj Training Centres, Ministry of Food and Agriculture and Cooperation, 1962.

India, Report on Public Administration by A.D. Gorwala, Planning Commission, 1962.

India, Report of the Sub-Committee of the Special Consultative Group of Members of Parliament on Administrative Reforms, on Administrative Tribunals and Machinery of Redress of Grievances at the Centre, 1965 (mimeo).

India, Report of the Committee on Prevention of Corruption (Santhanam Committee), 1964.

India, Report of the Study Team on Panchayati Raj Finance, Ministry of Community Development and Cooperation, 1963.

India Report of the Study Team on Nyaya Panchayats, Ministry of Law, 1962.

India Sadachar, Movement for Purity in National Life, Publications Division, 1964.

India, Seventh Report of Organisation and Methods Division, 1961-64, Ministry of Home Affairs.

India, Annual Reports of the Ministry of Home Affairs, 1964 to-date.

India, Annual Reports of the Central Bureau of Investigations, 1965 to-date.

India, Annual Reports of the Centeral Vigilance Commission, 1966 to-date.

India, Report of the Seminar organised by the Administrative Reforms Commission on District Administration, 27-29 September 1967, (mimeo).

India, Eighty-Fourth Report of Estimates Committee on Central Vigilance Commission (1968-69), Lok Sabha Secretariat.

India, Second Report of the Committee on Government Assurance, Lok Sabha Secretariat, 1968.

India, Annual Report of the Department of Communications, Posts and Telegraphs Board, 1968-69.

India, Second Report on Committee on Petitions, Lok Sabha Secretariat, 1968.

India, Address delivered by Dr. Zakir Hussain, President of India, to the Joint Session of both the Houses of Parliament, 12 February 1968.

India, The Lokpal and Lokayuktas Bill, 1969.

India, The Lokpal and Lokayuktas Bill, 1968, Report of the Joint Committee, presented to Lok Sabha on the 26 March 1969.

India, The Lokpal Bill, 1977.

India, The Lokpal Bill, 1977, Report of the Joint Committee presented to the Lok Sabha on 20 July, 1978.

India, Report of the Income Tax Appellate Tribunal, 1970, (mimeo).

India Interim Report of the Administrative Reforms Commission on Problems of Redress of Citizens' Grievances, 1966.

India, Report of the Administrative Reforms Commission on the Machinery of the Government of India and its Procedures of Work, 1968.

India, Report of the Administrative Reforms Commission on Centre-State Relationships, 1969.

India, Report of the Administrative Reforms Commission on State Administration, 1969.

India, Report of the Administrative Reforms Commission on Treasuries, 1970.

India, Report of the Administrative Reforms Commission on Posts and Telegraphs, 1970.

India, Report of the Study Team of Administrative Reforms Commission on Machinery of the Government of India and its Procedures of Work, 1968.

India, Report of the Study Team of Administrative Reforms Commission on Centre-State Relationships, 1967.

India, Report of the Study Team of Administrative Reforms Commission on Redress of Citizens' Grievances, 1966.

India, Report of the Study Team of Administrative Reforms Commission on District Administration, 1967.

India, Report of the Study Team of Administrative Reforms Commission on Administrative Tribunals, 1968.

India, Report of the Study Team of Administrative Reforms Commission on State Level Administration, 1968.

India, Report of the Working Group of Administrative Reforms Commission on Police Administration, 1967.

India, Report of the Task Force on Treasuries, Administrative Reforms Commission, 1968.

India, Office Memorandum No. 30/1/64-A.R., June 1964, Ministry of Home Affairs, for setting up the Complaints Cells and Enquiry-cum-Reception Offices.

India, Office Memorandum No. 30/1/68-PO, 9 May 1969, Ministry of Home Affairs, regarding the measures for dealing with grievances of citizens and procedure for inspection of complaint cells by Complaint Officers.

India, Resolution No. 24/7/64-AVD, 11 February 1964, Ministry of Home Affairs on the follow-up action on Public Grievances.

India, Fourth Commonwealth Law Conference, Occasional Papers, 1971.
India, *Reserve Bank of India Bulletin*, December, 1969.
Jammu and Kashmir, First Report of the Anti-Corruption Commission for Gazetted Government Servants, 1963 to 1967-68.
Jammu and Kashmir, the Jammu and Kashmir Government Servants' Prevention of Corruption (Commission) Act, 1962, Act No. XI of 1962.
Kerala Report of the Administrative Reorganisation and Economy Committee (Chairman, M.K. Vellodi) 1967, (mimeo).
Local Government (Scotland) Act, 1975.
Mauritius, Constitution Order, 1966.
Madhya Pradesh, The Madhya Pradesh Janch Ayukta (Lok Vyakti Avan Lok Sevak) Adhyadesh, 1968.
Maharashtra, Interim Report on the Working of the Sachivalya Administrative Reorganisation Committee, 1965.
Maharashtra, Report of the District Revenue Offices (Shri M.G. Pimputkar), 1959 (mimeo).
Maharashtra, The Lokayukta and Uplokayukta Act, 1971.
New Zealand, The Parliamentary Commission (Ombudsman) Act, 1962.
New Zealand, The Ombudsman Act, 1975, No. 9.
New Zealand, Reports of the New Zealand Parliamentary Commissioner, 1964 onwards.
Ontario Ombudsman Act, 1975.
Orissa, The Lokpal and Lokayukta Act, 1971.
Province of New Foundland, Annual Reports of the Ombudsman, published from 1975 (St. John's).
Province of Ontario, Annual Reports of the Ombudsman, published from 1976 (Toronto).
Rajasthan, Report of the Administrative Committee, 1963. Refer: Chapter III, Pt. B. The People and the Government.
Rajasthan, Annual Report of the Department of Removal of Public Grievances, Jaipur, 1965-66.
Report of the Select Committee of the Legislative Assembly to Review Legislation on the Ombudsman Act, Alberta, May 1977.
Sweden, Constitution of the Kingdom of Sweden, 6 June 1809 as amended—Articles 96-100.
The Swedish Parliamentary Ombudsman: Summary in English of Report for the period 1 January, 1976 to 30 June, 1976.
U.K., Annual Reports of the Commission for Local Administration in England from 1975.
U.K. Local Government Act, 1974.
U.K., Reports of the Parliamentary Commissioner for Administration 1967 onwards.
U.K., Reports of the Select Committee on the Parliamentary Commissioner for Administration, 1968 onwards.
U.K. Parliamentary Commissioner Act, 1967.
U.K., The Parliamentary Commissioner for Administration, 1965 (Omnd. 2767).

United Nations Seminar on *Judicial and Other Remedies against the Abuse of Administrative Authority with Special Emphasis on the Role of Parliamentary Institutions*, Sweden, 1962.

———, Remedies against the Abuse of Administrative Authority, selected studies, by C.J. Hanson and others, N.Y., UN, 1964.

United States, Senate Committee on the Judiciary, Sub-Committee on Administrative Practices and Procedures (89th Congress, 2nd Session), Ombudsman: Hearing, 7 March 1966.

Wisconsin, Legislative Referencc Bureau, Ombudsman, 1967.

C. ARTICLES

Aaron, Richard I., Ombudsman: the American Proposals". *Utah Law Review*, March 1967, (pp. 32-93).

Abraham, Henry J., *Annals of the American Academy of Political and Social Sciences*, May 1968, (pp. 55-61).

———, "People's Watchdog Against Abuse of Powers", *Public Administration Review*, Summer 1960, (pp. 152-7).

Abrahamson, M.W., "The Grievance Man in Ireland". *Administration* (Dublin), Autumn, 1960, (pp. 238-42).

Adams, J.C., "In Quest of the Ombudsman in the Mediterranean Area", *Annals of the American Academy of Political and Social Sciences*, May 1968, (pp. 97-103).

Advani, Ashok K., "Parliament and our Rights", Bombay, *Illustrated Weekly of India*, 6 May 1973, (pp. 28-31).

Agarwal, J.P., "Procuratorship", *Journal of the Indian Law Institute*, Jan-March 1961, (pp. 71-86).

Aikman, C.C., "The New Zealand Ombudsman", *Canadian Bar Review*, September 1964, (pp. 399-432).

Akthar, Mohd, "Democratic Totalitarianism", *Modern Review*, July 1973, (pp. 27-30).

Ameller, Michel, "The Ombudsman and Other Forms of Control", *Inter-Parliamentary Union Parliament*, 2nd ed., 1966.

Anderman, Steven D., "The Swedish Justice Ombudsman", *American Journal of Comparative Law*, Spring 1962, (pp. 225-38).

Anderson, Stanley V., "Connecticut Ombudsman?" *Case and Comment*, March-April 1965, (pp. 1-8).

"Ombudsman Proposals: Stimulus to Inquiry", *Public Affairs Report*, December 1966, whole issue.

———, "The Ombudsman: Public Defender Against Maladministration", *Public Affairs Report*, April 1965, whole issue.

———, "The Scandinavian Ombudsman", *The American Scandinavian Review*, December 1964, (pp. 403-9).

Andren, Nils, "The Swedish Office of Ombudsman", *Municipal Review*, December 1962, (pp. 820-1).

Angus, William H. and Kaplan, Milton, "The Ombudsman and Local Government", Stanley V. Anderson (ed.), (p. 115).

"Appeals Against Administrative Decisions" (a series of three articles). *Canadian Public Administration*, V. 5, 1962, (pp. 46-69).

Argylis, "Fusion of the Individual with the Organisation", American Sociological Review, Vol. 19, (pp. 67-72). "The Individual and Organization: Some Problems of Adjustment", *Administrative Science Quarterly*, Vol. II, 1956, (pp. 11-22).

———, "The Swedish Ombudsman", *Anglo-Swedish Review*, 1962, (pp. 97-103).

Arora, Ramesh Kumar, "Case For Ombudsman In India", *Commercium*, Jan. 1967, (pp 23-35).

———, "Development Administration Some Conceptual Issues", Jaipur *Prashanika*, April-June 1973, (pp. 39-48).

Arora, R.S., "Parliamentary Scrutiny: The Select Committee Device", *Public Law*, Spring, 1967, (pp. 30-41).

Ascher, C.S., "The Grievance Man or Ombudsman," *Public Administration Review*, June 1967, (pp. 174-7).

Awdry Daniel: "The Parliamentary Commissioner", *Occasional Papers, Fourth Commonwealth Law Conference*, 1971, (p. 19).

Bader, Helmut and Brompton, Henry, "Remedies against Administrative Abuse in Central Europe, the Soviet Union, and Communist East Europe (Ombudsman and others)". *Annals of the American Academy of Political and Social Sciences*, May 1968, (pp. 73-86).

Barrington, T.J., "Organization and Development", Dublin, *Administration*, Spring, 1973, (pp. 3-15).

Bexellius, Alfred, "The Ombudsman's Office and Other Means for Protecting Citizens' Rights in Sweden", *International Social Science Journal*, Vol. 18, No. 2, 1966, (pp. 247-51).

———, "The Swedish institution of the Justice-Ombudsman", *Administration* (Dublin), Winter 1961-62, (pp. 272-90).

Blix, Hans, "The Ombudsman: What He is and What He is Not". *Public Administration*, Kanpur, 3 July 1965, (pp. 303-6).

Blom-Cooper, L.J., "An Ombudsman Though Otherwise", *American-Swedish Monthly*, Vol. 57, 1963, (pp. 22-4).

———, "An Ombudsman for Britain", *Public Law*, 1960, (pp. 145-51).

Bologun, M.J., "A Framework of the Measurement of Government Efficiency", *Quarterly Journal of Administration*, October 1972, (pp. 21-34).

Broderick, A., "Ombudsman for Religions", *America*, 15 October 1966, (pp. 446-94).

———, Discussion, 5 November 1966, (pp. 527-8).

Brooke, P.F., "Danish Ombudsman", *Public Administration* (Kanpur), 19 June 1965, (pp. 227).

Brown, L. and P. Lavirotte, "Mediator: a French Ombudsman"; *Law Quarterly Review*, 1974, 1-26.

Bylin, James K., "The Ombudsman: He keeps Swedish officials in line: would it work here?" *Wall Street Journal*, 22 November 1966, (p. 18).

Caiden, Gerald E. and Raphaeli, Nimrod, "The Ombudsman Debate in Israeli Politics", *Parliamentary Affairs*, Summer 1968, (pp. 201-15).

———, "An Ombudsman for Australia?", *Public Administration* (Australia), June 1964, (pp. 97-116).

———, Ombudsman for Underdeveloped Countries" *Public Administration in Israel and Abroad*, 1967, (pp. 100-15).

Cains, Sidney and others, "The Citizen in Conflict With the State", *Royal Service Quarterly*, Vol. 36, No. 2, 1962.

Capell, Iris, "Ombudsman?", *Contemporary Review*, August 1960, (pp. 409-12).

Capozzola, J.M., "An American Ombudsman: Problems and Prospects", *Western Political Quarterly*, June 1968, (pp. 289-301).

Chapman, Bruce, "The Ombudsman", *Public Administration* (London), Winter 1960, (pp. 303-16).

Chapman, R.J.K., "The Machinery of Government; a Field for Public Enquiries and Scholarly Research", *New Zealand Journal of Public Administration*, Wellington, September 1972, (pp. 17-33).

Chatterjee, Dalip Kumar, "Origin of the Concept of Fundamental Rights in India", New Delhi, *Modern Review*, December 1973, (pp. 441-5).

Chaturvedi, S.N., "Machinery for Redress of Citizens' Grievances", *Indian Journal of Public Administration*, July-September 1966, (pp. 636-55).

Chaudhari, P.S., "Ombudsman: Its Desirability in India", *Supreme Court Journal*, November 1967, (pp. 77-82).

Cheng, Hingyong. "The Emergence and Spread of the Ombudsman Institution", *Annals of the American Academy of Political and Social Sciences*, May 1968, (pp. 20-30).

Chinkin, C.M. and R.J. Bailey, "The Local Ombudsman", Public Administration, 1976, (pp. 267-82).

Christensen, Bent, "The Danish Ombudsman", *University of Pennsylvania Law Review*, June 1961, (pp. 1100-26).

———, "The Citizen in conflict with the state", (A discussion to explore the possible need in U.K. for an appointment comparable with that of the Ombudsman), *Social Science Quarterly*, Autumn 1962, (pp. 41-8).

———, "Civil Service", (On proposed Parliamentary Commissioner for Administration), *Economist*, 16 October 1963, (p. 249).

———, "Complaint and Grievances Handling Procedure by Local Government", *Western City*, December 1968, (pp. 12-14).

Cohen, L.H., "Local Government Complaints: the M.P.'s Viewpoint", *Public Administration*, 1973, (pp. 175-83).

Colèman, Charles J., "Personnel: the Changing Function", *Public Personnel Management*, Chicago, May-June 1973, (pp. 186-93).

———, "A Council of State of Britain", *The Economist*, 15 August 1964, (pp. 623-5).

Cooper, Frank E., "The Need for an Ombudsman in State Government", Prospectus, April 1958, (pp. 27-44).

Das, S.R., "Is Justice Denied", *The Statesman*, New Delhi, 21 March 1970.

Davis, A.G., "The Ombudsman in New Zealand", *Journal of International Commission for Jurists*, Summer 1962, (pp. 51-62) Summer 1963, (pp. 34-42).

Davies, J.R., "A Newspaper Ombudsman" *Politics*, November 1967, (pp. 222-8).

Davis, Kenneth Culp "Ombudsman in America", *Public Law*, Spring, 1962, (pp. 34-42).

———, "Ombudsman in America: Officers to Criticise Administrative Action", *University of Pennsylvania Law Review*, June 1961, (pp. 1057-76).

Dennis-Jones, H. "An Ombudsman for Britain", *New Society*, 9 July 1964, (pp. 20-2).

Deshpande, V.S., "Rights and Duties under the Constitution", *Journal of the Indian Law Institute*; New Delhi, January-March, 1973, (pp. 94-108).

De Smith, S.A., "Anglo-Saxon Ombudsman?", *Political Quarterly*, January-March, 1962, (pp. 9-19).

Deutsch, Karl W., "Social Mobilization and Political Development", *American Political Sciences Review*, LV 3, September 1961, (pp. 493-94).

Disney, J., "Ombudsman in Australia", *Australian Quarterly*, 1974, (pp. 38-55).

Diwan, D.D., "Ombudsman: His Functions and Duties", *The Hindustan Times*, 3 November 1966, (p. 7).

Doctor, A.H , "A Lokpal for India", *Opinion*, 23 April 1968, (pp. 26-9).

Dube, S.C., "Bureaucracy and Economic Development", *Indian Journal of Public Administration*, Vol. XII, No. 3, July-September, 1966, (p. 349).

Egan, J., "Ombudsman: Danish Official to Protect the Private Citizen from Government", *Holiday*, November 1966, (p. 28).

Eisen Stadt, "Bureaucracy, Bureaucratization and Debureaucratization", *Administrative Science Quarterly*, Vol. 4, December 1959, (pp. 302-320).

Elcock, H.J., "Opportunity for Ombudsman: The Northern Ireland Commissioner for Complaints", *Public Administration*, 1972, (pp. 87-93).

Eller, J.N. "Swedes Have It: An Ombudsman", *America*, 19 March 1966, (p. 377).

Elman, P., "The Israel Ombudsman", *Israel Law Review*, 1975, (pp. 293-323).

Evens, Ganeth, "An Australian Bill of Rights", *Australian Quarterly*, March 1973, (pp. 4-34).

Evans, Roger Warren, "Ombudsman: France's way", *New Society*, 21 October 1965, (p. 21).

Farley, Marta Pisetska and Farley, Andrew N. "An American Ombudsman: Due Process in the Administrative State", *The Administrative Law Review*, Summer 1964, pp. 212-21).

Frampton, Geoffrey, "Citizen's Protection Against the State", *Hindu*, 6 November 1963, (p. 6).

———, "The Ombudsman", *New Statesman*, 23 October 1963, (pp. 560-1).

Frank, Bernard, "The British Parliamentary Commissioner for Administration: The Ombudsman", *Federal Bar Journal*, Vol. 28, Winter 1968, (pp. 1-24).

———, "Nebraska public counsel the Ombudsman", *Cumberland-Samford Law Review*, 1974, (pp. 30-58).

Friedman, K., "The Public and the Ombudsman: Perceptions and Attitudes in Britain and in Alberta", *Canadian Journal of Political Science*, Vol. X, September 1977, (pp. 497-525).

Friedmann, Karl A., "Commons, Complaints, and the Ombudsman", *Parliamentary Affairs*, Vol. 21, Winter 1967, (pp. 38-47).

Gajendragadkar, P.B., "Role of Administration in a Democratic Welfare State", *Indian Institute of Public Administration*, New Delhi, Vol. IX, No. 4, October-December, 1963.

Gangal, V.S., "Fundamental Rights", *Indian Finance*, New Delhi, 27 January 1973, (pp. 83-6).

Ganguly, Bangendu, "Citizens' Grievances: A New Machinery For Redress", *Indian Journal of Political Science*, April-June, 1968, (pp. 185-9).

Gellhorn, Walter, "Administrative Procedure Reform: Hardy Personnial", *American Bar Association Journal*, Vol. 48, 1962, (pp. 245-51).

———, "Finland's official Watchman", *University of Pennsylvania Law Review*, January 1966, (pp. 327-6).

———, "Norwegian Ombudsman", *Standford Law Review*, January 1966, (pp. 293-321).

———, "The Ombuds.ı an's Relevance to Ameriean Municipal Affairs", *American Bar Association Journal*, February 1968, (pp. 134-50).

———, "Protecting Citizens Against Administration in Poland", *Columbia Law Review*, February 1965, (pp. 1133-66).

———, "Settling Disagreements with Officials in Japan", *Harvard Law Review*, February 1966, (pp. 695-7).

———, "The Swedish Justice-Ombudsman", *Yale Law Journal*, November 1965, (p. 58).

"Germany's Army: Private Verdict", *The Economist*, 17 June 1964, (p. 1466).

Gilbertson, Forbes, "Will the Ombudsman Come to Canada?" *Canadian Business*, July 1964, (pp. 29-39).

Gopalakrishnan, M., "GoodA dministration An Urgent Need", *Journal of the National Academy of Administration*, Autumn 1972, (pp. 573-8).

Gorwala, A.D., "The Administrative Jungle", *Institute of Public Administration Journal*, Patna University, 1957.

Gordon, Phillip E., "The Municipal Ombudsman", *Municipal Attorney*, . October 1968, (pp. 145-8).

———, "The Grievance Man", *Civil Service Opinion*, November 1965. (p. 325).

———, "Grievance Man for U.S.? Ombudsman: Pro and Con Discussion", *Seminar Schologistic* (*Teacher* edition), 13 May 1966, (pp. 14-5).

Grossman, Howard J., "Do School Districts Need an Ombudsman", *American School Board Journal*, December 1967, (pp. 6-7).

Gwyn, William B., "The British PCA: 'Ombudsman or Ombudsmouse?' ", *Journal of Politics*, Vol. 35, February 1973, (pp. 45-63).

Hamilton, Randy H., "Can you Fight City Mall and Win?", (Local Government procedure for dealing with citizen grievances, their efficacy and recommended improvements), *Public Management*, October, 1967, (pp. 268-76).

———, "Ombudsman for What?", *National Civic Review*, March 1968, (pp. 132-7).

Hansen, J.P., "How to be an Ombudsman", *Manchester Guardian Weekly*, 7 January 1965, (pp. 14-5).

Hansen, Poul "The Ombudsman: A Watchdog of the Nation", *Statesman* (Calcutta), 21 January 1962, (p. 1).

Hanan, Ralph J., "How To Be an Ombudsman", *Manchester Guardian Weekly*, 7 January 1965, (p. 15).

Hewitt, Willian M., New York city's civilian complaint review board struggle, its history, analysis and some notes, *Police*, May-June 1967, (pp. 10-21); July-August 1967, (pp. 14-29); October 1967, (pp. 120-33).

Hiden, Mikael J.V., "Finland's Defenders of the Law", *Annals of the American Academy of Political and Social Sciences*, May 1968, (pp. 31-40).

Hill, Larry S., "The New Zealand Ombudsman's authority system", *Political Science*, September 1968, (pp. 40-51).

Hillson, Norman, "Ombudsman Idea is Gaining Favour", *Hitvada* (Nagpur), 6 January 1965, (p. 4).

Hoerning, Kaul H., "Development and Social Inequality: A Critique", Glasgow Co., November 1972, (pp. 135-46).

Holbrok George, "Parliament versus the Government?" *Civil Service Opinion*, April 1967, (pp. 108-9).

Holland, D.C., "A British Ombudsman", *Solicitor Quarterly*, Vol. 1962, (pp. 147-58).

Huang, S.M., "Control of the Executive Officers of Government", *Journal of Indian Law Institute*, April-June 1963, (pp. 171-90).

Hunter, A.A., De. C., "Ombudsman for Britain?" *Journal of the International Commission of Jurists*, Summer 1962, (pp. 150-9).

Hurwitz, Stephen, "Control of the Administration in Denmark; the Danish Parliamentary Commissioner for Civil and Military Government Administration", *Journal of the International Commission of Jurists*, Spring/Summer 1958, (pp. 224-43).

———, "The Danish Ombudsman and His Office" *The Listner*, 12 May 1960, (pp. 835-8).

———, "The Danish Parliament Commissioner for Civil and Military Government and administration", *Public Law*, Autumn 1958, (pp. 236-53).

———, "Denmark's Ombudsman: the Parliamentary Commissioner for Civil and Military Administration, *Wisconsin Law Review*, March 1961, (pp. 169-99).

———, "The Folketingats Ombudsman", *Parliamentary Affairs*, Spring 1959, (pp. 199-208).

———, "Public Trust in Government Services", *Danish Foreign Office Journal*, Vol, 20, 1956, (pp. 11-5).

———, "The Scandinavian Ombudsman", *Political Science*, March 1960, (pp. 121-42).

India, Parliament: Lok Sabha Secretariat, Research Branch, "The 'Ombudsman' in various Countries," *Journal of Parliamentary Information*, Vol. 4, 1964, (pp. 81-8).

"Indian Ombudsman", *Weekend Review*, 15 April 1967, (p. 7).

"Institution of Ombudsman", *Eastern Economist*, 14 July 1967, (p. 65).

Jagerskiold, Stig, "The Swedish Ombudsman", *University of Pennsylvania Law Review*, June 1961, (pp. 1077-99).

Jain, M.P., "Ombudsman in New Zealand, *Journal of Indian Law Institute*, April-June 1963, (pp. 307-14).

Jain. S.N., "Problems of Administrative Justice in India", Fourth Commonwealth Law Conference, *Occasional Paper*.

Kabad, B.K.R., "Ombudsman in New Dress an Uncoming Role", *Times of India*, (Bombay), 9 May 1968, (pp. 8).

———, "What will the Lokpal do?", *Public Administration*, February 1968, (pp. 1-2).

Kass, Benny L., "We can Indeed, Fight City Hall: The Office and Concept of Ombudsman", *American Bar Association Journul*, March 1967, (pp. 231-6).

Kastari, P., "The Constitutional Protection of Fundamental Rights in Finland". *Tulane Law Review*, Vol. 34, 1960, (pp. 695-710).

———, "The Parliamentary Ombudsman: His Function, Position and Relation to the Chancellor of Justice in Finland, *International Review of Administrative Sciences*, Vol. 28, No. 4, 1962, (pp. 391-8).

Kant V. Bhatt, "What Price Justice?", *The Himmat* (Bombay), 27 September 1968.

Kent, George, "Watchdog for the Common Man", *Rotarian*, July 1963. Condensed in *Reader's Digest*, August 1963, (pp. 82-5)

Klein, R., "Ombudsman into Mediateur", *Political Quarterly*, 1976, (pp. 92-4).

———, "The Health Service Commissioner: No Cause for Complaint", *British Medical Journal*, 1977, (pp. 248).

Kersell, J.E., "Parliamentary Ventilation of Grievances Arising Out of the Operation of Delegated Legislation", *Public Law*, Summer 1959, (pp. 152-68)

Korey, William, "Protecting Human Rights: A Global Ombudsman?", *Current*, November, 1967, (pp. 63-4).

"Labour Plan for Ombudsman", *Manchester Guardian Weekly*, 2 July 1964, (p. 4).

Lal, Diwan Chaman, "Ombudsman", *Indian Nation*, 6 November 1966, (p. 10).

———, "Ombudsman or a Commissioner", *Amrita Bazar Patrika*, Calcutta, November 1966, (p. 6).

Lawson, F.H. "An Inspector-General of Administration", *Public Law*, Summer 1957, (pp. 92-5).

Lefolii, Ken, "What the Right Ombudsman Would Do for Canada," *Maclean's* 18 April 1964, (p. 6).

Leambias, H.J. "Wanted—An Ombudsman in Canada", *Edge* (Edmonton-Canada), Spring 1964, (pp. 81-91).

Little Men's Champion: the Ombudsman", *Newsweek*, 12 December 1966.

"Lokpal", by D.V.G., *Public Affairs*, May 1968, (pp. 97-8).

Macalestair, Charles, "The British Version of Ombudsman", *National Herald* (Lucknow), 27 November 1965, Supplement, (p. 1).

Mandlesar, B.R., "The Lokpal Bill", *Hitavada* (Nagpur), 10 January 1968, (p. 4).

Marican, Y. Mansoor, "The Bureaucratic Power in India and Japan", *Philippine Journal of Public Administration*, Manila, April 1972, (pp. 204-23).

Marre, Sir A., "Some Reflections on an Ombudsman", *Social and Economic Administration*, 1975, (pp 3-12).

Marshall, Geoffrey, "The British Parliamentary Commissioner for Administration", *Annals of the American Academy of Political and Social Sciences*, May 1968, (pp. 87-96).

———, "A Critique of the Ombudsman Report," *The Lawyer*, London, Vol. 4, 1961, (pp. 29-32).

———, "The New Zealand Parliamentary Commissioner (Ombudsman) Act, 1962", *Public Law*, Spring 1963, (pp. 20-1).

———, "Should British Have an Ombudsman", *The Times*, (London) 23 April 1963, (p. 13).

Meane, Ingunn N., "Norwegian Ombudsman", *Western Political Quarterly*, December 1968, (pp. 624-50).

McBride, J.J. "Nova Scotia Ombudsman", *Delhousie Law Journal*, 1975, (pp. 182-200)

McKeown, Robert, "Why Canada Needs an Ombudsman", *Weekend*, Vol. 14, No. 2, (pp. 2-3).

Menon, K.P.S.: "How Much Freedom Should There Be in a Democracy?" *Capital*, January 1973, (pp. 35-8)

Merton Robert K., "The Unanticipated Consequences of Purposive Social Action", *American Sociological Review*, 1936, (pp. 894-904).

———, "Bureaucratic Structure and Personality", *Social Forces*, Vol. XVIII, 1940, (pp. 560-68).

Mehta, B., "Parliament and the Administrator", *Journal of Constitutional and Parliamentary Studies*, October-December 1967, (pp. 21-32).

Middleton, K.W.B., "The Ombudsman", *Judicial Review Edinburgh*, Vol. 5, 1960, (pp. 298-306).

Milne, A.J.M. "Philosophy and Political Action: The Case of Civil Rights", *Political Studies*, December 1973, (pp. 453-66).

Miller, J. Bonnett, "Administrative Necessity and the Abuse of Power", *Public Law*, Winter 1966, (pp. 330-45).

Minathur, Joseph, "Ombudsman in India", *Supereme Court Journal*, 15 May 1968, (pp. 37-47).

———, "Ombudsman in Mauritius", *Journal of Constitutional and Parliamentary Studies*, January-March 1969, (pp. 12-9).

Miranshah, W.P., "What Will be This Lok Pal", *Assam Tribune*, 4 June 1968, (p. 4).

Mitchell, J.D.B., "The Ombudsman Fallacy" *Public Law*, Spring 1962, (pp. 24-33).

Monteiro, J.B., "Case for an Ombudsman In India", *Economic Weekly*, 14 December 1963 (pp. 2039-40).

———, "Comment, (Ombudsman for India)", *Public Law*, Summer 1965, (pp. 81-8).

———, "Logic of India's Ombudsman Fever", *Public Administration*, (Kanpur), 6 March 1965, (pp. 116-7).

———, "The Ombudsman And its Relevance to India", *Modren Review*, March 1962, (pp. 326-28), May 1962, (pp. 406-10).

Mor, M.B., "Ombudsman versus Procuracy", *Hitavada* (Nagpur), 26 July 1966, (p. 411).

Morgan, Glenn G., "The Soviet Procuracy's General Supervision Functions", *Soviet Studies*, October 1959, (pp. 143-72).

Mundell, D.W., "Ombudsman for Canada", *Canadian Bar Journal*, June 1964, (pp. 179-209).

Murray, C.H., "The Grievance Man: In Scandinavia", *Administration*, Dublin, Autumn 1970; (p. 11).

Nader, Ralph, "An Answer to Administrative Abuse", *Harvard Law Review*, 20 December 1962, (p. 13).

Nanda, Gulzarilal. "Citizens' Grievances", *Public Administration*, Kanpur, June 1963, (pp. 14-7).

Narasimha, R.L., "Law & the Commonwealth", *Fourth Commonwealth Law Conference*, New Delhi, 1971, (pp. 29-30).

———, "The Indian Ombudsman Proposal: A Critique", a paper presented at the Fourth Commonwealth Law Conference, 1971.

National Academy of Administration, Mussoorie, Syndicate Report on "An Ombudsman System for India"? *Journal of the National Academy of Administration*, October 1963, (pp. 41-120).

Navaratne, G., "The Ombudsman and Administrative Corruption in Ceylon", *Eastern World*, November 1965, (p. 11).

Nelson, Dalmas H. and Price, Eugene G., "Realignment, Readjustment, Reform; the impact of the Ombudsman on American Constitution and political and Social Sciences'', May 1968, (pp. 128-38).

New Zealand, "Grievances Man v. Bureaucracy", *Time*, 24 August 1962.

New Zealand, "The Ombudsman in Action", Round Table, March 1963, (pp. 185-90).

Newman, Frank C., "Ombudsman and Human Rights: The new U.N. Treaty Proposals", *The University of Chicago Law Review*, Summer 1967, (pp. 951-62).

Noorani, A.G., "Citizens and State: Redress of Grievances", *Indian Express*, (New Delhi), 27 October 1963, (p. 6).

———, "Citizen's grievances", *Indian Express*, (New Delhi), 24 May 1967, (p. 6).

———, "The Grievance Man", *Opinion*, 29 March 1966, (pp. 21-4).

———, "India must have a 'Grievancé Man' ", *Indian Express* (New Delhi), 16 May 1965, (p. 6).

———,"Needed, Director of Prosecutions", *Indian Express* (New Delhi), 13 January 1967, (p. 6).

———, "The Ombudsman: the People's Tribune Badly Needed in India" *Indian Express* (New Delhi), 4 July 1962, (p. 6).

———, "The Lokpal Bill", *Indian Express* (New Delhi), 1 August 1977, (p. 6).

———, "The Lokpal Bill—in Battered Shape", *Indian Express* (New Delhi), 20 August 1978.

Northey, J.F., "A New Zealand Ombudsman?" *Public Law*, Spring 1962, (pp. 43-51).

———, "The Manitoba Ombudsman Act 1969", *Manitoba Law Journal*, 1970, (pp. 206-12).

Norton, P.M., "Tanzanian Ombudsman", *International and Comparative Law Quarterly*, 1973, (pp. 603-31).

Olson, Bruce T., "Ombudsman on the West Coast: an Analysis and Evaluation of the Watchdog Function of the California Grand Jury", *Police*, November-December 1967, (pp. 12-20).

Oluyede, P., "Redress of Grievances in Tanzania", *Public Law*, 1975 (pp. 8-26).

"The Ombudsman", *Manchester Guardian Weekly*, 7 December 1961, (p. 9).

"Ombudsman", *Your Government*, 15 January 1968, (pp. 1-8).

"The Ombudsman: A Symposium", *The Administrative Law Review*, November 1966, (pp. 6-106).

"Ombudsman at Work", *The Economist*, 23 June 1962, (p. 1222).

"Ombudsman: Best Device to End Corruption", *The Tribune*, (Ambala) 19 August 1963.

"Ombudsman for the Dead", *New Society*, 14 September 1967, (pp. 349-50)

"The Ombudsman in New Zealand", *New Administrator*, January 1964, (pp. 27-9).

"Ombudsman: Not So Much What he Says", *The Economist*, 23 December 1967, (p. 1209).

"Ombudsman Proves His Worth", *Manchester Guardian Weekly*, 25 June 1964, (p. 7).

"Ombudsman in Britain", *Commerce*, 23 October 1965, (p. 744).

"Ombudsmanship," *The Economist*, 4 November 1961, (pp. 413-4).

"Organisations for dealing with Citizens' Grievances in Foreign Countries", *Congress Forum*, 20 September 1963, (pp. 38-44).

Osborn, Robert J., "Citizen versus Administration in the USSR", *Soviet Studies*, December 1965, (pp. 226-37).

Parker, R.S., "The Ombudsman and Ministerial Responsibility", A Comment, *Public Administration*, March 1964, (pp. 69-76).

"Parliamentary Commissioner", Comment, *Public Law*, Winter 1965, (pp. 299-303).

Pattabhiram, M., "Lokpal Proposal Runs into Hurdles", *Hindu*, 3 April 1968, (p. 5).

Patterson, A.D., "The Ombudsman U.B.C." *Law Review*, April 1963, (pp. 777-81).

Pedersen, I.M., "The Danish Parliamentary Commissioner in Action", *Public Law*, Summer 1939, (pp. 115-27).

———, "The Parliamentary Commissioner: A Danish View", *Public Law*, Spring 1962, (pp. 15-23).

"Post-Ombudsmanship", *Christian Century*, 28 December 1966, (p. 1619).

Powles, Guy, "Aspects of the Search for Administrative Justice, with particular reference to the New Zealand Ombudsman", *Canadian Public Administration*, June 1966, (pp. 133-57).

———, "A Citizen's Rights Against the Modern State and its Responsibilities to him", *New Zealand Journal of Public Administration*, March 1969, (pp. 1-33).

———, "Common Justice", *The Guardian*, 14 May 1964, (p. 10).

———, "The Office of Ombudsman in New Zealand", *Journal of Administration Overseas*, January 1968, (pp. 287-92).

"Problems of Redress of Citizens' Grievances", (Interim Report of Administrative Reforms Commission), *Public Administration* (Kanpur), December 1966, (pp. 1-5).

Pruger, Robert, "The Good Bureaucrat", *Social Work*, (New Year), July 1973, (pp. 26-32).

Pugh, Sir Idwal, ICCB, "The Ombudsman—Jurisdiction, Powers and Practice", *Journal of the Royal Institute of Public Administration*, Summer 1978.

Rajagopalachari, C., "Savings Citizen from Executive Tyranny", *Civic Affairs*, March 1962, (pp. 9-11).

Rangarajan, S., "Judicial Creativity and the Ombudsman", *Lawyer*, November 1963, (pp. 199-212).

Raphaeli, Nimrod, "The Ombudsman of the City of the Jerusalem", *Studies in Comparative Local Government*, Winter 1968, (pp. 41-9).

Reuss, Henry S., "An Ombudsman for America" *New York Times Magazine*, 13 September 1964, (p. 30).

———, "A Trouble-shooter for Congress", *The Progressive*, 17 February 1966, (pp. 23-5).

———, "The Ombudsman: Tribune of the People," *Annals of the American Academy of Political and Social Sciences*, January 1966, (pp. 44-55).

Ridley, F., "Parliamentary Commissioner for Military Affairs in the Federal Republic of Germany", *Political Studies*, February 1964, (pp. 1-20).

Roberts, James S., "An Ombudsman for Pakistan?", *NIPA Reporter*, August 1963, (pp. 13-7).

Robson, William A., "The Constraints on British Government", London, *Political Quarterly*, April-June 1973, (pp. 117-26).

Rolph, C.H. and Whitaker, Ben, "Ombudsman in Danger", *New Statesman*, 26 February 1965, (p. 308).

Rosenblum, Victor G., "Controlling the Bureaucracy of the Antipoverty Programme", *Law and Contemporary Problems*, Winter 1966, (pp. 187-210).

Rosenthal, Albert H., "The Ombudsman—Swedish 'Grievance Man'," *Public Administration Review*, December 1964, (pp. 226-9).

Roth, Julius A., "The Right to Quit", *Sociological Review*, August 1973, (pp. 381-96).

Rowat, Donald C., Finland's Defenders of the Law: The Chancellor of Justice and the Parliamentary Ombudsman", *Canadian Public Administration*.

———, "Finland's Defenders of the Law: A Postscript", *Canadian Public Administration*, December 1961, (pp. 412-415).

———, "Ombudsman for North America", *Canadian Journal of Economics and Political Science*, November 1962, (pp. 543-56).

———, "The Parliamentary Ombudsman: Should the Scandinavian Scheme be Transplanted?", *International Review of Administrative Sciences*, Vol. 28, No. 4, 1962, (pp. 399-405).

———, "Recent Developments in Ombudsmanship: A Review Article", *Canadian Public Administration*, March 1967, (pp. 35-46).

———, "We Need a New Defence Against So-Called Justice", *Maclean's*, 7 January 1961, (p. 10).

———, "The Ombudsman Plan—Essays on the Worldwide Spread of an Idea", McClelland and Stewart, 1973.

Ruthnaswamy, M., "An Ombudsman for India", *Swarajya*, 5 May 1962, (pp. 3-4).

Sahay, S., "A Close Look—By No Means An Omdudsman", *The Statesman* (New Delhi), (p. 6).

Sanders, Ake, "An Ombudsman for the United States", *Annals of the American Academy of Political and Social Sciences*, May 1968, (pp. 104-10).

Sanders, Morion K., "Sweden's Remedy for Police Brutality', *Harper's Magazine*, Vol. 229, 1969, (pp. 132-6.)

Santhanam, K., "Ombudsman for India", *Swarajya*, Annual No. 1967, (pp. 61-4).

Sapru, R.S., "Ombudsman: Best Devise to End Corruption", *Tribune*, 19 August 1963, (p. 4).

Sarkar, Subash Chandra, "Civil Liberty in an Unjust Society", *Modern Review*, May 1973, (pp. 340-5).

Satyanarayana, P., "Ombudsman for India: Lokpal and Lokayukta", *Radical Humanist*, 18 June 1967, (pp. 227-8).

Sawer, Geoffrey, "The Ombudsman and Related Institutions in Australia and New Zealand," *Annals of the American Academy of Political and Social Sciences*, May 1968, (pp. 62-72).

Secher, H.P., "Controlling the New German Military Elite: The Political Role of the Paliamentary Defence Commissioner in the Federal Republic", *Proceedings of the American Philosophical Society*, April 1965, (pp. 64-84).

Setalvad, M.C., "The Ombudsman", *Journal of the National Academy of Administration*, April 1963, (pp. 1-9).

Seth, Vinod, "Freedom of the Press: a Ciritique of Benet Coleman Case", *Indian Political Review*, January 1974, (pp. 27-40).

———, "Scope and Function of Lokpal", *Hindu*, 4 July, 1968, (p. 6).

Shakdhar, S.L., "Administrative Accountability to Parliament", *Indian Journal of Public Administration*, July-September 1966, (p. 356-77).

Sharpley, George R., "Ombudsman: A Representative Democracy's Finest Hour", *Police Chief*, January 1969, (pp. 12).

Shearer, Ann, "The Case for an Ombudsman", *Manchester Guardian Weekly*, 13 June 1968, (p. 13).

Sheppard, C.A., "An Ombudsman for Canada", *McGill Law Journal* Vol. 10, No. 4, 1964, (p. 42).

Shukla, V.S., "The Ombudsman Hysteria", *Supreme Court Journal*, May 1967, (pp. 84-86).

Sinding-Larsen, T., "The Storting's Ombudsman for Public Administration," (cyclostyled) Oslo, 1977.

Singhvi, L.M., "Ombudsman for India", *Indian Nation*, (pp. 557-9); 26 August 1965, (p. 4).

———, "Plea for Ombudsman in India", *Indian Review*, November 1965, (pp. 557-9).

———, "Towards Controlling the Bureaucracy", *Shakti*, June 1965, (pp. 7-9).

Sington, Anne, "Denmark's Ombudsman", *Public Administration*, Kanpur, May 1966, (pp. 5-7).

Sinha, V.M., "Ombudsman and India", *Political Science Review*, May 1964, (pp. 135-41).

Smith, Austin, "What this country needs is an Ombudsman", *Association Management*, Vol. 15, 1963, (pp. 40-2).

Smith, Maurice H., "Thoughts of a British Consell d'etat (for the redress of administrative wrongs)", *Public Administration*, Spring 1967, (pp. 23-42).

Stewart, Michael, "The Ombudsman", *New Statesman*, 25 September 1964, (p. 430).

Storing, James A., "The Norwegian Ombudsman for Civil Affairs; The

First Three Years, 1963-66", *Western Political Quarterly*, June 1968, (pp. 302-24).

"Suggestions for a Russian Ombudsman", by Monitor, *Statesman*, Calcutta, 10 May 1966, (p 6).

"The Swedish Justice Ombudsman", *American Journal of Comparative Law*, Spring 1962, (pp. 225-38).

Thornberry, Cedric, "Protecting the Citizens", *Socialist Commentary*, March 1965, (pp. 26-7).

Thorson, K., "What about an Ombudsman?", *Sakatchewan Bar Review*, December 1963, (pp. 169).

Thuné, Sverre, "The Norwegian Ombudsman for Civil and Military Affairs", *Annals of the American Academy of Political and Social Sciences*, May 1968, (pp. 41-54).

Tripathi, P.K., "Lokpal: the Proposed Indian Ombudsman", *Journal of the Indian Law Institute*, April-June 1967, (pp. 135-52).

"U.S.S.R. Decree of the Presidium of the U.S.S.R. Supreme Soviet: on the Procedure for Examining Citizens' Proposals, Petitions and Complaints", *Current Digest of the Soviet Press*, 15 May 1968, (pp. 7-8).

"The Ombudsman in the States", *Annals of the American Academy of Political and Social Sciences*, May 1968, (pp. 111-21).

"Value of Ombudsman proved in New Zealand", *The Times*, London, 15 May 1964, (p. 12).

Venkatesan, G., "Ombudsman", Fight Against Corruption, *Youth Congress*, March 1969, (pp. 9-11).

Vijayalakshmi, "Ombudsman—Lesson For Us". *Indian Express* (New Delhi), 11 March 1962, (p. 14).

Wade, H.W.R., "The Council on Tribunals", *Public Law*, Winter 1969, (pp. 351-66).

———, "The Ombudsman: The Citizen's Defender", *Occasional Papers* Fourth Commonwealth Law Conference, New Delhi, (pp. 15-16).

Walnum Jacob, "The Institution of Ombudsman", *Amrit Bazar Patrika*, (Calcutta), 17 May 1968.

Walker, Richard L., "The Control Systems of the Chinese Government, *The Far Eastern Quarterly*, Vol. II, 1947-48.

Weir, A.B., "The Legislative Ombudsman", *Alberta Law Review*, 1976 (pp. 256-65).

Wennergren, Bertil, "The Rise of growth of Swedish institutions for Defending the Citizen against Official Wrongs", *Annals of the American Academy of Political and Social Sciences*, May 1968, (pp. 1-9)

Wheare, K.C., "The Redress of Grievances", *Public Administration*, Summer 1962, (pp. 125-8).

"Whose Pal is Lok Pal", *Thought*, 2 September 1967, (pp. 11-2).

Whyatt, John, "The Public and the Administration", *The Economist*, 4 November 1961, (pp. 413-4).

Wold, Terje, "The Norwegian Parliament's Commissioner for the Civil Administration", *Journal of the International Commission of Jurists*, Winter 1959/Spring-Summer 1960, (pp 21-9).

Yamamoto, Shotaro, "Ombudsmen in Japan", *Kwansei Gakuin University Annual Studies*, Nov. 1963, (pp. 75-91).

"A Year with the Grievance Man", *Manchester Guardian Weekly*, 17 October 1963, (p. 7).

Zeidler, Frank P., "An Ombudsman for Cities", *Annals of the American Academy of Political and Social Science*, May 1968, (pp. 122-7).

Zweig, Franklin M., "The Social Worker as Legislative Ombudsman", *Social Work*, January 1969, (pp. 25-33).

Index